NIKI LAUDA
HIS COMPETITION HISTORY

To Sarah
Without whose unstinting support and understanding I would have been unable to disappear into the office for hours on end to complete the manuscript when deadlines loomed. Thank you for indulging my obsession.

All rights reserved. No part of this publication may be reproduced or stored in a retrieval system or transmitted, in any form or by any means, electronic, mechanical, photocopying, recording or otherwise, without prior permission in writing from Evro Publishing.

© Jon Saltinstall

Published in November 2019

ISBN 978-1-910505-46-5

Published by Evro Publishing
Westrow House, Holwell, Sherborne, Dorset DT9 5LF, UK

Edited by Mark Hughes
Designed by Richard Parsons

Printed and bound in Slovenia by GPS Group

Every effort has been made to trace and acknowledge holders of copyright in photographs and to obtain their permission for the use of photographs. The publisher apologises for any errors or omissions in the credits given at the back of this book and would be grateful to be notified of any corrections that should be incorporated in future reprints or editions.

www.evropublishing.com

Cover images
Front 1982 Detroit Grand Prix.
Back Helmet evolution: 1971 International ADAC-Eifelrennen F2; 1973 Nürburgring Six Hours; 1976 German Grand Prix; 1978 Belgian Grand Prix; 1982 South African Grand Prix; 1984 Belgian Grand Prix.
Frontispiece On the threshold of achieving his ambition to be World Champion, Niki prepares for the start of the 1975 Italian Grand Prix.

NIKI LAUDA
HIS COMPETITION HISTORY

EVRO
PUBLISHING

JON SALTINSTALL
FOREWORD BY JOHN WATSON
AFTERWORD BY KURT BERGMANN

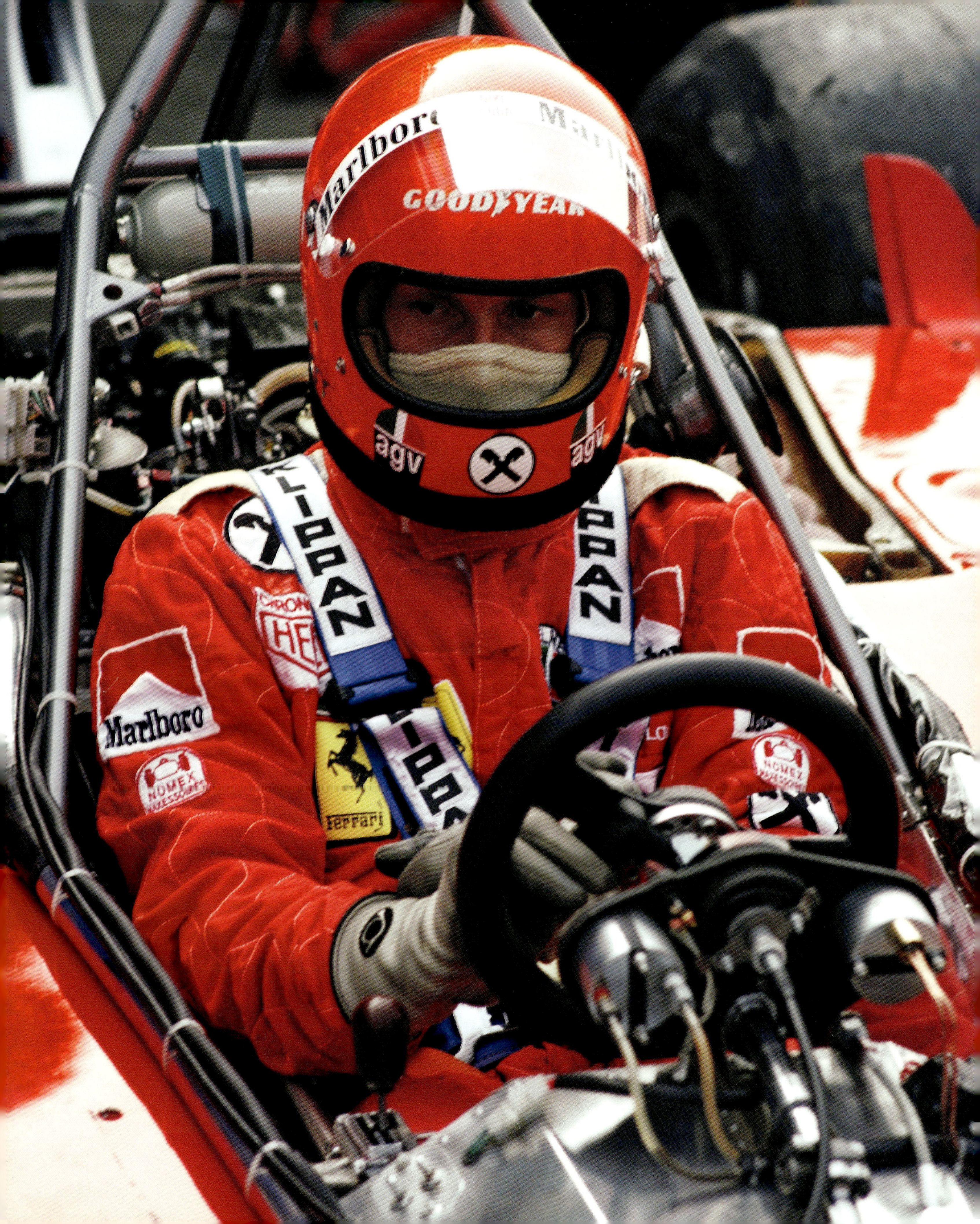
Marlboro
GOODYEAR
agv
agv
KLIPPAN
Marlboro
Ferrari

CONTENTS

	FOREWORD BY JOHN WATSON	6
	PREFACE BY DOUG NYE	9
	INTRODUCTION	12
1968	BEGINNINGS	14
1969	CLIMBING THE LADDER	26
1970	A FIELD OF MADMEN	42
1971	RITES OF PASSAGE	62
1972	BUYING A FUTURE	80
1973	BRM AND BMW	112
1974	LEARNING HOW TO WIN	138
1975	THE STARS ALIGN	160
1976	THE MORAL VICTORY	180
1977	THE PHOENIX RISES	204
1978	CHANGING HORSES	226
1979	ALSO-RAN... AND CHAMPION	248
INTERLUDE	SCRATCHING THE ITCH	274
1982	THE SECOND CAREER	276
1983	MARKING TIME	292
1984	AS CLOSE AS IT GETS	308
1985	THE LAST LAP	330
	LATER TESTS & DEMONSTRATIONS	346
	LIFE BEYOND THE DRIVING SEAT	360
	'NEARLY RACES'	363
	RUMOURS & POSSIBILITIES	366
	STATISTICS	367
	ACKNOWLEDGEMENTS	370
	PHOTO CREDITS	371
	BIBLIOGRAPHY	372
	INDEX	373
	AFTERWORD BY KURT BERGMANN	376

FOREWORD
JOHN WATSON

The first time I met Niki Lauda was at Mallory Park in 1971 in the European Formula 2 Trophy race. March had entered a five-car team led by Ronnie Peterson, and among the other four was this young Austrian chap who I thought was some wealthy kid, who rocked up in a new Porsche 911S with a stunningly beautiful girlfriend in tow. Based on that first impression, how could I take him seriously? Instead, what appeared over the course of the season was a formidable competitor both in and out of the car. Rather than just driving around problems, he quickly showed an ability to communicate, especially with Robin Herd, the chief designer, in a manner that the engineers could understand. His skill in generating sponsorship was the thing that had got him into the team, but it was this accomplishment in communicating technically that set him apart and made him the go-to guy for the engineers.

Ambitious, focused, confident — all these descriptions are true. Having got together the funds to buy a Formula 1 drive, he quickly realised that March was not the place to be. At Monaco in 1973 I watched him hustling the BRM around the place in the performance that got the attention of Enzo Ferrari, whose cars had been pretty useless all that year. Niki was the first of a generation of drivers who went to the Scuderia and proved able to pinpoint problems with the car in testing before getting a contract. His key skill then was recognising that he couldn't do it all himself; it was the triumvirate of Mauro Forghieri, Luca di Montezemolo and Niki that put the team back on track. His vision, ambition, understanding and ability to get people around him engaged was what set him apart.

He would have won the 1976 World Championship by a country mile had it not been for the Nürburgring accident. I was one of the first drivers to arrive at the scene after the other guys involved had got him out, and I helped to cradle him until the ambulance arrived. But having done all that, we got back into the cars and started all over again — that was what Formula 1 was like in those days. Of course, at the time we didn't realise the seriousness of the damage to his lungs.

To me, what Niki did at Monza six weeks later is the single most courageous act by any sportsman in any sport; to overcome his demons and get back behind the wheel to race again so soon after almost being killed. I am familiar with what tests he had to undergo to prove himself fit to race in Italy, so his performance seems even more remarkable to me. Then there was his brave decision to pull out of the race at Fuji: it was never fully explained at the time just how damaged his eyes were, and, remember, he was not just withdrawing himself from the World Championship race but Ferrari too. After all this, he had to go back to Ferrari in 1977 and race alongside Carlos Reutemann, who the management had employed as number one driver in his place. Niki dug deep into his resolve and dismantled Reutemann comprehensively during the season, taking the World Championship before walking out on the team.

At Hockenheim in 1977, Bernie Ecclestone flagged me down and asked what I thought about Niki joining Brabham. I told Bernie that as long as he would guarantee me parity of equipment, it was fine with me. What I hadn't appreciated, having never had a team-mate like Niki who was a double World Champion, was his ability to shape the team around him. He brought his personal sponsor, Parmalat, as title sponsor to the team and this, together with the political skills he had developed at Ferrari, confirmed him as the guy the management dealt with and the *de facto* team leader. As Bernie said to me later, 'Look at the hat', which carried Parmalat's logo. That told me who the go-to guy was.

I'd left for McLaren at the end of 1978 and Niki stopped at the end of 1979 when the second love of his life — aviation — became his preoccupation. He'd put a deposit down on a DC10, and the terms of the lease meant that as long as he could fill the aircraft and make the payments, he was in business. I think this was becoming a challenge by 1981 and made him consider his options. By this time, McLaren was in the Ron Dennis/

John Barnard era and there were rumours that Niki might be considering a return. The potential upsides were phenomenal for Marlboro and McLaren. Ron had worked with Niki before with the Project Four BMW Procar and knew what he could bring to the team. The pitfall was that it might just be a flight of fancy, so they agreed a three-race contract that either side could then cancel. He won the third race, signed a two-year contract and the rest is history.

At first there was a bit of a love-in between Niki and the McLaren guys, but what I'd come to realise, having been with the team for some time, was that Ron's ambitions were always for McLaren. Niki was no more or less than part of that aspiration. When we got to Las Vegas at the end of 1982, I was slightly better placed than Niki to take the title, so on the Saturday Ron took him aside and told him that if I came up behind and was faster, he was to let me pass. Niki was shocked: it was a watershed

ABOVE Friends as well as team-mates: Niki and John Watson in the Monza pits before the 1983 Italian Grand Prix.

moment for him as he'd never been asked to do this before and at that point he realised that he couldn't manipulate the team as he'd done elsewhere. He rather went through the motions in the race and couldn't wait to leave afterwards.

Niki's focus in 1983 was getting the TAG turbo engine into a Formula 1 chassis as soon as possible. This was resisted by John Barnard, who wanted to do things his way, so Niki did something high-risk by going to Marlboro and telling them that they had paid for an engine to be developed alongside going racing but that it wasn't being done, so they needed to put pressure on the team to do so. This caused a significant issue with Ron Dennis and John Barnard, but it was typical of Niki, who realised that if he waited for John to be ready at least three

FOREWORD 7

LEFT 'Things are different these days…' John and Niki chatting behind the pits at Montréal during qualifying for the 2005 Canadian Grand Prix.

months of track time would be lost. In hindsight, his decision was probably the right one and his World Championship in 1984 vindicated it, but he didn't win many friends at McLaren.

After his retirement at the end of 1985, his love affair with the airline was rekindled; his operation was in many ways a template for what small regional operators would later do. He overcame huge resistance from Austrian Airlines and the national government, both of whom played all kinds of dirty tricks to keep him from operating. He faced another awful situation when one of his Boeing 767s crashed on the way back from Thailand, killing everyone on board.

The third strand of his working life was his role at Mercedes-Benz, which he got mainly through Bernie's involvement. Niki and Bernie became strong friends during his time at Brabham and remained so for the rest of his life. Bernie wanted to have eyes and ears at Mercedes-Benz; when Ross Brawn left the team and Toto Wolff arrived, Niki was made joint team principal. His clarity of thought and ability to cut through the bullshit with brutal honesty was his skill. The success of Mercedes-Benz since 2014 is due in no small part to his involvement.

It's hard to say what Niki's legacy is: his record as a driver, his airline businesses or his role as a racing team boss? Each is equally important and feeds off the others. It's a great sadness for me as well as for his family that he's no longer around. It was strange for me to have a friendly relationship with a team-mate — normally one's main rival — and after 1983, when I left McLaren, it was a friendship I continued to enjoy. He was bright, intelligent and quick-witted — although there would occasionally be times when I could turn the tables on him. He was great company too, with a fine sense of humour. He was also the most indiscreet man I've ever known — you could never tell him a secret. Although I've not been directly involved in Formula 1 in recent years, I would always meet Niki for a coffee (or sometimes he'd have a whisky) and we'd pick up just where we had left off.

Niki was an outstanding competitor, a remarkable man at all levels and a good friend whose company I enjoyed. There are not many people who packed as much into 70 years as he did. He maxed out on life in all respects. This book is a timely reminder of all that he achieved in a long and diverse competition career.

John Watson

AUTHOR'S NOTE
John Watson was Niki Lauda's team-mate at Brabham in 1978 and at McLaren in 1982–83, during which time they formed a close personal friendship. He is Northern Ireland's most successful Grand Prix driver and gave both Roger Penske and Ron Dennis their first Formula 1 victories. A veteran of 151 Grands Prix, he won five of these; he was a contender for the 1982 World Championship until the final race. His most famous victories came after starting from the back of the grid, from 17th at Detroit in 1982 and 23rd in Long Beach a year later, the latter a record that still stands as the win from the lowest starting position.

PREFACE
DOUG NYE

The true standard setters of a motor racing era can be counted on one's fingers. Over four decades following the end of the Second World War one can cite in sequence Jean-Pierre Wimille, Alberto Ascari, Juan Manuel Fangio, Stirling Moss, Jim Clark, Jackie Stewart and Ronnie Peterson as having been that standard setter… plus, of course, Andreas-Nikolaus 'Niki' Lauda.

Following Stewart's retirement at the end of 1973, we wondered who would emerge as the new standard setter. Peterson had stolen some of the wee Scot's glory during that final, careful season of 1973. But then through 1974 Ronnie progressively lost his talisman — despite some still-wonderful winning drives, his John Player Lotus cars foundered — and young Lauda simply 'clicked' for Ferrari.

During that year the slightly built young Austrian qualified his Ferrari on pole position for nine of the 15 World Championship Grand Prix races. He led eight of them and won two. During a typical season following the retirement of one great champion, Niki was consistently the fastest among those whom Stewart had left behind to claim his former supremacy.

To those of us who watched Niki so closely, and who listened attentively to those working with him, and racing against him, it was already clear that here was someone extra special.

And his pace in the latest Ferraris was not only the pace of a mere hotshoe, hired to drive a dominant car. Niki's pace was to a great degree the result and reward of totally focused, intense dedication to testing, to experience, to analyse, to amend, and to test again… and again… and again. His ambition was to win the World Championship, and then to win it again — and again. He left no stone unturned.

He had dedicated, modified, built and rebuilt his life to achieve that end — and with it would come what perhaps most drove him; not fame, but fortune, and sheer winning… inherent, inborn competitive hunger.

Niki was naturally highly intelligent. His piercingly analytical

ABOVE Doug Nye at the wheel of a gullwing Mercedes-Benz 300SL at the Goodwood Festival of Speed — one of his regular haunts.

mind had absorbed so much experience over his formative racing years, from 1969 to 1973, that he broke into top-line Formula 2, and thence into Formula 1, abundantly aware. Whatever he could do on track, and however the stopwatch might measure his talents, he had also to maximise his manipulative background skills as far-sighted politician, diplomat and dynamic driver of men. His personal drive and ambition won him influential like-minded support, not least from Luca di Montezemolo, Fiat-Ferrari's frenetically rocket-fuelled management game changer.

From convincing sceptical bankers that he could indeed sustain a massive loan, to winning a war of wits (and of case-hardened negotiating toughness) against the long-unmatched guile of an ageing Enzo Ferrari, to entrancing the Marlboro tobacco money men, to matching the always calculated abrasiveness and determination of Bernie Ecclestone, to massaging maximum support from such competitive obsessives as Ron Dennis and John Barnard — Niki Lauda had few equals.

After being regarded merely as a convenient income source by March Engineering in 1971 Formula 2, he then worked assiduously to schmooze sponsors Marlboro and BRM Formula 1 team principals Louis and Jean Stanley alike to secure a credible launch pad into the premier league. That came in his 1973 season with the British Marlboro-BRM team. Summoning all the elaborately theatrical charm perceived to be inborn into a Viennese gentleman, he had kissed team owner Jean Stanley's hand. Bingo! For him it worked like a dream.

This was the same 'player' who then emphasised his personal drive and ambition to his new BRM mechanics. Demonstrating what for a racing driver was both untypical self-awareness, and the target dedication so crucial to securing total commitment from mechanics, Niki broke the ice with them by declaring: *'I know right now you all think that I am just a vanker. But I tell you — vun day I vill be World Champion!'* And he made direct ice-blue eye contact with each of those BRM boys, and they knew he meant it.

Teamed alongside veterans Jean-Pierre Beltoise and Clay Regazzoni in ageing V12-engined BRMs, the young Lauda quickly made his mark. His technical feedback proved valuable, his racing commitment admirable, his natural talent hugely promising. After scoring his first World Championship points with fifth place in the 1973 Belgian Grand Prix, he stormed into a fighting third place at Monaco, only for his car to fail. In the British Grand Prix at Silverstone he briefly led after a restart. He then out-qualified his senior team-mates for the German Grand Prix on the mighty Nürburgring. He held fourth place for a lap there before crashing heavily, through little fault of his own. He had become 'a player', a man to watch. One of those watching, with interest, was Enzo Ferrari.

Naturally fast, and ambitious, Niki had formed through that BRM season a strong personal tie with former Ferrari star Regazzoni. They were similarly committed — and both were warriors. But the younger Lauda would prove more dedicated, more intense — and more adept at politicking his own goals. When Regazzoni returned to Ferrari for 1974, he recommended the young Austrian as his team-mate. And so Niki joined Ferrari, and two of his three World Championship titles would follow.

After his 1976 German Grand Prix crash, in which he was so badly burned and his lungs so scorched that at first he was not expected even to survive, the warrior Lauda truly emerged, to insist upon racing again as early as that year's Italian Grand Prix at Monza, only six weeks hence.

In the paddock there, I examined his battered AGV crash

LEFT The drivers' press conference was an environment in which Niki Lauda and journalists often met. This is the briefing after Niki's final Grand Prix victory, in Holland in 1985. He is flanked by second-placed Alain Prost and third-placed Ayrton Senna.

helmet, torn from his head in the accident, its visor part-melted, blistered and flame-blackened. Protected only by his overalls and balaclava, he had slumped far longer, unconscious in that fireball. Yet out on the pitlane here he was, wheeling into the Ferrari pit in his 312T2 car. Our friend Alan Henry and I looked on. Those penetrating blue eyes, slightly bloodshot, flicked to mechanic 'Mannu' Cuoghi, gloved right hand on the steering wheel, his left waving an impatient index finger. Alan turned to me and just said it all: 'He's back. Look — same old Niki.'

Years later, it was quintessentially Niki for him to abruptly opt out of racing with a mere, unexpected phone call to Brabham team chief Bernie Ecclestone during Canadian Grand Prix practice, declaring he no longer wanted — needed? — just 'to drive round in circles'. He had a new airline to run and had to focus on that.

Two years later, it was also quintessentially Niki to change his mind, to negotiate a record fee with McLaren and to make a comeback, eventually to win his third World Championship title before finally retiring from racing at the end of 1985.

His new life in aviation, which had begun as a progressively absorbing hobby, had seen him create Lauda Air in 1979. He developed it well, but on 26 May 1991, the company's Flight 004 Boeing 767 broke up in mid-air and crashed in Thailand, killing all 223 on board. Niki rushed to the scene, and unstintingly offered support to grieving relatives while vowing to identify the cause. His quest — against entrenched obfuscation — highlighted fault by both aviation authority and engine manufacturer and eventually an engine thrust-reverser's uncommanded deployment in flight was verified as the disaster's most probable cause. Niki's implacability had again prevailed. His humanity towards the relatives is still remembered.

After Niki's death was announced, the reaction and sentiment expressed was as marked, and in many cases as heartfelt, within both the motor racing and aviation communities.

One witness of his reaction to the Flight 004 catastrophe posted this tribute on the professional pilots' network website: 'In late May and June of 1991 I had the experience of meeting Niki Lauda at the Hilton in Bangkok. I saw him every day for a few weeks as he met the families of those lost in the Lauda Air plane crash of May 26. He sat there alone — with no lawyers — and his empathy was obvious to all. Every day I witnessed his grief and his sympathy.

'I never met him again — but the memory of this physically scarred man with the "*jai dee*" (good heart) as they say in Thailand will live with me forever. RIP Niki Lauda…'

In 1993 Montezemolo attracted him back to Ferrari as a

ABOVE The second love of his life — aviation. Niki stands proudly before a new Boeing 767 soon after its delivery to Lauda Air in 1988.

celebrity consultant. In 2000 Lauda Air became a wholly owned subsidiary of Austrian Airlines, and Niki then changed horses to co-manage the infant Jaguar Formula 1 team through 2001 and '02, for Ford. That rare miscalculation saw his political skills stretched to breaking, numerous colleagues left unimpressed.

Late in 2003 he then founded a new airline, Niki, which merged with Air Berlin in 2011. Irrepressibly, the three-times Formula 1 World Champion then acquired charter airline Amira Air in 2016, and renamed it LaudaMotion. It absorbed the Niki brand after Air Berlin's insolvency. In parallel Niki Lauda had, in 2012, become non-executive Chairman of the Mercedes AMG Petronas F1 Team, where he played a crucial role in attracting Lewis Hamilton to join them.

All the great standard-setting drivers of their time have been cast in the warrior mould. Yet very few of that already select band was ever more truly tested, more tempered, more hard-tried than Niki Lauda. What follows traces this great man's story.

AUTHOR'S NOTE

Doug Nye began writing about racing cars at *Motor Racing* magazine in 1963–64. Today he is a multiple award-winning motor sports journalist and author of over 50 years' experience, with some 70 books to his name. He is Goodwood Motorsport's founding Historian and consultant and fulfils similar roles for Bonhams Auctioneers and the Collier Collection/Revs Institute in Naples, Florida, USA. He is a member of the National Motor Museum Advisory Council at Beaulieu, Hampshire, and is a regular columnist for *Motor Sport* magazine, while contributing to many other specialist periodicals worldwide.

INTRODUCTION

For those with little more than a passing interest in the history of Formula 1 motor racing, Niki Lauda is the man who survived a near-fatal conflagration at the Nürburgring in 1976 and came back to win the World Championship a year later, having lost out to James Hunt following the accident.

Those concerned with the history of the sport in a little more depth know of him as the teenager who started racing against the wishes of his family, bought a March works drive, blagged his way into BRM and, having shown his mettle there, got the call from Ferrari just when things were on the up and was able to shape a winning team around him. A man who turned his back on the Scuderia (after two world titles) much as Enzo Ferrari had done to him following the accident, went to Brabham in a big-money deal with Bernie Ecclestone, then walked away from the sport and went off to run his own airline. A man who then came out of retirement two years later and took a third world title before retiring for good, but stayed close to the sport with roles as a TV presenter and a team principal.

But a closer analysis of Lauda's career on a race-by-race basis reveals a lot more than this. It shows a man who was always fiercely assured of his own capabilities, but who from the earliest days had a level of self-control and racecraft that would epitomise his career. He had a well-developed awareness of the sport's risks — he got out of Formula 3 in the last year of its 'screamer' era as he found it inhabited by madmen — but was as quick as anyone on the great unsanitised road circuits at Spa, Brno and the Nürburgring; indeed, he holds the outright Formula 1 and touring car lap records for the *Nordschleife*.

He was a versatile all-rounder who won hillclimbs on alpine mountains and grass-roots 'Flugplatzrennen' on concrete airfields, who competed successfully in Group 6 sports prototypes and who was acknowledged as one of the best touring car drivers of his day. In Formula 2 and later Formula 1 he had to measure himself against a team-mate who was regarded at the time as the fastest in the business, Ronnie Peterson, and he emerged also with a reputation as a great test and development driver. In 1979, while enduring a season in one of the least reliable Formula 1 cars of his career, he had the motivation and competitiveness in more equal machinery to win the concurrent Procar Championship.

His status as the definitive 'comeback king' stands up not just in the context of his return to racing after his Nürburgring accident in 1976, but perhaps, more significantly, in his return to the cockpit after retiring from the sport in 1979. Few other drivers have delivered championships in different eras, let alone after having a two-year hiatus when they did not compete at all. Formula 1 in the 1980s was a very different sport from the one it had been in the 1970s, requiring a step-change in driving style and technique; Lauda not only adapted to it, he mastered it.

Much can be said of a driver who wins races and championships with the best equipment of the day placed at his disposal, but there are many who consider that the mark of true greatness is to be victorious in inferior cars. There is little doubt that the 1977 Ferrari 312T2 was no more than the fifth-best car that year, yet Lauda still managed to deliver three Grand Prix victories and win the World Championship. Equally, his world title in 1984 was a triumph of experience, mechanical sympathy, guile and strategy over a younger, quicker team-mate who had yet to hone his own racecraft to the level that the Austrian had long since developed.

In an era before telemetry, when race engineers could not analyse a driver's every input and reaction from the pit wall, the relationship between the two was based on trust and co-operation. A team could not necessarily disprove a driver's account of what had happened and some were more honest than others. Lauda's almost brutal candour and practicality earned him respect and authority in equal measure.

At heart he was a racer, and a purist one at that. He was a trenchant critic of the artifices of modern-day DRS (Drag Reduction System), which he viewed as a sticking plaster

12 NIKI LAUDA

RIGHT The author, pictured with part of his collection of largely self-built scale models of the cars raced by Niki Lauda throughout his career.

over the problem that cars should basically have more power than grip. Although he had been at the forefront of the safety campaign that had eliminated much of the sport's lethal nature, he despised the halos that were introduced in 2018 and objected to the fact that cars leaving the track in the modern era could simply drive though extended asphalt run-off areas and rejoin without any real physical penalty, which he considered a factor in declining standards of driver behaviour. When he had raced, mutual respect was more prevalent and contact with other cars was likely to result in a serious accident.

This book is not intended to be a retelling of Lauda's life and exploits, which have been covered at length in his own noteworthy autobiographies and in numerous interviews elsewhere. Instead, it is a chronological account of each race in which he took part, drawn from contemporary reports and publications to obtain as accurate a view of his performances as possible, informed by the accounts of observers at the time. With the benefit of hindsight and the knowledge of his later achievements, these provide an insight into the experiences that shaped his development as a racing driver. With a handful of exceptions, each account is supported with a photograph from the event to illustrate the variety of the machinery in which he competed and how this also evolved over a career that spanned 16 seasons. These images also tell a story of the evolution of the tracks on which he raced, with an almost total absence of safety arrangements in his earliest days. Also included are the later test sessions and demonstration events in which he participated, adding to the eclectic mix of cars he experienced.

These days, we are used to reading forensic race reports, with individual lap times broken down to thousandths of a second in sector-by-sector assessments supported by highly detailed technical drawings and pin-sharp digital photography. The flip side to this coin is that access to drivers is much more rigorously controlled, policed by marketing minders to make sure that answers are carefully scripted and nothing is given away.

Things were rather different when Lauda started racing, and remained so for much of his career. Old-school journalists plied their trade in the traditional way, reporting what they had witnessed first-hand out on the track and in the pitlane as much as what was fed to the primitive press facilities in which they worked. They talked to the drivers and team personnel to get the inside story of what had actually happened, although this could lead to some mischief-making and misinformation. The inevitable result was that some accounts differ from others, that reporters formed alternative perspectives on what had happened, and that few people ever had the whole story. To get a comprehensive picture of any given weekend's activity, it is necessary to study all the available reports; between them, the journalists of the day had pretty much everything covered.

In researching this book, I examined not only official entry and results lists but also reviewed all contemporary European motor sport magazines and newspapers (and some from further afield) in order to get as fully rounded a view as possible of what happened, and to try to establish the truth where any discrepancies arose. I hope, therefore, that the outcome is a comprehensive record that is as accurate as possible.

1968
BEGINNINGS

Whether or not his family believed in his abilities as a racing driver, Niki Lauda certainly did. Self-confidence was never an issue for the young Viennese, who built his career entirely independently from the wealthy background into which he was born. Living on his wits and his undoubted street-wise intelligence, he later said that in the beginning he was always one car ahead of his career (and his bank account); the one he was actually racing at any one time had not yet been paid for.

The foundation for his first racing season is a story that has entered motor racing folklore. In late-night high jinks on an icy road, he wrote off a Mini belonging to school friend Peter Draxler's father, then bought the wreck for 38,000 schillings that he borrowed from his grandmother, and almost immediately part-exchanged it for a full-blown two-year-old Group 2 racing Austin Mini Cooper S from state champion Fritz Baumgärtner.

Baumgärtner hit it off with the forthright youngster and helped him reassemble the Mini's 1,275cc engine in the garage of the Lauda residence, Niki's parents having been persuaded that he was merely looking after the machine for a friend and that working on it would help him develop his engineering skills. His ability to talk his way out of trouble was already well-developed…

1968

1 Bad Mühllacken hillclimb (A)

15 April 1968, Group 2
Mini Cooper S • #128
Result: 2nd in class

Listed in the programme as 'A.N. Lauder', the young Austrian's first motorsport event was the Bad Mühllacken hillclimb, organised by the Motorsportclub Rottenegg. He took part in his ex-Baumgärtner Mini that he and the car's former owner had fettled to deliver some 100bhp. The purchase price had included a few exploratory laps at the Semperit tyre company's Kottingbrünn test track, where, to the surprise of the Mini's vendor, Lauda had immediately found the ideal line, showing none of the hasty over-excitement so often displayed by newcomers. Baumgärtner, one of the quickest touring car drivers in Austria at the time, was impressed, but cautioned the youngster that as these few laps represented his only experience of the car, for his first competitive outing he should use no more than 8,000rpm rather than the 9,000rpm the engine would accept.

Lauda surprised more experienced drivers at Bad Mühllacken with his self-discipline as he dutifully stuck to his self-imposed speed limit to avoid overreaching himself — and also to avoid incurring any damage that he could ill afford to pay for. A clean, steady first ascent was good enough for third quickest time. Using another 500rpm, his second run was fastest outright and gave him second place on aggregate in his class, 1.5 seconds adrift of the overall victor. He reflected later that he could have gone quicker; the car still had something to spare.

ABOVE Before it all started: Niki looks over his ex-Fritz Baumgärtner competition Mini Cooper S at the Lauda family home in Vienna's Pötzleinsdorferstrasse before setting off to participate in his first hillclimb at Bad Mühllacken. At this point, his father believed he was looking after the car for a friend.

ABOVE Lauda tackles the Bad Mühllacken hillclimb, taking care not to overreach either himself or his Mini Cooper S. His name was spelled incorrectly in the programme.

BEGINNINGS   15

ABOVE Hitched to the back of the BMW saloon loaned by Alfred Schwab, the stepfather of his friend Stefan Culen, Lauda's Mini Cooper S is readied for the journey to Dobratsch, where he would record his first victory in only his second event. Among those standing in the garage are the car's former owner, Fritz Baumgärtner, Stefan Culen and another school friend, Alfons Kammerlander.

2 Dobratsch hillclimb (A)

25 April 1968, Group 2
Mini Cooper S • #10
Result: 1st in class

Fearing that the 9.3-mile (15.0km) Dobratsch course was too difficult for a beginner, with its dangerous corners and at one point a sheer drop to the valley floor, Baumgärtner had a crisis of conscience and told Lauda's father of the youngster's activities. Nevertheless, Lauda entered the event regardless of domestic disapproval, helped by the gift of 1,000 schillings for fuel and the loan of an elderly BMW V8 saloon as a tow car from his friend Stefan Culen's stepfather, Alfred Schwab. The event was a round of the national hillclimb championship and attracted many well-established drivers, including Lambert Hofer and Peter Peter. As Lauda had no mechanic of his own, he enlisted the help of one of Hofer's men to successfully cure a persistent misfire in practice.

Lauda's first victory was achieved by a narrow margin ahead of Hofer, who was something of a local celebrity and had been expected to win in his own Mini. The result was as much of a surprise to Lauda as it was to the others, as the final times were not immediately released and the winner was only revealed when the organiser placed the laurel wreath around his neck. Any desire to keep things low-key was scotched when a race report in the *Kurier* newspaper was read by his family the next day, but vehement opposition from his patriarchal grandfather was not going to thwart his motorsport ambitions.

3 Alpl hillclimb (A)

5 May 1968, Group 2
Mini Cooper S • #157
Result: 1st in class

After his victory at Dobratsch, Lauda approached Hans Ortner, an acknowledged star in the national hillclimb series driving for the strong Abarth team, to enquire about opportunities at the Italian outfit. Although Ortner was unable to assist, the ambitious youngster had already decided to set himself a benchmark in each class in which he competed. In hillclimbs, he had to be faster than Lambert Hofer, who was five years his senior, came from a similar background and was already an established name. If Hofer had beaten him just once, he alleged, he would have had to give up.

His first goal always was to win his class, which he assuredly achieved at the 4.0-mile

1968

(6.4km) Alpl course in beating runner-up Hans Himmetsburger by the huge margin of 11 seconds in his class, which comprised 13 runners.

Although Lauda's efforts were starting to gather momentum, at this stage few people took him seriously. Despite its meticulous preparation, the Mini was still tailored to Baumgärtner, its owner had no spare parts, and he kept the car at Hofer's garage.

4 Engelhartszell hillclimb (A)

26 May 1968, Group 2
Mini Cooper S • #139
Result: 1st in class, 5th overall

Before this event, it later transpired, Lauda had reconnoitred the mountain course and noted every little bump and surface change. His future rival, Helmut Marko, subsequently observed that although this was a relatively unimportant hillclimb, Lauda had prepared for it as if it had been the final of the European Mountain Championship, showing a level of professionalism that was unusual in such a young driver. Lauda's thoughtful approach paid off as he was fastest in practice, not only in his class but overall.

Heavy rain dominated the following day's competition. Wet conditions were new to him but, if anything, they magnified his talent and he won both runs in his class confidently from Hofer, after his key rivals Martin Forster and Herbert Grünsteidl crashed out. He was now attracting comment in the sporting press, with *Austro Motor* applauding his wet-weather driving and adding that his performance had exceeded expectations. During these early days, his name always appears in contemporary reports as 'Nicki' rather than 'Niki', a style he was to adopt a little later.

5 Kasten-Vichtenstein hillclimb (A)

9 June 1968, Group 2
Porsche 911S (W2-879) • #103
Result: Retired (accident)

Having been beaten in the overall rankings at Engelhartszell by the title-winning Porsche 911S of Peter Peter, Lauda decided that a faster car was needed if he was to progress. In the face of further opposition from his family he pulled off another outrageous deal, this time selling the Mini Cooper S to Helmut Koinigg and using the proceeds as a deposit to acquire the Porsche from Peter, who generously agreed that the youngster could pay off the balance when he sold it. He arranged for the 911S to be prepared by hillclimb specialist Gerhard Mitter so that it could be tuned to the optimum — Lauda's perfectionist nature was becoming apparent.

Meticulous preparation did not pay great dividends this time. Having only driven some 300km (about 200 miles) in the Porsche — on public roads — he was second fastest on the first ascent after a furiously quick run in another rain-affected contest. On his second run, having

ABOVE LEFT Lauda's Mini Cooper S is captured at speed on one of the few straight sections of the tricky Alpl hillclimb course.

ABOVE RIGHT At the picturesque Engelhartszell hillclimb, Niki recorded his third and final class win in the Mini Cooper S. He was already looking to upgrade.

BEGINNINGS 17

ABOVE Lauda was one of several competitors whose cars left the road on the unprotected drops of the steep, narrow Koralpe mountain road, the difference being that he still managed to emerge victorious in his class with his newly acquired Porsche 911S.

RIGHT Sharing his compatriot Lambert Hofer's Mini, Lauda heads a gaggle of cars during his first-ever circuit race, on the challenging Nürburgring *Nordschleife*.

set the quickest time at the mid-point, he over-reached himself, came off the road and ended up in the bushes. A damaged fuel tank meant that he recorded the first retirement of his career.

6 Koralpe hillclimb (A)

23 June 1968, Group 2
Porsche 911S (W2-879) • #149
Result: 1st in class, 5th overall

Lauda's competition programme was almost derailed at the Koralpe hillclimb. Whereas most competitors had brought their cars on trailers, he had driven his to the event and had forgotten that, after fitting the 911S with its racing exhaust, the Porsche would accelerate rather more quickly. The inevitable happened soon after his run started. Overcooking things on a fast bend, he bounced the Porsche off a wall and shot down the mountainside into a ditch. With the help of spectators, he manhandled the car back onto the road and surprised the opposition by breezing through to win the Group 2 class. His excellent time was quicker than all the more powerful Group 5 machinery and gave him fifth place overall. *Austro Motor* was already describing him as the sensation of the year.

7 Nürburgring Six Hours (D)

7 July 1968, Group 2
Mini Cooper S (with Lambert Hofer) • #73
Result: Retired

Now came Lauda's first attempt at a circuit race — a daunting and ambitious one. Lambert Hofer, his hillclimb rival, entered his Mini Cooper S in the prestigious annual six-hour marathon at the Nürburgring, on the *Nordschleife*, and invited Lauda to partner him. It was Niki's first motorsport foray outside Austria, over 550 miles (900km) from Vienna.

To make sure they were properly prepared, the two Austrians spent the week before the race completing endless laps of the circuit, taking turns as driver and (regularly car-sick) passenger to learn the 14.2-mile (22.8km) course. Noting what the professional teams did, Lauda then spent the untimed Friday practice setting up the car and was one of the 90 successful qualifiers from the huge entry of 120.

For once the weather in the Eifel mountains was beautiful, but that also meant he was making his début in front of an enormous crowd. To add to the pressure of challenging 43 other hopefuls in the Division 2 class, he was also the youngest driver in the six-hour race. Although the Mini Cooper S failed to make it to the finish, Lauda's willingness to take on big challenges was already apparent.

18 NIKI LAUDA

1968

8 Preis der Shell-Austria AG (A)

Tulln-Langenlebarn, 14 July 1968, Group 2
Porsche 911S (W2-879) • #30
Result: Retired (engine)

Lauda entered his first solo circuit race much nearer home, on the concrete expanses of the Langenlebarn military airbase close to the town of Tulln on the River Danube about 15 miles (25km) upstream of Vienna. Rain early in the day made this rudimentary course, marked out by straw bales, rather treacherous but the weather improved in time for Lauda's 20-lap race. His race suit now was one of Jochen Rindt's old ones that had been given to him.

After a good start, he ran a strong second behind Sigi Pust's similar 911S and ahead of eventual winner Klaus Reisch's Alfa Romeo GTA, but before long his engine expired. After the race, he considered buying Pust's 911S as a replacement when his rival announced that business commitments meant he would be giving up racing.

9 Tauplitz hillclimb (A)

4 August 1968, Group 2
Porsche 911S (W2-879) • #40
Result: 1st in class, 7th overall

Next came an event near Graz on the 6.1-mile (9.8km) Tauplitzalm Alpine toll road, a challenging mountain course used on the European Hillclimb Championship trail. While practice took place in bad weather, the day of timed runs dawned fine. Early on, however, proceedings were marred when the popular Kary Seitz crashed his Porsche RSK fatally.

Pushing aside any misgivings about the narrow mountain road and its unprotected drops, Lauda took a comfortable class win and seventh place overall. Impressively, his time was quicker than those achieved by the winners of the classes for over 2-litre Sports & Special Touring, GT and Formula Vee cars.

ABOVE Lauda's Porsche 911S is fuelled and checked ahead of his first solo race, on the rough concrete of Tulln-Langenlebarn's aerodrome.

BELOW Safety facilities are almost non-existent for both drivers and spectators as the Porsche 911S negotiates the Tauplitz hillclimb, where Lauda scored another class win.

BEGINNINGS 19

ABOVE Niki powers the Porsche away from the start line in his first run up the fast, challenging Stainz hillclimb.

RIGHT At the Walding hillclimb, one of the premier events on the national calendar, Lauda steered the Porsche 911S to another class win — and to the attention of Kaimann boss Kurt Bergmann.

10 Stainz hillclimb (A)

11 August 1968, Group 2
Porsche 911S (W2-879) • #51
Result: 1st in class, 9th overall

This was the only event in which Lauda and his childhood hero Jochen Rindt actually drove against each other, not in wheel-to-wheel competition but instead racing against the clock. For Lauda it was only his 10th contest of any description but, after his class wins in hillclimbs and two track appearances, the establishment was starting to take notice of the promising newcomer.

A strong entry included local hero Helmut Marko, but Rindt's surprise late participation in a Formula 2 Brabham BT18 attracted another 10,000 spectators to the twisty ascent through vineyards outside Graz, boosting the crowd to 35,000. As the competition neared its climax, racing was interrupted for half an hour by undisciplined fans constantly crossing the course and several drivers complained vociferously, some suggesting the event should be postponed. Lauda, unfazed by either the big-name competition or the minimal safety arrangements, drifted the Porsche through the narrow bends to beat Sigi Pust's 911S to the class victory. His final time was good enough for ninth place overall.

11 Walding hillclimb (A)

15 August 1968, Group 2
Porsche 911S (W2-879) • #33
Result: 1st in class, 6th overall

Although this hillclimb was not part of the national championship, it was the Austrian motorsport federation's 'Golden Ribbon' event so the country's leading club drivers were present. The first ascents took place in the dry but rain set in by the time of the second runs. Once again, Lauda took the class win, and finished sixth overall.

More significantly, his uncle now gave him a helping hand. Heinz Lauda, director of Veitscher Magnesitwerke, a big mining company, recommended his nephew to Kurt 'Master' Bergmann, boss of the Kaimann racing team. Despite some initial scepticism about the slender youth in the Styrian hat, Bergmann was sufficiently impressed by his confident performances against strong competition to invite the youngster to try out one of his Formula Vee single-seaters.

20 NIKI LAUDA

1968

12 STAMK Flugplatzrennen (A)

Zeltweg, 25 August 1968, Group 2
Porsche 911S (W2-879) • #2
Result: 1st in class, 1st overall

This national-level competition, a round of the national touring car championship, was run directly after the 500km international sportscar race, the feature event of this last-ever meeting at Zeltweg's bumpy airfield circuit. Lauda had now gained some modest backing from Valvoline to assist with his hand-to-mouth racing budget, but his convincing win in the 35-lap race — his first outright victory on a circuit — owed as much to Berndt Brodner's continued record of mechanical failures as it did to his own driving skill and expensively tuned 911S. Brodner was leading by half a lap when his Porsche failed, leaving Lauda to take the flag some eight seconds ahead of Klaus Reisch's Alfa Romeo GTA. As a result, the championship was still far from decided: Reisch, Hofer and Lauda all still had a real chance of taking the title.

13 Finland-Austria Challenge (SF)

Keimola, 8 September 1968, Formula Vee
Kaimann Mk3 (V680X) • #4
Result: 4th

This was the second leg of a contest between national teams from Austria and Finland, the first having taken place at Zeltweg. Kaimann boss Kurt Bergmann was prepared to take chances with young talent, albeit on a highly selective basis, and decided to give Lauda his single-seater break in one of the works Formula Vee cars. It was also a test of the youngster's resolve, as Lauda was required to drive the team's Opel Blitz race-car transporter and trailer — the usual driver was on holiday — to Finland and return everything in one piece, a round trip of 14 days. Austria's five-car team comprised Günther Huber, Helmut Marko and Lauda in works Kaimanns, Walter Bussek in a private Kaimann and Lothar Schörg in an Austro.

The Kaimanns had more powerful engines than the local cars and from the start Huber and Marko were in a class of their own, pulling out a gap of over 20 seconds in a race lasting just over 30 minutes and staging a dead heat at the finish line. Lauda held off a concerted challenge from Matti Järvi, whose Veemax pressed him hard from lap 4 onwards, and steadily closed up on third-placed Schörg to finish right on his tail, just 0.9 second behind in fourth place. He had acquitted himself well, finishing ahead of all the strong Scandinavian contingent and fellow Kaimann driver Bussek in eighth place. He had also achieved the goals he had set himself for his single-seater baptism: he had not tried to win but had driven a flawless race to finish without

ABOVE Niki's Porsche 911S heads the Mini Cooper S of Herbert Grünsteidl (winner of Lauda's début hillclimb at Bad-Mühllacken) in the national touring car championship race during the last-ever meeting at the Zeltweg airfield course.

BELOW First time out in a single-seater: Niki awaits the start of practice at Keimola in Finland in his works-entered Formula Vee Kaimann Mk3, having driven the factory's race-car transporter and trailer all the way from Austria.

BEGINNINGS 21

ABOVE During the 1968 Donau Pokal race at Aspern, Horst Löhner's private Kaimann Mk3 leads Niki's works car and Alfred Vogelberger's Olympic around a bend delineated by straw bales.

damage, gain experience, and show Bergmann that he could be relied upon.

More importantly for Bergmann, Lauda brought the cars home safely despite a breakage on the rusty trailer during the return journey. It happened at 70mph in the wet on the bumpy Hamburg *Autobahn* but Lauda managed to bring the ensemble safely to a halt, even if there was no hard shoulder on which to take refuge. He and his compatriots had little choice but to abandon the wrecked trailer in adjacent woodland and hitch the Kaimann that it had been carrying directly to the transporter's towing hook to get it back to the factory.

14 Donau Pokal (A)

Aspern, 6 October 1968, Formula Vee
Kaimann Mk3 (V680X) • #11
Result: 8th

Traditionally, the two aerodrome meetings at Aspern and Innsbruck completed the national season on consecutive weekends, known as 'Austrian Speed Week' in a nod to the famous Bahamas event. Lauda took part in two races at each venue.

The 10-lap Formula Vee race at Aspern attracted a highly competitive 18-car entry, with all the best national drivers once again present and fighting for championship positions. Lauda's entry via the Kaimann works team meant that he avoided the 'ID Card' category for amateur Formula Vee competitors and was pitted straight away against the serious drivers. The hard-fought race was thrilling, with so much contact between the jostling competitors that several observers commented on its resemblance to a stock-car event. On his way to a creditable eighth place, Lauda managed to avoid separate three-car tangles among the leaders on the seventh and eighth laps, one of which involved Austro driver Werner Riedl overtaking Helmut Marko while airborne. It was all very close, with fourth to ninth places covered by just six seconds at the flag.

15 Preis der Firma Generale (A)

Aspern, 6 October 1968, Group 2
Porsche 911S (W2-879) • #36
Qualifying: 4th • Result: 3rd in class, 3rd overall

In his second race at Aspern, Lauda qualified well in a large field for the 20-lap combined

22 NIKI LAUDA

1968

Special Touring Group 2/Group 1 and GT event, which comprised a high-quality but small entry of only five runners in his over-1,600cc division. An outside tip for victory, he had a race-long duel with Klaus Reisch and eventually finished third in both his class and overall, half a minute adrift of second-placed Berndt Brodner's similar 911S. Neither was able to keep up with Ernst Furtmayr's flying Schnitzer-prepared BMW 2002, which set a new lap record *en route* to victory. Although Lauda was nearly a minute behind the BMW at the flag, he did finish the race six laps ahead of his old sparring partner Lambert Hofer, whose Mini won the 1,300cc division

16 Preis der Formel Vau Europa (A)

Innsbruck, 13 October 1968, Formula Vee
Kaimann Mk3 (V680X) • #9
Qualifying: 12th • Result: Retired

At Innsbruck's bumpy 1.7-mile (2.7km) aerodrome course, where practice and

ABOVE Niki surveys the rear of his Porsche 911S as he prepares for the Preis der Firma Generale Group 2 Special Touring race on the Aspern aerodrome.

BELOW Alfred Vogelberger's Olympic heads Niki's Kaimann Mk3 and the duelling pack around another rudimentary course marked out by straw bales; this time the venue is the Innsbruck airfield and the race the Preis von Tirol.

BEGINNINGS 23

ABOVE Lauda takes avoiding action as Lothar Schörg spins his Austro in front of him on the slippery concrete of Innsbruck's aerodrome.

BELOW In the Preis von Tirol at Innsbruck, Niki's Porsche 911S leads Sigi Pust's similar car from Reinhardt Stenzel's works Alfa Romeo GTA, Berndt Brodner's very quick Porsche 911S and the Alfa Romeo GTA of Klaus Reisch.

qualifying took place between aircraft landings, Sunday morning's 15-lap Formula Vee race — the concluding round of the five-race national championship — attracted a field of 39 cars, more than twice the number than had competed at Aspern.

Lauda started from the inside of the fourth row, having qualified 1.9 seconds off the pole time. In an attempt to curb the recklessness that had pervaded the Formula Vee season so far, OSK officials equipped with two-way radios were stationed around the course and were instructed to enforce driving standards, by use of the black flag if necessary. While this made the drivers' behaviour generally more circumspect, it made little difference to Lauda as someone punted him off anyway. Meanwhile, Helmut Marko, his future nemesis, won the slipstreaming contest at the very last corner in his Kaimann.

Lauda finished ninth in the championship standings, equal on points with his friend Gerold Pankl (Austro), who took eighth place by virtue of a better finishing record.

17 Preis von Tirol (A)

Innsbruck, 13 October 1968, Group 2
Porsche 911S (W2-879) • #58
Qualifying: 3rd • Result: Retired

For his second race at the Innsbruck-Kranebitten airport, held during the afternoon, Lauda entered his Porsche 911S under the banner of Valvoline RAR Racing Team. He qualified a strong third behind the factory entries of Ernst Furtmayr (BMW) and Reinhardt Stenzel (Alfa Romeo), although he was 1.3 seconds off the pole time. Once again all the Special Touring Car categories competed together in the 15-lap race and the cars in his over-1,600cc class proved faster than the Formula Vee racers; Lauda's pace in what was basically a production car was underlined by the fact that his time would have been good enough for ninth on the grid in the combined Group 5 and GT headline event.

The field was large and boisterous, even if

there were only five starters in Lauda's class. He was making up ground behind the merciless battle between the sister Porsches of Sepp Greger, Holger Zarges and Stenzel, helped when Furtmayr spun away the lead, when he posted the race's sixth retirement. Local reports noted that he had handled the Porsche very effectively.

18 Dopplerhütte Hillclimb (A)

27 October 1968, Group 2
Porsche 911S (W2-879)
Result: 1st in class, 9th overall

In good late-autumn weather, large crowds flocked to the 'Grand Mountain Prize of Vienna' event and once again all the big names of local motorsport were present for what was a purely Austrian affair (the usual German contenders had not been invited). This was Lauda's last meeting of the season and again he competed in both his Porsche and the Kaimann.

For the first time in a hillclimb, he entered the Porsche in two different classes, winning the Group 2 division ahead of his season-long 911-mounted rival Brodner and placing ninth overall in the touring category. Yet again his performance demonstrated that he was capable of beating Group 5 competition with a much less sophisticated Group 2 machine.

It had been a good season in his well-prepared Porsche and he had shown his potential strongly, achieving decent results against more competitive fields in higher-profile events.

19 Dopplerhütte Hillclimb (A)

27 October 1968, Formula Vee
Kaimann Mk3 (V680X)
Result: 2nd in class, 9th overall

Getting to grips with the single-seater Kaimann, this time at a hillclimb rather than a circuit, Lauda again featured prominently in his second contest of the weekend. The Group 9 (Formula Vee) class had the busiest entry of all, with 13 starters. As expected, Helmut Marko won the class in his Kaimann but Lauda provided the biggest surprise of the meeting, his aggregate time from two runs just 1.5 seconds behind the local champion, beating Erich Breinsberg and four other drivers in identical Kaimann Mk3s even if poorer conditions meant that his run was three seconds slower than he had achieved in his Porsche earlier in the day. His team-mates were impressed: finishing runner-up in his class and ninth overall again was his reward for thorough preparation of his works-run car and careful study of the hillclimb course.

SUMMARY

In its annual appraisal of Austrian drivers for 1968, *Powerslide* magazine commented that Lauda had 'attracted the attention of many with his performances in a Mini Cooper S and a Mitter-fettled Porsche 911; a very talented young man who in his first season surprised in Formula Vee.' Having gained the confidence of Kurt Bergmann, who would become his first mentor, and with a seat in a competitive works team for 1969, he could look forward to the new season.

ABOVE Still a relatively unfamiliar environment for the young Austrian; the cockpit of Lauda's Formula Vee Kaimann Mk3 before practice at Dopplerhütte.

1969
CLIMBING THE LADDER

By 1969 Kurt Bergmann's Kaimann team had proved itself to be the class of the field in European Formula Vee racing, both in its engineering standards and the professionalism of its organisation. It was a good fit for the young Lauda, whose personal values concerning the optimum preparation of his cars matched those of his employer.

Paired with the experienced Erich Breinsberg, who was nine years his senior, Lauda got down to the serious business of learning his racecraft in closely matched machinery against ambitious and varied competitors. There was no room for faint-heartedness; steely nerves and strong determination would be needed in the no-holds-barred world of Formula Vee racing. The racing would take place on some of Europe's most challenging and famous circuits as well as others where the safety improvements that were receiving attention at the sport's upper echelons had not yet permeated.

Lauda would also need to learn how to establish his own position within the team. Breinsberg was well-ensconced at Kaimann, a close personal friend of its founder and clearly the number one driver. In order to progress, Niki would not only have to beat all the other hotshoes on the grid, but he would also need to demonstrate that he could outperform his well-regarded team-mate.

Despite his early reputation for seriousness and thorough attention to detail in the preparation of his cars, young Lauda had his wild side too: the season would see him become one of the 'rat pack' of Austrian Formula Vee drivers — others included Peter Peter, Gerold Pankl and Lothar Schörg — who partied their way around the Central Zone qualifying races for the European Cup. It was an education of sorts, and one that would stand him in good stead when he moved to England a couple of years later.

1969

20 AvD Deutschland Trophy (D)

Hockenheim, 12 April 1969, Formula Vee
Kaimann Mk4 (V690X)
Qualifying: 1st • Result: 4th (fastest lap)

Strong Austrian/German rivalry was evident in this supporting event for Hockenheim's high-profile Jim Clark Memorial Formula 2 race. This Formula Vee contest, the first Central Zone preliminary for the European Cup finals, seemed like premeditated lunacy on the full Hockenheim course with its long, flat-out sections, and the expected slipstreaming battles soon developed.

Lauda made a fine start to his new season by qualifying on pole position. By lap 6 he headed the leading group from Alfred Vogelberger (Olympic), Gerold Pankl (Austro) and Lothar Schörg (Austro), all fighting incredibly hard for positions that changed hands constantly. Niki stayed in front for much of the distance before spinning in the stadium section on the last lap, but he recovered to finish fourth, just one second off a podium place and five seconds behind team leader Erich Breinsberg. At least he had fastest lap to show for his efforts. Later, he admitted that his spin had been the result of foolish over-confidence.

21 Preis von Wien (A)

Aspern, 13 April 1969, Formula Vee
Kaimann Mk4 (V690X) • #7
Result: Retired (accident)

The day after the Hockenheim race, Lauda was at Aspern, a mere 460 miles (730km) away and close to home in Vienna. For drivers who had been at Hockenheim, the organisers arranged an extra practice session on race morning, and Lauda was keen to make his mark early. Lapping quickly and weaving his way around the many cars that were circulating the short airfield course, he arrived too fast at a corner that was already blocked by two spun

BELOW Some last-minute words of advice from Kurt Bergmann before Niki goes out on his qualifying run at Aspern. If the advice was to take things steadily, it was ignored.

CLIMBING THE LADDER   27

22 Belgrade Grand Prix (YU)

Belgrade, 20 April 1969, Formula Vee
Kaimann Mk4 (V690X)
Result: 2nd

For this Formula Vee support race at the first of three European Touring Car Championship rounds behind the Iron Curtain, 15 of the 17 entrants were from Austria and Germany. The venue, a 2.7-mile (4.35km) street circuit laid out in Belgrade, then capital of Yugoslavia but now Serbia's capital, was far from safe, with many of the 40,000 spectators sitting right next to the track.

In very wet conditions, practice showed just how quick the Formula Vee cars were becoming, as Lauda and Erich Breinsberg almost matched the times of the turbocharged BMW touring cars, their works Kaimanns comfortably the fastest cars in the field. The race was held after one of the two hour-long touring car feature events, the end of which had seen spectators swarm onto the track, leaving several inches of mud and litter across the already rain-soaked tarmac. Consequently, the start of the Formula Vee race was held up while people were persuaded to return to the spectator areas and the worst of the mess was cleared up.

When the flag fell, Lauda and Breinsberg immediately pulled clear but by lap 3 Gerold Pankl had caught up with them and passed Breinsberg to take second place. Lauda maintained a firm lead until the last lap when, after losing concentration under pressure from Pankl, he spun on a patch of mud. Pankl

ABOVE Niki speeds across Aspern's concrete runway during the additional practice session that was laid on for drivers who had raced at Hockenheim the previous day. Shortly afterwards, he somersaulted into straw bales, obliging a photographer to run for cover. Despite the spectacular shunt — captured here by a television camera — he escaped virtually unscathed.

RIGHT The starting grid forms up for the Belgrade Grand Prix, watched by throngs of spectators wrapped up in cold April weather against the backdrop of some rather grim Eastern Bloc architecture.

cars. He was unable to avoid a collision and his Kaimann somersaulted spectacularly into the outfield, landing upside down and in the process causing his helmet to scrape on the track. Marshals righted the car to find Lauda drenched in petrol (the fuel cap had become dislodged) but unhurt apart from a damaged finger. He readily accepted responsibility for the incident.

Lauda's immediate concern was whether the car could be fixed in time for the race. Repairs were hastily completed by the Kaimann mechanics and he just made it onto the back row of the grid, but in the rush no one noticed that a cooling fan baffle had been bent. This caused the air-cooled engine to overheat, forcing him to retire while running fifth, ahead of Peter Peter's Austro. That evening the accident appeared on a TV sports broadcast and caused his family yet more worry.

1969

squeezed through to take the win while Lauda lost time having to reverse before resuming, but nevertheless he finished a comfortable second ahead of Dieter Quester, who, as a works BMW driver, had won the larger-capacity touring-car race. Although Lauda's talent was evident, and here measurable against the established Quester, he still lacked the experience to avoid making mistakes at crucial moments.

23 Budapest Nagydija (H)

Népliget Park, 11 May 1969, Formula Vee
Kaimann Mk4 (V690X) • #9
Result: 4th

This was another supporting race for the European Touring Car Championship, this time in Hungary's capital city for the Grand Prix of Budapest. A crowd of 50,000 lined the demanding and dangerous tree-lined roads of this 3.3-mile (5.3km) circuit around the city's municipal park.

The Formula Vee race attracted drivers from five different countries and the Austrian contingent again fared well. During a torrentially wet Saturday practice session that left the track awash with deep puddles of standing water, Lauda qualified on the front row. The following day's race, fortunately in dry, sunny weather, was blighted by engine failures and spins, but Lauda managed to keep up with the leaders, behind a fierce tussle at the front between Gerold Pankl and Alfred Vogelberger, and Manfred Schurti's third-placed Austro. After a steady drive, Lauda duly finished fourth in the tough 20-lap competition.

ABOVE Niki's Kaimann Mk4 lines up on the Budapest starting grid alongside the older Mk3 of Helmut Bross. The casually placed straw bales offer little protection for the fragile Formula Vee cars against the tree-lined avenues of Népliget Park.

ZOLDER
1 JUNE 1969

Prior to Zolder's Western Zone qualifying round for the Formula Vee European Cup, the works Kaimann team decided to go to the Belgian circuit with Lauda for pre-race testing in order to get useful track time ahead of their own Central Zone qualifying round later in the month. His Kaimann Mk4 dominated the time sheets amid grumbles from some other competitors who wanted to have the Austrian's engine checked for legality.

Lauda was then asked to try out a Formula Vee Austro. Belgian enthusiasts Etienne der Clerk and Michael van Wassenhove had purchased two Austros that they loaned to, among others, reigning Belgian national champion Bernard Goffinet (pictured at the wheel here). The two patrons persuaded Lauda to do some laps in Goffinet's car, whereupon he set exactly the same time as he had achieved with his Kaimann.

This was sufficient to convince the complainers that Lauda's speed in the Kaimann was down to him, not any spurious engine advantage.

In a separate experiment later in the day, the Belgian benefactors spent some time watching the line Lauda was taking in a particular bend. Placing a matchbox near the point where he made his apex, they were astounded at his precision, finding that on every lap he passed the matchbox to within a centimetre.

CLIMBING THE LADDER 29

ABOVE The Rossfeld–Berchtesgarten mountain road was as challenging a hillclimb as any; here Niki attacks one of its many fast bends in his Formula Vee Kaimann Mk4.

BELOW Kaimann team leader Erich Breinsberg's Mk4 heads Niki's sister car during their no-holds-barred duel in the Rhein-Pokal race at Hockenheim. No team orders were given and Lauda was not fazed by the challenge of his much more experienced team-mate.

24 Rossfeld hillclimb (D)

8 June 1969, Formula Vee
Kaimann Mk4 (V690X) • #27
Result: 5th in class, 32nd overall

After 108 hours of rain and snow, there were doubts as to whether this prestigious hillclimb meeting would be run, but event day dawned clear and the course dried progressively. The Formula Vee runners went out first and on the still-slippery surface their times were some 30 seconds slower than the winning Ferrari prototype would later achieve.

The Kaimanns were not as suited to the 3.7-mile (6.0km) course as the Olympics and Austros of their German rivals and could not match them this time. Lauda was fifth fastest on his first run, 1.2 seconds slower than team-mate Erich Breinsberg, but after adjustments to his transmission — one presumes a change of final-drive ratio — he was just 0.17 second slower than Breinsberg on the second ascent, and nearly five seconds quicker than the next-quickest Formula Vee car. However, with the prototypes, GTs and touring cars all running in better conditions later in the day, this was only good enough for 32nd in the overall rankings.

25 Rhein-Pokal-Rennen (D)

Hockenheim, 15 June 1969, Formula Vee
Kaimann Mk4 (V690X)
Result: 2nd

Before racing began, Lauda completed several demonstration laps to showcase the difference between a VW Beetle and his Formula Vee Kaimann, his time in the single-seater some 30 seconds faster than in the saloon — powered by the same air-cooled engine — around Hockenheim's short course.

A huge entry of 80 hopefuls was split into two practice sessions (for even-numbered and odd-numbered cars), with 25 qualifying from each group. Come the race, from the outset

Lauda appeared determined to win it. He calmly held second place, despite experiencing severe understeer, as he and team leader Erich Breinsberg pulled out a 30-second lead in the now-familiar Kaimann 'train'. On the last lap they traded the lead three times before entering the *Sachs-Kurve* side by side, whereupon Breinsberg gave the late-braking Lauda a nudge and they both spun into the infield. Rejoining, a disgruntled Breinsberg chopped across Lauda's nose to take victory, afterwards demanding to know what the youngster thought he was doing. Brushing off requests from the older driver to impose team orders, Bergmann refused to chastise his junior pilot, preferring to let them decide matters on the track.

26 ADAC-Hansa Pokal (D)

Nürburgring, 29 June 1969, Formula Vee
Kaimann Mk4 (V690X) • #84
Result: 4th

This Central Zone qualifying round for the European Cup was run over seven laps of the Nürburgring's 4.8-mile (7.7km) *Südschleife* and was dominated by the Austrian quartet of Lauda and Erich Breinsberg in their works Kaimanns together with Helmut Marko (McNamara) and Peter Peter (Austro). From the start, these four pulled clear of the field with Lauda holding third place. They drove an unexpectedly fair race despite furiously jockeying for position in a no-quarter-given battle that saw cars frequently go off the road.

All four were in contention for victory when, towards the end of the last lap, they went into the *Nordkehre*. Breinsberg led but Peter half-spun as he fended off Marko, who in turn went off the track as he took avoiding action. Marko rejoined right in front of Lauda, forcing him to brake to a standstill, and when the group got going again only two seconds covered them at the flag. Although Lauda did not make the podium, all four had done enough to qualify for the finals of the European Cup. Just after the finish line they were also lucky to avoid hitting an official with the red flag who decided to stop them in order to avoid the wasted time of cars completing a slowing-down lap; the unfortunate Christian Dietrich, however, crashed his Olympic when trying to miss the man.

27 Sopron Grand Prix (H)

Sopron, 6 July 1969, Formula Vee
Kaimann Mk4 (V690X)
Result: 1st

Hungary's second international Formula Vee meeting of the year was held on Sopron's fast and hazardous 3.2-mile (5.1km) public road circuit. Although the event did not count towards the European Cup, it still attracted a strong Austrian contingent from just over the border, Sopron being only 50 miles (75km) from Vienna.

The race was a run at frantic pace, the fastest lap completed at 95mph with the leaders covered by no more than two seconds throughout the entire 15 laps. In almost tropical heat, once again it was a closely fought duel, but this time Lauda headed the 'Kaimann Express' with his team-mate pressing him hard all the way. Breinsberg waited in vain for him to make a mistake but he drove perfectly to take his first win in a single-seater. To celebrate his success, he took team boss Kurt Bergmann on a lap of honour, the grinning 'Master' sitting astride the Kaimann's engine cover.

28 Internationales Flugplatzrennen (A)

Tulln-Langenlebarn, 13 July 1969, Group 2
Opel Rekord 1900 'Black Widow' • #41
Qualifying: 11th • Result: Retired (engine)

The infamous 'Black Widow' was Opel's unofficial works car that had been given to Kaimann boss Kurt Bergmann (minus its 180bhp engine) when the programme was abandoned at the end of 1968. It was an aluminium-bodied Rekord Series C that had been built out-of-hours at the Opel factory. Created as a 'ringer' to challenge the works BMWs, in various hands

ABOVE & RIGHT Street racing at its most basic: Niki's Kaimann is shadowed by the sister car of team leader Erich Breinsberg as they pass the unprotected kerbs, ditches and lamp-posts of Sopron. This time the younger driver made no mistakes and scored his first victory in a single-seater. As captured in this still from a fuzzy home video, he took team boss Kurt Bergmann for a lap of honour astride the car.

KOTTINGBRÜNN
9 JULY 1969

Kurt Bergmann's network of contacts included useful connections with Semperit, which used an old military airfield next to its plant at Kottingbrünn, near Vienna, for tyre testing. Although Semperit had no racing programme, Bergmann was able to use the facility to try out his cars, so Lauda had become very familiar with the course on which he had had his first-ever turn at the wheel of a competition car, trying out Fritz Baumgärtner's Mini Cooper S before purchasing it early the previous year.

In preparation for a move up to Formula 3 in 1970, the rival McNamara team rented the Semperit test track to try out its new car, the Mk3B. As Lauda had proved a tough opponent in Formula Vee, he was invited to the test, which also gave the team the chance to evaluate him. Peter Arundell, the former Grand Prix driver who was now McNamara's racing manager, was also on hand, reportedly offering the youngster advice on his driving technique.

it regularly out-ran Porsche 911s as well.

After acquiring the car, Bergmann installed a new Kaimann-tuned engine and entered it at Tulln-Langenlebarn for his young Formula Vee driver. Starting from 11th on the grid and having made a rather poor getaway, Lauda was soon the fastest man in the 20-lap race, passing car after car until he was stopped by engine failure midway through. He later remarked that it was the worst car he ever drove; there is no evidence that it ever won a race, so it certainly did not live up to its hype.

29 Internationales Flugplatzrennen (A)

Tulln-Langenlebarn, 13 July 1969, Formula Vee
Kaimann Mk4 (V690X) • #33
Result: 3rd

In the afternoon, Langenlebarn's rather grim military airbase hosted the second *Flugplatz* (aerodrome) race of the Formula Vee season. As the event was part of the national championship development programme for potential Formula 2 drivers, it attracted a big entry of 33 cars.

The Austrian hopefuls engaged in a mêlée, jostling and banging wheels and sometimes squeezing each other off the course. Very quickly, a trio comprising Peter Peter, Erich Breinsberg and Lauda broke away from the rest but the two works Kaimann drivers were unlucky with traffic. Peter was able to thread his Austro through the backmarkers more effectively and avoided some hairy moments to win the 20-lap scramble from Breinsberg and Lauda, who was 13 seconds behind his team leader at the chequered flag.

ABOVE Lauda's Opel Rekord 'Black Widow' lines up at Tulln-Langenlebarn alongside the Mini Cooper of Helmuth Pechtl. On the row behind are Günther Breyer's Porsche 911 and Roland Moser's Ford Escort.

BELOW Niki's Kaimann Mk4 charges across the bumpy, rippled concrete of Tulln-Langenlebarn's military aerodrome.

ABOVE The sweeping curves of the new Österreichring were too much for the little Formula Vee cars, which had to run flat out for most of the lap. Here, Niki leads a typical squabbling, slipstreaming bunch — Peter Peter's Austro, an unidentified Kaimann Mk4, Alfred Vogelberger's Olympic and Wolfgang Bulow's McNamara — through the downhill plunge of the *Boschkurve*.

BELOW The race of the year: Niki has his Kaimann locked in battle with Helmut Marko's McNamara during the Continental Preis at the Nürburgring.

30 Europa Trophäe (A)

Österreichring, 27 July 1969, Formula Vee
Kaimann Mk4 (V690X)
Result: 8th

The organisers at the newly built Österreichring had attracted the third and last Central Zone qualifying round for the European Cup to their inaugural race weekend. Qualifying was brutal as a huge 56-car entry fought over 26 starting places; there was plenty of contact as some drivers had realised that a blow to the rod protruding from the back of the gearbox of the car in front would make it jump out of gear.

In reality, this magnificent new circuit was too fast for Formula Vee cars and there were many retirements of over-stressed machinery. A tight pack of eight drivers scrapped for the lead throughout, with the positions changing on every lap. The slipstreaming battle for placings was undecided until the last lap, but Helmut Marko's McNamara eventually proved quicker than the Austros and Kaimanns and pulled away to win, with Lauda finishing eighth.

31 Continental Preis (D)

Nürburgring, 3 August 1969, Formula Vee
Kaimann Mk4 (V690X) • #10
Result: 2nd

Helmut Marko and Lauda were in a class of their own in this supporting race for the German Grand Prix on the full Nürburgring *Nordschleife*. The battle between the two Austrian hotshoes had added spice as Marko was paid a retainer by McNamara while Lauda — five years his junior — was unpaid at Kaimann, and both were aware that the Formula 1 team bosses were watching. Lauda was the first driver to break the 10-minute Formula Vee lap record in practice, but Marko was only a fraction slower. Both started on the front row in a field of 50 cars.

Lauda was in front at the end of lap 1 but the

34 NIKI LAUDA

1969

LEFT Niki at speed in the Kaimann Mk4 on the Nürburgring *Nordschleife*.

BELOW A decidedly disgruntled Lauda looks on as Helmut Marko celebrates his Nürburgring victory in company with third-placed Peter Peter.

lead changed constantly as he and his compatriot shadowed and slipstreamed each other. Their terrific duel lasted the whole race: every one of the six laps was run faster than their qualifying pace, and Marko established the new Formula Vee lap record on the final lap as the battle reached its climax. Down the *Döttinger-Höhe* straight for the last time, Marko forced Lauda onto the grass in his attempt to get past and took the win by 15 seconds as his rival recovered. Their pace had been so fast that they finished nearly a minute ahead of the field.

The atmosphere on the podium was icy and the Kaimann team considered a protest against Marko's robust tactics, but in the absence of any eye-witnesses to the incident Bergmann decided against it.

32 Österreichring 1,000km (A)

10 August 1969, Group 4
Porsche 910 (010) (with Otto Stuppacher) • #25
Qualifying: 16th • Result: 21st

The Österreichring's first full international meeting was a prestigious one as the spectacular new circuit hosted the final round of the International Championship of Makes, the name by which the world championship for sports cars was then known. For this 1,000km race, styled the Grosser Preiss von Österreich, the Bosch Racing Team gave Lauda a one-off drive in its Porsche 910, partnered by Otto Stuppacher, the car's owner. The combination qualified fastest of the 2-litre runners, although some doubts were raised over the accuracy of the timekeeping during official practice and times were only given for each car and not for individual drivers.

Stuppacher took the start and handled the first stint of this 170-lap contest, although his efforts were unremarkable and left Lauda with some work to do when he took over. After two

CLIMBING THE LADDER 35

RIGHT Sharing his compatriot Otto Stuppacher's Porsche 910 in the Österreichring 1,000km, Niki is followed by the Alfa Romeo T33/3 of Ignazio Giunti and Nanni Galli. The Austrian pairing finished 21st, having completed 133 laps of the 170.

BELOW Niki seems more interested in his crash helmet than the camera as he lines up with Kaimann team boss Kurt Bergmann, mechanic Thomas Haberson, lead driver Erich Breinsberg and chief mechanic Lazi Bühler together with the Mk4 Formula Vee cars and the infamous Opel Rekord 'Black Widow' outside the Kaimann factory before the first leg of the European Cup Final at Mantorp Park in Sweden.

stints each, the duo finished ninth in their class and 21st overall, the last finisher still running, 37 laps behind the winning Porsche 917 driven by Jo Siffert and Kurt Ahrens. This was, incidentally, the legendary 917's first victory.

33 Nordic Challenge & European Cup Final (Part 1) (S)

Mantorp Park, 31 August 1969, Formula Vee
Kaimann Mk4 (V690X) • #96
Result: Retired (fuel pump)

Sweden's Mantorp Park hosted the first round of the two-part Formula Vee European Cup Final, contested by teams comprising the six most successful drivers from preliminary rounds in each of the four European zones (North, South, West and Central). The three works Kaimanns were among a six-strong Austrian contingent in the large, cosmopolitan field but they were on the back foot from the beginning as their Continental tyres were completely outclassed by the new

1969

ABOVE Concentration is etched into Niki's face as he navigates his Kaimann out of the Mantorp Park paddock ahead of the first European Cup Final. The Austrian cars were outclassed and he did not make it to the chequered flag.

Goodyears and racing Dunlops available to the local competitors. Qualifying produced some rather suspect times, but it made little difference to the eventual result.

Scandinavians dominated the slipstreaming contest and from the outset Bertil Roos (RPB), Lasse Sirviö (Austro) and Alfred Vogelberger (Olympic) left the rest of the field behind. Lauda — for whom the Kaimann team had held great hopes after his performance at the Nürburgring — came away empty-handed when his fuel pump failed only eight laps into the 25-lap race.

34 Festival Auto Monza (I)

14 September 1969, Formula Vee
Kaimann Mk4 (V690X)
Result: 1st

This was a private race run behind closed doors at Monza away from the prying eyes of the sporting press. The event was organised at the invitation of the Italian Automobile Club with the aim of comparing the relative performances of the various national junior formulae, including Formula Vee, Formula Ford and the short-lived 'Formula Baby' cars tuned by Ernst Prinoth. As one of the successful Formula Vee manufacturers, Kaimann was well represented and Lauda was Kurt Bergmann's chosen driver for a singleton works entry, Erich Breinsberg having taken a holiday. For Lauda, it was also a good opportunity to get to know Monza, a track that featured on the calendars of all major race series.

Kaimanns dominated the event, mainly because of their stiffer chassis frames and visibly better grip, so the race was a simple exercise for Lauda, his works car winning comfortably from the private versions of Christian Dietrich and Manfred Schurti. The only downside for the Austrian was the theft of his new Speed-Pilot stopwatch from his hotel room the night before the race, while he was asleep.

CLIMBING THE LADDER 37

ABOVE At the Salzburgring's inaugural meeting, Niki's Kaimann Mk4 leads the Austros of Peter Peter, Gerold Pankl and Horst Miedaner through the *Semperit-Kurve* during the Preis von Salzburg race. Slipstreaming battles became a regular feature of racing at the Salzburgring.

35 Preis von Salzburg (A)

21 September 1969, Formula Vee
Kaimann Mk4 (V690X) • #8
Qualifying: 2nd • Result: 3rd

Motorsport was booming so strongly in Austria that the country saw not one but two new circuits open during 1969, this inaugural meeting at the Salzburgring quickly following the Österreichring's early fixtures. Formula Vee in particular had quickly gained huge popularity in the country and had been one of the motivating factors for the construction of the 2.6-mile (4.2km) Salzburgring. At this meeting, Lauda wore for the first time a red/orange helmet, a colour that would become his trademark; he said later that he had chosen the colour as it would make him easier to find if he crashed into undergrowth at a circuit such as the Nürburgring.

Dieter Quester was uncatchable in the race, his privately entered Kaimann fitted with the same Goodyear tyres that had dominated in Sweden; Quester had had them flown in from England especially and they were unavailable to other drivers. As the works Kaimann team was contracted to Continental, whose tyres were far less effective, Erich Breinsberg and Lauda were somewhat outclassed, Quester winning by nearly 10 seconds. Nevertheless, the works Kaimann pair had a tremendous scrap in Quester's wake with Lauda losing out to his team-mate by just 0.2 second at the flag.

36 Preis von Tirol (A)

Innsbruck, 5 October 1969, Formula Vee
Kaimann Mk5 (V690X) • #8
Result: 2nd

This race was eagerly anticipated as it would decide the national championship and complete the 'Formula Vee to Formula 2' programme, so all the local elite were present

38 NIKI LAUDA

1969

in the large entry. Lauda was in contention for the title along with Erich Breinsberg, Peter Peter, Gerold Pankl and Harald Ertl.

Pankl stormed away at the start and only the Kaimanns — now Mk5 versions — of Lauda and Breinsberg on their new 'red spot' Continental racing tyres could stay with him, snapping at his heels. Eventually, Ertl's Austro closed on them and an intense four-way fight developed. On the last lap Pankl spun out of the lead, forcing the unlucky second-placed Lauda to take drastic avoiding action that allowed Breinsberg to squeeze through to snatch the win. Lauda crossed the line eight seconds behind his team-mate to take the runner-up position.

37 Eifel Cup & European Cup Final (Part 2) (D)

Nürburgring, 12 October 1969, Formula Vee
Kaimann Mk5 (V690X)
Qualifying: 5th • Result: 20th

This was the second and deciding round of the European Cup Final, run over 15 laps of the narrow, hilly Nürburgring *Südschleife*. Fog shrouded the Eifel course early in the morning, putting the race in doubt, but it had cleared by the time the Formula Vee contest started. Lauda, who was one of the pre-race favourites although he had no chance of outright success in the European Cup following his car's retirement at Mantorp Park, qualified on the inside of the second row, one of eight drivers who went faster than the 1968 lap record.

After a hectic start and a first lap characterised by bumping and wheel-banging between some of the drivers, Lauda pitted with a broken throttle cable, losing almost a lap while the problem was fixed. He managed to resume but finished a distant (and lapped) 20th out of 24 finishers, bitterly disappointed. However, he managed to assist works team-mate Erich Breinsberg and Kaimann-mounted Helmut Bross when they came up to lap him, delaying Per-Olov Broström's RPB enough for the Swede to lose the tow from the Kaimann pair.

ABOVE Niki could have won at Innsbruck, had it not been for Gerold Pankl's spin in front of him.

BELOW The raw dangers of the tree-lined Nürburgring *Sudschleife* are all too apparent in this shot of Niki holding off the RPB of Per-Olov Broström, who is a lap ahead after the Austrian's long pit stop early in the Eifel Cup race.

CLIMBING THE LADDER 39

38 Internationales ADAC-Flughafenrennen (D)

München-Neubiberg, 26 October 1969, Group 5
Opel Rekord 1900 'Black Widow'
Result: 5th

Although Neubiberg's jarring concrete 3.5-mile (5.7km) airfield course, a former Luftwaffe base in the south-east outskirts of Munich, was hardly a top-line venue, BMW was happy to spice up the occasion by fielding some of its 2002 saloons in the headline events. Thanks in part to a decent prize fund, these races were well-supported with large entry lists. Lauda took part in the now-infamous Opel 'Black Widow' as a wild card to challenge the BMWs and other minor opposition in the Group 5 class.

He came home fifth in the 10-lap race after a torrid scrap. The chequered flag was shown a lap early, but this made little difference as the field ignored it and kept going. Shortly afterwards, the 'Black Widow' was stolen from the Kaimann works, but nobody went looking for it.

39 Internationales ADAC-Flughafenrennen (D)

München-Neubiberg, 26 October 1969, Formula Vee
Kaimann Mk5 (V690X) • #855
Result: 1st

There was also a Formula Vee event at Neubiberg. Practice showed that a chicane contrived with straw bales after the start line was far too narrow and several collisions occurred there, leading the organisers to widen the obstacle. Nevertheless, the drama continued and by the end of the meeting the track was littered with straw from bales destroyed by errant cars. Some drivers discovered that the most effective way to get in front was not to brake at all for the chicane on the final lap and

RIGHT Neubiberg's surface was made more hazardous as it became strewn with straw dislodged by collisions with the bales. Here Peter Peter (Austro) and Lauda pick their way through the debris.

1969

ABOVE On his way to winning the first heat of the Formula Vee race at Neubiberg, Lauda outbrakes fellow works Kaimann driver Dieter Basche.

take the flag regardless, invariably out of control.

As a safety precaution, the race was divided into two heats. In the first, Lauda, Dieter Basche (briefly in a Kaimann seat) and Peter Peter broke away from the pack to indulge in a private fight. Their battle was completely open, with the lead changing constantly until three laps from the end, when Lauda managed to extend his advantage and take a clear win. The second heat was less frantic and Lauda came home third having shadowed a duel between Alfred Vogelberger (Olympic) and Fritz Böhler (Austro). His margin of victory in the first heat was sufficient to give him the overall win on aggregate.

SUMMARY

As Lauda had no karting experience, some observers had been sceptical of his transition to Formula Vee. Kurt Bergmann himself commented that he expected all his drivers to deliver wrecked cars back to him at some point and Lauda certainly did so with his somersault at Aspern early in the year. Subsequently, though, his driving in Formula Vee was very consistent: he had only one further retirement (due to mechanical failure) and did not crash again.

The statistics for Lauda's 18-month Formula Vee career during 1968–69 read pretty well: 20 races, two wins, seven podiums, seven other placings and one fastest lap. His much-reported duel with Helmut Marko on the Nürburgring *Nordschleife* in the supporting event to the German Grand Prix was widely acknowledged as 'race of the year'.

By 1969, *Powerslide* magazine had uprated its opinion of him: 'Young, greedy for victory, without big financial worries… that's how (he) goes racing. Lauda has not had much serious experience, but he is not complacent (though often already shows cheekiness). Learning some tactical lessons would sometimes help…'

It was during 1969 that Lauda's commitment to working closely with his engineers to improve the car first became apparent. Bergmann spotted his high level of technical understanding and observed that he would spend hours in discussion with his mechanics. Austrian journalist and sometime Formula Vee driver Rainer Braun stated: 'From the beginning I had noticed that he had an incredible interest in his car, asked a hundred times why this is so and that way and not otherwise. We all did not care; we just sat in the pits and drove off. Niki, however, found small gains here and there and would not allow something to be a little bit wrong. It soon became clear to us that he did more than anyone else and was also smarter than anyone else.'

In his first full year in a single-seater, Lauda had finished third in the national championship and 10th in the European Cup. He now wanted to turn his attention to bigger things and by the end of 1969 the junior Formula Vee driver was laying plans for a Formula 3 campaign.

CLIMBING THE LADDER **41**

1970
A FIELD OF MADMEN

In a Viennese coffee house in February 1970, the hopeful and ambitious trio of Niki Lauda, Gerold Pankl and Werner Riedl met with Peter Urbanek, who headed the Austrian branch of the English racing management company Paul Watson Racing, to formulate their plans for the forthcoming season. Lauda, shrewdly as he thought, had decided to enter the European Formula 3 Championship. Pankl-Lauda Racing was formed and with financial support from his father — now partially reconciled to his racing ambitions — he purchased a new McNamara chassis and a 1-litre Ford engine.

McNamara was a somewhat obscure manufacturer, based in Lenggries, Bavaria, and had enjoyed success in Formula Vee in 1969 with Helmut Marko, the man Lauda saw as his main rival. After his test at Kottingbrünn the previous July, McNamara had offered Lauda a Formula Vee seat for 1970 and he accepted on the condition that the company also sold him a Formula 3 car that his private mechanic could work on at the factory. In fact the Formula Vee ride never materialised as McNamara turned its focus to Indianapolis, no doubt because the company's owner, Francis McNamara, was American, and based his embryonic enterprise in Germany simply because he was a soldier stationed there. McNamara's resources were stretched and the Formula 3 cars suffered regular defects and poor reliability, factors that in no small part would lead Lauda to his next change of direction.

Formula 3 in 1970, the final year of 1,000cc regulations, was still a fiercely competitive breeding ground for young talent, a tough environment where racecraft was still being learned. A driver who survived the craziness of its starts and who sustained his concentration while heading the scrambling, slipstreaming packs that developed would need to be lucky as well as brave; being talented was not always enough on its own.

1970

40 Coupe de Printemps (F)

Nogaro, 29 March 1970, Formula 3
McNamara Mk3B (002/70) • #11
Result: Did not start (accident in practice)

ABOVE The Pankl-Lauda Racing team in 1970. Sadly the optimism of Niki and his friend Gerold Pankl was not translated into a successful Formula 3 campaign.

BELOW Niki lowers himself into the cockpit of his McNamara Mk3B ahead of his Formula 3 début at Nogaro. Only four minutes into the first practice session the car was destroyed after a tangle with his team-mate.

Lauda's Formula 3 début typified his entire season in the category. In company with his friend Gerold Pankl, he drove for 36 hours to Nogaro in south-west France towing a flat-bed trailer carrying their two race cars; they were the only Austrians represented in a field of 30 locals. On his first practice lap, Lauda slotted into Pankl's slipstream, closed up and pulled out to pass just at the moment Pankl's engine cut out. Niki's left front wheel hit Pankl's right rear, which launched his car into the air. It cleared a marshals' post before landing on the verge just before the guardrail and then ploughed along the barrier for 100 metres, losing all four wheels and leaving little intact but the chassis.

His first Formula 3 appearance had lasted just four minutes — and involved no racing.

A FIELD OF MADMEN

ABOVE A study in concentration as Niki pilots the McNamara Mk3B around the rain-sodden Nürburgring *Nordschleife*. Unfortunately, his focus wavered later in the race, resulting in a spin that dropped him to 16th and last place.

41 ADAC 300Km / Goodyear Pokal (D)

Nürburgring, 19 April 1970, Formula 3
McNamara Mk3B (007/70) • #18
Qualifying: 15th • Result: 16th

The field for this race was relatively small because few entrants wanted to commit their fragile Formula 3 cars to the rigours of the Nürburgring *Nordschleife* and there was also a date clash with the inaugural race at the new Paul Ricard circuit. Having obtained a new spaceframe chassis from the McNamara factory in order to repair the damage incurred at Nogaro, Lauda qualified on the outside of the sixth row in a field that also included Formula Vee machinery.

The cars were held on the grid too long, causing some to overheat, and in a shambolic start Lauda was involved in a tangle with Gerold Pankl that eliminated his friend. Having got going again, he climbed to sixth place by the end of the first lap, but when running alone in fifth he spun out at the fast *Hatzenbach* bends, saying later that he never figured out why. He cautiously manoeuvred the McNamara back over an embankment to rejoin the race and catch up again, but his off-track excursion meant that he completed only three of the five scheduled laps and was classified 16th and last.

42 Criterium de Nivernais (F)

Magny-Cours, 3 May 1970, Formula 3
McNamara Mk3B (007/70) • #7
Qualifying: 11th • Result: 6th in heat; 5th in final

Suffering gear-selection problems during qualifying, Lauda managed to shift down instead of up, resulting in a blown engine and gearbox. His showing thereafter was rather better, the racing involving two 20-lap heats and a 35-lap final.

For much of his heat, the second, he duelled with Gerold Pankl for sixth place until his team-

RIGHT The paddock at Magny-Cours. Niki appears to be inflating the rear tyre of his McNamara Mk3B with a foot pump while Gerold Pankl (next to the transporter) looks on. Both are wearing sports jackets and flannels, despite having just driven from Vienna to the south of France and being required to do their own spanner work. Different times…

44 NIKI LAUDA

1970

LEFT Niki's McNamara Mk3B heads Etienne Vigoureux's Tecno 69 and Brendan McInerney's Chevron B15 in a typical slipstreaming pack of Formula 3 'screamers' at Magny-Cours.

mate retired on lap 15, leaving him to retain the position until the finish although he was closing on Denis Dayan's GRAC at the flag. His sixth place put him 11th on the grid for the final. In a more competitive race, he was soon in a nine-car pack contesting the lead, although the best three broke away after 18 laps. Although he passed Brendan McInerney's Chevron with two laps to go to take fifth place, he finished a fairly distant 10 seconds behind the fourth-placed Lotus 59 of James Hunt, his future rival. It was already apparent that the undeveloped McNamara chassis could not really compete with the more advanced Tecnos and Brabhams.

43 Internationale DMV Mai Pokal Rennen (D)

Hockenheim, 10 May 1970, Formula 3
McNamara Mk3B (007/70) • #18
Qualifying: 3rd • Result: Retired (accident)

Despite the main Formula 3 contenders attending the more prestigious Monaco Grand Prix supporting race, a large field of 31 starters was present at Hockenheim. The focus was on the fight between the Austrian McNamara drivers, Werner Riedl, Gerold Pankl and Lauda, who would have enjoyed a walkover had they not agreed for the race distance to be reduced from 30 to 22 laps so as to allow the other cars with smaller fuel tanks to be able to complete the distance.

Run over the long circuit with many slipstreaming groups chasing each other, this was an exciting race of high attrition that saw only 13 cars finish. The three McNamara drivers fought each other intensely, running virtually flat out from the start, but on lap 15 Lauda was eliminated when Siegfried Schreider collided with him, the Tecno pilot having panicked and lost control while being lapped.

BELOW Hockenheim's stands are packed with spectators as Niki powers through the stadium; a collision with another car meant that he failed to finish.

A FIELD OF MADMEN 45

ABOVE The McNamara Mk3B on the grid awaiting the start of the first heat of the Preis von Steiermark at the Österreichring. This time Lauda made it to the finish, in sixth place.

BELOW Early in the race on the fast and dangerous Brno road course, Niki chases after the leading Chevron B17 of Jürg Dubler, which has already pulled out an advantage.

44 Preis der Steiermark (A)

Österreichring, 17 May 1970, Formula 3
McNamara Mk3B (007/70) • #8
Qualifying: 7th • Result: 6th

Although there was a strong 41-car entry at the Österreichring, the paucity of starting money meant that only 17 contenders actually arrived, so the race was divided into two 15-lap parts in the hope that more of the fragile cars would finish.

Lauda ended lap 1 of the first race in fourth place and spent the next 14 laps in a closely fought, zig-zagging, six-car battle to finish sixth, dead-heating with Ulf Svensson's Brabham BT28 on the line. With the grid order for the second race set by the results of the first one, there was another equally frantic slipstreaming spectacle. Fourth again after lap 1, Lauda came home seventh at the end of a race run at a quicker pace, with places changing several times a lap. The aggregate times placed him sixth overall, just 3.2 seconds behind the winner.

45 Mezinárodni Závod Automobils (CZ)

Brno, 24 May 1970, Formula 3
McNamara Mk3B (007/70) • #10
Qualifying: 4th • Result: 2nd

A huge field of 40 entrants was padded out with a number of local hopefuls and a handful of the top European drivers. The race was run over 10 laps of the fast, daunting 8.7-mile (13.7km) Brno circuit, held on public roads.

At the end of the first lap the leading group comprised a dense pack of nine cars with Lauda in the thick of it. He scrabbled past the Lotus of Freddy Kottulinsky and Werner Riedl's sister McNamara, then got himself ahead of Mikko Kozarowitzky's Titan before chasing down pole-sitter Jürg Dubler's quasi-works Chevron for the lead. They engaged in a desperately hard-fought duel and when Lauda got ahead he pulled out a small advantage that he retained for several laps. With three laps to go, Dubler made a charge, breaking the lap record to catch up again, and on the last lap squeezed through under braking at the narrowest point on the track. To the Swiss driver's surprise, Lauda then forced his way past again at the Serpentine curves, frantically holding his car on opposite-lock. The experienced Dubler recognised that his only remaining opportunity was on the run to the flag and he slipstreamed past Lauda on the final straight, the two drivers almost dead-heating, a mere 0.3 second apart after almost an hour of fierce racing.

46 XII Hämeenlinnan Ajot (SF)

Ahvenisto, 14 June 1970, Formula 3
McNamara Mk3B (007/70) • #5
Result: 4th

After competing in the Formula Vee race at Keimola in Finland in 1968, Lauda and Lothar Schörg had driven to Hämeenlinna to have a look at the Ahvenisto circuit, which had only opened the previous year. Apparently they did not like what they saw, so they turned back and skipped the Formula Vee race that was to take place there the following weekend. But when the chance of a Formula 3 expedition to the two-race Finnish Speed Week came two years later, with a decent prize fund at stake, Lauda decided to make the long trip. He finished fourth in the race, although a distant 20 seconds behind third-placed James Hunt's well-driven Lotus.

By this time, Pankl-Lauda Racing was largely funding McNamara's Formula 3 programme and was as much a privateer effort as it was a works team, which made challenging for the top positions harder.

47 II Keimolan Juhannusajot (SF)

Keimola, 21 June 1970, Formula 3
McNamara Mk3B (007/70) • #5
Result: Retired

The second part of Finnish Speed Week was Keimola's 'Midsummer Fair'. The track was covered in mud after the frantic Formula Vee race that preceded the poorly supported Formula 3 event, which had just 13 starters. Practice was chaotic and produced an unlikely set of times that led to many protests, although Lauda was

ABOVE The jostling Formula 3 pack dives through the first turn at Hämeenlinna, as Niki's McNamara Mk3B takes the inside line from Jean Johansson's Tecno 69 ahead of the March 703 of Harald Ertl.

A FIELD OF MADMEN 47

satisfied with his performance and the grid slot he was given. In the 25-lap race he held station behind the tightly packed leading bunch, which was engaged in the usual frantic scrap, but neither representative of the Pankl-Lauda Racing team had a satisfactory result this time, both retiring.

48 200 Meilen von Nürnberg (D)

Norisring, 27 June 1970, Interserie
Porsche 908/2 (008) • #39
Qualifying: 11th • Result: 3rd in class, 5th overall

By now, Lauda had decided that he would take part in the Interserie, a new European championship for 'big-banger' sports cars inspired by the success of the spectacular Can-Am in North America. For the purpose he acquired a secondhand Porsche 908/2 — a 3-litre spyder that Porsche had developed for the 1969 season — and ran it under the umbrella of Austria's Bosch Racing Team. Lauda was only able to afford the

ABOVE James Hunt's Lotus 69 (right) and Conny Andersson's Brabham BT28 head Niki's McNamara Mk3B and Jean Johansson's Tecno 69 at Keimola. His second race in Finland within a week ended in retirement.

BELOW Niki's newly acquired Porsche 908/2 leads the similar car of Karl von Wendt through the *Dutzendteich* corner during the inaugural Interserie race at the Norisring.

48 NIKI LAUDA

1970

car thanks to help from a Swiss businessman seeking an association with his father: Niki agreed to intervene on the man's behalf in return for funding, naturally without Lauda Senior being aware of the arrangement. During the first part of the 1970 season this particular 908/2 had been campaigned by Alain de Cadenet in International Championship for Makes races, including the Daytona 24 Hours.

The inaugural round of the Interserie was the big annual fixture at the Norisring, a 2.45-mile (3.94km) circuit laid out amid Hitler's Nazi parade grounds in Nürnberg (Nuremberg). It was a 200-mile contest split into two parts, each comprising 41 laps, with the final results determined on aggregate. The 25-strong field was of high quality, featuring many well-known drivers and spectacular cars.

While big-engined Group 5 and Group 7 machines such as Porsche 917s and Lola T70s filled the top eight places on the grid, Lauda was third quickest of the 3-litre Group 6 runners, lining up 11th. His 908/2 was among five such cars in the field, but only of them, driven by Pedro Rodríguez, out-qualified him.

During the first race, he was soon involved in a very close battle for seventh place with the three 908/2s that he had beaten in qualifying, driven by Karl von Wendt, Helmut Marko and Helmut Leuze. He had got the better of both von Wendt and Leuze when, on lap 19, Marko collided with a Porsche 907 they were lapping. Lauda finished sixth, lapped once.

The start of the second race was delayed by 20 minutes after a gale left debris on the track, but when the action got going Lauda found himself in another slipstreaming battle. Running between seventh and ninth places for much of the time, he eventually came home sixth once again, his same three 908/2 rivals occupying the next three places. His aggregate result was fifth, and an impressive third in the 3-litre category behind class winner Rodríguez and Herbert Schultze's works Alfa Romeo T33/3.

In later years, he commented that the 908/2 was the car that impressed him the most in his early career.

NORISRING
27 JUNE 1970

While at the Norisring, Lauda briefly drove his compatriot Helmut Marko's Olympic during practice for the Formula Vee race. Marko had switched from McNamara for the 1970 season, but by now was finding that the MAHAG-Olympic team seemed to be losing its motivation. Having long since buried the hatchet with Lauda after their fracas at the Nürburgring the previous summer, Marko — aware of his countryman's growing reputation for mechanical understanding — sought his opinion of the German car. Lauda's feedback must have been useful, for Marko went on to win the following day. In this photo, Niki rounds the old *Grundig* hairpin, a corner that would disappear from use when the circuit was shortened after Pedro Rodríguez's fatal accident a year later.

49 Südwest Pokal, Europa-Marken-Trophäe (D)

Hockenheim, 5 July 1970, Interserie
Porsche 908/2 (008) • #21
Qualifying: 19th • Result: 4th in class, 12th overall

As a driving force behind the introduction of the Interserie, the Motorsport-Club Stuttgart — organisers of this Hockenheim meeting — had proved itself open to new ideas and remained one of the few organisers supporting the rather neglected German Formula 3 championship, so Lauda was able to take part in two races in a colourful weekend of racing.

The 30-lap Interserie race was held on the longer circuit and was dominated, as expected,

A FIELD OF MADMEN 49

ABOVE Blasting along one of Hockenheim's tree-lined straights, Niki's Porsche 908/2 heads for 12th place in the Europa-Marken-Trophäe.

BELOW In the second Formula 3 race of the year at Hockenheim, the Solitude-Rennen, Niki charges into the stadium section in his McNamara Mk3B.

by the more powerful Group 5 and Group 7 machinery, whose drivers were intent on a rematch of the previous weekend's competition at the Norisring. Lauda was still finding his feet in the category, learning his racecraft in a 3-litre class that was dominated by another Porsche 908/02, the Martini entry of Gérard Larrousse, alongside a large number of similarly well-funded privateers. Pacing himself carefully, Lauda avoided a huge oil slick at the *Sachs-Kurve* that caused many other drivers to spin. After running in the lower midfield throughout the race, he finished 12th, two laps behind Vic Elford's winning McLaren M6B, but his fourth place in Group 6 was creditable.

50 Südwest Pokal, Solitude-Rennen (D)

Hockenheim, 5 July 1970, Formula 3
McNamara Mk3B (007/70) • #11
Qualifying: 11th • Result: 5th

The fastest 30 drivers from the large entry were able to take the start after two practice sessions, the first of which was so wet that no drivers could find suitable gear ratios to use. As usual at Hockenheim, the start and the first lap of this 25-lap contest were frantic but Lauda, having qualified on the inside of the fifth row, was soon making up places in a very competitive field. After two laps he was among the 10-car leading group and then after five laps he found himself in a private duel with Ulf Svensson's Brabham that lasted for the rest of the race.

50 NIKI LAUDA

1970

ABOVE Lauda's Alpina BMW 1602 lifts its inside wheels as he tackles the Nürburgring *Nordschleife* in the last year of its unrefined form during the 1970 Six Hours for touring cars.

With a lap to go, Svensson towed past Lauda for seventh place but on the final lap they came across David Purley's slow-moving Brabham, its engine having expired while running second. Lauda used the moment to squeeze by Svensson and beat him to fifth place by just 0.2 second, albeit nearly a minute adrift of the winner.

51 Nürburgring Six Hours (D)

12 July 1970, Group 2
BMW 1602 (with René Herzog) • #61
Result: Retired (distributor)

Lauda had intended to make his first racing appearance in Britain for the third round of the Interserie at Croft but instead took up the offer of a paid seat with the Alpina BMW team in the more prestigious Nürburgring Six Hours the same weekend. Originally the Alpina team had planned to pair Paul Bergner and René Herzog in a 1602 model in its bid for the 1,600cc Division 2 crown against 93 other hopefuls, but after a series of breakages in practice Bergner switched to a private 2002Ti and Lauda was installed in his place. The race was run at record speed and was dominated by works Alfa Romeos after the failure of all the best BMWs, that of Lauda/Herzog included. After a fairly nondescript run, their engine expired before half distance due to distributor failure and they posted the race's 37th retirement. Coincidentally, the sister Alpina entry of Lauda's Formula 3 racing buddy, Gerold Pankl, stopped on the same lap with a broken engine mounting.

52 British Grand Prix support race (GB)

Brands Hatch, 17 July 1970, Formula 3
McNamara Mk3B (007/70) • #57
Result: Retired (accident in Heat 1)

A week after his aborted entry for the Croft Interserie round, Lauda did race in Britain for the first time, at the Formula 3 International Trophy supporting event to the British Grand

A FIELD OF MADMEN 51

RIGHT On the grid for the first heat of the Brands Hatch International Formula 3 Trophy, a supporting race to the British Grand Prix, Niki's McNamara Mk3B (57) lines up with Torsten Palm's Brabham BT28 (5), Martin Warren's Chevron B15 (33) and Max Bonnin's Tecno 69 (67).

ABOVE & RIGHT At Brands Hatch, Niki's McNamara Mk3B was eliminated in a heavy impact at Clearways at the end of his heat and the damage prevented him from starting in the final. Here he is looking straight at the photographer, Alois Rottensteiner, whom he had advised to stand at this corner as somebody was bound to crash there…

Prix at Brands Hatch. The Shell Super Oil British Formula 3 Championship was very competitive, more so than the European series in which Lauda had been competing, and the opportunity to perform in front of Formula 1 team bosses drew a huge entry of 59 cars, such that the event was run as two 10-lap heats and a 20-lap final on the Friday before Sunday's big race.

Lauda, one of a handful of drivers who got under the 1m 40s barrier in practice on Brands Hatch's Grand Prix circuit, ran in Heat 1 alongside 24 other hotshoes. He was involved in a race-long dice with Steve Matchett (Chevron) and Tom Walkinshaw (March) until baulked by Mikko Kozarowitzky's Titan going into Clearways on the penultimate lap. Forced to cut in sharply, he collided with Eddie Jacobsson's March, which clipped the rear wheel of the McNamara and propelled the car into a hard impact with the bank.

Lauda crashed right in front of his friend, the photographer Alois Rottensteiner, at the very point where he had advised him to stand as there was every chance of an incident there. Again, the car was a virtual write-off and there was no chance of repairing it for the final.

52 NIKI LAUDA

1970

53 Internationales Flugplatzrennen (D)

Diepholz, 19 July 1970, sports cars and GTs
Porsche 908/2 (008) • #61
Result: 1st (fastest lap)

Two days after his Brands Hatch crash, Lauda was at Diepholz for the short 25-lap 'Flugplatzrennen' sports car and GT race in support of the main Formula 3 event. The youngest driver in the field, he had very little opposition in the Group 5/Group 6 class apart from David Prophet's ostensibly faster McLaren-Chevrolet M12, the rest of the large field being locals mainly driving a variety of Porsches and modified touring cars. Despite wet conditions, he set a new lap record on his way to victory, improving on the previous best by nearly 10mph.

Lauda was also on the entry list for the Formula 3 race but did not contest it because the McNamara had been too badly damaged at Brands Hatch. Somewhat ironically, his erstwhile McNamara team-mate Gerold Pankl narrowly won this event on a weekend dominated by Austrian drivers.

54 Grand Prix Sverige (S)

Karlskoga, 9 August 1970, Group 5 & 6 sports cars
Porsche 908/2 (008) • #6
Qualifying: 11th • Result: Retired (gearbox)

Lauda now spent three consecutive weekends in Scandinavia and this first one was overshadowed by a dreadful crash in the preceding touring car race that killed five spectators and led to a two-hour delay in racing

BELOW Niki's Porsche 908/2 pursues local hero Joakim Bonnier's Lola T210 past Karlskoga's packed spectator banks during the 1970 Swedish Grand Prix for sports cars.

A FIELD OF MADMEN

before the organisers decided to continue, mainly to keep the large crowd calm and in place. In the interests of safety, the fields for the sports car and Formula 3 races were reduced to just 16 starters.

Lauda's Porsche 908/2 sat towards the rear of the truncated grid for the 32-lap sports car race. He ran in midfield, duelling with Teddy Pilette's Lola T70 for much of the distance. They had just been promoted a place by the retirement of Ronnie Peterson's Porsche 908 when both were forced to pit with problems after 26 laps. When Lauda's engine was restarted, there was a large cloud of smoke and, although he got going again, on the next lap his car stopped at the back of the circuit with a seized gearbox.

55 Kanonloppet (S)

Karlskoga, 9 August 1970, Formula 3
McNamara Mk3B (007/70) • #20
Qualifying: 8th • Result: 3rd in Heat 2 (fastest lap), 5th in Final

Lauda's repaired McNamara was now back in action, wearing new pale blue bodywork in place of its usual green. As at Brands Hatch, the size of the entry meant the event was run as two 16-lap heats and a 32-lap final.

Lauda took part in Heat 2 and qualified fifth. Although he got away slowly, dropping to 10th, he was soon duelling hard with David Purley (Brabham), the pair slicing through the field. Lauda passed five cars, including his team-mate's, and on lap 11 lay fourth, right behind the leading trio, Purley among them. When Purley's car lost its nose on the last lap, the Austrian was elevated to third place and also took fastest lap; he finished only 12 seconds adrift of Gerry Birrell's dominant wing-assisted Brabham.

As his heat had been a little slower than the first, he started eighth on the grid for the final. Driving carefully on a track made slippery with oil, he ran seventh from the start but lost a place to Sten Gunnarson's Brabham on lap 3. Promoted by a couple of spinners, he fought with Gustaf Dieden (Brabham) for sixth place and by lap 18 both had moved up again so he was then fifth, a position he held to the flag.

BELOW Running wide to avoid a spinner, Niki's McNamara Mk3B — now painted pale blue after the Brands Hatch crash — kicks up the dirt as he charges through the field in the first heat of Karlskoga's Kannonloppet Formula 3 event, taking fastest lap *en route* to third place. He would finish fifth in the final.

1970

56 Knutstorp Cup (S)

Knutstorp, 16 August 1970, Formula 3
McNamara Mk3B (007/70) • #36
Qualifying: 1st • Result: 7th (fastest lap)

In a field of 47 mainly Scandinavian entrants, Lauda was the big surprise of the meeting, despite being uncomfortable with both his car and the circuit during practice. Going quickly from the outset, he qualified on pole position for the first time in Formula 3, ahead of the experienced Ulf Svensson.

He led away when the flag fell but on lap 2, with the whole field bunched together behind him, he braked too late at Velodrome bend and spun. The closely following Torsten Palm had to take avoiding action and over-revved his Brabham's engine in the process. Lauda resumed at the back, ending his high hopes for a good result, but he charged through the field, breaking the lap record in the process. By the end he had worked his way up to seventh place, albeit some 35 seconds behind the winner. Once again, his inexperience when leading a race had cost him dearly.

57 Finnish Grand Prix (SF)

Keimola, 23 August 1970, Interserie
Porsche 908/2 (008) • #61
Qualifying: 6th • Result: Retired (wheel bearing)

After three rounds in as many weeks, the Interserie had taken a prolonged break to allow its protagonists to compete in other events before the series resumed in Finland. The event had been well-promoted and attracted the biggest crowd ever seen at the Keimola track, which Lauda had experienced only a couple of months earlier in the Formula 3 race there.

Although the main Interserie title contenders were all present, he did very well in qualifying, his Porsche 908/2 proving to be the fastest of the 3-litre runners and quicker than such luminaries as David Piper (Porsche 917K) and Leo Kinnunen (McLaren M7), both in more powerful machines. He maintained his grid position at the start and ran sixth early on, but his closely fought duel with the similar 908/2s of Gérard Larrousse and Helmut Marko ended within five laps when his car suffered a front wheel-bearing failure.

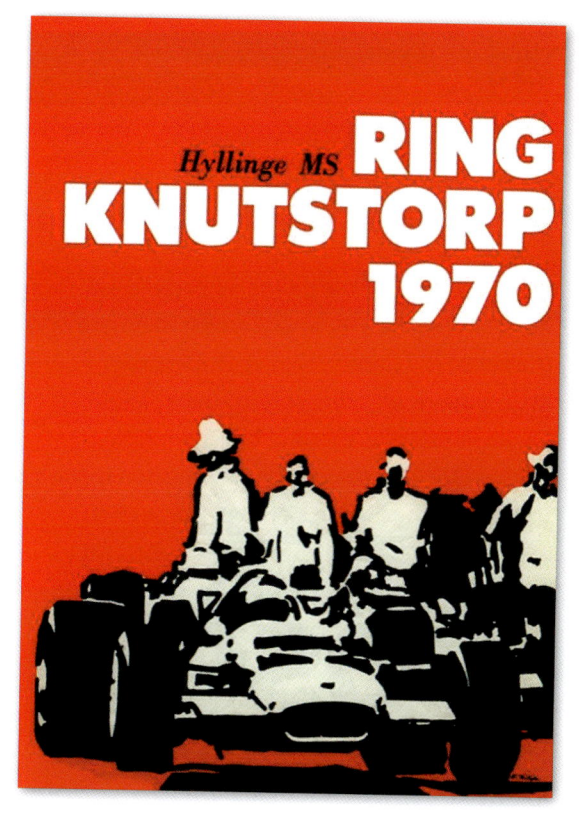

BELOW The small field of starters assembles ahead of the Finnish Grand Prix. From left: Lauda's Porsche 908/2; the Lola T70s of Ronnie Peterson and Teddy Pilette; Helmut Kelleners's March 707 and the Porsche 917Ks of Gijs van Lennep and Jürgen Neuhaus.

A FIELD OF MADMEN 55

58 Zandvoort Trophy (NL)

Zandvoort, 30 August 1970, Formula 3
McNamara Mk3B (007/70) • #25
Qualifying: 12th • Result: 4th

On a hectic weekend for the continental drivers who were also racing in Britain the next day, Lauda recorded an identical qualifying time to that of team-mate Gerold Pankl, but started ahead of him from 12th place on the grid having set his time first in the extremely windy conditions. He fended off those around him to hold his position into *Tarzan* and enjoyed another race-long battle with the Brabham of Ulf Svensson. Promoted by the retirements of Freddy Kottulinsky (Lotus) on lap 11, Roger Keele (Palliser) on lap 22 and James Hunt (Lotus) on the 24th and final lap, he finished a solid fourth. The race was dominated by Jürg Dubler's Chevron but only six of the 28 starters made it to the chequered flag.

By now, the McNamara operation was seriously overstretched in its efforts to support the Indianapolis project as well as its European activities and, with no factory support for his Formula 3 programme, Lauda was gradually losing patience.

59 Guards International Trophy (GB)

Brands Hatch, 31 August 1970, Formula 3
McNamara Mk3B (007/70)
Qualifying: 23rd • Result: 13th in Heat 2, retired in Final (handling)

Again using Brands Hatch's full Grand Prix circuit, a large entry of over 50 drivers was split in half for two 15-lap qualifying heats, with the best 15 finishers from each heat making the 30-lap final. Fighting a rearguard action against the stronger Chevrons and Brabhams, Lauda was the only McNamara driver to make the start, his car back in its dark green bodywork. He qualified 15th for the second heat and, outpaced, came home 13th, which was just

BELOW Niki hurls his McNamara into the hairpin before *Hunzerug* in his pursuit of Ulf Svensson's Brabham during the Zandvoort Trophy, while team-mate Gerold Pankl follows at a distance.

sufficient to secure a place in the final. Starting 23rd, his troubled weekend was completed when he was pushed onto the grass at South Bank early in the race, causing handling problems that subsequently forced him to retire.

60 Coupe de l'Avenir (B)

Zolder, 6 September 1970, Formula 3
McNamara Mk3B (007/70) • #26
Qualifying: 8th • Result: Retired (accident)

Fastest by a huge margin in free practice, Lauda could only manage eighth in the quicker conditions of qualifying. The race was a disaster for him and a defining moment for his next career choice.

On lap 3 of the first heat, the 10-car pack in which he was embroiled crested the blind brow behind the pits at 130mph to find an ambulance on the track, trundling *en route* to a crash involving Hannelore Werner's Eifelland-March. Three cars somehow squeezed past but a fourth hit the ambulance and spun into Lauda's car, pitching him into another collision and leaving him stranded in the middle of the track just as the next group of slipstreaming cars arrived. Warned only by a white flag with no waved yellows displayed, the squabbling bunch did not so much as lift and Lauda awaited the impact.

In fact it never came, although one car did

ABOVE As the flag drops for the start of the Formula 3 Guards Trophy at Brands Hatch, Niki gets away from 23rd on the grid; his McNamara Mk3B is at the back on the right-hand side.

LEFT Brands Hatch in 1970 was not a happy place for Lauda. Suffering handling problems after being forced off the track at South Bank, he ran wide at Clearways on his way to another retirement.

A FIELD OF MADMEN 57

ABOVE In his Porsche 908/2, which he shared with Freddy Kottulinsky in the Imola 500km race, Niki powers around the rather basic circuit on his way to a respectable fifth place.

BELOW An impressive and combative drive at Thruxton saw Niki's Porsche 908/2 take fifth place in the Yellow Pages Trophy Interserie race.

shoot over his McNamara's nose. He undid his seat belts and jumped clear of the wreck, declaring his intention to get out of Formula 3 — which, he had concluded, was full of maniacs. The previous day Jochen Rindt had been killed at Monza and Lauda was suddenly aware that having talent did not make a driver immune. An ongoing dispute with McNamara over the lack of spare parts and the absence of any help with repairs also played a part in his decision, although his father later paid the factory 14,000 DM to settle a counter-claim for breach of contract and parts ordered but not paid for.

61 Imola 500km (I)

13 September 1970, Interserie
Porsche 908/2 (008) (with Freddy Kottulinsky) • #35
Qualifying: 12th • Result: 5th

After his decision to abandon Formula 3, Lauda turned his attention to sports car events for the rest of the season. At Imola, with Swedish Formula 3 rival Freddy Kottulinsky as his co-driver, he qualified an encouraging 12th in an impressive field that included works entries from Porsche, Alfa Romeo and Ferrari.

Kottulinsky took the start and handled the first half of the race, moving up to sixth place by lap 50 and handing the car over to Lauda some four laps down on the leader. By lap 60, Lauda had overtaken Gianpiero Moretti's Ferrari 512S for fifth, a position he held to the flag having narrowly avoided the spinning Martini Porsche of Gérard Larrousse/Rudi Lins. Although his 908/2 could not keep pace with the best of its class rivals, fourth in the Group 6 category was a very respectable achievement considering that the class winner was a works Alfa Romeo and the two 908/2s in second and third places were run by the well-funded Martini Racing Team. The overall winner, meanwhile, was Brian Redman, driving solo in his Gulf Porsche 917K, seven laps ahead of the Austrian–Swedish pairing.

62 Yellow Pages Trophy (GB)

Thruxton, 20 September 1970, Interserie
Porsche 908/2 (008) • #8
Qualifying: 5th • Result: 5th

This 25-lap Interserie round had a reduced field, with many drivers preferring to race at Zandvoort's non-championship Trophy of the Dunes fixture. Although Lauda's 908/2 had won at Thruxton earlier in the year in the hands of Alain de Cadenet, the competition was much stronger this time — and he always took things carefully in the car because he was so conscious of the amount of money he had invested in it.

58 NIKI LAUDA

1970

He ran fourth initially, having instantly gained a position when pole-sitter Jürgen Neuhaus fluffed his start in the powerful Porsche 917K and dropped to the back. Lauda kept up well with the front runners in the early laps and became involved in a battle with three other 908/2s — those of Helmut Marko, Rudi Lins and Michel Weber — and a pair of 2-litre Lolas driven by Chris Craft and Terry Croker. On lap 5 Craft spun at Segrave and dropped behind the Austrian, who held him at bay for a while and also engaged in a memorable duel with Croker. Although it took less than 16 laps for Neuhaus to regain the lead in his 917K, Lauda drove a committed race to finish fifth, just 34 seconds behind the winner, with the two Lolas and Marko's 908/2 ahead of him.

63 Österreichring 1,000km (A)

11 October 1970, International Championship for Makes
Porsche 908/2 (008) (with Peter Peter) • #12
Qualifying: 12th • Result: 6th

Although Lauda had taken part in his home country's round of the International Championship of Makes a year earlier, this time he did so in his own car and invited Peter Peter, a long-time sparring partner in single-seaters, to join him. In qualifying he managed 12th quickest in an exciting field of 44 where his Porsche 908/2 was among seven 3-litre prototypes, including works Alfa Romeos, and fearsome 5-litre contenders in the form of a works Ferrari 512 and works-backed Porsche 917Ks.

ABOVE The recently built Österreichring looks like a country road as Niki's Porsche 908/2, shared in this race with Peter Peter, sweeps through the *Texaco-Schikane*.

LEFT The JW Automotive-run Porsche 917K of Pedro Rodríguez/Leo Kinnunen, lights ablaze, bears down on Niki's 908/2 during the Österreichring 1,000km.

A FIELD OF MADMEN 59

He ran 13th initially but stopped on lap 16 with a cracked exhaust manifold and again four laps later. However, he decided to continue despite the car being significantly down on power and it ran reliably for the rest of the race. The Austrian pair reached fifth place at one point and finished a most respectable sixth, nine laps behind the winning 917K. In the 3-litre prototype category they were beaten only by better-funded rivals in the shape of a works Alfa Romeo and two 908/2s run by the Martini Racing Team for Gérard Larrousse/Rudi Lins and Reinhold Joest/Gerold Pankl.

64 SCM-Rundstrecken-Rennen Aachen (D)

Nürburgring, 18 October 1970, Sports/GT
Porsche 908/2 (008) • #17
Qualifying: 4th • Result: 3rd (4th and 3rd in two parts)

This was a national race at the Nürburgring organised at short notice by the Automobilclub von Deutschland to take place on the less-used *Südschleife* while some reconstruction work on the *Nordschleife* was being completed. The event was organised as two 15-lap parts with the result determined on aggregate.

Part 1 was rather processional with the top four places remaining unchanged throughout. Lauda finished an untroubled fourth, behind three much more powerful V8-engined cars driven by winner Helmut Kelleners (March 707), Chris Craft (McLaren M8C) and David Prophet (McLaren M12).

Part 2 was much more combative and Lauda was involved in a big seven-car battle that proved to be the highlight of the afternoon. Soon he was hounding Herbie Müller's Lola T70 for third place, getting ahead on lap 5, but then had to work overtime to fend off the Lola T210 of Joakim Bonnier, who finally passed him on lap 11 after a frantic side-by-side duel. On lap 14 the Swede was held up lapping two older Porsches and Lauda was able to force his way past again, holding the place to the finish to prevail by a mere 0.2 second, while Kelleners and Craft again took the top two places. Lauda's combined performances gave him a well-deserved third place on aggregate.

65 Preis der Martha (A)

Österreichring, 25 October 1970, Sports/GT/Touring
Porsche 908/2 (008)
Result: 1st

As a new initiative by the Österreichring's owners to create versatile races with a variety of vehicle categories to appeal to wider audiences, the 'Martha Grand National' — as much a festival as a race meeting — was a noteworthy effort and a welcome promotional platform for Austrian motorsport. There was a large field comprising multiple classes of Group 1 and 2 touring cars, GT and sports cars, all racing together in a 10-lap competition, driven by various representatives of the Austrian racing elite. The race, which was enlivened by a frantic duel between Gerhard Krammer's Alfa Romeo and Sepp Manhalter's BMW in a rerun of a recent Langenlebarn event, saw Lauda's Porsche 908/2 win its class convincingly, a minute clear of Helmut Marko's similar Martini Racing machine.

SUMMARY

The only worthwhile results Lauda achieved in his 15 Formula 3 starts in 1970 were second place at Brno, fourth place at Zandvoort and fifth place

BELOW Niki's Porsche 908/2 braves it out with Herbie Müller's Ecurie Bonnier Lola T70 into the *Südkehre* at the start of the late-season SCM-Rundstrecken-Rennen Aachen race held on the Nürburgring *Südschleife*.

1970

at Hockenheim — and three destroyed McNamara chassis. In an interview in 1971, Lambert Hofer explained: 'Niki only had those accidents because he was involved in them; he did not cause them. His competitors on the track were all kamikaze, but he was already worried about having the car perfectly tuned. He concerned himself with every last detail of the car, discussing earnestly with his mechanics… the vehicle he was driving was a jewel; he had the engine rebuilt after 600 laps and he was always responsible, I think he understood right away what the true nature of motorsport is: first, finish the races; second, do so always with the least possible effort, and think about the next race, to be able to continue.'

Fortunately, his results with his Porsche 908/2 spyder were more promising. There were victories at the Österreichring and Diepholz and third place at the Nürburgring before his season culminated in a fine sixth place against the world's best sports car racers in Austria's round of the International Championship for Makes. Because the car itself was the security for the loan that had allowed him to purchase it, he had to take great care of it and during all these races he never so much as spun, commenting later that 'one accident would have finished me'. Even though at the end of the year he sold the car and repaid the borrowing, he was still broke — but his reputation was growing.

A year earlier, Kurt Bergmann had observed that Lauda's performances relative to his competitors became better each time he got into a more powerful car. This certainly appeared true when comparing his outings in the Porsche spyder with those in his McNamara. Logically, a step up to Formula 2 would see a similar exponential improvement…

ASPERN
AUTUMN 1970

With a new Formula Super Vee category due in 1971, Aspern-based Kaimann held a press launch at the airfield circuit to show off its new contender. Happy to return to the team that had given him his break in single-seaters, Lauda was present and completed a few laps to evaluate the car. His feedback as a development driver had been recognised by Kurt Bergmann from an early stage and this exercise was certainly not inconvenient for Lauda as Aspern was so close to his home in Vienna.

ABOVE In this promotional photograph, Kurt Bergmann makes adjustments to the new Kaimann Formula Super Vee car while a helmetless Niki sits in the bare chassis and the Kaimann crew look on.

A FIELD OF MADMEN 61

1971
RITES OF PASSAGE

Rumours abounded in November 1970 of a planned 'Team Austria' Formula 2 équipe, to which the emergent Niki Lauda's name was linked. Following the wishes of her late husband, Nina Rindt had established the Jochen Rindt Foundation with the goal of benefiting Austrian motorsport. Among its activities, the Foundation planned to support an Austrian National Formula 2 team, running two Lotus 69s — provided by its benefactor's F1 employer — with the drivers expected to be Helmut Marko and Lauda. Funding was to come from various Jochen Rindt Racing Car Shows, which continued to draw large crowds, with the balance pledged by Austria-based companies including Shell, Bosch and Erste Österreichische Sparkasse. However, the inability to find suitable management thwarted the project before it had even got off the ground.

No sooner had the Team Austria project faded, in January, than the young and ambitious March team's Formula 2 plans for 1971 were announced. John Coombs, a long-established and very successful team owner, would alleviate the ever-present financial burden by running the works team with the drivers of its 712s being Ronnie Peterson and Dieter Quester, while in addition the factory would maintain two more 712s for Lauda and Mike Beuttler. In the event, however, terms could not be agreed between March's management and Coombs, so the status quo was restored.

If either of these projects had got off the ground, Lauda might have been saved a significant amount of debt. Instead, with typical resourcefulness he organised a bank loan equating to £20,000 — a big sum at the time — to pay for a seat in March's works Formula 2 squad. The story of how his grandfather, who was on the board of the bank in question, vetoed the loan, forcing Lauda to go elsewhere for his borrowing, has been told at length in his autobiographies, but it illustrates the level of self-belief and commitment that the young Austrian had in his own abilities. Both would be tested during the new season.

1971

ABOVE Niki's works March 712M rounds Mallory Park's Shaw's Hairpin during the season-opening Speed International Trophy.

66 Speed International Trophy (GB)

Mallory Park, 14 March 1971, Formula 2
March 712M/9 • #33
Qualifying: 10th
Result: Race 1, not classified (fuel pump); Race 2, retired (engine)

Lauda was an impressive third fastest in first practice for his first Formula 2 race, an early-season non-championship round, having proved to be quicker than most in sorting out the best gear ratios for the little 1.35-mile (2.17km) Mallory Park circuit with its contrasting mix of very fast and very slow corners. However, a broken inlet trumpet on his Cosworth FVA engine then intervened and left him only 10th on the grid for the first of two 40-lap races, with the overall result to be determined on aggregate. A late hitch also occurred during the warm-up when the engine's fuel pump had to be replaced.

In the first race he went well until a fuel pipe came loose on lap 20 and cost him eight laps in the pits having it refitted. Although he was still running at the finish, and keeping up with the leaders, he was unclassified. Starting from the back row in the second race, he diced with the Brabham of Brian Hart for much of the distance and reached fourth place by lap 27, but his engine broke a con rod as he passed the pits on lap 29, signalling his retirement.

67 Jim Clark Memorial Trophy (D)

Hockenheim, 4 April 1971, Formula 2
March 712M/9 • #29
Qualifying: 14th
Result: Race 1, 5th; Race 2, retired (clutch)

Lauda performed decently well in his second Formula 2 outing — the opening round of the European Formula 2 Championship — to qualify 14th out of 39 entrants, nine of whom missed the cut for this two-part contest.

He got away well in the first 20-lap race at the much-criticised Indy-style rolling start, surviving an assault by Vittorio Brambilla's Brabham at the *Sachs-Kurve* that saw the Italian spin off,

RITES OF PASSAGE **63**

RIGHT The Formula 2 front runners pose next to a helicopter in the Hockenheim paddock (from left): Jürg Dubler, Niki, Tim Schenken, Gerry Birrell, Mike Beuttler and Wilson Fittipaldi.

BELOW Shorn of wings in an effort to reduce drag along the fast Hockenheim straights, Lauda's March 712M is prepared in the pits ahead of the Deutschland Trophy/Jim Clark Memorial race.

1971

and was up to seventh place by lap 15. Driving superbly in the closing laps, he raced hard with Tim Schenken (Brabham) and Patrick Depailler (Tecno), overtaking both and then holding off the Australian to finish fifth.

Race 2 saw him eighth at the end of the first lap. He repeatedly led his slipstreaming group as places switched several times a lap, but his strong effort ended with clutch failure after only three laps. Although he was unclassified on aggregate, he had made an impact with the established Formula 2 stars. The partisan Austrian press was already talking of a Formula 1 début.

68 BARC Yellow Pages 200 (GB)

Thruxton, 12 April 1971, Formula 2
March 712M/9 • #38
Qualifying: 8th
Result: Heat 1, retired (brake line); Final, 10th

Thruxton was where Lauda had impressed his March bosses in his first test for the team earlier in the year, when he had matched Jochen Rindt's best time from the previous season. Now he was back for the circuit's big Easter Monday fixture, where the European Formula 2 Championship round, run as two 28-lap heats and a 50-lap final, topped the bill.

Niki qualified eighth fastest for the second heat. He passed Vittorio Brambilla on lap 1 to take seventh place and held the position comfortably until exactly half distance, when he was forced to retire with a broken brake line. He qualified for the final as one of the 10 fastest lappers who had not finished in the top 10 in their heat, so that meant a lowly grid position, just 26th.

The race soon settled into several distinct groups. Lauda ran hard in the fourth bunch, which comprised five cars, and spent most of the race scrapping with the well-financed Automovil Club Argentina Brabham of Carlos Reutemann. He passed Tetsu Ikuzawa's Lotus on lap 20 and relentlessly chased the next duelling pack to eventually finish 10th, a lap down on winner Graham Hill's Brabham.

69 International ADAC-Eifelrennen (D)

Nürburgring, 2 May 1971, Formula 2
March 712M/9 • #32
Qualifying: 8th • Result: 6th

The Eifelrennen Formula 2 race was one of the first meetings to be held after the *Nordschleife*'s 'upgrade'. With a dry wit that was to prove spookily prescient, Lauda commented, 'The removed hedges and trees have made the Nürburgring much clearer, but now you can see how far you can fall down in some places, for example at *Bergwerk*.' He was eighth quickest in qualifying despite a tired engine, his car having been taken over by Jean-Pierre Beltoise for the previous weekend's non-championship Pau Grand Prix before coming to the Nürburgring with an unchanged and over-worked engine. At least a new clutch was fitted for the race.

He got away cleanly at the rolling start and ran seventh between the Brabhams of Carlos Reutemann and Peter Westbury, then soon got

ABOVE Niki's March 712M leads Alistair Walker's Brabham BT30 through Thruxton's Campbell corner during the BARC Yellow Pages 200 Formula 2 race.

RITES OF PASSAGE **65**

ABOVE The nose of his March 712M lifting under acceleration, Niki heads onto the Nürburgring pit straight during the ADAC-Eifelrennen on his way to sixth place.

RIGHT Although Helmut Marko was older than Niki by six years, their paths into the sport's upper echelon converged. Having first competed against each other in hillclimbs and then in Formula Vee, the compatriots — seen at the Jarama Formula 2 race — both made their Formula 1 débuts in the 1971 Austrian Grand Prix. Marko held a Doctorate in Law and after his career was ended by injury, he accompanied Niki to Maranello at the end of 1973 to help negotiate his first Ferrari contract. Ironically, Marko himself had been under consideration for a Ferrari seat.

ahead of Henri Pescarolo when the Frenchman's March lost its brakes on lap 3. Dieter Quester's March passed him for sixth but Lauda regained the place when his compatriot's gear-change broke. By half distance he had been promoted to fourth by the retirements of Derek Bell and Ronnie Peterson, both in Marches. The final laps of the race saw a riveting duel between Lauda, Graham Hill and Westbury as they chased down Reutemann, getting on the tail of the Argentine driver when he had to slow for an ambulance on the track. At the flag it was Westbury who prevailed, edging out Hill's Brabham for fourth place, but Lauda had been at the head of the group for seven laps and dropped to sixth on the last lap only because of a broken anti-roll bar.

70 Gran Premio de Madrid (E)

Jarama, 16 May 1971, Formula 2
March 712M/9 • #9
Qualifying: 19th • Result: 7th

For this fourth round of the European Formula 2 Championship, only 18 starters were permitted for the single 60-lap race. Having suffered a misfire throughout qualifying, Lauda could only manage a reserve slot for the grid but

66 NIKI LAUDA

he was in good company as several recognised aces also failed to make the cut.

However, Lauda's canny observation got him a place in the race. Jean-Pierre Beltoise had scraped onto the last row after his Pygmée's overheating engine allowed him only a few practice laps. After the warm-up lap, Lauda spotted that Beltoise's engine would not fire up again, so 30 seconds before the start he sneaked past the stranded Pygmée to claim a place at the back of the grid just as the flag fell.

As it was notoriously difficult to overtake at Jarama, positions did not change much. Lauda nevertheless got himself up to 10th place by half distance, behind Wilson Fittipaldi's Lotus. He tussled with the Brazilian for several laps but his March was still hampered by a slight misfire and he was unable to pass. With some forceful driving and aided by retirements ahead, their fight brought them to within five seconds of fifth-placed Jean-Pierre Jaussaud's March, putting Lauda seventh at the flag, the last unlapped finisher.

71 Tauernpokal (A)

Salzburgring, 23 May 1971, 2-litre sports
Chevron B19 (71-07) • #6
Qualifying: 5th • Result: 1st (Heat 1, 1st; Heat 2, 2nd)

Austrian race organiser Willy Lowinger wanted Lauda at 'his' round of the European 2-litre Sports Car Championship and arranged an entry via the well-regarded Red Rose Racing alongside John Hine, the Lancashire-based team's regular driver. The event was organised as two 45-lap races with the results determined on aggregate.

An assertive Arturo Merzario (Abarth) led away in Race 1 but Lauda passed him after the hairpin to lead at the end of the first lap. The pace was frantic: Helmut Marko's Lola led briefly before retiring with loss of fuel pressure, then Lauda and Vic Elford traded the lead until the Englishman pitted his Lola on lap 21. After being pressed by John Burton, whose Chevron took the lead with 10 laps to go, Lauda played

ABOVE An opportunistic move by Niki saw him sneak onto the grid at Jarama, taking advantage of his position as first reserve. Here he tackles the arid course outside Madrid on his way to seventh place.

RITES OF PASSAGE 67

a waiting game until the last lap, slipstreaming past to score a well-judged victory just ahead of Merzario, who was glued to his tail.

Conditions were wet at the start of Race 2 but Lauda and Elford opted for dry tyres while most of the field chose intermediates; it was a good decision, as the rain soon stopped. Once again Merzario led from the start while his Abarth team-mate Ernesto 'Tino' Brambilla kept Elford and Lauda at bay, but the Englishman forced his way to the front and broke away to win by eight seconds. Initially fifth, Lauda gained a place when Brambilla suffered a puncture after a collision with Hine in the second Red Rose entry; he then fought a long duel with his team-mate, whom he passed on lap 20. As his tyre advantage improved, he overhauled Merzario, who was still on wets, on lap 34. With Hine between him and the Italian, his second place gave him overall victory by 1.4 seconds on aggregate. Having never previously sat in a Chevron and not driven at the circuit for two years, he had beaten first-class opposition.

ABOVE Niki took an excellent victory in the 2-Litre Sports Championship at the Salzburgring, having driven a canny and strategically managed race.

BELOW Crystal Palace basks in May sunshine as the field awaits the start of Heat 2. Niki's March 712M (33) lines up alongside Richard Scott's Lotus 69 (57); neither would qualify for the final.

68 NIKI LAUDA

1971

72 London Trophy (GB)

Crystal Palace, 31 May 1971, Formula 2
March 712M/9 • #33
Qualifying: 9th • Result: Heat 2, 8th; Final, did not start

This highly competitive European Formula 2 Championship round was run in hot conditions at London's fast, short and tight Crystal Palace circuit, the healthy field having to be split into two 45-lap heats from which the best 16 would go through to a 50-lap final. There were separate qualifying sessions for each heat and the first such session had to be suspended when a broken water main flooded the track. Qualifying for the second heat was unaffected and unsurprisingly provided faster times, Lauda ending up ninth on the grid.

Come the race, his March was not running well and he spent most of the time scrapping with the Brabham of John Watson, finishing a lapped eighth. This was not good enough to qualify for the final, as only the first six finishers from each heat plus the next four fastest lappers (whether or not they finished) went through.

Years later, Lauda admitted that Crystal Palace was the only track he disliked and he could never properly get going there.

73 Gran Premio Della Lotteria (I)

Monza, 20 June 1971, Formula 2
March 712M/10 • #31
Qualifying: 13th
Result: Heat 1, retired (gearbox); Heat 2, retired (gearbox)

The arrangements for this year's Lottery event at Monza were unusual, and not just because the entry combined Formula 2 and Formula 5000. Race 1 was to be contested by the first 20 Formula 2 qualifiers and Race 2 was for the next six Formula 2 qualifiers plus all Formula 5000 entrants. Each of these races was split into two parts, with aggregate results, to reduce stress on the fragile engines of the smaller cars.

BELOW With wings removed to reduce drag for the annual Monza Lotteria slipstreamer, Niki's works March 712M (31) and Carlos Pace's similar Frank Williams-entered car (33) wait at the end of the pitlane for practice to start. Niki qualified for the primary all-Formula 2 races, while the Brazilian could only make it into the combined Formula 2/Formula 5000 secondary events.

RITES OF PASSAGE **69**

Monza's slipstreaming challenge meant that practice times did not count for a great deal and, as was customary in this period, wings were removed from the cars to reduce drag.

Using 712M/10 rather than his usual 712M/9, Lauda qualified for Race 1 and was immediately jockeying for position at the rolling start for the first heat. The contest quickly evolved into a fierce slipstreaming battle between the 10 leading cars and Lauda was in the thick of it, but he was forced to retire after only four laps when a gearbox bearing failed. Although the transmission was repaired in time for the second heat, he suffered precisely the same failure after only two laps and his weekend was over.

74 Grand Prix de Rouen-Les-Essarts (F)

Rouen, 27 June 1971, Formula 2
March 712M/9B (entered as '10') • #12
Qualifying: 3rd • Result: 4th, 1st in Heat 1

BELOW Niki leads his team-mate Ronnie Peterson through the temporary chicane at Paradis in the first heat of the Rouen Grand Prix, a race that marked him out as a man to watch.

For this sixth round of the European Formula 2 Championship, Lauda's March 712M was a new chassis, built up in four days, Howden Ganley having destroyed the Austrian's original 712M/9 in a heavy testing accident at Thruxton. The new chassis was numbered '9B', but it was entered here at Rouen as 712M/10, perhaps to suit documentation already drawn up for customs. At subsequent races the car was entered under the previous 712M/9 identity.

Rouen had been one of Europe's fastest and most challenging road courses, often featuring slipstreaming battles, but it had also witnessed much tragedy, none worse than the previous year's Formula 3 race in which two drivers had been killed and one seriously injured. As a consequence, two chicanes had been introduced to slow down the cars, on the entry to the ultra-quick *Grésil* bend and at the fast kink at *Paradis*.

As had become commonplace this season, the large field required the event to be run as two heats, each of 16 laps, and this time there was a 25-lap final for the fastest men. Despite missing one practice session when March team-mate Jean-Pierre Jarier blew up the engine earmarked for his new car, Lauda qualified an excellent second for his heat, the first, even though he had had little time to acclimatise to the nuances of his unfamiliar car.

In his heat, Lauda got past Mike Beuttler's March on lap 2 and quickly closed on team-mate Ronnie Peterson, the leader, soon becoming involved in a private race with the Swede. Lauda's March had a regular rear wing whereas Peterson's had a smaller one that gave an overall speed advantage, but Lauda found he had the upper hand in faster corners and swept past on lap 10 to take the lead, much to the concern of March team manager Alan Rees, who signalled frantically for him to get back behind the senior driver. Lauda finished a close second, having made another challenge on the last lap that almost collected the flagman, and he set fastest lap. His car stopped on the slowing-down lap with a broken throttle linkage so he hitched a ride back to the pits with Peterson, astride his team-mate's engine cover.

Lauda started third on the grid for the final. Getting away fourth, he managed to hold off Dieter Quester, whose March then pushed him

1971

ABOVE The BMW 2800 CSs were a handful during the Nürburgring Six Hours; Niki's Alpina car tries to lift a front wheel as he battles on towards a podium place.

almost off the road on the flat-out run down to the *Nouveau Monde* hairpin, costing him a couple of places. Sixth at the end of lap 1, he moved up to fifth when Carlos Reutemann's Brabham broke its throttle linkage on lap 20. After a long dice with Tim Schenken's Brabham, he gained another place when the Australian's engine dropped a valve. Suffering a bad misfire towards the end of the race, he pressed on regardless to finish fourth.

This was the first showing of his true potential against the best drivers in a top-line event.

75 Nürburgring Six Hours (D)

11 July 1971, Group 2
BMW 2800 CS (with Günther Huber) • #5
Qualifying: 4th • Result: 3rd (2nd in class)

Despite a clashing Interserie round at the Norisring, there was a strong entry for this Nürburgring classic, for which BMW Alpina invited Lauda back after his promising début with the team at this fixture the previous year. Driving one of BMW's big new coupés, fitted with a 3-litre engine, he was paired with an old Formula Vee rival, Austrian Günther Huber. They found the revised *Nordschleife* much quicker than before and qualified fourth in a huge field, 19 seconds behind the pole-sitting Ford Capri RS 2600.

Running on durable Dunlops to try to save a tyre change, Lauda and Huber settled into a fairly lonely fourth position, moving up a place when the Capri of Rolf Stommelen — the runaway leader — burst a tyre and crashed. By half distance they had slipped to fifth place but, driving with bravado and promoted by retirements, they finished third (and second in class) after their pace had forced the similar but faster Schnitzer-entered coupé to overstress its engine. They had been the only convincing BMW runners, crossing the line just under four minutes behind the winning Capri after six hours' racing.

RITES OF PASSAGE

76 Spa 24 Hours (B)

Spa-Francorchamps, 24 July 1971, Group 2
BMW 2800 CS (with Gérard Larrousse) • #10
Qualifying: 2nd • Result: Retired (gearbox)

There was a stellar entry for the Spa 24 Hours, the year's most important race for touring cars, with 10 of BMW's big coupés pitted against the fast but fragile Ford Capris. This time sharing his Alpina entry with Gérard Larrousse, Lauda proved his considerable class as a touring car driver by securing second place on the grid early in practice on Friday, although an engine vibration at high revs concerned him.

Slow at the start of the race, he lay fifth into *Eau Rouge* as the field streamed away but made up a place by the end of the first lap. The Alpina BMW featured strongly in the six-car leading group, but right from the start Lauda's car continued to be afflicted by the engine vibration and after an hour and a half he was in the pits. Despite the best efforts of the Alpina technicians, the problem could not be solved and he rejoined well down the field.

He was soon making up ground, the fastest man in the race, but at around 10pm he lost third gear completely and spent 35 minutes in the pits having the gearbox changed. When the replacement gearbox broke, before midnight, another was cannibalised from Günther Huber's crashed sister car, but it was then found that a brake line had also failed. Facing Spa's flat-out sections with only one brake circuit was not an option, so the car was retired.

77 Mantorp Trophy (S)

Mantorp Park, 8 August 1971, Formula 2
March 712M/9B (entered as '9') • #7
Qualifying: 5th
Result: Unclassified (Race 1, 7th; Race 2, retired [clutch])

After a six-week gap, the European Formula 2 Championship resumed in Sweden, for

BELOW Occupying the middle of the front row, the BMW 2800 CS that Lauda shared with Gérard Larrousse is readied for the Spa 24 Hours.

1971

another two-part event with results decided on aggregate. During practice late on Friday fellow Austrian Dieter Quester collided with Lauda, aggravating their national rivalry, and mechanical gremlins afflicted the rest of his practice. He qualified fifth with a time equal to John Watson's, both two seconds off Ronnie Peterson's pole.

The first 36-lap race was run in the wet after a downpour arrived shortly before the start. Lauda passed Jean-Pierre Jaussaud's March on lap 2 as the leading pair streaked away and by lap 18 he was running in the five-car group that had formed behind them, taking fifth place from Quester. A robust battle with the March driver lasted for several laps but then Lauda's engine went off-song and on lap 25 Quester retook the place; both were then passed by Tim Schenken on lap 27. Lauda eventually finished seventh, just 0.2 second adrift of Quester and with only 5.5 seconds covering the four places ahead of him.

There was confusion about the starting order for the second race but the drivers all eventually found their correct positions. Lauda circulated on his own in seventh place for several laps and reached fifth by half distance, again duelling with Quester. On lap 25 he stopped out on the back straight with a broken clutch. Although 13th on aggregate, he was unclassified.

78 Austrian Grand Prix (A)

Österreichring, 15 August 1971, Formula 1
March 711/1 • #26
Qualifying: 21st • Result: Retired (handling)

With Jochen Rindt gone, the organisers of the Austrian Grand Prix arranged for Lauda to make his Formula 1 début in his home race, a plan that had been announced by the March team at the Eifelrennen in May as a reward for his Formula 2 performances. His old rival Helmut Marko also made his first Formula 1 appearance, with BRM, almost two years to the day after their memorable Formula Vee duel at the Nürburgring.

A blown engine on the first day meant that Lauda missed second practice awaiting a replacement and when the new one was finally installed it lost most of its lubricant after a pipe became detached and sprayed oil over the exhaust system. Although he was able to refix the offending pipe out on the track, a wise move that saved the Cosworth DFV from terminal damage, he then had to trade engines with Mike Beuttler and that meant he had to sit out the final qualifying session. As a consequence he started on the back row, the only man slower than him being Jackie Oliver, whose McLaren had crashed after completing just six laps.

The dummy grid was set so far back that the flag fell before the 'proper' grid was fully in position, so those towards the back effectively made a rolling start. After ending the first lap in 18th place, Lauda pitted after only five laps

ABOVE Niki prepares to climb aboard his March 712M in the Mantorp Park pitlane. Mechanical gremlins would leave him unclassified at the flag.

RITES OF PASSAGE 73

NIKI LAUDA

1971

OPPOSITE Lauda made his Formula 1 début at his home Grand Prix in a rent-a-drive March 711 and qualified second from last. When the flag fell for the start, the back of the grid had not finished forming up and he was the slowest to get away.

LEFT Niki tackles the majestic Österreichring. By this stage the March team was running on a shoestring and his 711 was poor, its ill-handling chassis fitted with a tired engine and dud tyres, so he was undeterred by his inevitable retirement.

with handling problems that the team tried to address by fitting new front tyres. Now running at the tail of the field, he stopped again three laps later and one of the replacement front tyres was changed again. At the 20-lap mark, just after one-third distance, he decided to retire because the handling shortcomings could not be resolved.

He later claimed he was undeterred by his unimpressive début as he knew the car he had been given was poor.

79 Swedish Gold Cup (S)

Kinnekulle-Ring, 22 August 1971, Formula 2
March 712M/9B (entered as '9') • #2
Qualifying: 6th • Result: 7th (Race 1, 7th; Race 2, 7th)

This was an opportunistic non-championship addition to the Formula 2 calendar following the cancellation of the traditional meeting at Enna in Sicily. It was supported by most of the usual front runners, although many of the Formula 1 drivers who did Formula 2 as well gave it a miss. The narrow Kinnekulle-Ring was so short, measuring just 1.29 miles (2.07km), that the contest was inevitably run as more than one race, the chosen method this time being to have two 48-lap parts with the final results, unusually, calculated by adding the placings in the two parts and dividing the sum by two (and using total race times to split any drivers who finished 'equal').

Lauda qualified sixth, the third of three drivers who all set exactly the same time of 51.1 seconds. Four laps into the first race, he accidentally knocked his ignition switch off — possibly due to one of the circuit's many severe bumps — and was passed by eight cars before he could restart the engine. He fought his way back to finish seventh, 43 seconds behind the winner.

In the second race he made a steady start, outbraking John Watson for seventh place on lap 3 and ran in a tight, duelling four-car group to finish in that position, this time only 23 seconds adrift. So the average of his positions gave him seventh overall.

BELOW Niki fights his way back through the field on his way to seventh place in the first heat of the Swedish Gold Cup race at Kinnekulle-Ring.

RITES OF PASSAGE 75

80 Rothmans International Trophy (GB)

Brands Hatch, 30 August 1971, Formula 2
March 712M/9B (entered as '9') • #22
Qualifying: 7th • Result: 7th

It had been four years since Brands Hatch had hosted a Formula 2 race and a big crowd turned out for this non-championship event on Bank Holiday Monday. With larger, repositioned rear wings to improve downforce, the Marches were handling better and in fiercely competitive practice sessions on the morning of the race Lauda was one of five drivers who set exactly the same time.

After he had done his quick lap, his engine blew at the end of the final session. The March team only had one spare engine, a well-used one, and there were two claims upon it, the other from James Hunt on a guest outing with the works team. It looked briefly as though Lauda would have to withdraw and the situation gave rise to quite an argument between Max Mosley and Robin Herd, March's principals, over who should receive the one available engine. Although Lauda later claimed that he could not remember how the conflict was resolved, he believed the decision went his way because his sponsors were paying more. So a frenetic engine change in the limited time available got him on the grid for the afternoon's race.

Ronnie Peterson streaked off into an unassailable lead in the early laps, so the real battle was for second place, with Graham Hill (Brabham), Emerson Fittipaldi (Lotus), Wilson Fittipaldi (March), Gerry Birrell (Lotus), Carlos Reutemann (Brabham), Lauda and Peter Westbury (Brabham) all in line together. Eventually Hill, Reutemann, Birrell and Westbury pulled away in a group and Lauda, having to hold fourth gear in place, gradually fell back. He was overtaken easily by Reine Wisell's Lotus on lap 28 and towards the end, with the tired engine misfiring badly, he was almost caught by John Watson's old Brabham.

BELOW Niki's March 712M pictured at the Brands Hatch August Bank Holiday meeting.

1971

ABOVE Rain dominated proceedings at the Tulln-Langenlebarn airfield race. Here Niki tries to keep the cockpit from flooding as he chats to his engineer; in the race, he was one of many who spun on the streaming wet concrete.

81 Jochen Rindt Memorial Trophy (A)

Tulln-Langenlebarn, 12 September 1971, Formula 2
March 712M/9B (entered as '9') • #11
Qualifying: 7th
Result: Unclassified (Race 1, 9th; Race 2, retired [spin])

Press hype about the expected battle between the Austrian trio of Helmut Marko, Dieter Quester and Lauda was deflated when BRM, Marko's new Formula 1 team, refused to let him take part in this European Formula 2 Championship round.

Morning practice was dry and the fastest 10 runners were covered by less than a second, but torrential rain prevailed throughout the afternoon for the two 35-lap races and made the already slippery concrete utterly treacherous.

In Race 1, Lauda got a bad start from the middle of the third row and dropped to 14th at the end of lap 1. Ronnie Peterson was almost the only driver not to spin and in a virtuoso performance of car control he dominated the contest while Lauda could only finish ninth, the last unlapped finisher. Race 2 was little better on the streaming wet track and Lauda's race ended on only lap 6 when he spun at the chicane and was unable to restart his engine, which had been suffering low fuel pressure throughout the afternoon. Retirement meant that he was unclassified in the aggregated results.

82 Grand Prix d'Albi (F)

Albi, 26 September 1971, Formula 2
March 712M/9B (entered as '9') • #17
Qualifying: 12th • Result: Retired (suspension wishbone)

This ninth round of the European Formula 2 Championship was run as a single 63-lap race with only the fastest 20 qualifiers from 32 participants able to start. After a poorly organised practice session, Lauda qualified midfield (12th) on the closely matched grid. His performance in practice had not been helped by

RITES OF PASSAGE

the fact that the March team's efforts were, quite understandably, focused on Ronnie Peterson as he was challenging for the championship title.

Niki made up a place to lie 11th after five laps and by lap 21 he was mixing it with the front runners, having got up to fourth in the slipstreaming battle. After Patrick Dal Bo retired his Pygmée on lap 26 and Peterson pitted his March on lap 28, Lauda was left holding an excellent second place, closing steadily on Emerson Fittipaldi's works Lotus for the lead while holding off Peter Westbury (Brabham) and François Migault (March). However, his car was suffering severe vibrations resulting from mismatched brake discs and calipers, and on lap 32 he was forced to let Westbury through. Ten laps later this took its toll when the March's lower right front wishbone fractured under heavy braking and the suspension collapsed. His was only one of many mechanically-related retirements that decimated the field, as just eight of the 20 starters made it to the chequered flag.

BELOW Albi was another slipstreaming fest; Niki's March 712M, wearing its front fin assembly in place of the rear wing in an improvised attempt to reduce drag, leads the Brabham BT36s of Peter Westbury and Carlos Reutemann down the long but relatively narrow *Pajol* straight.

83 Gran Premio di Roma (I)

Vallelunga, 10 October 1971, Formula 2
March 712M/9B (entered as '9') • #8
Qualifying: 18th • Result: 7th (Race 1, 11th; Race 2, 5th)

This European Formula 2 Championship round at the newly revised Vallelunga circuit was run in two 35-lap parts for 22 cars, seven missing the cut. Having set his quickest practice time on Friday, Lauda failed to improve on Saturday morning after going off and slightly bending the March's monocoque — his only mistake of the season. Prior to the incident he had experienced the same vibration as at Albi, but changing the discs and calipers seemed to cure the problem. He missed the afternoon qualifying session but the team was able to repair the car in time for the race, although he started from the ninth row of the grid.

Fighting handling problems resulting from the accident damage, he raced hard with John

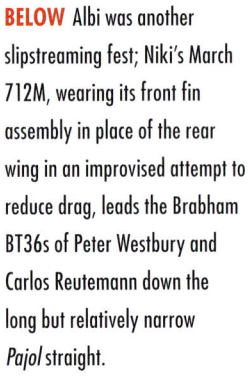

1971

Cannon (March) in the first contest and despite a spin finished 11th amid a dense pack. The handling difficulties persisted in the second race, but he did rather better, helped by an improved grid position based on results in the first race. After a spirited duel with Gerry Birrell (Lotus) and Jean-Pierre Jaussaud (March), he got the better of both, and lost out to Mike Beuttler for fourth place by just 0.7 second after a late charge. Seventh place on aggregate came after a hard afternoon's work.

Rather oddly, the following weekend the Vallelunga circuit hosted another European Formula 2 Championship round, the last of the season, but Lauda was among various drivers who gave it a miss.

SUMMARY

Lauda had driven a clean and consistent Formula 2 campaign in 1971, his only real error coming in his last race of the season at Vallelunga. Obviously very much the number two in the March team, with the consequent lack of priority for components and car preparation that went with the position, he accepted the situation and made his response on the track. He learned from his mechanics and especially from his team leader Ronnie Peterson, who became European Formula 2 Champion. The two drivers got on very well, Lauda later revealing that the Swede taught him the technique of left-foot braking. He studied Peterson's driving intently to learn where and why he was quicker. Tenth place in the European Formula 2 Championship was probably less than he deserved.

While he still lacked the experience (and financial clout) of many of his rivals, contemporary observers commented that by the end of 1971 he had matured into a very good racing driver. Although his Formula 1 début at his home Grand Prix ended with a lamentable (but predictable) technical failure, he had announced his arrival in the sport's upper echelon. The Austrian press in particular noted that where previously they had spoken of Helmut Marko or Dieter Quester as Jochen Rindt's successor, Lauda was now just as hot a prospect. Even the somewhat circumspect *Autosport* commented, 'Of all the drivers except Peterson, Niki Lauda showed the most long-term potential.'

Looking ahead to 1972, March designer Robin Herd had hoped to carry out a full-scale development programme on the team's new Formula 2 challenger much as he had done in his previous role at McLaren, but lack of funds prevented it. However, the testing and development work that could be done was undertaken largely by Lauda after Mike Beuttler's initial run in the 722.

The Austrian's consistent approach and candid feedback — skills he had learned early from his Formula Vee days — were becoming evident and he was also building a good relationship with one of the engineers, Harvey Postlethwaite, who would go on to make a name for himself as one of Formula 1's most successful designers. After a test at Thruxton, where Peterson set a series of times that Lauda repeatedly beat, Herd later reflected, 'I realised we were in trouble because we had two superstar drivers, and we couldn't even afford one of them.'

ABOVE Niki's Cosworth-engined works March 712M leads Dieter Quester's BMW-powered, Eifelland-entered sister car in the Gran Premio di Roma at Vallelunga. Quester finished second while the best Lauda could manage was seventh after damaging his car's monocoque in practice.

RITES OF PASSAGE 79

1972
BUYING A FUTURE

Lauda faced a busy year. Number two to Ronnie Peterson in the March works team, he was going to contest full seasons in both Formula 1 and Formula 2. On paper, at least, this time he had a better chance of challenging for the title in the European Formula 2 Championship, which was now run to a 2,000cc limit rather than the previous 1,600cc; like all 'graded' drivers, Peterson, the reigning champion, could no longer earn points.

Of course, Lauda's opportunity was not just the reward for some good performances in 1971; a hefty financial contribution to the March team's finances, provided by the 22-year-old courtesy of increasing his loan from the Austrian Raiffeisenkasse bank by an eye-watering £100,000, was the defining factor. His plan was that loan repayments would come primarily from his share of Formula 1 starting money, helped by an internal agreement between the Raiffeisenkasse's credit and advertising departments to offset the loan interest against a sponsorship deal — with the added collateral of a life-insurance policy on the youngster in case he did not survive his chosen career.

At the beginning of December 1971, Lauda announced that on the few weekends when he was not committed to March, he would contest European Touring Car Championship races. Ford Germany and BMW had both been in discussions with him, but an offer from Burkard Bovensiepen's Alpina team secured his services for the Bavarian marque, for which he had already raced occasionally in the two previous seasons. At least he was being paid a retainer for his tin-top activities and his financial woes were eased a little further when the jeans company Levi's also agreed a sponsorship deal with him.

1972

84 Argentine Grand Prix

Buenos Aires, 23 January 1972, Formula 1
March 721/2 • #15
Qualifying: 22nd • Result: 11th

Lauda began his first Formula 1 World Championship season with the March 721, a simple stop-gap development of the previous year's 711, still with the characteristic 'tea-tray' front wing at this stage. At Buenos Aires he was the first driver out on the track in practice, having incentivised his mechanics by means of a crate of beer to prepare his car promptly. Fighting severe understeer, he wisely did not attempt any heroics in qualifying on the unfamiliar circuit and started from the rear of the grid.

In the race he took things steadily at first, moving up the field as others retired while having a private joust for last place with old sparring partner Helmut Marko. The two Austrians fought as if the title depended on the outcome, Marko throwing his BRM all over the place in an attempt to stay ahead of the March and at one point mistaking Peterson for Lauda

ABOVE Now a fully fledged Formula 1 driver, Niki turns the March 721 into the infield section of the Buenos Aires autodrome on his way to 11th place in the Argentine Grand Prix.

BELOW Niki and March designer Robin Herd discuss progress in the Buenos Aires pits.

BUYING A FUTURE 81

at the hairpin when being lapped, forcing the Swede into a spin. Towards the end, Marko's brakes were shot but he just held off Lauda at the flag, by mere inches. That meant Niki finished 11th, two laps behind, having done all that was required of him.

85 South African Grand Prix

Kyalami, 4 March 1972, Formula 1
March 721/2 • #4
Qualifying: 21st • Result: 7th

For this race the March 721s were fitted with a different style of nose, of more conventional wedge-shaped configuration with separate canard wings. During practice Lauda went through six front brake discs in an effort to cure a persistent vibration and in the end well-used discs from Argentina were refitted for final qualifying. Forced to use an old Cosworth DFV after one of the better engines had been damaged while being unloaded at the docks, he was allowed to use Peterson's (which had 600rpm more available) to set a time but was brought in after three laps; at least he was not on the back row this time.

Early in the race he shadowed Jacky Ickx (Ferrari) before he slipstreamed past into Crowthorne like a veteran and pulled away from the Belgian. He determinedly chased down Graham Hill's Brabham, although the Englishman made his car very wide, shutting the door every time Lauda made any move to overtake. Ultimately the Austrian finished less than half a car's length behind the sixth-placed former double World Champion, who subsequently apologised for his blocking tactics. Just missing out on a championship point was an excellent achievement that exceeded expectations.

BELOW A combative performance in the South African Grand Prix at Kyalami saw Niki just miss out on a championship point after a long battle with Graham Hill for sixth place.

86 Mallory Park (GB)

12 March 1972, Formula 2
March 722/5 • #2
Qualifying: 5th • Result: 2nd (Race 1, 2nd; Race 2, 2nd)

For Formula 2's new 2,000cc limit, the Ford BDA engine was the only feasible option for most competitors and almost all teams adopted it, using various engine tuners who bored out the standard 1,601cc unit to varying degrees. However, an acute shortage of suitable BDA engines meant that more than half of the intended entries did not turn up for this season opener, which doubled as the first round of both the European Formula 2 Championship and the new five-round John Player British Formula 2 Championship, and was run as two 50-lap parts. Lauda's efforts in practice were hampered by his March repeatedly jumping out of fifth gear, resulting in a frightening spin in the long, fast Gerard's right-hander, but he still qualified strongly on the second row.

In the first race he was involved in a fierce dice with Dave Morgan (Brabham) and Wilson Fittipaldi (March), the trio progressing with the retirements of Ronnie Peterson and Jody Scheckter (McLaren). As Lauda harried Morgan, their pace brought them up behind race leader Carlos Reutemann's Rondel Brabham. Morgan squeezed through on lap 35 to take the lead and two laps later Lauda forced his way past as well for second place, but worsening oversteer meant he had to settle for that position behind the flying Morgan.

With a front-row grid position for the second race, Lauda was poised to do well but Reutemann, his Brabham on fresh tyres, got in front and dominated, leaving the Austrian to engage in a

ABOVE Flanked by Jody Scheckter's McLaren M21 and the Brabham BT36 of Richard Scott, Niki's March 722 lines up on the Mallory Park grid for his first Formula 2 race of the year.

BUYING A FUTURE 83

four-way battle for second place, maintaining a gap of between two and four seconds to Morgan. Although Niki closed right up to the leader by lap 30, he was unable to shake off Morgan and in the last five laps he was hindered by the loss of third gear. Had he got ahead of Reutemann, it might have given him enough margin for overall victory; as it was, Morgan followed him home just one second behind, close enough to give the Englishman the win on aggregate.

87 Oulton Park (GB)

31 March 1972, Formula 2
March 722/5 • #2
Qualifying: 2nd • Result: 1st

Oulton Park's 40-lap Good Friday event, the second round of the John Player British Formula 2 Championship, only had a small field, most competitors saving their cars for the more important Thruxton meeting that started the next day. Lauda was quickest in the wet first practice session despite a blown engine gasket in his Race Engine Services-prepared BDA and wound up second after the next dry session.

It began to rain heavily during warm-up and in torrential conditions he made a tremendous start to lead from Tim Schenken's Brabham and John Surtees's eponymous TS10. Although Schenken initially stayed with him, Lauda soon pulled away and by lap 16 he had lapped all but the top four, increasing his lead further when Schenken was delayed by a spin. Driving superbly in the appalling weather, he splashed round to take a dominant victory by nearly a minute, with only six of the 14 starters making it to the finish.

88 BARC 200/Jochen Rindt Trophy (GB)

Thruxton, 3 April 1972, Formula 2
March 722/5 • #23
Qualifying: 7th • Result: 3rd (Heat 1, 1st)

Thruxton's Easter Monday fixture, a round of both the European Formula 2 Championship and the John Player British Formula 2

BELOW Plunging through torrential rain, Niki heads for his first Formula 2 win, in the John Player British Formula 2 Championship race at Oulton Park.

84 NIKI LAUDA

ABOVE *En route* to victory in the first heat of the BARC 200/Jochen Rindt Trophy, Niki brakes his March 722 for Thruxton's chicane.

Championship, was run as two 28-lap heats and a 50-lap final. After only six laps of practice, Lauda's Race Engine Services-prepared engine died and the replacement unit had a misfire, so he was only able to qualify seventh for his heat.

After a storming start he was third at the end of the first lap of Heat 1. On lap 10 he made a daring move, staying in the slipstream of Carlos Pace's Pygmée to follow as it passed Gerry Birrell's new March for the lead. These two then pulled away, sharing a new lap record in the process before the Pygmée began to misfire. Lauda took the lead on lap 25 and went on to secure a comfortable win.

Third on the grid for the final, he got away in second place behind Ronnie Peterson and ran in close formation with François Cevert, both of these rivals using Formula 1 rear tyres on their Marches. On lap 9 the Frenchman passed him at the chicane, putting him third. After 15 laps his car started to trail oil from a breather pipe so he paced himself and settled for his third place, albeit a lap down and with just two finishers behind him in a race that saw very heavy attrition.

As Peterson and Cevert were 'graded' drivers, which meant they could not score points, Lauda secured the maximum nine available for the European Formula 2 Championship and took the lead in the title race. His third place also gave him four points in the John Player British Formula 2 Championship, which he also now led comfortably after three of its five rounds

89 Deutschland Trophy/Jim Clark Memorial (D)

Hockenheim, 16 April 1972, Formula 2
March 722/5 • #16
Qualifying: 1st
Result: Heat 1, retired (fuel pump); Heat 2, retired (final drive)

The ever-present dangers of the sport were brought home to Lauda when Bert

BUYING A FUTURE 85

Hawthorne was killed after his Leda crashed during practice out on Hockenheim's fast, brutal and isolated forest section. Lauda had reported to the pits that there were two cars crashed and on fire with no-one attending the scene, but it took two further laps for officials to respond. The incident fuelled his resolve to support the safety crusade, which by then was gathering momentum. Practice ended with Lauda on pole position, his car fitted with the absent Ronnie Peterson's Cosworth-tuned engine rather than his usual Race Engine Services version.

The contest was run in two 20-lap parts. In the first race Lauda led Henri Pescarolo (Brabham) out of the first corner and they raced closely in the early stages, the Frenchman taking the lead on lap 4 but Lauda regaining it a lap later. On lap 12, while leading comfortably, he failed to appear from the woods, having stopped with a broken fuel pump belt.

Starting 16th on the grid for the second race, he was an astounding seventh at the end of the first lap and, towing works team-mate Jochen Mass in his slipstream, he stormed through to second place by lap 4. Meanwhile, race leader Jean-Pierre Jaussaud (Brabham) knew the Austrian could not beat him overall and let him retake the lead on lap 9. Although Lauda soon pulled out a two-second gap, he signalled to his pit that his tyres were going off and giving him severe handling problems. However, after nine laps it was his transmission that failed. His only consolation for twice retiring from the lead was fastest lap, set in the second race.

ABOVE Niki's March 722 emerges from the echoing sound-box of Hockenheim's pine forest and into the stadium section during the Jim Clark Memorial Trophy meeting.

BELOW Wrestling the recalcitrant March 721X around the twisty Jarama circuit, Niki only managed to complete seven laps of the Spanish Grand Prix before retiring.

90 Spanish Grand Prix

Jarama, 1 May 1972, Formula 1
March 721X/1 • #24
Qualifying: 25th • Result: Retired (stuck throttle)

By now Robin Herd's much-vaunted new 721X, a complicated design with a transverse gearbox using Alfa Romeo internals, was available. Although the team completed two days of testing at Jarama a week before the race, only one of the two 721Xs was present — Lauda's was delayed at the factory — and the Austrian was obliged to watch as Ronnie Peterson circulated. Right at the end of the second day he was finally given his chance at the wheel, for just five laps, and very quickly he had two uncharacteristic spins and reported the car to be undriveable. It had extreme initial understeer on turn-in followed by snap oversteer when power was applied, a problem that was found to worsen as fuel load lightened.

Lauda's tribulations were not helped by the fact that when his 721X — the first to be built — finally arrived, it proved to be 18kg heavier than Peterson's. His dismay was compounded by gear-selection problems during practice and he qualified last, some 6.5 seconds slower than Jacky Ickx's pole time in his Ferrari. He made up three places at the start, even getting ahead of his team-mate, but dropped back to retire after just seven slow laps while enduring a sticking throttle cable and a faulty differential.

91 Grand Prix Automobile de Pau (F)

Pau, 7 May 1972, Formula 2
March 722/5 • #29
Qualifying: 7th • Result: Heat 1, 2nd; Final, retired (driveshaft)

Pau's 1.71-mile (2.76km) street circuit hosted the fourth round of the European Formula 2 Championship, run as two 37-lap heats and a 70-lap final. During practice Lauda was hampered first by a misfiring engine (a Race Engine Services unit) and then, following an engine change, a blow-up of the replacement Cosworth-prepared version after only four laps. With a third BDA installed, he qualified seventh.

The start of the first heat was rather chaotic. Jean-Pierre Beltoise's March was push-started but avoided disqualification, while Lauda banged his rear wheel against Henri Pescarolo's front, bending a suspension top link and giving the wheel negative camber; he continued undaunted but the Frenchman pitted to have his Brabham

ABOVE Lauda's excellent second place in the first heat at the picturesque Pau street circuit did not translate into a similar success in the final, from which he retired early with driveshaft failure. Following him here are Gerry Birrell's March 722 and Andrea de Adamich's Surtees TS10.

BUYING A FUTURE 87

ABOVE The 1972 Monaco Grand Prix was one of the wettest on record, but at least this meant it was run at a very slow pace that disguised some of the March 721X's shortcomings. Niki splashes his way towards 16th place.

checked. Lauda took fifth place from David Purley (March) on lap 4 and set about Jody Scheckter (McLaren), whom he outbraked into the hairpin on lap 6. He soon caught and passed Reine Wisell's GRD, then sat on the tail of Gerry Birrell's March for five laps before forcing his way past into second place and pulling away, although he was unable to make any impression on Patrick Depailler's winning March. Only six cars completed the heat.

Starting the final from fourth on the grid, he completed the first lap in fifth place after a big wheel-banging incident shuffled the pack. On lap 6 he was delayed after sliding on oil dropped by Graham Hill's Brabham, although he made up a place as Jean-Pierre Jaussaud (Brabham) also hit the oil and spun in front of him. He had moved up to third by lap 10, but oil on his tyres prevented him from making much progress in catching second-placed Depailler. His race ended when the right-hand driveshaft broke as he powered up the hill on lap 20.

92 Monaco Grand Prix

Monte Carlo, 14 May 1972, Formula 1
March 721X/1 • #4
Qualifying: 22nd • Result: 16th

This was another dismal Formula 1 outing for Lauda, who had never raced at Monaco. It was obvious that the 721X was almost impossible to handle and a complete rebuild with new components did nothing to mitigate the fundamental flaws in its design. The car's extreme — and insoluble — understeer was not what was needed for the twists and turns of the Monte Carlo circuit. Nevertheless, this time Lauda managed to avoid the back of the grid as there were three more Marches behind him.

Torrential rain on race day only exacerbated the 721X's handling problems; even at 5mph he struggled to get his car round Station Hairpin. Lauda passed Graham Hill (Brabham) on lap 1 but spun on lap 4, damaging a wheel rim and

1972

requiring a pit stop for a new wheel. Thereafter he ran near the tail of the field, with his overalls soaked in petrol leaking from a broken fuel gauge, but he plugged on to finish 16th, six laps adrift. At least he collected some much-needed prize money.

93 Grand Prix Brno (CZ)

Brno, 21 May 1972, Group 2
BMW 2800 CS • #6
Qualifying: 3rd • Result: Retired (engine)

Lauda returned to the BMW Alpina team for this European Touring Car Championship round at Brno, a relatively local race for him as the Czech venue was just across the border from Vienna. His desire to achieve a good result was no doubt enhanced by a new bonus system introduced by BMW, giving a driver 50,000 DM for a victory and 10,000 DM for a top-three grid position. His old friend Gerold Pankl was originally listed as his co-driver but instead raced the team's 2002 in the 2-litre class, leaving Lauda to drive alone.

Saturday practice took place in very wet conditions, but despite fluctuating oil pressure and handling issues caused by the big coupé's inboard rear brakes, he responded to challenges from the pit wall to take third on the grid.

For Sunday's two-hour race, there was drizzle as the start approached and three warm-up laps were allowed to give everyone an idea of where the long 8.66-mile (13.94km) road circuit was wet or dry. Many drivers decided to change to intermediate tyres, but as Lauda's car was already in place on the grid officials prevented him from swapping his rubber. At the end of the first lap he pitted with engine woes. Although the Austrian was initially accused of over-revving his car's 3-litre motor, Alpina technical director Dr Fritz Indra confirmed he had authorised him to use the 8,200rpm showing on the rev counter's tell-tale. The problem turned out to be a broken valve rocker and he was forced to retire.

LEFT Alpina boss Burkard Bovensiepen listens intently to Niki as his BMW 2800 CS is worked upon in the Brno pits.

BELOW Niki steers his Alpina-run BMW 2800 CS past some very substantial-looking local architecture during the Brno touring car race.

BUYING A FUTURE   89

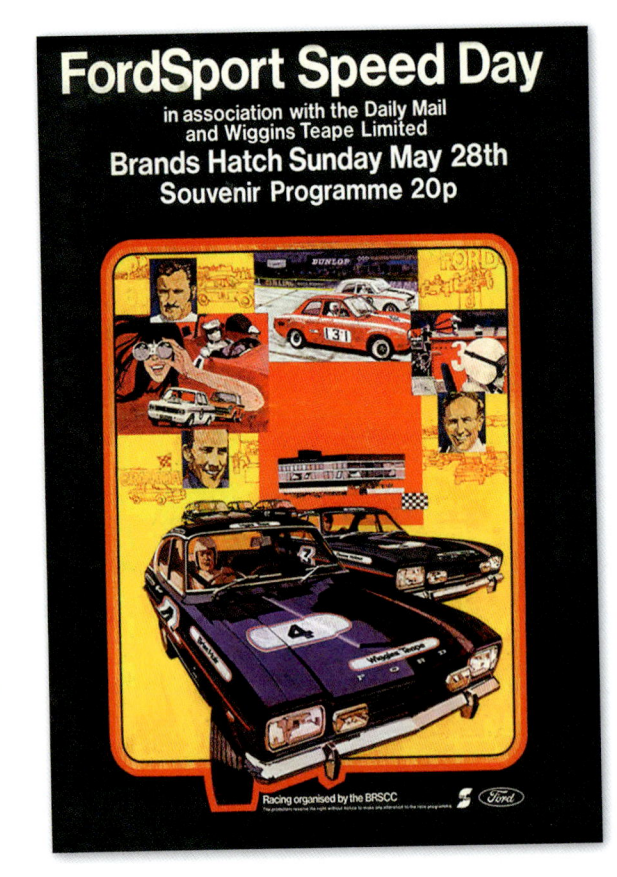

BELOW Fighting for grip in a road-specification Ford Capri 3000E, Niki attacks the Brands Hatch short circuit during the Fordsport Day Capri Trophy Race. Note the misspelled 'Nicki' on the car's front wing.

94 Fordsport Speed Day, Capri Trophy (GB)

Brands Hatch, 28 May 1972, 'pro-celebrity' race
Ford Capri 3000E (RWC 399K) (with Bill Stone) • #12
Qualifying: 15th (ballot)
Result: 5th=; Heat 1, 7th (Lauda); Heat 2, 3rd (Stone)

Ford provided 16 identical road-specification Capri 3000E models for a cohort of Formula 1 drivers and team managers to share in a 'pro-celebrity' race on the 1.24-mile (1.99km) Brands Hatch 'short' circuit. There were two 10-lap races, one for the drivers, the other for the team managers, with the result determined on aggregate. As grid places were decided by ballot, practice times meant little and for his race Lauda started from the back row alongside Gerry Birrell.

Niki had a great dice with Emerson Fittipaldi — both on and off the grass — that involved plenty of contact and soon engulfed Tom Belsø. Drifting the car around the circuit, which had

90 NIKI LAUDA

1972

been made slippery by a full day's racing, Lauda finished seventh ahead of Fittipaldi and in line astern behind François Cevert, Vince Woodman and Birrell. For the second race, March team manager Bill Stone took over the car and benefited from the grid being reversed. His third place put the duo joint fifth on aggregate.

The cars were then auctioned off, all looking rather battered after the afternoon's general hooliganism.

95 Greater London Trophy (GB)

Crystal Palace, 29 May 1972, Formula 2
March 722/5 • #23
Qualifying: 6th
Result: Heat 1, retired (crankshaft); Final, did not qualify

This event, the last-ever international race held at Crystal Palace, doubled as the fifth round of the European Formula 2 Championship and the fourth round of the John Player British Formula 2 Championship.

It was not a memorable weekend for Lauda. Working with fellow March driver Gerry Birrell during practice to compare different tyres and armed with an engine prepared by Cosworth rather than the usual Race Engine Services, the Austrian qualified sixth for the first of two 45-lap heats.

At the start he dived onto the grass and got past Birrell into the first corner to slot in behind John Surtees, completing lap 1 in third place. Despite a wheel damaged by debris, he held off the Marches of Patrick Depailler and Mike Beuttler for seven laps and took second place when Surtees's engine failed. On lap 9, however, his engine expired when its crankshaft broke at Ramp.

A replacement engine was quickly installed for the 50-lap final but he was denied a place in the race. An error by the time-keepers meant that he had not been credited with his best race lap, which would have been good enough to qualify him for the final. Instead, he was made third reserve, but this was not enough to get him into the race.

ABOVE Firing his March 722 past the unyielding sleepers of the tight Crystal Palace circuit in the first heat of the Greater London Trophy, Niki heads for retirement with yet another engine failure.

BUYING A FUTURE

ABOVE Last time in the woeful March 721X; Niki drags the car to the finish at Nivelles using only four gears, but at least he can now put the frustrating experience behind him.

96 Belgian Grand Prix

Nivelles, 4 June 1972, Formula 1
March 721X/1 • #12
Qualifying: 25th • Result: 12th

As the classic Spa-Francorchamps circuit was now considered too dangerous for Formula 1, the Belgian Grand Prix was transferred to the new and rather characterless Nivelles circuit near Brussels. Lauda still had the original March 721X with its troublesome gearbox and all its attendant handling problems, whereas Ronnie Peterson had a much-modified car that was, in fact, little better. The Austrian missed final practice and last place on the grid was the result, almost two seconds adrift of the next-slowest qualifier and five seconds away from the pole-position time. Persistent gear-selection problems led the team to blank off fifth gear for the race.

Lauda made up three places on lap 1 thanks to problems for others, then passed Mike Beuttler's Formula 2-based 'hybrid' March 721G on lap 15 and Nanni Galli's recalcitrant Tecno two laps later. A duel with Galli continued for much of the race, until the Italian crashed, leaving Lauda to finish a lonely and distant 12th, three laps behind Emerson Fittipaldi's winning Lotus. The 721X's understeer was so bad that at the exit from the circuit's hairpin, which led into the main straight, the car regularly pushed itself onto the grass under acceleration.

The one thing Lauda salvaged from the 721X débâcle was an enhanced reputation as a test driver. The March engineers finally realised that the forthright Austrian had been right all along about the car's flaws, so they increasingly listened to his technical assessments rather than those of his superstar team-mate.

GOODWOOD
31 MAY 1972

After the Crystal Palace fiasco, Lauda tested his Formula 2 March 722/5 at Goodwood with newly designed Formula 3 bodywork. The experiment was not entirely successful; with too much downforce at the front end, the 150cm maximum body width that applied to the more junior category was just not substantial enough to counteract the pressure. This caused the rear end to become decidedly skittish and his test session ended with a big spin.

1972

97 Rhein-Pokalrennen (D)

Hockenheim, 11 June 1972, Formula 2
March 722/5 • #8
Qualifying: 1st
Result: Unclassified (Race 1, 13th; Race 2, retired [electrics])

During practice for this sixth round of the European Formula 2 Championship, Lauda was lucky not to collide with Peter Gethin's Chevron when they spun simultaneously in the stadium section. As at Hockenheim's previous Formula 2 contest two months earlier, Lauda again used Peterson's usual — and superior — engine to aid his cause and was credited with an astonishing lap time that gave him pole position; he pointed out that it was two seconds faster than he had actually gone, but officials insisted that the time stood.

The customary two races were shortened to 15 laps each (from 20 laps) due to heavy rain and poor visibility. In the first, Lauda's Goodyears kept him in touch, allowing him to run second behind Emerson Fittipaldi (Lotus), but by lap 3 he was passed by Gethin and Dave Morgan (Brabham). With his engine refusing to run cleanly in the wet conditions, he dropped further and further back and after missing the first chicane late in the race he received a one-minute penalty that meant his eventual eighth place became 13th. The weather was even worse for the second race and drowned electrics on the first lap caused his retirement, so he was unclassified on aggregate.

Ever since his fine start to the European Formula 2 Championship season, with second place at Mallory Park and victory at Thruxton, Lauda had led the title chase, but now Jean-Pierre Jaussaud (Brabham) took over at the top of the table thanks to scoring maximum points for his second place on aggregate.

BELOW In more wet weather at Hockenheim for the Rhein-Pokalrennen European Formula 2 Championship race, a combination of mechanical problems and driver error meant another fruitless afternoon for Niki.

BUYING A FUTURE 93

ABOVE Lauda had an older March 721 (rather than the unloved 721X) for the non-championship Gran Premio Della Repubblica Italiana at Vallelunga but shortly after this practice photograph was taken the car was written off in a high-speed accident following a tyre failure.

RIGHT Mike Beuttler gives Niki a few pointers about his hybrid March 721G, which the Austrian tried out during practice at Vallelunga.

94 NIKI LAUDA

1972

98 Gran Premio Della Repubblica Italiana (I)

Vallelunga, 18 June 1972, Formula 1
March 721/1 • #8
Qualifying: 7th • Result: Did not start (accident)

Only eight Formula 1 cars contested this non-championship race at Vallelunga on the date originally scheduled for the cancelled Dutch Grand Prix. The number was reduced to seven during practice when Lauda wrote off his old-specification March 721 after a tyre suddenly deflated; the car went straight on at the fast *Curva dei Gemini* right-hander, removing all four wheels and damaging the monocoque. Although the Austrian was unhurt, the car was too badly damaged to repair so he sat out the race. This was a disappointment: despite having been delayed by a leaking oil cooler, he had been setting impressive times that had put him third quickest in the first session.

There was another reason for the trip to Italy. For Mike Beuttler's privateer Clarke-Mordaunt-Guthrie-Durlacher 'stockbroker' team, March had produced a 721G, a hybrid using a Formula 2 monocoque fitted with Formula 1 running gear, a concept that followed on from the March 72A, a similar one-off Formula 5000 creation for John Cannon using an Oldsmobile engine. Having briefly sampled Beuttler's 721G at Nivelles, Lauda completed several more laps with it early in practice at Vallelunga and despite a broken third gear he quickly judged that it was a better prospect than the disastrous 721X. After both he and Peterson further assessed Beuttler's car at Silverstone, March built more 721Gs for works use.

99 Grand Prix de Rouen-Les-Essarts (F)

Rouen, 25 June 1972, Formula 2
March 722/5 • #27
Qualifying: 6th • Result: Retired (engine); Heat 1, retired (engine)

Due to the construction of an *autoroute*, the Rouen road circuit was dramatically changed for 1972, with a new section between *Grésil* and *Paradis* shortening the circuit from

BELOW Niki's March 722 was quick again at Rouen-les-Essarts but he was halted by engine failures in his heat and in the final. Here he leads a trio of Brabham BT38s piloted by Bob Wollek, Richard Scott and Wilson Fittipaldi through the fast uphill bends between *Nouveau Monde* and *Sanson*.

BUYING A FUTURE   95

4.07 miles (6.54km) to 3.44 miles (5.54km). As one of the first drivers to go out in practice on the revised track, Lauda set a series of fast laps in poor weather, but in drier conditions the best he could manage was only 10th fastest. His practice was ended by a collision with John Surtees at *Nouveau Monde* that incurred the Englishman's wrath and damaged his Surtees TS10.

The event was organised as two 20-lap heats with a final and Lauda's qualifying performance put him sixth on the grid for the second heat. He was enjoying a dice with Patrick Depailler (March) when his BDA engine blew up on lap 7; at that point he had recorded the third-fastest race lap and this meant he was eligible for the 30-lap final. Commandeering the engine from Jochen Mass's sister car, he started 17th and climbed to 11th by the end of the first lap. After David Purley (March) and Depailler clashed on lap 13, he was elevated to eighth place but almost immediately the replacement engine began to emit smoke and, having dropped to 10th, he was forced to quit with a blown cylinder head gasket on lap 16.

BELOW Niki's factory-development March 721G suffered a driveshaft failure early in the French Grand Prix at Clermont-Ferrand.

100 French Grand Prix

Clermont-Ferrand, 2 July 1972, Formula 1
March 721G/2 • #14
Qualifying: 21st • Result: Retired (driveshaft)

March had finally admitted failure with the 721X and two new 721Gs had been built in record time in readiness for the French Grand Prix, held at the picturesque 5.0-mile (8.1km) Clermont-Ferrand road circuit. Lauda's car for this race, 721G/2, was intended to be the development chassis, with a new one planned to be available to him for the following race. The introduction of a new car mid-season was always going to give the over-stretched March team limited scope to sort out any problems and Lauda was never happy with his car.

It suffered major brake problems in practice and then a fuel leak and a troublesome loose driveshaft emerged in Sunday's warm-up. There was no time to replace the driveshaft so Lauda's race was compromised from the outset and he quickly slipped to the back. At the end of the second lap he pitted briefly to have the car checked and after two more laps he withdrew.

Four laps later, his old rival Helmut Marko, driving for BRM, was behind Emerson Fittipaldi's Lotus when it threw up a stone that pierced the Austrian's visor and permanently blinded his left eye, ending his racing career.

101 Jochen Rindt Trophy (A)

Österreichring, 9 July 1972, Formula 2
March 722/5 • #3
Qualifying: 12th • Result: Retired (engine)

Although Lauda had consumed 10 engines in seven Formula 2 races so far, he had high hopes for his home round of the European Formula 2 Championship as his was the only works March entry, but the hot weather and fast circuit were again hard on engines. He went through five in practice, with the final blow-up being an engine that had been stripped down

1972

and rebuilt in the paddock from the remains of others. With no other reserve engines available, a replacement unit from Chris Amon's new engine-preparation business was flown out but this too failed to run well, so an old Race Engine Services-prepared mill was reinstalled.

Lauda was lucky that the event was taking place in Austria; the organisers validated Friday's practice times for qualifying so his best lap from that day (which equalled Watson's 'official' 11th) got him into the race. However, his bad luck continued and after getting away in 10th place he retired with loss of oil pressure after only seven laps, having made no further progress.

His hopes in the European Formula 2 Championship were now waning fast as he had not scored any points since the second round, the six subsequent races having all ended in retirement, and he now lay fourth in the standings. After the Österreichring, Mike Hailwood (Surtees) took over at the top of the table, having scored maximum points in two consecutive races, followed by Carlos Reutemann (Brabham) and Jean-Pierre Jaussaud (Brabham).

ABOVE Ahead of the Jochen Rindt Memorial Formula 2 race at the Österreichring, Niki ponders his chances of finishing with an engine intact.

LEFT At a boiling hot Österreichring, Lauda's March 722 lines up ahead of Carlos Ruesch's Surtees TS10 in readiness for the start of the Jochen Rindt Memorial Formula 2 race.

BUYING A FUTURE 97

ABOVE While waiting for his new chassis to be delivered to Brands Hatch for the British Grand Prix, Niki tried out Mike Beuttler's prototype Clarke-Mordaunt-Guthrie-Durlacher March 721G during Thursday afternoon practice.

BELOW The March 721G was significantly better than the 721X but was still far from perfect; struggling with unpredictable handling, Niki had a troubled run to ninth place in the British Grand Prix.

102 British Grand Prix

Brands Hatch, 15 July 1972, Formula 1
March 721G/4 • #4 (practice only: March 721G/1 • #31)
Qualifying: 19th • Result: 9th

As Lauda's new race chassis, 721G/4, was not ready when the March works team arrived at Brands Hatch, by mutual agreement with the Clarke-Mordaunt-Guthrie-Durlacher team he borrowed Mike Beuttler's prototype 721G/1 for the second half of Thursday afternoon's practice session so that he could at least set a time (in case the later sessions were washed out).

His own car was ready for Friday's practice and he soon made some progress with it, although it had been set up by Ronnie Peterson on the short circuit and had the wrong spring and damper settings. The car was a real handful, leaping dramatically over the track's undulations and wandering on the straights; he managed a

1972

wild spin on the rapidly deteriorating surface at Druids, fortunately without damage. At least this time he qualified in the top 20 and so was eligible for full starting money.

On the first lap of the race, Chris Amon's Matra and Beuttler's March touched going into Druids and Lauda was forced onto the grass to avoid them. With the car still handling unpredictably over bumps, he was at his quickest early in the race, passing Dave Charlton's privateer Lotus on lap 8. He spent the next 16 laps scrapping with and eventually passing Rolf Stommelen's Eifelland-March, then a brief joust with Arturo Merzario's Ferrari shortly afterwards was resolved in the Italian's favour. Although the March's handling steadily deteriorated, he progressed as high as eighth thanks to the retirement of others. On lap 72 Carlos Reutemann (Brabham) got past, leaving him ninth, and he finished in that respectable position, three laps behind the winner.

103 Gran Premio Città di Imola (I)

Imola, 23 July 1972, Formula 2
March 722/5 • #32
Qualifying: 7th • Result: 3rd (Race 1, 8th; Race 2, 5th)

For the European Formula 2 Championship round at Imola, Lauda was again March's only works entry. Race Engine Services was given a final chance to build a reliable engine, but this was still down on power so Lauda switched to an Alan Smith-prepared BDA to set his best time before the block cracked and he had to revert to the weaker Race Engine Services version for the race, run as two 28-lap parts.

In the first race he lay fifth at the end of lap 1 amid a strong four-car battle with the Brabhams of Dave Morgan, Bob Wollek and Peter Westbury, but he found his engine losing out on the straight. He dropped back to eighth and was just able to hold off Andrea de Adamich's

BELOW In scorching heat at Imola, the mechanics check over Lauda's March 722 during practice for the European Formula 2 Championship race.

BUYING A FUTURE

Surtees to keep that position at the flag. After being passed by Graham Hill and John Surtees — the only two 'graded' drivers in the field — in the second race, he managed to haul his March home in fifth place. Nearly half of the cars failed in the almost tropical temperatures, but for once Lauda's engine survived the distance and he was as surprised as anyone to find himself in third place on aggregate. He was even happier to score six championship points as the second-placed non-graded driver.

104 German Grand Prix

Nürburgring, 30 July 1972, Formula 1
March 721G/4 • #23
Qualifying: 24th • Result: Retired (split oil tank)

BELOW Niki's March 721G pulls out of the Nürburgring pits during practice for the German Grand Prix.

Following a redesign of the 721G's suspension, the car looked more competitive at the Nürburgring and Lauda was smiling for the first time since the start of the season. However, he completed only a handful of practice laps as his car was plagued by fuel-pressure problems and he missed Saturday's final session altogether, eventually qualifying more than 20 seconds behind team-mate Ronnie Peterson's very encouraging time, which put the Swede fourth on the grid.

The lack of fuel pressure was traced to a faulty non-return valve in the central fuel collector tank that prevented air from being expelled, so petrol could not enter from the pannier tanks. Early on Sunday morning Lauda took advantage of a short free-practice session around the pits 'loop' to try his now healthy car and felt more optimistic for the race.

He made up four places on the first lap, one of them because Chris Amon's Matra started from the pitlane. By lap 4 he had progressed to 18th, in the middle of a duelling six-car group, but then had to pit because his Cosworth DFV engine was losing oil through a split in the tank and oil pressure had all but vanished by the end of the lap. The car was retired immediately.

1972

105 Mantorp Grand Prix (S)

Mantorp Park, 6 August 1972, Formula 2
March 722/5 • #2
Qualifying: 22nd
Result: Retired (Race 1, did not qualify; Race 2, retired [engine])

During untimed practice on Friday, Lauda spun into the catch fencing and bent a wishbone, causing him to miss most of the afternoon session. Serious engine trouble on Saturday coupled with rain during the qualifying session that had been allocated to even-numbered cars meant that he did not set a time, so he was second reserve for the first of the two 36-lap races at this European Formula 2 Championship qualifier. He was allowed to complete the two warm-up laps in case any drivers ran into last-minute trouble but was not called for.

A spate of retirements meant there were only 16 participants left for the second race, so Lauda was invited to join in — some consolation for having travelled so far. Starting from the back row, he tore through the field and reached sixth place by lap 18. But his efforts were to little avail. He was hounding Jean-Pierre Jaussaud (Brabham) for fifth place when his Race Engine Services-prepared engine suffered yet another cracked block, forcing his retirement.

ABOVE Seen drifting the March 722 through a fast curve at Mantorp Park, Niki stormed up to sixth place in the second of the two Formula 2 races, having been allowed to start from the back of the grid in a much-reduced field, but his charge ended in yet another retirement.

BUYING A FUTURE 101

ÖSTERREICHRING
11 AUGUST 1972

Matra arrived early for the Austrian Grand Prix, wanting to carry out pre-race tyre testing. The French team brought its usual two cars for Chris Amon — the regular MS120D race car and an older MS120C spare — and both were prepared and ready to go on the day preceding official practice. However, Amon himself was missing, so the team invited Lauda to try out the newer car, knowing of his technical understanding and his familiarity with the Österreichring. Just as Lauda was getting ready to leave the pits, Amon appeared, so the Austrian was instead sent out in the older car, MS120C/4, which had been unused for three races. He came past the pits only once: on his second lap the engine exploded, even though he was running it some 3,000rpm below the limit he had been given, and he was forced to abandon the car out on the circuit.

ABOVE Niki had a brief run in Chris Amon's Matra MS120C before official practice for the Austrian Grand Prix until the car's V12 engine blew up after one and a half laps.

1972

106 Austrian Grand Prix

Österreichring, 13 August 1972, Formula 1
March 721G/4 • #4
Qualifying: 22nd • Result: 10th

Extensive tests at Goodwood with the March 721G had not resulted in any meaningful progress and Lauda, struggling to cope with the car's handling deficiencies as stoically as team-mate Ronnie Peterson, could not really impress his home crowd at the Österreichring. March's strained finances meant that Lauda was given 'used' front tyres that caused his car to understeer violently; in addition his tired Cosworth DFV simply was not good enough for this power circuit and his promised new engine was given to Peterson when Mike Beuttler refused to honour a previous agreement to share his motor with the Swede. Lauda's mood was not improved when his car caught fire in the paddock while it was being cleaned.

Come the race, there was more consternation when his March's fuel metering unit had to be changed on the grid, Lauda lining up 22nd out of 25 starters. Despite everything, he moved up to 14th position by half distance, mainly aided by retirements, although he did overtake Peter Gethin's BRM on lap 16 and Jacky Ickx's misfiring Ferrari three laps later. He spent much of the second half of the race impressively hounding François Cevert after the Tyrrell driver had pitted, but the March was labouring to accelerate out of corners and he slipped back to finish 42 seconds behind the Frenchman, in 10th place and a lap behind the winner.

107 Levi's Challenge (NL)

Zandvoort, 27 August 1972, Group 2
BMW 2800 CS (with Gerold Pankl and Toine Hezemans) • #12
Qualifying: 6th • Result: 3rd

Lauda returned to the BMW Alpina team for the four-hour Zandvoort Trophy, the sixth round of the European Touring Car Championship, driving a 2800 CS with his old Formula 3 team-mate Gerold Pankl. During practice he was third quickest of the BMW drivers and the car lined up sixth on the grid.

After a careful start, he initially ran sixth before determinedly hunting down and passing Chris Craft's Ford Capri and John Fitzpatrick's Schnitzer BMW despite his car's poor handling. Less than an hour into the race, he was punted off at *Tarzan* while lapping an Alfa Romeo, puncturing a rear tyre and damaging the wheel rim. A stop to change the wheel and take on fuel

SILVERSTONE
25 AUGUST 1972

Following his return from Austria, Lauda gave March's new 2-litre sports challenger, the 73S, its first run at Silverstone. His team-mates at March, Ronnie Peterson and Jochen Mass, were both contracted to Ford's touring car programme and were thus precluded from driving this BMW-engined car, whereas Lauda, with his BMW connections through his touring car activities, was ideally placed to evaluate the power unit for which March would have exclusive use the following season. The focus of the team's BMW tie-up was Formula 2, with the sports car created purely to allow March to use its engine order quota to the full.

Initial tests of the 73S were promising as Lauda immediately broke Silverstone's 2-litre lap record. He went on to carry out an *ad hoc* development programme with the car for the rest of the year, as and when March's strained finances permitted.

OPPOSITE The Österreichring was very much a 'power' circuit but Niki's March 721G was anything but a 'power' car and he finished a lapped 10th in his home Grand Prix.

BUYING A FUTURE 103

ABOVE It was a hard afternoon's work for Niki in the four-hour Levi's Challenge at Zandvoort, sharing this Alpina-entered BMW 2800 CS with Gerold Pankl and Toine Hezemans.

cost him a lap, but gradually he caught up again, underlining his quality as a first-rate touring-car driver. Seventh after 35 laps, he was back up to fourth when he handed over to Pankl at the two-hour mark. With half an hour to go, local hero Toine Hezemans, whose sister Alpina-run BMW had retired, took over the car when Pankl pitted for a new tyre. The Dutchman brought the big coupé home third — a good result.

RIGHT Niki and Ronnie Peterson enjoyed a relaxed, open relationship, the Austrian saying later that he had learned a lot from his March team leader — albeit probably not a great deal about testing as technical feedback was not among the Swede's many strengths.

108 Festspielpreis der Stadt Salzburg (A)

Salzburgring, 3 September 1972, Formula 2
March 722/5 • #4
Qualifying: 6th • Result: 6th (Race 1, 6th; Race 2, 8th)

Despite the works March team having by now abandoned Race Engine Services as its supplier, at this European Formula 2 Championship round the cars were still down on power, a shortcoming exemplified for Lauda in particular by him being unable to keep in fifth gear on the circuit's long uphill sections.

This was another contest run in two parts. From sixth on the grid for the first race, Lauda ran fifth at the end of lap 1 in a 10-car train within which positions shuffled constantly

1972

BUYING A FUTURE

as the race settled into a typical Salzburgring slipstreaming battle. After a scrap with Ronnie Peterson, which the watching Helmut Marko thought was a little too heated with some intra-team 'fouling', Lauda finished the first race in sixth place, in close company with the Brabhams of Graham Hill and Carlos Reutemann behind the leading trio, but well clear of the rest.

After changing the Alan Smith-prepared engine to a Geoff Richardson-built unit for the second race, he found the replacement engine weaker still and, as in practice, had to change down to fourth gear on the uphill straight behind the pits. He fought with Peter Gethin for fifth place before dropping back and thereafter he could only benefit from the failures of others. He just managed to hold off Bob Wollek (Brabham) and Hiroshi Kazato (March) to finish eighth, enough for him to be classified sixth on aggregate.

109 Italian Grand Prix

Monza, 10 September 1972, Formula 1
March 721G/4 • #4
Qualifying: 20th • Result: 13th

ABOVE With the nose of his March 722 carrying the scars of his scrap with Ronnie Peterson's sister car, Niki heads for sixth place in the first heat of the Festspielpreis der Stadt Salzburg against the photogenic rural backdrop of the Salzburgring.

BELOW Wearing the little-used front-radiator nose configuration, Lauda had to make a recovery drive in his March 721G in the Italian Grand Prix, having lost time while his engine's throttle slides were cleaned out after the car was showered with dirt in a first-lap incident.

For Monza, Lauda's race chassis had been converted to a front-radiator layout with full-width nose that he had previously tested at Goodwood and that Ronnie Peterson had tried out on the spare car in Austria, where the wide nose was considered to give insufficient downforce. This was a less of an issue at Monza; worn-out Cosworth DFVs were a bigger problem.

After enjoying a trouble-free practice for once, Lauda outqualified team-mate Ronnie Peterson for the first time, 20th to the Swede's 24th. He was nearly eliminated on the first lap of the race when Peterson took to the grass to avoid Jackie Stewart's ailing Tyrrell and rejoined the track in uncomfortably close proximity, spraying a cloud of dirt over the Austrian's car. This clogged the throttle slides of Lauda's engine and he had to pit to have them cleaned out, resuming five laps down. After a brave solo pursuit at the back of the field, he eventually finished 13th and last.

110 Oulton Park (GB)

16 September 1972, Formula 2
March 722/5 • #4
Qualifying: 4th • Result: 2nd (joint fastest lap)

With a superior Ford BDF engine courtesy of Cosworth Engineering finally fitted to his March 722, Lauda went into this fifth and final round of the John Player British Formula 2 Championship as the clear points leader and with high hopes of taking the title. As with the European Formula 2 Championship, this one-off British series used the 9–6–4–3–2–1 scoring system, and the rankings ahead of this race were Lauda on 19 points, Dave Morgan and Jody Scheckter equal second on 12, and Ronnie Peterson fourth on nine. But all four men had a chance because double points were on offer for this 40-lap finale.

Despite a harmless spin that caused him to miss half of practice, Lauda qualified well for fourth spot on the grid and was involved in a four-car train in the early laps. Scheckter's title challenge evaporated when he retired his McLaren from the lead on lap 15. When Tim Schenken (Brabham) dropped out of contention on lap 19, it left a frantic and enthralling three-car battle at the front between Peterson in the lead, James Hunt's second-placed March and Lauda in third. The Austrian maintained a watching brief as Hunt shoved his year-old Hesketh-run March into the lead on lap 36 but Peterson regained it on the next lap with a very late braking move at the Esso Hairpin, in the process forcing Hunt onto the marbles and allowing Lauda through into second place. As the Swede started to struggle with selecting third gear, Lauda made up ground and was glued to his team-mate's gearbox until the end, crossing the line just 0.2 second behind. It was enough for Lauda to take the John Player title with 31 points to Peterson's 27.

ABOVE Lauda's works March 722 exits Old Hall Corner at Oulton Park during the final round of the John Player British Formula 2 Championship. Second place gave him the title.

BUYING A FUTURE 107

ABOVE Niki's March 721G is a lap behind race winner Jackie Stewart's Tyrrell 005 in the Canadian Grand Prix as he tries to make up ground after his early stop with jammed throttle slides.

111 Canadian Grand Prix

Mosport, 24 September 1972, Formula 1
March 721G/4 • #26
Qualifying: 19th • Result: Disqualified

As at Monza, Lauda's 721G arrived at Mosport with front-mounted radiators, but after he crashed it in practice and damaged the front end it had to be rebuilt in the original side-radiator configuration. Practice was run in foul weather and after his engine dropped a valve he qualified 19th, 2.8 seconds adrift of team-mate Ronnie Peterson on the front row.

Having ingested dirt thrown up at Turn 1 on the first lap of the race, his car stopped with its throttle slides jammed shut. The March mechanics came out to the stranded Austrian and talked him through the remedial work, which took 15 laps to complete. Thereafter he drove an excellent race to finish 15th, lapped only once more. However, his efforts proved to have been in vain when he was disqualified because his mechanics were deemed to have given illegal outside assistance in helping refasten his seat belts while out on the circuit. To make things worse, this outcome brought financial disadvantage: as no starting money was paid and only the first 20 drivers earned prize money, his disqualification meant that he received only the nominal consolation payment granted to the last five starters.

112 Preis von Baden-Württemberg und Hessen (D)

Hockenheim, 1 October 1972, Formula 2
March 722/5 • #9
Qualifying: 14th • Result: 9th

Despite a strong showing early in practice with fourth quickest time, Lauda's Cosworth-prepared BDF engine did not deliver good enough top-end performance on the long Hockenheim circuit's fast stretches. In an effort to compensate, he twice left his braking too late at the end of the main straight and had to take to the escape road. Having failed to find a clear lap in the tightly packed qualifying session, he ended up a disappointed 14th on the grid.

Unlike the season's two previous European Formula 2 Championship rounds at Hockenheim, this one was run as a single race, of 32 laps. After the bumping and jostling of the rolling start had resolved itself, by lap 5 Lauda was running behind the leading group, in an eight-car pack, and with his engine still down on power he fell back steadily as the race progressed. A charging Graham Hill (Brabham) passed him on lap 21, and then he also lost out to Andrea de Adamich's Surtees and Henri Pescarolo's Rondel-run Brabham after lengthy duels with both. He finished a lonely ninth.

113 United States Grand Prix

Watkins Glen, 8 October 1972, Formula 1
March 721G/4 • #5
Qualifying: 25th • Result: Not classified

For the last World Championship round of the season, Lauda qualified 25th in a larger-than-normal field of 31, and again he was ahead of team-mate Ronnie Peterson on the grid. On the Friday, his Cosworth DFV was 1,300rpm down and he was slowest through the speed trap, some 15mph (about 25kph) adrift of the fastest car, but a new engine for the next session improved the situation and meant that he could at least reach fifth gear on the main straight.

After making up a couple of places at the start of the race, his fuel metering unit played up and on lap 5 the fuel pressure zeroed, stranding him out on the circuit for over a minute. He was able to restart and made a long pit stop on lap 11 for adjustments, but the problem persisted despite another stop two laps later and he spent most of the race circulating at the rear of the field. Towards the end, both he and Mike Hailwood (Surtees) had to take avoiding action at Turn 11 (the last corner before the pits) to steer around Mike Beuttler's wayward March, and they spun into each other, the resulting collision breaking the Surtees's rear suspension. Still running at the finish but 10 laps behind Jackie Stewart's victorious Tyrrell, Lauda was unclassified. It must have been somewhat galling that Peterson, meanwhile, had a trouble-free run from his lowly grid position and climbed all the way to fourth place at the finish.

ABOVE His March 722 carrying a much smaller rear wing than usual in an effort to reduce drag, Niki swings through Hockenheim's stadium section on his way to ninth place in the Preis von Baden-Württemberg und Hessen.

BELOW As he approaches Watkins Glen's Turn 10, Niki's March 721G is about to be lapped by Peter Revson's McLaren M19A during the United States Grand Prix.

BUYING A FUTURE

ABOVE A one-off outing in the March 73S 2-litre sports car in the Kyalami Nine Hours yielded an unexpected fourth place for Niki and co-driver Jody Scheckter.

SILVERSTONE TESTING
OCTOBER TO DECEMBER 1972

Lauda worked closely with engineer Harvey Postlethwaite to complete most of the development testing of March's next Formula 2 contender, the 732 with its punchy BMW motor, although he would not reap the benefits of his efforts. Instead, it was in Jean-Pierre Jarier's hands that the car went on to walk the 1973 European Formula 2 Championship with ease. The 732 tests ran concurrently with those for the 73S 2-litre sports car, which used a version of the same BMW power unit.

114 Kyalami Nine Hours (ZA)

4 November 1972, Group 5
March 73S (with Jody Scheckter) • #6
Qualifying: 4th • Result: 4th

The first March 73S 2-litre sports car to see action was campaigned in South Africa by Lucky Strike Racing for rising local star Jody Scheckter in the five-round Springbok Trophy Series. This winter championship kicked off with the Kyalami Nine Hours, a long-established race that finished in darkness and required two drivers, so Lauda — the man who had done most of the development testing of the 73S — was invited to partner Scheckter. Despite extensive pre-race testing and setting a time that was a second quicker than his team-mate's, Lauda was pessimistic about their prospects because tyre problems caused the car — the only 2-litre participant on Goodyears — to switch from understeer to oversteer without warning.

After qualifying fourth, Lauda took the start and held an impressive third place early on behind two of the season's all-conquering works Ferrari 312PBs and with nearly 12 seconds in hand over the fourth-place duel. However, the March was soon in trouble and he pitted after only eight laps with low oil pressure and an overheating engine that was 800rpm down on normal, even though the BMW unit had been changed twice during practice. Having lost five laps while the engine was checked and oil replenished, he rejoined to find the revs slightly increased and his pace improved. By the time of his planned pit stop to hand over to Scheckter, he had caught and passed the Chevron of Peter Gethin/John Love for fourth place, but the position was lost during the stop when the BMW engine refused to restart, wasting another four minutes.

Taking over again after five hours, Lauda regained fourth place when Gethin hit fuel pump problems, the new March still running despite enduring trouble with brakes, fuel filter and tyres. Staying out on slicks during a brief shower towards the end of the race when others pitted for rain tyres was a brave move, one that looked

110 NIKI LAUDA

1972

PAUL RICARD, DRIVER EVALUATION
4 DECEMBER 1972

March wanted Lauda to stay as a paid driver for 1973, but then STP cut its funding and the team could only offer him a Formula 2 contract and a Formula 1 testing role supporting Chris Amon, the proposed new lead driver following Ronnie Peterson's departure to Lotus. So, with no Formula 1 race seat for 1973, Niki persuaded BRM to let him join its driver-evaluation test at the new Paul Ricard circuit in the south of France. BRM's first choice had been Roger Williamson, but after his mentor Tom Wheatcroft vetoed the approach (he wanted Williamson in a Cosworth-engined car) the Bourne team cast the net a little wider.

Lauda had never been to Paul Ricard, so BRM new recruit Clay Regazzoni showed him the lines in his Ferrari Daytona road car before spinning on the sandy track, much to the Austrian's amusement. While Regazzoni and Vern Schuppan tested updated P160Bs for two days, Lauda was given 20 laps in the newer but ineffective P180 on the third day. His times in P180/1 were faster than Schuppan's despite having a car that BRM's Tim Parnell admitted was at least 2.5 seconds a lap slower than the older model. After this impressive performance, Marlboro's Patrick Duffeler arranged a deal for Lauda to join the team on merit but with no retainer, and with a contribution of personal sponsorship that Lauda was required to make but in fact never existed.

as if it might pay dividends when John Hine's third-placed Chevron pitted with electrical trouble. However, when Hine rejoined, the Englishman still had six laps in hand over the Lauda/Scheckter March, which finished fourth, third of the 2-litre runners, albeit 35 laps down on the winning Ferrari of Clay Regazzoni/Arturo Merzario. The team was delighted that the car's problems had all been minor and its drivers had brought it home to the flag against expectations.

SUMMARY

March had survived 1972 largely thanks to the money Lauda had brought to the team, but a litany of mechanical failures and retirements in both Formula 1 and Formula 2 had done little to enhance his reputation as a racing driver. In the lower category, engines had been a major issue, both in performance and reliability. While Emerson Fittipaldi had averaged three races with the same Cosworth-prepared engine, several times Lauda had used three or more engines at one meeting. Although he won the lesser John Player British Formula 2 Championship, he could only manage fifth in the European Formula 2 Championship, amassing less than half of Surtees-equipped champion Mike Hailwood's tally. The consistent reliability of the more conservative Brian Hart-built 1,850cc unit used by Team Surtees was the main factor in Hailwood's title.

As for Formula 1, the uncompetitiveness of March's compromised designs ensured that Niki did not pick up a single World Championship point. *Autosport* commented, 'After a disappointing season, we are unlikely to see him in an F2 car again.' The magazine's reporter was correct, but for reasons that were different from those he imagined. On a more positive note, one of the more telling summaries came from Alpina's technical chief, Dr Fritz Indra, who acknowledged the Austrian's commercial savvy as well as his technical appreciation in and out of the car: 'Working with him was a dream; [he was] always the first in the pits, always knowing exactly when to go fast — something important when sponsors were watching. He was motivating for the whole team. How he treated the mechanics, how he cared for the preparation of the car, he electrified all those involved.'

BUYING A FUTURE

1973
BRM AND BMW

Lauda's move to Marlboro-sponsored BRM was announced at a press conference in Geneva on 10 January 1973. His new team had spent most of the previous Formula 1 season unsuccessfully fielding more cars than anyone else and continued in a similar vein, with three regular entries in 1973 compared to everyone else's two.

Already Lauda harboured concerns about BRM's ability to prepare three of its V12-engined cars to a suitable standard and despite the bluster and bravado of the team's principal, Louis Stanley, he was alert to the limitations that its finances posed on car development. He had already seen at first hand how this affected performance on the track during his days with cash-strapped March and was determined that, one way or another, he would make sure he was in a position to demand the best of whatever was available.

Lauda's switch to BRM meant that his Formula 2 commitment to March ceased, so he would have time to contest touring car races for BMW Alpina alongside his Formula 1 appearances. This was good news for his finances, as the Group 2 contract was well paid and would allow him to make inroads into his still-heavy bank loan. In effect he earned nothing from BRM: his contract with the team included payment of a personal financial contribution — from a supposed sponsor that never existed — in instalments timed to fall due just after receipt of his share of start and prize money, so he was banking on earning enough to cover this commitment.

1973

115 Argentine Grand Prix

Buenos Aires, 23 January 1973, Formula 1
BRM P160C/05 • #34
Qualifying: 13th • Result: Retired (oil pressure)

Against expectations, the Firestone-shod BRM was well-suited to the Buenos Aires track. Lauda adapted quickly to the well-balanced P160C chassis and was among the quick runners in first practice. He was delighted with the car in qualifying, apart from it exhibiting rather too much roll for his liking, and a mid-grid position was a big improvement over his average performances with March in 1972.

In 12th place at the start, he ran at the back of the second squabbling bunch for a long time without showing much potential to progress. In common with both of his BRM team-mates, Clay Regazzoni and Jean-Pierre Beltoise, he encountered tyre problems later on and these allowed Wilson Fittipaldi's Brabham to get past. He retired after 66 of the 96 laps when he saw the BRM V12 engine's oil pressure sag.

116 Brazilian Grand Prix

Interlagos, 11 February 1973, Formula 1
BRM P160C/05 • #16
Qualifying: 13th • Result: 8th

Lauda was pleased with his BRM in first practice, using a similar set-up to the one that had initially worked well in Buenos Aires. On Saturday he only managed to complete four laps before the engine blew out all of its water but

ABOVE Jacky Ickx's Ferrari 312B2 gives chase as Lauda gets to grips with the BRM P160C during practice for the Argentine Grand Prix.

BELOW Niki heads for his first Formula 1 finish in a BRM; his P160C is pictured *en route* to eighth place at Interlagos.

BRM AND BMW 113

nevertheless he again qualified quite well, in 13th spot. During Sunday warm-up, the P160C broke a stub axle and lost its right rear wheel, causing a spectacular spin.

After completing the first lap of the race in ninth place, he steadily improved his position, aided by retirements ahead. At around half distance he stopped out on the circuit when his engine died but he was somehow able to revive it by fiddling with the electrics, losing two laps in the process. Then he had to make a pit stop to have his seat belts tightened, although this was not done correctly and he was rather shaken around in the cockpit for the rest of the 40-lap race. He finished eighth.

117 South African Grand Prix

Kyalami, 3 March 1973, Formula 1
BRM P160D/01 • #17
Qualifying: 10th • Result: Retired (engine)

Lauda was allocated a new P160D chassis (04), but Clay Regazzoni tried it in testing and took it over — much to the Austrian's dismay — because he preferred it to his own. So Niki, as the team's junior member, reluctantly had to accept Regazzoni's South American chassis (01), which he felt was some two seconds a lap slower. Nevertheless, he was still fastest of the BRM cohort on the first day, Thursday, although miffed by the team's refusal to allow him to run in cooler conditions later in the afternoon, when a tail wind was blowing down the straight. Further annoyance came when he was not given a chance to use the quicker Firestones that his team-mates received, allowing them to leapfrog him on the grid. Despite a tired engine, he put in many more laps than either Regazzoni or Jean-Pierre Beltoise to qualify on the fourth row late in the final session. By now he was already expressing concerns about the dilution of BRM's scarce resources in running a three-car team.

Hampered by an excessively tall first gear, he lost three places at the start, although both of his team-mates fared much worse as they dropped to the back of the field. He soon recovered to seventh, holding his position determinedly in the leading group of cars before passing Carlos Reutemann's Brabham for sixth place on lap 24. His race was short-lived as two laps later his engine exploded in a cloud of white smoke on the approach to Crowthorne.

BELOW Now equipped with the moderately updated BRM P160D, Niki's promising showing in the South African Grand Prix ended with engine failure.

114 NIKI LAUDA

1973

ABOVE A front-row grid position and fastest lap during the Race of Champions at Brands Hatch flattered Niki's BRM P160D, as its Firestone tyres worked well but did not last the race distance.

118 Race of Champions (GB)

Brands Hatch, 18 March 1973, Formula 1
BRM P160D/01 • #61
Qualifying: 2nd • Result: Retired (electrics/tyres) (fastest lap)

The BRMs worked well at Brands Hatch's traditional early-season non-championship Formula 1/Formula 5000 fixture. After the P160Ds were fitted with special Firestone qualifying tyres, the team claimed the first three grid positions, with Lauda second fastest.

Although he seemed to move first as the flag dropped, Lauda got away third and was running well for the first dozen laps, challenging team-mate Jean-Pierre Beltoise for second place as the pair, with leader Ronnie Peterson (Lotus), pulled out a 15-second lead over the pack. Niki then dropped back noticeably, tyre wear problems and a rear puncture forcing him to pit after 16 laps. Rejoining a lap down in 13th place, he was soon making up time but was eventually forced to retire from eighth place on lap 30 when a battery lead worked loose. He had the consolation of setting fastest lap, although Peterson and Beltoise subsequently matched his time.

119 Monza Four Hours (I)

25 March 1973, Group 2
BMW 3.0 CSL (with Brian Muir) • #6
Qualifying: 7th • Result: 1st

For this opening round of the European Touring Car Championship with a high-quality cast of drivers, Lauda teamed up with Brian Muir in a Malcolm Gartlan-prepared, Alpina-entered BMW 3.0 CSL, a lightweight version of the previous year's BMW coupé. Although the car was underpowered relative to other CSLs with its old 3-litre motor and was severely delayed in practice by two engine changes and by hydraulic issues, Lauda still took seventh on the grid, having been faster than Muir throughout.

As the works Capris set the pace, Lauda lay fifth in the early part of the race until the retirement of Hans Stuck's BMW after an hour promoted him to fourth, albeit some way adrift of the leading trio. Muir took over for the middle stint but, after being lapped soon after the halfway mark, was brought in early to hand the car back to Lauda for the final push, the car now

BRM AND BMW 115

RIGHT Seen in practice, Niki's beautifully prepared Alpina BMW 3.0 CSL, shared with Brian Muir, took a surprise victory in the Monza Four Hours, having been driven harder and faster than any of the opposition expected.

LEFT At the end of the opening race of the touring car season, Niki and Brian Muir celebrate their victory against a rather imposing Monza backdrop.

lying third. Soon after, at 99 laps, Jody Scheckter's Capri was delayed by a botched tyre change that required him to revisit the pits three laps later, allowing Lauda to sweep through into a clear second place, between two works Capris. With just over an hour to go, he was a lap behind the leader, Jackie Stewart, and 75 seconds ahead of third-placed Jochen Mass.

Driving flat out, he chased down Stewart's Capri, which broke a camshaft with 45 minutes to go. That left Lauda with a one-minute lead and even after a last-minute precautionary stop for fuel he took the flag 20 seconds clear to win the fastest ETCC race to date, run at an average 126.1mph (202.9kph). Both team and driver were surprised by their victory; the Alpina car had been so quick that the rival Schnitzer team demanded that its engine be checked.

120 Preis von Wien (A)

Aspern, 1 April 1973, Group 1
BMW 2002 • #15
Qualifying: 7th • Result: Retired (tyres)

The organising ÖASC had revived its airfield races at Aspern the previous year and for this fixture wanted to have a showdown between local heroes Dieter Quester and Lauda. Quester was entered in the Group 2 and Formula 3 races, but Lauda could not take part in either: Alpina was not willing to supply his Monza-winning BMW 3.0 CSL for the saloon race and Formula 3 participation was not possible because his contract with BRM did not allow him to race other single-seaters.

Instead, the Aspern event's supremo, Willy Lowinger, came up with a different idea: Quester and Lauda would compete in BMW 2002Tis in two Group 1 touring car races — the first at Aspern, a second at Innsbruck — whose fields would be padded out by locals in BMWs and Alfa Romeos. When the 'duel' was announced, media hype attracted a big enough crowd to Aspern to cover the cost.

The Aspern contest was exciting but did not last very long. Lauda was soon hampered by technical problems, his 2002Ti refusing to run properly, and then suffered a puncture that forced him to quit, leaving Quester's quicker Pankl-prepared car to take an unchallenged win.

121 Daily Express International Trophy (GB)

Silverstone, 8 April 1973, Formula 1
BRM P160D/01 • #14
Qualifying: 9th • Result: 5th

Still in a D-specification chassis while team-mates Clay Regazzoni and Vern Schuppan had upgraded E-specification cars for this non-championship event, Lauda qualified on the fourth row of the grid, just 0.1 second behind Regazzoni, after being delayed by a left rear puncture in qualifying. Compared with Brands Hatch a month earlier, the team's Firestones were nowhere near as effective.

In seventh place from the start, he was blocked by David Hobbs's Formula 5000 Lola at Copse but got ahead in a very late braking move at

ABOVE Fighting tyre problems, Niki hurls his BMW 2002Ti around Aspern's rudimentary airfield circuit during his pursuit of Dieter Quester's similar, but faster, car in the first leg of their Willy Lowinger-engineered 'duel'.

ABOVE Obliged to persevere with the older P160D in the non-championship International Trophy race, Niki hurls the BRM through one of Silverstone's fast curves. He finished fifth after battling with some of the Formula 5000 runners in the same race.

BELOW Niki's BMW 3.0 CSL set provisional pole-position time for the Austria-Trophäe at the Salzburgring before the meeting had to be abandoned when a blizzard left the circuit blanketed in snow.

Becketts, forcing his way past with wheels locked up as the Englishman took to the grass. He caught up with the leading pack and was briefly elevated to fifth when Jackie Stewart spun his Tyrrell, but his tyres deteriorated and the recovering Stewart passed him again. For much of the rest of the race he was locked in a tense battle with Brett Lunger's Formula 5000 Lola, until the American retired at three-quarters distance. Thereafter Lauda had a fairly lonely run to fifth place, persevering with a shredded left rear tyre and ignoring pit signals to change it as the race ended in snowy conditions.

122 Austria-Trophäe (A)

Salzburgring, 22 April 1973, Group 2
BMW 3.0 CSL • #5
Qualifying: 1st • Result: race postponed

Lauda was again paired with Brian Muir in the Alpina BMW 3.0 CSL at the

1973

Salzburgring, where Friday practice started on a soaked track. Quick to use some of the limited supply of intermediate tyres as soon as the track began to dry, he was comfortably the fastest driver that day. Overnight, however, a sudden blizzard dumped 18 inches of snow on the course and, despite great efforts to clear it, further snowfalls during Saturday forced officials to postpone this second round of the European Touring Car Championship.

The four-hour race was rescheduled for 19 May, a date left free by the cancellation of the Brno round, the Czech circuit having failed a drivers' safety inspection. As the new date clashed with the Belgian Grand Prix, Lauda was unable to take part and Toine Hezemans took over his seat in a much-reduced field.

123 Spanish Grand Prix

Montjuïc, 29 April 1973, Formula 1
BRM P160E/01 • #16
Qualifying: 11th • Result: Retired (tyres)

The BRM drivers all endured handling problems in practice at Barcelona's street circuit, with their cars leaping all over the place; at one point, Lauda, now with a P160E, landed within inches of a marshals' post and it was hastily moved back as a result. He also tried the spare car (05) in the final session but that was just as bad, although after overnight work on his race car he was fifth quickest in warm-up.

From 11th on the grid, he was initially sixth after a great start and ran ahead of a tight pack, but he found the BRM's handling dreadful on full tanks and was quickly overtaken by Emerson Fittipaldi's Lotus. After a four-way battle with Peter Revson (McLaren), Carlos Reutemann (Brabham) and team-mate Jean-Pierre Beltoise, he was forced to pit with overheating Firestones after only 15 laps. He had to stop again — for good — on lap 28, unable to keep the BRM on the road because the new rubber had also deteriorated. Initial reports that he quit in disgust were wide of the mark; in fact he was refused any further tyres — he had shredded six in all — because the team wanted to make sure there were enough available for Beltoise in case he ran into similar difficulties. In the event, the Frenchman, who finished fifth, drove more conservatively and was the only BRM driver to escape tyre problems.

124 Coupes de Spa (B)

Spa-Francorchamps, 5 May 1973, Group 2
BMW 3.0 CSL • #28
Qualifying: 1st • Result: 1st (fastest lap)

The traditional 15-lap Group 2 race, a warm-up event for the following day's 1,000km, had a somewhat depleted field with the favourites Jacky Ickx (BMW) and Ronnie Peterson (Ford Capri) absent. Lauda was quickest in practice in his Alpina-run BMW 3.0 CSL but needed an engine change to achieve it.

The start saw Lauda's BMW and Jochen

ABOVE Frustrated by insoluble handling problems, Niki pitches his BRM P160E into the *El Angulo* hairpin at the Montjuïc circuit during the Spanish Grand Prix.

BRM AND BMW

Mass's Capri run away from the field, lapping increasingly quickly and swapping the lead continually in a tremendous duel. Lauda set a new touring car lap record before Mass got ahead of him on lap 10, but on the penultimate lap one of the Capri's rear wheels came adrift with the half-shaft still attached as the German driver turned into *La Source* hairpin. Lauda was able to cruise to an easy victory, nearly a minute ahead of Claude Bourgoignie's Capri.

125 Spa 1,000km (B)

Spa-Francorchamps, 6 May 1973, Group 2
BMW 3.0 CSL (with Hans Stuck) • #60
Qualifying: 18th • Result: 7th (1st in touring class)

At this World Championship for Makes race, Lauda was originally due to share Alpina's sister BMW 3.0 CSL with Brian Muir but

ABOVE In the Coupes de Spa, Niki's BMW 3.0 CSL and Jochen Mass's Ford Capri RS 2600 fought a dramatic, race-long duel that ended in mechanical failure for the German and victory for the Austrian.

BELOW Cocking a wheel through Spa's Malmedy curve in the class-winning BMW 3.0 CSL he shared with Hans Stuck in the 1,000km race, Niki is chased down by the works Ferrari 312PB sports prototype of Arturo Merzario/Carlos Pace.

switched before practice to partner Hans Stuck. They qualified their car in midfield, four places behind the other Alpina car, for which Stuck was also a nominated driver. Interestingly, the best times for both BMWs were inferior to Lauda's lap record in the previous day's Coupes de Spa race, in the Austrian's case by six seconds.

Niki's showing in this important endurance race was equally strong. From lap 18 onwards he engaged in a tremendous battle with Gijs van Lennep's works Porsche Carrera RSR, which could only just keep up with the flying BMW, moving ahead only when Lauda pitted and going on to finish fifth. With Stuck dividing his time between both Alpina entries, the Austrian drove for three hours — nearly three-quarters of this high-speed race — and beat all the other Porsches to deliver a comprehensive victory in the touring class, and seventh place overall.

126 Belgian Grand Prix

Zolder, 20 May 1973, Formula 1
BRM P160E/08 • #21
Qualifying: 14th • Result: 5th

The Belgian Grand Prix had another new home, Zolder, where the track had been resurfaced only a week before the race. Lauda had a new BRM P160E chassis and Firestone produced a much-improved tyre of new construction, helping him to post third fastest time early on Friday, before the new surface started to break up. After remedial work by the organisers and lots of debate among drivers about whether they felt the race should even take place, practice on Saturday finally saw everyone start going for times, although they had to tread warily and keep to a slender racing line. To add to the general frustration, some of the time-keeping was suspect and there were protests,

BELOW Niki's BRM P160E takes the chequered flag at Zolder to finish fifth and claim his first World Championship points. He followed Andrea de Adamich's Brabham BT37 across the line, the BRM pit having failed to advise him that the Italian was actually ahead rather than a lap behind, costing him another point.

leading to revised figures being issued shortly before the race. Lauda lined up 14th on the grid although he had been fifth fastest unofficially.

Driving forcefully on the patched-up track, he carved his way up to fourth place, passing François Cevert's brake-troubled Tyrrell *en route*, but with four laps to go he was forced to pit with the BRM almost out of fuel. While he was stationary, Andrea de Adamich's Brabham took the place from him but the BRM pit crew failed to inform their driver, who resumed thinking he was a lap ahead of the Italian and held station even though he could easily have repassed had he known. With Emerson Fittipaldi also in trouble, Niki could perhaps have snatched third at the flag, but fifth place was still his best showing so far in Formula 1 and brought his first World Championship points.

127 Nürburgring 1,000km (D)

27 May 1973, Group 2
BMW 3.0 CSL (with Brian Muir) • #70
Qualifying: 26th • Result: Did not start

A practice time of 8m 38.00s by Lauda would have been good enough for 26th on the grid, which was pretty impressive with 46 sports prototypes and GTs alongside the 13 touring cars in the field. However, co-driver Brian Muir, who was new to the Nürburgring, then crashed at *Wehrseifen*, leaving the rear of the car too badly damaged to be repaired in time for the race.

Lauda commented that he would not have minded so much if his partner had been going quickly, but grumbled that the Australian had been driving slowly and had still come off the track. Even more disgruntled were the Alpina mechanics, who had spent all week welding a new rear end onto the car after Muir had shunted it at the postponed European Touring Car Championship round at the Salzburgring the previous weekend.

128 Monaco Grand Prix

3 June 1973, Formula 1
BRM P160E/08 • #21
Qualifying: 6th • Result: Retired (gearbox)

Fuel-pressure problems in first practice forced Lauda into the spare car (05) and his times were unremarkable. When final practice was held late on Saturday afternoon, after the

RIGHT Pictured in practice for the Nürburgring 1,000km race, Niki's BMW 3.0 CSL tackles the *Karussell*. Soon after, co-driver Brian Muir wrecked the car, leaving them unable to take the start.

Formula 3 heats had left the circuit rather greasy, times were generally a second or so slower, so the most commented-upon performance was Lauda's remarkable second-fastest time in the session, the Austrian placing his car inches from the guardrails even though he had 'flu. Comfortably the fastest BRM driver in qualifying despite transmission trouble near the end of practice, he started from sixth spot on the grid.

He showed huge commitment in the race. He worked his way up to third place by the ninth lap, with only Jackie Stewart and Emerson Fittipaldi ahead of him, and easily kept Jacky Ickx's hard-charging Ferrari at bay. Still in touch with the leaders on lap 24, he was just about to lap the tail-enders when he stopped at the Station hairpin with a broken gearbox. His magnificent effort earned him the Jo Siffert Award for driver of the day and BRM boss Louis Stanley was sufficiently impressed to offer to waive the rest of Lauda's pay-driver instalments provided he signed a three-year contract. More significantly, his performance was watched on television by Enzo Ferrari, who took note.

129 Swedish Grand Prix

Anderstorp, 17 June 1973, Formula 1
BRM P160E/08 • #21
Qualifying: 15th • Result: 13th

Promised improvements to the V12 engines yielded little and the BRMs struggled in qualifying. Starting two-thirds of the way down the grid, Lauda soon made up ground and

ABOVE A career-defining moment for Niki: after working his BRM P160E into third place, he kept the Ferrari 312B3 of Jacky Ickx at bay for 15 laps until his race ended with gearbox failure. Watching on television, Enzo Ferrari was impressed — and the phone call from Maranello came shortly afterwards.

BRM AND BMW 123

Later he fell back with fuel pick-up difficulties; a breather flap was playing up and letting out petrol as well as vapour. Turning on the electric pump failed to make any difference and, having slipped to a lowly 10th, he was forced to make a late stop for fuel with 12 laps to go, dropping to 13th. He struggled home in that position, five laps adrift.

130 Nürburgring 24 Hours (D)

23–24 June 1973, Group 2
BMW 3.0 CSL (with Hans-Peter Joisten) • #29
Qualifying: 2nd • Result: 1st (fastest lap)

This year's Nürburgring 24 Hours was of that duration only on paper, as this was a '3x8' event comprising two eight-hour periods of racing and an eight-hour break between, with the overall result determined on aggregate. There were two reasons for this procedure: firstly, to address safety concerns, in particular the fact that most accidents in previous races had happened in the early morning, when fatigue was at its worst; secondly, to counter complaints

ABOVE Thoughtful or just bored? Niki remains in the cockpit of the BRM while adjustments are made during practice at Anderstorp.

his long-running duel with Howden Ganley's ISO-Williams enlivened the middle order for many laps. Running sixth behind Jackie Oliver's Shadow as the race progressed, he was hounding the Englishman and by half distance the two of them had closed on the battle for fourth between François Cevert (Tyrrell) and Denny Hulme (McLaren).

RIGHT The Swedish Grand Prix was another troublesome race for Niki, fuel pick-up issues leaving his BRM P160E lagging a long way behind at the finish.

124 NIKI LAUDA

about noise from the residents of Breidscheid, a village roughly halfway round the circuit. Lauda shared one of two BMW Alpina entries with Hans-Peter Joisten, their big coupé now fitted with an enlarged 3.3-litre engine.

An extraordinary 105 cars started the race at 5pm on Saturday. Hans Heyer's works Ford Capri took the lead initially, but the Austrian soon outbraked it into the *Nordkehre* and quickly pulled away. Second time around, Lauda set the fastest lap of the race in a stunning 8m 39.6s, an achievement that was all the more impressive because the car still had a full fuel tank, and after one more lap his lead was an incredible one and a half minutes. Just as impressively, in one spell during his first stint he recorded the same time to within a tenth of a second on three successive laps. When, after the race, a baffled Burkard Bovensiepen, Alpina's owner, asked him how this was possible, Lauda's simple explanation was that he had been driving on the limit all the time.

After two hours, only the first four cars remained on the same lap as the weather deteriorated, drizzle becoming rain. Lauda's decision to stay out on slicks proved to be a bad one because he hit standing water at the left-hander following the *Fuchsröhre*, slid off the track and hit a bank. His seat was torn from its mountings but he managed to fix it well enough to drive back to the pits for repair. His advantage was such that he did not lose the lead and at the end of the first eight-hour contest Lauda and Joisten were the winners on 47 laps completed, with only the sister Alpina BMW of Brian Muir/Han Akersloot on the same lap. During the cessation, the mechanics were allowed to work on the cars for 90 minutes.

When racing resumed at 9am on Sunday, 77 cars took to the track. Lauda led again until he had to make a seven-minute stop to change a

ABOVE Niki throws the Alpina-prepared BMW 3.0 CSL into the *Südkehre* during the early stages of the Nürburgring 24 Hours; the car's special auxiliary lights for this race are still protected by covers.

BRM AND BMW 125

RIGHT The Alpina mechanics swarm round Niki's BMW 3.0 CSL, shared with Hans-Peter Joisten, during a routine stop in the Nürburgring 24 Hours race on the way to a resounding victory.

BELOW Illuminated by floodlights during the night-time cessation of racing activity at the Nürburgring, the BMW crews work on the 3.0 CSLs in readiness for the resumption of racing the following morning.

shock absorber, allowing the works Capri, at this point driven by Klaus Fritzinger, to move ahead, but only for one lap. A spin by Lauda at the *Karussell* on lap 7 allowed the Capri to pass again, but the Austrian got back in front a lap later. Thereafter he and Joisten remained unchallenged, winning comfortably by over a lap from the Muir/Akersloot sister car. Late in the race, the Alpina team's two BMWs were so far ahead of the third-placed works Capri — by about 90 miles (145km) on aggregate — that Bovensiepen discussed calling them in to have them washed so that they would look their best for the TV cameras at the finish. Lauda roundly disabused the team boss of this potentially arrogant tactic, reminding him that the race was not won until the chequered flag was waved.

131 French Grand Prix

Paul Ricard, 1 July 1973, Formula 1
BRM P160E/08 • #21
Qualifying: 17th • Result: 9th

After trying the spare car (05 again) in first practice to see if its engine was any better than the one in his allocated chassis, Lauda reverted to his race car. Although his was the fastest BRM on the first day of practice, it was still desperately slow on the Paul Ricard circuit's two significant straights; he improved slightly in the second and third sessions but, with his team-mates receiving better tyres, he was

1973

ultimately the team's slowest qualifier.

He drove a fairly nondescript race, languishing in the lower midfield unable to keep up with either Graham Hill's Shadow or Arturo Merzario's Ferrari, and easily passed by the Brabham of Wilson Fittipaldi. Retirements aided his progress and he finished ninth, the last runner on the same lap as the winner but nearly two minutes adrift. For once all the BRMs completed the race without making a single pit stop despite high tyre wear, but they were not very inspiring. Some blame was laid at Firestone's door, although the real problem lay in the underfunded team's need to fit used parts to the cars and run patched-up engines to save money.

ABOVE The arid landscape of the Paul Ricard circuit provides a rocky backdrop to Niki's BRM P160E as he heads for ninth place in the French Grand Prix.

BELOW Niki adjusts his helmet strap before setting off to demolish the touring car lap record for the Nürburgring *Nordschleife* in the Alpina BMW 3.0 CSL.

132 Nürburgring Six Hours (D)

8 July 1973, Group 2
BMW 3.0 CSL (with Hans-Peter Joisten) • #15
Qualifying: 1st • Result: 3rd (fastest lap)

BMW had finally homologated a 3.5-litre engine and full aerodynamic package

BRM AND BMW 127

ABOVE Yet to receive the scars of team-mate Hans-Peter Joisten's brush with a barrier, Niki's now bewinged BMW 3.0 CSL lifts its inside wheels as he tackles a right-hander during the Nürburgring Six Hours.

for its CSL, giving it a definite advantage over the lighter but now less powerful Ford Capri. The new bewinged CSL was experiencing considerable understeer, but after Lauda juggled suspension and roll-bar settings he was fastest by Saturday lunchtime, after a rain shower had washed the circuit clean.

He led away from pole at the rolling start and after a brief tussle with Jochen Mass, who got his Capri ahead for part of the first lap, pulled away to build a substantial lead after an hour's racing. Seeming very at ease, he was telling jokes on the radio, but three laps after Joisten took over the car a rear tyre punctured and caused a brush with a barrier, requiring a pit stop for repairs. The suspension at the affected corner needed attention and the Alpina pair dropped to sixth. Joisten then had a second off-road trip, necessitating a further pit stop. When Lauda took over again he was five laps adrift; tearing back through the field in spectacular style, he ignored the hazards of the oil-smeared track and made up a complete lap to eventually finish third. His fastest lap of 8m 21.3s, fully 18 seconds superior to his best lap two weeks earlier, was a new touring car record for the *Nordschleife*.

There was a sad footnote to Lauda's two successful Nürburgring races with Hans-Peter Joisten. Just two weeks later, the German driver was leading the Spa 24 Hours in an Alpina-entered BMW 3.0 CSL when he crashed fatally.

133 British Grand Prix

Silverstone, 14 July 1973, Formula 1
BRM P160E/08 • #21
Qualifying: 9th • Result: 12th

Benefiting from a new rear wing with streamlined side plates and having had a day of testing at Silverstone on the Tuesday before the race, during practice Lauda was the fastest of all the 12-cylinder runners — Ferraris included — despite having an engine that was down on power.

When he let in the clutch at the start, the left driveshaft snapped. His BRM hardly moved and as he sat helplessly on the grid he was hit by an unsighted Jackie Oliver, whose Shadow tore off the P160E's left rear wheel. It was beneficial to him that the race was stopped at the end of lap 1 when Jody Scheckter lost control of his McLaren at Woodcote and caused a massive crash that took out 11 cars. During the wait before the race could be restarted, the BRM mechanics were able to repair his battered car.

At the restart, Lauda took full advantage of a gap in front of him on the grid (where Scheckter would have sat) and, hugging the pit wall after a possible jumped getaway, he blasted up the inside line to take an incredible second place into Copse. However, his early charge overheated his tyres and Jackie Stewart (Tyrrell) outbraked him into Stowe on lap 2. Thereafter he fell back steadily through the leading group, eventually pitting on lap 24 to have a worn-out left front tyre changed. It was a long stop as two different wheels were tried in an attempt to get one to locate. He later had a huge spin at Club when the rev limiter started playing up; he stopped out on the track to do a makeshift repair, switching off the rev limiter, before halting again on lap 35 to have his seat belts refastened and change a rear tyre. After all that, he finished four laps behind, in 12th place.

Shortly after the British Grand Prix, Enzo Ferrari's newly appointed henchman, Luca di Montezemolo, met Lauda in London to progress negotiations.

134 Internationales ADAC-Flugplatzrennen (D)

Diepholz, 15 July 1973, Group 2
BMW 3.0 CSL • #100
Qualifying: 2nd • Result: Retired (gearbox/final drive)

Attracted by TV coverage and a large prize purse, Alpina made a surprise late entry for Lauda in this third round of the Deutsche Rennsport Meisterschaft, Germany's national

BELOW On the limit through Woodcote, Niki's BRM P160E leads Emerson Fittipaldi's Lotus 72D early in the restarted British Grand Prix, before tyre trouble forced him to drop back.

RIGHT Niki and Hans Stuck in their BMW 3.0 CSLs leave the rest trailing in their wake at Diepholz.

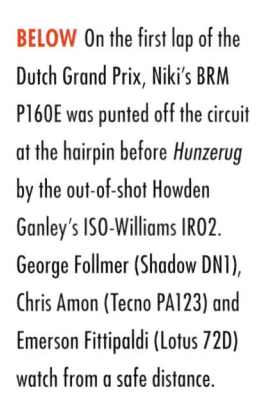

BELOW On the first lap of the Dutch Grand Prix, Niki's BRM P160E was punted off the circuit at the hairpin before *Hunzerug* by the out-of-shot Howden Ganley's ISO-Williams IR02. George Follmer (Shadow DN1), Chris Amon (Tecno PA123) and Emerson Fittipaldi (Lotus 72D) watch from a safe distance.

130 NIKI LAUDA

touring car championship. Having missed first practice while at the British Grand Prix, he flew in from Silverstone on Sunday morning and took part in a short qualifying session. Despite excessive understeer on his BMW 3.0 CSL, he was immediately as quick as pace-setter Hans Stuck's similar works entry and lined up alongside the German driver on the front row.

From the rolling start, these two favourites were in a race of their own and swapped the lead twice on the first lap, but from lap 2 Lauda was ahead, his car performing better under braking than Stuck's. After five laps, Stuck went off at the last corner with a broken suspension tie rod, leaving Lauda unchallenged. But he only lasted another 10 laps before his car's transaxle gearbox broke, even though a fresh one had been installed before the race.

135 Dutch Grand Prix

Zandvoort, 29 July 1973, Formula 1
BRM P160E/08 • #21
Qualifying: 11th • Result: Retired (fuel pump)

The BRMs had revised suspension for Zandvoort. Lauda was quickest in the very wet Friday practice, more than 0.5 second clear of the fastest Goodyear runner, but he was stopped out on the track by an electrical fault during the Saturday morning session and a comprehensive engine blow-up in the afternoon ruined his chances of a good qualifying position.

On the first lap he was halted by a traffic queue at *Hunzerug* and was punted off into the sandy infield by Howden Ganley's ISO-Williams, although he continued in last place with a dented oil tank. He made up a few of the lost places but suffered a host of issues that caused him to make several pit stops. These included an oil leak, tyre chunking (which caused two stops, as an unbalanced wheel was fitted first time) and two fuel-pump belt failures. He retired after 51 laps when the fuel pump finally broke, by which stage he was two laps down on Ronnie Peterson's leading Lotus.

After the race, Marlboro announced that it would not be continuing as BRM's sponsor for 1974, so the team's prospects for the following year looked even more parlous.

136 German Grand Prix

Nürburgring, 5 August 1973, Formula 1
BRM P160E/08 • #21
Qualifying: 5th • Result: Retired (accident)

Along with three other teams, BRM completed a test day on the Tuesday preceding the Grand Prix although Lauda claimed they learned little. Nevertheless, he produced an excellent performance in first qualifying, setting a cracking pace in a closely fought competition with Nürburgring specialist Jacky Ickx, who was having a one-off drive in a McLaren as his long-time relationship with Ferrari was souring. In qualifying fifth, Lauda was only 2.2 seconds behind runaway World Championship leader Jackie Stewart (Tyrrell) on pole position and fully eight seconds faster than both of his team-mates. By now, though, it was fair to describe him as a Nürburgring specialist as well, for he had competed in three long-distance races at the circuit in the preceding couple of months, and had raced there on 10 other occasions in earlier years.

BELOW After showing great form in both practice and the race during the German Grand Prix, Niki was unlucky to suffer a wrist injury when tyre failure pitched his BRM P160E into the barriers at *Kesselchen* at high speed.

AUSTRIAN GRAND PRIX
19 AUGUST 1973

To his great disappointment, as well as that of thousands of his spectating countrymen, Lauda could not take part in the Austrian Grand Prix because of his injured wrist. After only two practice laps on Friday morning, his car fitted with one of BRM's 'special' V12 engines for his home race, vibrations through the steering wheel caused too much pain to allow him to hold the rim properly and he was forced to withdraw. Louis Stanley unsuccessfully sought Jacky Ickx as a potential stand-in but, as it turned out, Clay Regazzoni switched to Lauda's unused P160E after his own suffered engine woes in practice and shortly afterwards the 'special' unit also failed.

Shortly after the Austrian Grand Prix, Lauda visited Maranello to meet Enzo Ferrari for the first time and to see the facilities in the racing department and at Fiorano, although he was frustrated that he could not do any laps of the test track because of his wrist. By this time, BRM team-mate Regazzoni, as exasperated as Lauda was by the British team's shortcomings, had already committed to a return to Ferrari for the 1974 season, after one disappointing season away.

ABOVE Niki in the paddock during practice for the Austrian Grand Prix. To the disappointment of the local crowd, the wrist injury that he sustained at the German Grand Prix precluded any meaningful involvement at the Österreichring.

Fourth at the start, he pursued Ickx closely around the first lap. Second time round through the tight, climbing right-hander at *Bergwerk* he felt something odd in the BRM's handling. Through the flat-out swerves at *Kesselchen*, the rear broke away and he veered off the road into a prolonged accident in which the car was severely damaged against the barriers. He emerged from the wreck looking distinctly unsettled and was found to have a cracked bone deep in his right wrist. It was suspected that a tyre had deflated.

137 Italian Grand Prix

Monza, 9 September 1973, Formula 1
BRM P160E/10 • #21
Qualifying: 15th • Result: Retired (accident)

The BRM team arrived from testing at Paul Ricard amid an air of despondency, having been unable to reproduce the lap times achieved there at the start of the season. The tests had been conducted with a new chassis, 10, which

1973

was allocated to Lauda for Monza now that his wrist had healed. The only noticeable difference was that this car carried smaller wings to reduce drag on Monza's long straights. He performed unobtrusively in practice, qualifying in midfield having suffered troublesome rear brakes.

In an attempt to avoid his engine ingesting dirt at the start as it had the previous year, a pair of ladies' tights was taped over his airbox, although this makeshift 'filter' was soon ruined by the slipstream of other cars. Only 18 laps into the race he was black-flagged for a loose brake duct; when he pitted for it to be fixed he also took on new rubber, but this proved disastrous.

As he braked for *Parabolica* on lap 34, the car suddenly darted away from him and cannoned into the guardrail very close to where Jochen Rindt had crashed fatally in 1970. Fortunately, there was now a two-tier barrier at this point and, although it bent upwards, it stopped the BRM from going underneath as the car slid along before coming to rest in a sand trap. From the tell-tale marks on the road it appeared that the left front tyre had burst but, whatever the reason, Niki had suffered his second severe crash in as many races through no fault of his own. At least this time he was unscathed.

ABOVE Niki's BRM P160E leads Graham Hill's Shadow DN1 into Monza's *Ascari* chicane during the Italian Grand Prix.

BELOW Niki shone in the wet at Mosport, where his BRM P160E is seen leading eventual winner Peter Revson's McLaren M23.

138 Canadian Grand Prix

Mosport, 23 September 1973, Formula 1
BRM P160E/08 • #21
Qualifying: 8th • Result: Retired (final drive)

After damaging his right front wheel when he hit an animal at 140mph in pre-race testing at Mosport Park, Lauda endured a problematic practice; an engine change made little difference and he lost the last 15 minutes of qualifying with an electrical fault. However, Niki had dug deep and despite the BRM's power deficiency on this challenging track he achieved a good eighth place on the grid, utterly out-performing similarly equipped team-mates Jean-Pierre Beltoise (16th) and Peter Gethin (25th), the latter having his first Formula 1 drive of the

BRM AND BMW

ABOVE Before the second leg of their head-to-head race, Niki and Dieter Quester chat in the Innsbruck paddock.

BELOW The scrap between the two Austrians in their (allegedly) identical BMW 2002Tis was very hard-fought; here Dieter Quester's leading car lifts its inside wheels as Niki harries him around the Innsbruck airfield circuit.

year as a one-off replacement for Clay Regazzoni, who, Ferrari-bound, had displeased Louis Stanley by criticising BRM in the media.

After heavy rain before the race, everyone started on wet-weather tyres. Aided by the efficacy of his Firestones, Lauda made a tremendous getaway from the fourth row and was third by the end of lap 1. After only four laps he took the lead from pole-man Ronnie Peterson (Lotus) and extended his advantage by three or four seconds on some laps. By lap 15 he was 23 seconds clear and still pulling away, but then a drying track and uncooperative backmarkers began to arrest his progress. Pitting on lap 20, his stop was slow and he was given intermediates instead of the slicks he wanted, so he made a second pit stop on lap 29 to change to slicks.

After Jody Scheckter (McLaren) and François Cevert (Tyrrell) collided on lap 33, spreading debris across the track, a minor Formula 1 landmark occurred when a safety car was deployed for the first time. However, its driver erroneously picked up Howden Ganley's ISO-Williams as the leader, and among those right behind the New Zealander's car was Lauda, so he had to endure more delay. A certain points finish — fifth was looking likely — was lost when he retired with transmission failure on lap 63. The Jo Siffert Award for his doughty performance was small consolation.

139 Preis von Tirol (A)

Innsbruck, 30 September 1973, Group 1
BMW 2002Ti • #26
Qualifying: Not known • Result: 1st

This race at the Innsbruck airfield circuit was the second instalment of organiser Willy Lowinger's 'duel' between Dieter Quester and Lauda. To further entertain the audience, the race was run in two parts; the original intention had been for the drivers to swap their Pankl-prepared BMW 2002Ti cars after the first 10-lap contest, but Quester's protest that this was outside the rules was accepted. Both wins went to Quester just ahead of Lauda, but then Quester refused a post-race technical inspection of his car's engine, claiming lack of time. Disqualification followed and Lauda inherited overall victory.

Meanwhile, his Ferrari future was being finalised. Two weeks later, after legal shenanigans with BRM had been resolved and an agreement reached to offset his unpaid race earnings against a claim for breach of contract, Lauda signed for Ferrari. Suddenly Austria had a new national hero.

140 United States Grand Prix

Watkins Glen, 7 October 1973, Formula 1
BRM P160E/08 • #21
Qualifying: 21st • Result: Retired (fuel pump)

Lauda missed most of practice owing to an engine that refused to run cleanly and, when it was eventually replaced, his gearbox was changed at the same time. That proved to be a bad decision as the replacement 'box was troublesome and the Austrian never displayed the sparkle he had shown of late, although François Cevert's fatal accident during Saturday practice no doubt played a part, especially as Lauda was first to arrive at the grisly scene. He was also annoyed that having organised himself a set of 'super-fast' Firestone qualifiers, which the team had apparently been unable to obtain, he found that when he was ready to use them they had been put on Jean-Pierre Beltoise's car and the Frenchman was already out on the track. However, in the knowledge of the impending departure of both Lauda and Regazzoni, perhaps it was unsurprising that most of the team's attention was focused on Beltoise.

Starting from near the back of the grid after his troubled practice, Lauda worked his way up to midfield before pitting on lap 17 with his engine running badly and dropped to last place. A series of electrical checks over three pit stops finally diagnosed a faulty mechanical fuel pump that took a further 20 laps to change, after which he gamely rejoined in a lonely pursuit. Although he was still running in 18th place at the chequered flag, he had completed only 35 laps and was too far back to be classified.

ABOVE Niki's BRM P160E tackles Watkins Glen's Anvil section during the United States Grand Prix.

RIGHT The ballot has just been drawn for the initial allocation of the RS 2600s for the Ford Capri Vergleich comparison race, part of the Österreichring Saisonfinale meeting. The drivers would swap their British-registered cars for the second heat, Niki receiving Dieter Quester's machine from the first heat.

ABOVE Niki's road-standard Capri RS 2600 understeers its way round the Österreichring on its way to victory in the first heat of the Saisonfinale 'Capri comparison'.

141 Ford Capri Vergleich, Saisonfinale Trophy (D)

Österreichring, 14 October 1973, Group 1
Ford Capri RS 2600 (XWC 713L and YOO 399L) • #1
Qualifying: Not known • Result: 1st (Heat 1, 3rd; Heat 2, 1st)

As Lauda's BMW contract had ended and he had signed with Ford for some touring car appearances in 1974, he was able to take part in a contest set up by the company at the season-ending national Group 1 meeting at the Österreichring. The occasion was a premier of the updated Capri RS 2600 at which four such cars were put in the hands of Austria's best drivers — Lauda, Dieter Quester, Helmut Koinigg and Kurt Rieder. The cars ran on standard tyres with soft shock absorbers and without limited-slip differentials and at last featured the rear spoilers that they had obviously needed all season to curb their wayward handling. The RS 2600s were allocated by ballot and used for two 10-lap races, with the results decided on aggregate.

Rieder and Quester scrapped for the lead in the first race, Rieder coming out on top, while Lauda had a fairly lonely run to third place. When the Capris were swapped around for the second heat, Lauda took over Quester's car. Koinigg led at first but soon retired with engine failure, leaving Quester and Lauda to put on a dramatic duel that had the spectators on their feet. Towards the end, Quester was able to break away but collided with Heinz Derflinger's Alfa Romeo and spun. Lauda forged past to take the win ahead of an angry Quester, the combined results from the two heats giving Niki victory on aggregate.

SUMMARY

BRM had been a trying experience for Lauda. While he got on well with Clay Regazzoni and Jean-Pierre Beltoise, his relationship with the team's management was less cordial and deteriorated as the season progressed. On several occasions his car was not fuelled sufficiently to complete the full race distance and his record of mechanical reliability was woeful, exacerbated by the team's strained finances and lack of resources. Lauda had made clear his financial conditions from the outset, with the sharing of start and prize money to be made punctually each month. The team's failure to comply gave him the lever to extricate himself from the contract when Ferrari came calling.

FIORANO
OCTOBER AND NOVEMBER 1973

Lauda's first Formula 1 test for Ferrari (pictured upper right) in late October confirmed his expectations about the tractability of the flat-12 engine but he was also surprised by the deficiencies of the 312B3's chassis compared with his BRM. Mercurial designer Mauro Forghieri had returned to the team with responsibility to address the problems inherent in the original 312B3, but progress had so far been hampered by a lack of funding, industrial unrest and no proper development programme.

It was at this test that the Austrian's celebrated directness came to the fore. Via Piero Lardi, who was acting as translator, he informed Enzo Ferrari that the car was 'shit' and needed development. A successful test a few days later, with revised suspension geometry and changed roll centres, delivered more than the improvement that Lauda and Forghieri had promised in response to Mr Ferrari's demands. He had now gained the *Commendatore*'s trust and had established the foundation for the team's renaissance.

During another Fiorano session on a foggy day in late November, Lauda was present for the first test of Forghieri's new sports prototype. When Regazzoni tried the 312PB-74 (pictured lower right in a rather grainy 'spy' shot), he declared it to be a significant improvement over its less-than-successful predecessor, while Lauda, who could not make any comparisons, claimed to be merely satisfied with it, although in reality he did not want anything to do with the project and was merely fulfilling his contractual obligations. However, demands by Fiat to reduce the racing budget meant that Ferrari could not afford to invest in both Formula 1 and sports car racing to the level that was needed, so Montezemolo — with no little pressure from Lauda — convinced Enzo Ferrari that winning the Formula 1 World Championship now required the company to focus exclusively on that aim for the first time in its history. The 312PB-74, therefore, never raced, although it was used for a further test at Paul Ricard in December, primarily to evaluate different Goodyear tyre widths.

Nevertheless, the Bourne team's well-balanced chassis had given him the opportunity to shine when conditions levelled the playing field for its underpowered V12 engines, such as at Monaco. *Autocourse* went so far as to suggest — on the evidence of his performances in practice at Zandvoort and in the early stages of the Canadian Grand Prix — that if every race had been wet in 1973, he would have been World Champion. A little far-fetched, maybe, but a recognition of his talent when given a fair crack of the whip.

Ford competitions boss Michael Kranefuss's coup in September by signing Lauda from under BMW's nose for the 1974 touring car season also gave him the unique position of simultaneously holding contracts with Ford and Ferrari, despite Enzo Ferrari's intense dislike of Ford after the American giant's failed attempt to buy his company 10 years earlier. Had Lauda's Ferrari deal been completed first, it is most unlikely that he would have been seen in a Ford cockpit in 1974.

The Lauda Plan was now in full swing. After only two full seasons in Formula 1 he was now driving for the sport's most illustrious team.

1974
LEARNING HOW TO WIN

Over the winter of 1973–74, Ferrari's Formula 1 development programme began in earnest with Lauda at its epicentre. For the initial runs at Vallelunga, unusually there was no crowd of enthusiastic and exuberant youngsters turning out for a Ferrari test, happy to be able to see the red cars up close. At this stage there was still uncertainty as to how the new driver/engineer combination of Niki Lauda/Clay Regazzoni/Mauro Forghieri would gel and if these highly touted recruits would be able to restore confidence to the previously toxic atmosphere at Maranello. Lauda, with his precise and meticulous approach, set the quicker times although it was clear that the partisan national press favoured his Italian-speaking Swiss team-mate.

An early session at Misano was ostensibly a tyre test, although Enzo Ferrari was in attendance to see his new 'pupil' at work. Lauda, who had two 312B3 chassis at his disposal, set times that were some way off the track's official Formula 1 lap record, which was held by Chris Amon's Tecno. Italian weekly *Autosprint* commented that this just went to show that nobody could work miracles, much less Lauda.

Alongside the customary Fiorano shakedowns, the pre-season testing programme included six days at Paul Ricard and a further session at Kyalami, with considerable focus on developing Goodyear tyres to suit the updated car's chassis; further modifications were then tested at Vallelunga. By the time the 312B3s arrived in Buenos Aires for the first round of the 1974 Formula 1 World Championship, almost 30 significant alterations had been made to the car from its configuration when Lauda joined the team.

1974

ABOVE New Ferrari driver: Niki poses with the 1974-specification 312B3 outside the famous farmhouse at Maranello. Note how dusty and dirty the car looks, like the Ferrari-liveried Fiat parked in the background.

BELOW Looking every inch the proud patriarch with his new charge under contract, Enzo Ferrari seems pleased with the progress Niki is making. The honeymoon is still in full swing.

142 Argentine Grand Prix

Buenos Aires, 13 January 1974, Formula 1
Ferrari 312B3/012 • #12
Qualifying: 8th • Result: 2nd

This year's Argentine Grand Prix used a different variation of the multi-format Buenos Aires autodrome, the 3.71-mile (5.97km) #15 circuit being rather longer than the 2.08-mile (3.35km) version used the previous year.

For the first practice session, the remodelled 312B3s were wearing the same Lotus-style low-line airboxes that had first been seen in Austria the previous year, but by the second session they were sporting a tall, slim style — as pioneered by Hesketh designer Harvey Postlethwaite — and this remained for the early part of the season. The speed of the Ferraris in Argentina's considerable heat surprised many and Lauda was quick from the outset, proving the value of the thousands of miles of testing he had completed over the winter. Hurling his new car around the track, he clocked third-fastest time in the opening session but eventually qualified eighth after encountering tyre problems in the quicker

LEARNING HOW TO WIN

BELOW Still wearing its original 1973-style airbox, Niki's Ferrari 312B3 sweeps through the infield of the Parc Almirante Brown circuit at Buenos Aires during practice for the Argentine Grand Prix.

BOTTOM Weeks of intensive testing and development paid off as Niki brought the Ferrari 312B3 home in a hugely encouraging second place in his first race for the Scuderia.

sessions. He was somewhat irked to be adrift of Clay Regazzoni, who put his Ferrari on the front row, and also just behind the Lotus of Jacky Ickx, the man he had effectively replaced at Maranello.

Avoiding the initial mêlée of the race start, he was seventh at the end of lap 1 and soon stole sixth from Carlos Pace's Brabham, gaining another place when Emerson Fittipaldi pitted his McLaren. Up to fourth by lap 14, he had a long dice with Ickx for third position, finally getting past when the Belgian was slowed by a puncture on lap 27. He had closed to within five seconds of second-placed Denny Hulme (McLaren) when Carlos Reutemann's leading Brabham suffered electrical failure two laps from the end, so he finished a close second to Hulme and claimed his first Formula 1 podium.

143 Brazilian Grand Prix

Interlagos, 27 January 1974, Formula 1
Ferrari 312B3/012 • #12
Qualifying: 3rd • Result: Retired (wing stay)

Despite complaining of a lack of straight-line speed on Friday, Lauda was definitely quick in the corners and was 0.3 second clear of the others through the long *Curva do Sol* alone. He appeared so committed and on the limit there that the marshals stood back from their posts as he came past. An engine change for the next session, to check if the Cosworth DFVs were indeed superior to the Ferrari flat-12 in a straight line, confirmed that this was indeed the case, so the original unit was rebuilt for the race and he consolidated his third position on the grid.

The start was shambolic. Having been delayed on the dummy grid, Lauda was still working his way through to his correct starting position when the startled flagman released the field early. Niki was swamped by the pack, ending the first lap in 10th place as his engine kept cutting onto 10 cylinders. The rebuilt motor had a broken valve spring; his race could have been different had he and the team left things alone. Two laps later he was out, a rear wing stay having broken due to the pounding it received from the notoriously bumpy Interlagos track.

144 Race of Champions (GB)

Brands Hatch, 17 March 1974, Formula 1 & Formula 5000
Ferrari 312B3/010 • #12
Qualifying: 3rd • Result: 2nd

Fresh from tests at Jarama where revised rear suspension and a modified rear wing had shown an improvement, Lauda was optimistic for this non-championship race. Having been fastest by 1.5 seconds in the wet on Friday, he was unable to get a clear lap on Saturday and qualified third, missing out on the 100 bottles of champagne awarded by Moët et Chandon for pole position.

He was superb in streaming conditions in the race, the Ferrari handling perfectly on its new Goodyear rainwear. He managed the traffic effectively to pass Emerson Fittipaldi (McLaren) for second place, then overtook Carlos Reutemann's brake-locking Brabham for the lead on lap 7. He maintained a 10-second margin over second-placed Jacky Ickx but towards the end of the race minor trouble developed when a bump stop in the rear suspension began to tear away. The blows that the car was now taking from Brands Hatch's notorious bumps were enough to shift the balance between the two drivers. Ickx closed in and six laps from the end the rainmaster

ABOVE The Brazilian Grand Prix at Interlagos was less satisfactory than his Ferrari début; after problems in practice and the race, he retired early with a broken rear wing mounting.

LEARNING HOW TO WIN 141

ABOVE In the torrential rain that prevailed throughout the Race of Champions at Brands Hatch, Jacky Ickx's Lotus 72D prepares to overtake Niki's Ferrari 312B3 in a steely move on the outside of Paddock Hill Bend.

BELOW Clay Regazzoni and Niki had enjoyed a good working relationship at BRM in 1973 and would share a productive three years together at Ferrari.

made a daring lunge to the outside in the braking area for Paddock Hill Bend. Lauda, recognising the inevitable, gave Ickx just enough room to get past and was forced to settle for second place.

145 South African Grand Prix

Kyalami, 30 March 1974, Formula 1
Ferrari 312B3/012 • #12
Qualifying: 1st • Result: 16th (not running at finish)

Testing at Vallelunga had delivered a new, more streamlined, all-enveloping engine cover and a deeper-chord single-plane front wing. Both proved a step forward, the new front wing giving the 312B3 improved turn-in that gained Lauda's approval and allowed him to set a new unofficial lap record at the Rome track.

Although the Ferraris did not look particularly fast in South Africa, Lauda started from pole position for the first time in his Formula 1 career, having spent much of practice cruising

1974

around in case anyone matched his time. He got a perfect start when the flag fell, holding off Carlos Reutemann (Brabham) into Crowthorne to sit firmly in the lead. But the Brabham was very quick on the straight and on lap 10 Reutemann squeezed through. The two cars ran close together for the next 60 laps, drawing away from the rest of the field. Then the Ferrari hit trouble, its oil pressure sagging at the tight Clubhouse left-hander. Accepting that it was better to finish, Lauda switched off his ignition there each lap and coasted through other corners. With just three laps to go, the flat-12 died out on the circuit when the ignition box failed; the fault was later attributed to a moment just before the race when the unit was accidentally splashed with coolant, causing its circuitry to become corroded.

146 Austria-Trophäe (A)

Salzburgring, 14 April 1974, Group 2
Ford Capri RS 3100 (with Jochen Mass) • #2
Qualifying: 3rd • Result: Retired (engine)

After signing for Ford in June 1973, Lauda had only managed a brief 10-lap test in the new Capri RS 3100 at Paul Ricard in February so he was delighted to be able finally to drive the improved model (with Jochen Mass) in this second round of the European Touring Car Championship, the works Ford team having had to miss the first round at Monza. In practice, the new V6 engine failed after Niki had completed only 12 laps and he qualified third behind the BMW of Hans Stuck (sharing with Jacky Ickx) and Ford team-mate Dieter Glemser (sharing with Toine Hezemans), whose Capri had a stiffer bodyshell than Lauda's and was markedly quicker as a result.

The lead changed five times on the opening lap and for 50 laps the contest continued to be enthralling. The trio of Stuck, Glemser and Lauda ran within a second of each other, the Austrian leading over the line for 10 of those laps as positions were traded constantly. When the Glemser/Hezemans car pitted with a jammed

ABOVE At Kyalami, Lauda took his first Formula 1 pole position and was set for a strong finish until sidelined by electrical failure.

BELOW During the four-hour Austria-Trophäe race at the Salzburgring, Niki's plan to collaborate with the sister Capri RS 3100 of Dieter Glemser/Toine Hezemans to keep the BMW 3.0 CSL of Hans Stuck/Jacky Ickx behind both works Fords has just come undone, as the second Ford drops behind with a jammed throttle.

LEARNING HOW TO WIN 143

throttle, rejoining a lap down, Lauda cannily allied with it to keep the rival BMW behind but after three hours the sister Capri retired with a broken crankshaft. Leading at the final pit stop, Lauda handed over to Mass with victory looking hopeful but then the Capri's engine started to emit smoke and Stuck went past. With 10 minutes of the race left, the Capri's V6 blew up.

147 Spanish Grand Prix

Jarama, 28 April 1974, Formula 1
Ferrari 312B3/015 • #12
Qualifying: 1st • Result: 1st (fastest lap)

Armed with a brand-new chassis, Lauda was the bookies' pre-race favourite and had been quick in testing at Jarama. Keen to claim the team's extra set of new qualifying tyres, he was unimpressed to find that Clay Regazzoni had already taken them in an attempt to cure persistent understeer on his own car. Nevertheless, he still took pole position and came within 0.01 second of Ickx's two-year old practice record. Job done, he sat out much of qualifying as others struggled to get close to his time.

Sunday dawned wet and although the rain had abated by the time the flag fell, slick tyres were not an option. Lauda made a decent start from pole but Ronnie Peterson made a better one and the Lotus led into the first corner with the Austrian tucked in tight behind. As the race developed and the track dried, Lauda was the more adept at using the damp parts of the circuit to keep his tyres cool. He led for one lap when the Swede stopped for new tyres, on lap 21, and pitted himself next time round. All the top runners stopped to change onto slicks within the space of four laps and, after everything had shaken out, the two Ferraris were left in charge thanks to shambolic work by Peterson's crew, with Lauda 20 seconds in front of Regazzoni and a full lap ahead of the rest. He quickly stretched his advantage to 30 seconds and thereafter ran unchallenged to the flag, troubled only by the

BELOW First Grand Prix victory: having started from pole position, Niki steers his Ferrari 312B3 to his maiden Formula 1 win in a wet/dry Spanish Grand Prix, claiming fastest lap *en route*.

1974

LEFT Niki celebrates his Spanish Grand Prix win, with Clay Regazzoni (Goodyear cap), his girlfriend Mariella Reininghaus and chief mechanic Ermanno Cuoghi (red jacket) close by.

BELOW Niki formed a very close working relationship with chief mechanic Ermanno Cuoghi, placing his total faith in the Italian's preparation of his car and defending him against some of the more extreme politicking that would later arise within the team.

lack of a rev counter, which had stopped working on the third lap. The slow conditions meant that the two-hour time limit came into play rather than the race running its scheduled distance, so only 84 of the 90 laps were covered.

Lauda had driven a textbook race to take his first Grand Prix victory, with a clean sweep of pole position and fastest lap too.

148 Belgian Grand Prix

Nivelles, 12 May 1974, Formula 1
Ferrari 312B3/012 • #12
Qualifying: 3rd • Result: 2nd

Ferrari rotated its cars to aid their preparation, a tactic learned from the sports car programme, so Lauda was back in his older chassis. His only complaint was finding a clear lap in practice, so he used his time to sort out the best rubber for the race; he went through more than 50 Goodyears to arrive at a matched

LEARNING HOW TO WIN 145

ABOVE Right on the tail of Emerson Fittipaldi's winning McLaren M23, Niki's Ferrari 312B3 is a mere three tenths of a second behind as the chequered flag falls on the Belgian Grand Prix at featureless Nivelles.

set that he liked, and then went out on soft tyres in the last 15 minutes of qualifying to earn his third place on the grid behind team-mate Clay Regazzoni on a rather suspect pole, with a time a full second quicker than everyone else.

In a tight pack at the start, Lauda got away fifth but passed Ronnie Peterson (Lotus) on lap 3 and quickly dealt with Jody Scheckter (Tyrrell) for third. The South African repassed on lap 25 when Niki was baulked while lapping backmarkers but he got ahead again on lap 38. When leader Regazzoni ran wide at the hairpin a lap later, Emerson Fittipaldi (McLaren) took the lead and Lauda slipped through too.

Running as hard as they could, they soon broke clear of the rest. Both were troubled by severe tyre vibration later in the race, in Lauda's case causing his hands to become blistered from trying to hold the steering steady in the corners. Nevertheless, towards the end the Ferrari was closing fast on the McLaren, quicker on the straights despite losing out through the turns. Fittipaldi mistook the position of the finish line and slowed after the final corner to take the flag just 0.35 second ahead, with Lauda's nose tucked under his rear wing.

149 Nürburgring 1,000km (D)

19 May 1974, Group 2
Ford Capri RS 3100 (with Jochen Mass) • #72
Qualifying: 19th • Result: Retired (lost wheel)

As there was no clashing Formula 1 commitment with Ferrari, Lauda was able to race for Ford in this round of the World Championship for Makes, in which Group 2 touring cars were eligible but never likely to be able to run near the front. In deference to the fuel crisis, this important long-distance fixture was shortened from its usual 1,000km to 750km. A Ford test day the week before had shown the works Capris to be quick, although their lap times were still outside Lauda's 1973 record for the *Nordschleife*.

1974

To the disappointment of the huge crowd, the touring cars were not quite as entertaining as the GTs this time. Another battle between Ford and BMW saw Dieter Glemser's lead Capri duelling with Hans Stuck's CSL early in the race until gearbox troubles eliminated the BMW, elevating the Lauda/Mass Capri. During the second hour, with Mass driving, a rear wheel came off the Capri at *Hatzenbach* (the securing nuts had worked loose) and left the car marooned with suspension damage.

150 Monaco Grand Prix

26 May 1974, Formula 1
Ferrari 312B3/012 • #12
Qualifying: 3rd • Result: Retired (electrics)

Quickest from the first practice session, the Ferraris locked out the front row with Lauda starting from pole despite some self-recrimination for shunting his favoured car (015) at the swimming pool section on the first day and wrecking the right-front corner. He used the spare (010) — and still headed the time sheets with it — while his Belgian Grand Prix car (012) was brought from Maranello for the race.

Annoyed that the race director refused to allow him to choose which side of the track pole position would be placed, Lauda tucked in behind Clay Regazzoni when the flag fell. Frantically trying to find a way around his slower team-mate, he harried him relentlessly until he finally squeezed by on lap 21 after pressuring the Swiss into a spin at *Rascasse*. Now holding off the hard-charging Ronnie Peterson (Lotus), he led convincingly until lap 32, when he suddenly slowed with electrical failure and stopped on the harbour front. A faulty alternator was overloading the battery and a well-deserved victory was lost.

A heated discussion in the team's hotel that evening cleared the air between the Ferrari drivers, but it was evident that Lauda was not prepared to accept that he was anything other than the team leader.

ABOVE Despite its size, the Ford Capri RS 3100 still manages to take to the air at *Brünnchen* as Niki manhandles it round the Nürburgring *Nordschleife* during the 1974 1,000km race.

BELOW Jochen Mass's Surtees TS16 follows at a distance as Niki's Ferrari 312B3 heads along the Monaco harbour front.

LEARNING HOW TO WIN 147

151 Swedish Grand Prix

Anderstorp, 9 June 1974, Formula 1
Ferrari 312B3/012 • #12
Qualifying: 3rd • Result: Retired (transmission)

Having been fastest in tyre testing at Dijon, Lauda was quickest at Anderstorp on Friday despite unsettled weather. The next day the Tyrrells dominated and he settled for third on the grid without even going out in the afternoon, so sure was he that it would rain. Telephone calls in the evening to Mauro Forghieri, who remained at Maranello, did little to find a solution to the cars zig-zagging under braking so he went to the grid expecting a hard afternoon's work.

Running third behind the Tyrrells from the start, he held off a charging James Hunt in the Hesketh but from lap 10 he realised something was wrong. The Ferrari's handling was deteriorating as a rear suspension top-link mounting point had torn away from its weld, giving rise to huge understeer as the wheel leaned inwards. To compound his problems, gearbox difficulties set in around lap 40.

After visibly struggling for most of the race, he was finally forced to concede third place to Hunt on lap 66, just 14 laps from the end, and three laps later his unhappy race ended when third gear broke.

152 Dutch Grand Prix

Zandvoort, 23 June 1974, Formula 1
Ferrari 312B3/015 • #12
Qualifying: 1st • Result: 1st

Lauda was half a second slower than Clay Regazzoni on Friday, but such was Ferrari's superiority at the Dutch track that he was still second on the time sheets. The role reversal was due to the Austrian having chosen the wrong tyres; with the correct ones fitted, he took pole a full second quicker than the nearest Ford-

BELOW Squaring up for an on-track rivalry that would reach its zenith two seasons later, Niki's Ferrari 312B3 leads James Hunt's Hesketh 308 at Anderstorp in a duel that lasted for more than 60 laps.

ABOVE Amid Zandvoort's sand dunes, Niki's Ferrari 312B3 exits *Gerlach* on the way to his second win of the year in dominant style.

powered rival, Emerson Fittipaldi (McLaren), and it was clear that only misfortune would stop him running away with the race. Sunday morning warm-up was cancelled to placate an anti-noise lobby in the seaside community around Zandvoort and Lauda took the opportunity to change his car's set-up to achieve better handling on full tanks.

He made an excellent start and comfortably beat his team-mate off the line, pulling away relentlessly to extend his lead to 10 seconds in as many laps. However, he was forced to drive flat-out for virtually the whole race to retain a cushion over Regazzoni, who kept him under constant pressure throughout and clawed back a few tenths whenever the Austrian showed any sign of restraint. Niki never put a wheel wrong and maintained the gap at eight seconds, the pair unchallenged for the rest of the afternoon. With 10 laps to go, the Swiss finally settled for second place so Lauda eased off slightly, cruising home to a satisfying victory. The demonstration had been demoralising for all but Ferrari fans.

153 French Grand Prix

Dijon-Prenois, 7 July 1974, Formula 1
Ferrari 312B3/012 • #12
Qualifying: 1st • Result: 2nd

Building up slowly in Friday morning practice before using his soft tyres, Lauda was soon quickest in the afternoon, and at the end of qualifying he was the only man in the 58-second bracket on this short track, just 2.04 miles (3.29km) in length. He had one moment of concern when a rock thrown up by José Dolhem's spinning Surtees narrowly missed him.

He led superbly from pole at the start, an intense duel with Ronnie Peterson (Lotus) drawing them both away from the pack. However, the Ferrari was suffering a worsening front-end vibration — due to a faulty tyre with uneven tread thickness — that put him off-line in corners, allowing the Swede to close up. At the end of lap 16 the Ferrari ran slightly wide coming onto the straight, giving Peterson the

LEARNING HOW TO WIN 149

ABOVE Against a cloudless sky, Niki powers along Dijon's main straight on his way to second place in the French Grand Prix.

chance to get very close and outbrake him into the next corner. Buckling down to the challenge, Lauda nursed his mishandling car without losing a place for another 64 laps to finish six seconds ahead of team-mate Clay Regazzoni, although the vibration jarred his vision on the straight.

He had gone into the race five points behind Emerson Fittipaldi in the World Championhip standings, so his six points and the Brazilian's failure to finish put him at the top of the table for the first time.

154 Nürburgring Six Hours

14 July 1974, Group 2
Ford Capri RS 3100 (with Jochen Mass) • #6
Ford Capri RS 3100 (with Dieter Glemser/Toine Hezemans) • #7
Qualifying: 1st • Result: Retired (accident) and 2nd (1st in class)

For this fourth round of the European Touring Car Championship, Lauda again shared his works Ford Capri RS 3100 with Jochen Mass and qualified second, a good 15 seconds quicker than the sister car of Dieter Glemser/Toine Hezemans. In Saturday practice he crashed at *Brünnchen*

RIGHT After Jochen Mass crashed the works Capri RS 3100 he was sharing with Lauda in the Nürburgring Six Hours touring car race, Niki was put in the delayed sister car of Toine Hezemans/Dieter Glemser. His charge through the field to take a class win was the highlight of the race. Here, on the right, Mass (in race overalls) and Ford competitions boss Michael Kranefuss (pale trousers) take a keen interest as Lauda is installed in the car.

150 NIKI LAUDA

1974

LEARNING HOW TO WIN

trying an ambitious pass of a slower NSU whose driver failed to see him, the resulting collision with the guardrail causing unseen minor damage that forced Mass to pit for a new fuel pump early in the race. After that incident, the German was making up time when, at *Breidscheid*, he came across two crashed cars that had been caught out by a sudden heavy shower; he spun in avoidance, went off the road and came to rest with his wrecked car on top of a barrier.

Prospects looked bright for the sister works Capri, but on lap 26 Hezemans pitted with a broken differential and the Ford mechanics set about replacing it, a task that took 28 minutes. As the team's fastest driver, Lauda was put in the car to do his best. He flung it round the *Nordschleife* as if contesting a sprint, reprising his practice form by circulating 15 seconds a lap faster than anyone else on the track. Despite a slow puncture on the flat-in-fifth *Dottinger Höhe* straight on the last lap, he passed a works Ford Escort RS 1600 with Mass at its wheel to take second place against all expectations.

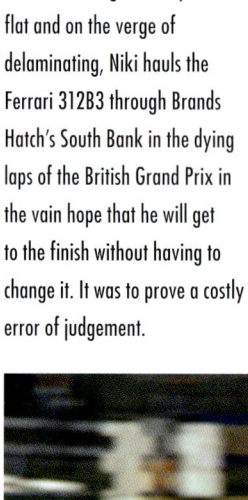

BELOW His right rear tyre flat and on the verge of delaminating, Niki hauls the Ferrari 312B3 through Brands Hatch's South Bank in the dying laps of the British Grand Prix in the vain hope that he will get to the finish without having to change it. It was to prove a costly error of judgement.

155 British Grand Prix

Brands Hatch, 20 July 1974, Formula 1
Ferrari 312B3/015 • #12
Qualifying: 1st • Result: 5th (fastest lap)

McLaren boss Teddy Mayer made a scarcely veiled threat on race morning that if a Ferrari won again, he would demand that its engine was checked for legality. This was of no consequence to Lauda, who was on pole again having set a time that was later equalled by Ronnie Peterson (Lotus).

As at Monaco, the Austrian asked to have his start position moved, to the left-hand side of the grid, but to no avail. He still arrived at Paddock Hill Bend in the lead and ended the first lap two seconds ahead of an unsettled Jody Scheckter (Tyrrell). The Ferrari then dominated the race until 20 laps from the end when a tiny puncture formed in the right rear tyre and a long, slow deflation began. Nursing the car through left-handers but able to take the right-handers and straights almost as normal, the Austrian ignored signals to pit for a replacement, gambling on staying out, but on the penultimate lap the overworked tyre exploded.

Driving on the rim, he fell to third place before diving into the pits. The wheel was changed in 15 seconds but as he roared away he found the pitlane exit blocked by bystanders and an official car. A marshal (incorrectly) showed him the red flag and he climbed out of his 312B3 in disgust. Although he was classified ninth, an FIA appeal — heard in September — elevated him to the rightful fifth place he occupied when halted.

156 German Grand Prix

Nürburgring, 28 July 1974, Formula 1
Ferrari 312B3/015 • #12
Qualifying: 1st • Result: Retired (accident)

In private testing at the Nürburgring in May, Lauda had unofficially become the first man ever to lap the *Nordschleife* in under seven minutes. He did not quite repeat the feat during a trouble-free practice for the German Grand Prix but his lap of 7m 0.8s did yield his seventh pole position of the year and left him brimming with confidence for the race.

At the start, he lagged as he gave the engine insufficient revs and Clay Regazzoni led away with Jody Scheckter (Tyrrell) passing him under braking for the *Südkehre*. Keen not to allow his team-mate to break away, Lauda used the Ferrari's power to draw alongside Scheckter on the straight behind the pits and they approached the *Nordkehre* together, with Lauda in a narrowing gap on the inside. Forgetting he had a new, unscrubbed right front tyre that had been fitted just before the start after he had picked up a puncture in the paddock tunnel, he was slightly ahead when he hit the brakes. The cold tyre gave little grip and braking pulled his car to the right, his rear wheel on that side hitting the Tyrrell's left front. The Ferrari was thrown into the air, snapped to the right and was pitched into the catch fencing at the outside of the curve. His race was over after just 20 seconds and two corners.

Regazzoni, meanwhile, won and moved to the top of the World Championship standings, while Lauda's lack of points-scoring finishes saw him slump to fourth place behind Scheckter and Fittipaldi.

With typical self-analysis, on Sunday evening Niki flew to the ARD television studios in Cologne to study slow-motion footage of the incident, over and over again, so as to properly understand his error.

157 Austrian Grand Prix

Österreichring, 8 August 1974, Formula 1
Ferrari 312B3/015 • #12
Qualifying: 1st • Result: Retired (engine)

In very hot conditions, Lauda's engine had a con rod come through the side of the block during first practice and, relegated to the spare car (011), he was fourth quickest initially. His problems were exacerbated by a set-up error;

ABOVE Niki's Ferrari 312B3 exits the inner banking of the *Karussell* during practice for the German Grand Prix. He would not make it this far on the first lap of the race.

LEARNING HOW TO WIN 153

ABOVE Lauda sits patiently in the Österreichring pits while the Ferrari mechanics tend to his 312B3, before going out to claim yet another pole position.

despite extensive pre-race testing at his home circuit, the ride height was set too high on both Ferraris. Order was later restored and after three stunning laps late in qualifying he was quickest once again, with Carlos Reutemann's Brabham alongside him on the front row.

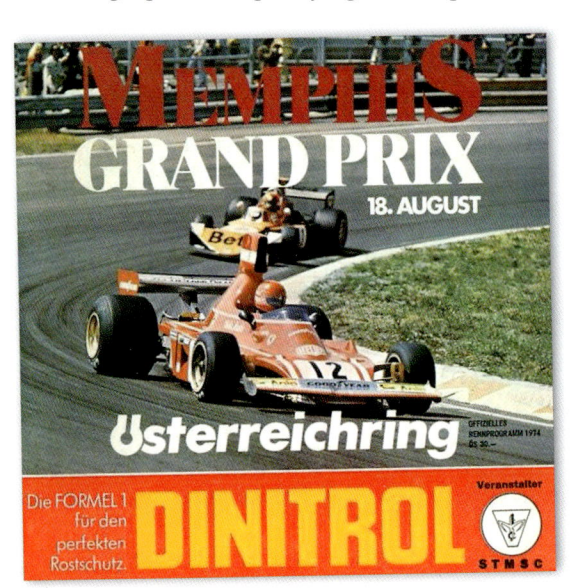

Out-dragged up the hill by Reutemann at the start, he settled into second place and pressured the Argentine driver relentlessly; the Ferrari was quicker through the fast sections but the Brabham had the edge through the infield *Texaco-Schikane*. On lap 13 Lauda suddenly slowed as his engine went off-song but he struggled on until he bowed to the inevitable and pitted on lap 16. After losing a lap while the mechanics fiddled with the flat-12's ignition, he briefly rejoined for one more stuttering lap before retiring, the engine having dropped a valve.

Of the top four in the World Championship battle, Regazzoni was the only to score points — he finished fifth — and therefore extended his lead at the top of the standings while Lauda remained fourth.

1974

158 Italian Grand Prix

Monza, 8 September 1974, Formula 1
Ferrari 312B3/015 • #12
Qualifying: 1st • Result: Retired (engine)

With the very real possibility that one of its drivers could win the World Championship, an atmosphere of chaos pervaded the Ferrari team at Monza.

Speculation that Lauda believed his teammate was receiving preferential treatment proved unfounded and it was Ferrari v Brabham again, with Lauda, as in Austria, edging out Carlos Reutemann to take pole position. Reutemann had the advantage during Friday practice, scotching the Austrian's plans to spare his engine that day, but overnight rain washed the track clean and Lauda secured pole by 0.1 second. The unusual decision was made to install a brand-new engine in his car before the race; he was then quickest in the warm-up after Ferrari made a breakthrough with a thinner-section rear wing that could be run flatter, reducing drag without upsetting the car's handling.

After apparently jumping the start, Lauda held a huge lead at the end of lap 1 and started to pull away from the pack, which was headed by Regazzoni — a Ferrari 1–2 for the home fans! Although he was keeping his revs well below the limit, after 20 laps his oil and water temperatures

MONZA
AUGUST 1974

Ferrari, like several other teams, did a lot of testing at Monza ahead of the Italian Grand Prix and completed more laps than most. Low drag was clearly on Mauro Forghieri's mind, evidenced in this poor-quality but interesting photo by a new cockpit surround incorporating engine air scoops either side, where the mirrors were usually positioned. This apparently failed to give good results and the regular tall airbox was reinstated. Lauda and Clay Regazzoni (pictured) then spent the rest of the time evaluating a variety of rear wings of different shapes and sizes.

LEFT Out of the shadows: Niki's Ferrari heads up the gentle hill towards the *Ascari* chicane in the heart of Monza's Royal Park before engine failure ended his race.

LEARNING HOW TO WIN

began to rise. Thinking that litter was clogging his radiators, he dropped his revs further while still maintaining the gap, but exhaust smoke on the overrun heralded a bigger problem. On lap 30 he was overtaken by his team-mate and a couple of struggling laps later he pitted for good amid plumes of smoke, the engine having lost its coolant because of a cross-threaded water-pump connection.

At least the *Tifosi* could still cheer a red car at the front, but not for long as Regazzoni's car also expired with engine failure on lap 40.

BELOW Gearbox trouble scuppered what looked like certain victory for Niki's Ford Capri RS 3100 at the Norisring. Here he powers around the Nürnberg street course in front of massed spectators.

159 200 Meilen von Nürnberg (D)

Norisring, 15 September 1974, Group 2
Ford Capri RS 3100 (GA ECPY 19999) • #3
Qualifying: 3rd • Result: Heat 1, 6th; Final, retired (gearbox)

Ford and BMW attached a great deal of prestige to the traditional Norisring event, which drew huge crowds. A high-quality field for the Deutsche Rennsport Meisterschaft touring car race was also attracted by the lure of a 100,000 DM prize fund for the combined final, which would be contested by the fastest 20 cars from two 65-lap heats, split for cars in Division I (over 2 litres) and Division II (under 2 litres).

Having set an unofficial lap record before practice, Lauda qualified third for the large-capacity heat with an identical time to second-placed Hans Stuck (BMW) while fellow Ford man Toine Hezemans claimed pole. Niki got past Stuck on lap 2, quickly closed on Hezemans and took the lead on lap 8. He looked to have the race sewn up, but his early pace had over-stressed the car; with five laps to go, he lost all but fourth gear and limped home to take sixth place.

In the 74-lap final, with a fresh gearbox and extra cooling provision, he ran comfortably in second place from the start but pitted after 15 laps when gear-selection problems returned. He resumed on lap 22 but only got halfway round the circuit before stopping at the side of the track.

160 Canadian Grand Prix

Mosport Park, 22 September 1974, Formula 1
Ferrari 312B3/015 • #12
Qualifying: 2nd • Result: Retired (accident)

After trying both his own car and the spare (014) in third practice, Lauda would have taken his 10th pole position of the year had it not been for a sudden rain shower late on when he had been biding his time for a last run in his frantic battle with Emerson Fittipaldi (McLaren) to top the time sheets — so he had to settle for second spot on the grid.

Despite a cautious start, Lauda took the lead and pulled out a small advantage over Fittipaldi. Behind them, Clay Regazzoni (Ferrari) initially ran third from Jody Scheckter (Tyrrell), but the South African passed on lap 3. From that point until well after half distance, the top four World Championship contenders ran in those positions, which, if maintained to the chequered flag, would have set up an intriguing four-way fight for the title at the last round, with Lauda the slight underdog on 47 points facing the other three on 49. It was not to be.

Lauda was using a higher gear than normal at some points on the circuit to protect his engine from a rattle at high revs that had developed in the morning warm-up, and this may have cost him dearly. Holding a five-second lead, on lap 68 he came over the brow into the sweeping Turn 3 right-hander to find the track covered with dirt scattered by John Watson's errant Brabham, which had gone off the road. With less engine braking available than usual because he was in a higher gear, and with no flags displayed to warn of the hazard, he slid helplessly into the barrier. To add insult to injury, when Lauda failed to respond immediately to a request to throw the electrical cut-out switch (he had jumped over the barrier and was waiting for the next group of cars to go past), a marshal activated the Ferrari's on-board fire extinguisher and filled the car with powder.

While his hopes of the title were shattered, winner Fittipaldi and runner-up Regazzoni went into the last round tied on points, while Scheckter, seven points behind them, also still had a chance.

161 United States Grand Prix

Watkins Glen, 6 October 1974, Formula 1
Ferrari 312B3/015 • #12
Qualifying: 5th • Result: Retired (shock absorbers)

After Clay Regazzoni bent his race car's chassis in testing, bruising his leg, the original 312B3 (010) was sent over from Italy for use as a new spare. This was significant for Lauda, who had to resort to it in qualifying after the oil pressure in his own car dropped. The replacement car was insufficiently prepared, suffering persistent understeer and a down-on-power engine. He could not improve his Friday time in it and a place on the third row was the result. The night before the race, Ferrari switched engines in all three cars, tripling the chances of a

ABOVE The grid forms up at Mosport under overcast skies with Emerson Fittipaldi's McLaren M23 on pole alongside Niki's Ferrari 312B3. Lining up behind are Jody Scheckter's Tyrrell 007, Carlos Reutemann's Brabham BT44, the partly obscured Shadow DN3 of Jean-Pierre Jarier, Clay Regazzoni's Ferrari 312B3 and the rest.

LEARNING HOW TO WIN 157

FIORANO
27 SEPTEMBER 1974

This is the first sight of a world-beater, with Enzo Ferrari present in the background and designer Mauro Forghieri (hands in pockets) overseeing his contender for 1975. After a presentation to the sporting press of the new 312T with transverse gearbox (hence the 'T'), Lauda gave the far from raceworthy prototype its first shakedown at Fiorano. He later conceded that he had been lukewarm about the 312T when he first saw the drawings, admitting that he harboured bad memories of the March 721X, another pioneering design with a transverse gearbox. However, when he immediately lapped within a second of the Fiorano record despite running on hard tyres, he began to appreciate what a major step forward the car was, although his ability as a development driver and his willingness to adapt his style contributed to its success.

Testing of the 312T continued at Fiorano, Vallelunga and Paul Ricard throughout the autumn and winter, although the programme was disrupted when Regazzoni wrote off the second chassis (019) at the Rome circuit. The first serious tests at Fiorano (on 10 October) were made with the car unmodified from the guise seen at the press conference and Lauda completed some 30 laps, setting a time just shy of the well-developed 312B3's best. On the first day of testing at Vallelunga, he went a full second quicker than the B3 had ever managed. The team then moved to Paul Ricard for back-to-back comparisons with the older car and more intensive tyre testing. Although the 312T proved to be quite nervous when driven close to the limit, that limit was much higher than most of the opposition, and Lauda would hone his style to drive for prolonged periods at the edge of its neutral handling.

RIGHT By the end of 1974, the mercurial, emotional Mauro Forghieri and the intense, committed Niki Lauda had formed the most effective engineer-designer/racer-developer partnership in the pitlane.

1974

problem, as Lotus's Peter Warr put it.

In this race, Lauda needed to help his teammate's World Championship chances if possible, although Regazzoni started only ninth on the grid. At first Niki, running fourth ahead of title contenders Jody Scheckter and Emerson Fittipaldi, went as slowly as he could to allow his seventh-placed team-mate to keep in touch, but Regazzoni's 312B3 was handling badly due to a shock-absorber problem and slipping back. By lap 10 Lauda was told by the pit wall to forget the strategy and he quickly pulled away from Scheckter, but then similar shock-absorber trouble began to afflict his car and he too dropped back. After a pit stop on lap 24 to try to rectify the issue, he retired after 38 laps when the engine started to tighten. Regazzoni kept going to finish a lowly 11th, four laps down.

Ferrari's worst weekend of the year had occurred just at the worst moment. Not only had Regazzoni missed out on becoming World Champion, the honour falling instead to Fittipaldi, but McLaren's win and Ferrari's *nul points* meant that the Italian team had also failed to secure the constructors' title, which it had led since early in the season.

SUMMARY

It had been a pivotal year for Lauda, who had announced his presence as a title contender having dominated qualifying throughout the season and taken two excellent victories. Comparison of his key season statistics with those of World Champion Emerson Fittipaldi is instructive as Lauda was comfortably ahead on most counts: he out-qualified the Brazilian for 13 of the 15 races; he took nine pole positions to Emerson's two; he led eight races while Fittipaldi led only three but, crucially, won those three; and, perhaps most telling of all, Lauda led 338 race laps during the year compared with just 77 for the World Champion.

Of course, Niki had endured more than his share of unreliability and he had made mistakes that had cost him dearly. For some observers, the errors meant that a question mark remained over his judgement under pressure, although there were no such doubts about either his speed or his self-confidence. Lauda later conceded that 1974 had been as much about learning how to lose as it had been about learning how to win, accepting that his dominant performances in South Africa and Monaco had seen certain victories lost to technical failures.

He now understood that every little aspect of car and driver performance needed to come together to ensure success. He was now also firmly ensconced as Ferrari's number one driver, despite his Swiss team-mate's better finishing position in the World Championship. He was ready to challenge for the sport's biggest prize.

ABOVE Watkins Glen's autumnal trees form a colourful backdrop as Niki's Ferrari 312B3 sets off after the leaders, with Carlos Reutemann's Brabham BT44 giving chase.

LEARNING HOW TO WIN 159

1975
THE STARS ALIGN

Luca di Montezemolo had made a big impact at Ferrari during 1974 and under his direction the team had a stable management structure for the first time in many years. Much of the chaos and infighting that had bedevilled the Scuderia had been eliminated, allowing individuals to focus on doing their jobs rather than political jockeying and this in turn translated into a more effective operation.

For 1975, Lauda's new Formula 1 contract contained a clause ensuring he was exclusively a Ferrari driver, so he could not accept Ford's invitation to race again in the European Touring Car Championship. He accepted the situation with equanimity; in any case, Mauro Forghieri had scheduled such an extensive testing programme that he was happy instead to gather his strength on his few free weekends, especially now that he had cleared most of his debts and the need for other income had diminished.

On paper, with a strong tally of pole positions and victories in 1974, Ferrari looked like favourites for the World Championship, but over the winter the opposition had not stood still. McLaren had pursued an equally intensive development programme with the M23 that had carried Emerson Fittipaldi to the title in 1974, and Brabham's Gordon Murray had come up with a lightened, improved 'B' version of its swift, nimble BT44. What neither of them, nor indeed any of the other teams, had was the superbly powerful, tractable and — most importantly — reliable Ferrari flat-12 engine.

Equally significant was the fact that no other team had a driver who was prepared to put quite as much personal commitment into finding marginal gains, both in the car and in himself. Lauda invested a huge number of hours pounding round Fiorano testing new components and tyres; when not in the car, he pursued the rigorous personal training regime devised by Austrian ski-team coach Willi Dungl. Confident that he was as well prepared as possible, and with the secret weapon that was the 312T waiting in the wings, the Austrian held high hopes for the new season.

162 Argentine Grand Prix

Buenos Aires, 10 January 1975, Formula 1
Ferrari 312B3/020 • #12
Qualifying: 4th • Result: 6th

A brand new 312B3-specification chassis with updated aerodynamics, revised suspension, bigger brakes and improved cooling was made available for Lauda, although his practice was delayed when the seat belts did not fit. Ferrari's expectation that the uprated version of the previous year's car would be good enough was proved wrong. Lauda suffered from persistent oversteer and by the end of the first day he was third quickest, having spent much of the time tuning the car on full tanks in preparation for the race. His grid time came from a late run for which he said he had had to drive like a madman, as he had found the car struggling to generate heat in its tyres.

After pole-sitter Jean-Pierre Jarier failed to take the start, his Shadow having broken its final drive *en route* to the grid, Lauda was third at the off, jostling for position behind the Brabhams of Carlos Reutemann and Carlos Pace, but he was overtaken by James Hunt's Hesketh on lap 8. By now the Ferrari was suffering because its left rear tyre was deteriorating, due to a manufacturing fault, causing the handling to suffer as a rear damper gradually failed. Eventual race winner Emerson Fittipaldi (McLaren) soon passed him and with 10 laps to go Patrick Depailler (Tyrrell) slipped by as well, but Lauda did manage to haul his erratically handling car to the finish, in sixth place, the last unlapped runner.

He only just made it: the suspension was so askew that the inside edge of the tyre was nearly worn through to the carcass.

ABOVE New bottle, old medicine. Niki steers his Ferrari 312B3 — a new chassis but still the 1974 design — through the twisty infield section of the Buenos Aires autodrome on his way to sixth place.

THE STARS ALIGN 161

ABOVE Niki sweeps through the infield curves at Interlagos.

163 Brazilian Grand Prix

Interlagos, 26 January 1975, Formula 1
Ferrari 312B3/020 • #12
Qualifying: 4th • Result: 5th

After wasting most of the first day with a car that was found to have been set up with the wrong ride height at the rear, Lauda tried the spare car (012) with hard springs and soft tyres in an attempt to mitigate nervous handling over the bumps of Interlagos. A delay on race morning might have helped him as an oil-pump drive sheared during the warm-up and the team thought it wise to change the engine. The mechanics accomplished the task — by grafting the whole rear end of the spare onto his race car — in a remarkable 66 minutes. There was no time to tune the handling on full tanks, so Niki was rather frustrated as he took to the grid.

Running sixth from the start, he was off the pace from the outset. Emerson Fittipaldi (McLaren) passed him after four laps and by lap 19 he lay eighth. The car was not properly balanced after its hasty rebuild, its wayward handling causing it to weave on the straights, and from the third lap there was also a nasty vibration from the front end. He persevered until the end of the race, although he backed off in the final laps. As attrition removed some of those ahead of him, he eventually finished fifth.

164 South African Grand Prix

Kyalami, 1 March 1975, Formula 1
Ferrari 312B3/014 (practice only) • #12T
Ferrari 312T/018 • #12
Qualifying: 4th • Result: 5th

Having refused to send the 312Ts to South America, Mauro Forghieri conceded that the 312B3 was no longer the force it had once been and brought forward the new car's introduction from its planned Spanish début. Lauda was so keen to start practice with it that

162 NIKI LAUDA

ABOVE The old and the new. The spare Ferrari 312B3 allocated to Niki appears relatively bulky alongside Clay Regazzoni's svelte new 312T in the pitlane at Kyalami. The Austrian was forced to run the older car in practice after his race car was damaged.

LEFT Last-minute checks for Niki's 312T before he heads to the grid. A slipping belt for the fuel metering unit left the engine short on power in the race and disguised the car's true performance.

THE STARS ALIGN 163

he was in a virtual drag race with Jean-Pierre Jarier (Shadow) to get out on track as soon as the pitlane opened. Once a broken throttle linkage was sorted, the 312T looked very competitive and Lauda set quickest time during the first session, enjoying a kind of private race with Emerson Fittipaldi until late in the Thursday session when the McLaren's engine exploded while the Ferrari was right behind, the resulting oil slick sending Lauda spinning backwards into the catch fences at Sunset Bend. Although still driveable, the car was too badly damaged for immediate repair so he had to use the spare 1974-specification 312B3 for final qualifying. This was when most drivers set their quickest times and in the older car he was unable to improve on his earlier effort.

FIORANO
EARLY APRIL 1975

In the week before the International Trophy at Silverstone, Lauda tested a new rear wing at Fiorano, but most significant was the fitting of a de Dion rear end to the 312T. This was the first time the system, which had been devised by Mauro Forghieri for the following season's car and would absorb many hours of Lauda's time in testing, had been seen on a modern Ferrari. Before the crew packed up and headed off to Silverstone, Lauda spent a few laps enjoying himself aboard a modified Ford Escort belonging to former Abarth aerodynamicist Francesco Guglielminetti. A rare event indeed — precious few Fords can have lapped Fiorano during Enzo's lifetime.

Lauda was back in the repaired 312T for the race but was troubled by a down-on-power engine. He was eighth after the first lap and passed Ronnie Peterson's ageing Lotus for seventh place on lap 8, but then made no further progress even though the car was handling well and was as reliable as usual. Only when Fittipaldi pitted on lap 39 did his position improve and eventually he came home a disappointed fifth, having moved up one place when his team-mate retired with eight laps to go.

Examination of the car after the race revealed a slipping metering unit belt, which had caused the engine to run 85bhp down — a problem that was exacerbated by Kyalami's rarefied atmosphere. Reassured by the discovery, Lauda suggested that he should carry out back-to-back tests against the 312B3 as soon as the team returned to Fiorano; within a few laps he broke the lap record in the 312T. The team's morale, which had been sapped by negative reports in the Italian press suggesting that the new car was no good, was restored immediately.

165 Daily Express International Trophy (GB)

Silverstone, 12 April 1975, Formula 1
Ferrari 312T/022 • #12
Qualifying: 2nd • Result: 1st

Ferrari was present at the International Trophy for the first time since 1969 with a single-car entry for Lauda. After experiencing issues with the 312T's left-side springs over-compressing, he was soon fastest but was edged out for pole by James Hunt in the final session. Hunt got the better start but Lauda stayed right with the flying Hesketh, the leading pair closely pursued by Emerson Fittipaldi (McLaren). At half distance he was still being pressured by the Brazilian and briefly turned off the rev limiter to try to gain an edge, but it made no difference.

On lap 25 Hunt's engine exploded at Copse and Lauda took the lead. Into the last quarter of the race, the Ferrari's handling deteriorated, with worsening understeer caused by a vibration

1975

ABOVE Flat-out through Woodcote, Niki holds off Emerson Fittipaldi's McLaren M23 during their epic duel in the late stages of the International Trophy race at Silverstone. This was the last time that Formula 1 cars used this 150mph corner in its pre-chicane glory.

from the front wheels, and his slender lead, just a couple of car lengths, was reduced to nothing. Nose to tail with Fittipaldi for the last five laps, Lauda defended superbly and despite a last-lap wobble at Abbey that allowed Fittipaldi to pull alongside into Woodcote, he crossed the line a tenth of a second ahead. It was a deserved victory after withstanding huge pressure for the entire race.

166 Spanish Grand Prix

Montjuïc, 27 April 1975, Formula 1
Ferrari 312T/022 • #12
Qualifying: 1st • Result: DNF (accident)

Lauda was as dismayed as most of his competitors to find that guardrails at the picturesque Barcelona parkland circuit were badly fixed with many bolts missing and in some places the rails were not even attached to the uprights. As there had been three fatalities in just over a year as a result of barrier failures, the drivers were uncompromising and refused to practise until things were put right. With five miles of two-tier Armco to secure, a quick solution was impossible and practice was cancelled.

The following day an army of Formula 1 mechanics and team personnel got stuck in and eventually the most crucial points on the circuit were attended to. Although things were far from ideal, the FIA stewards accepted that the circuit was ready for racing. Encouraged by his Silverstone win, Lauda quickly set the pace in the much-reduced qualifying session, duly annexing pole position despite his misgivings. However, his race was brief and unpleasant.

As the flag fell for the start, Vittorio Brambilla optimistically tried to shove his March inside Mario Andretti's Parnelli but only succeeded in ramming the American's car, just as Andretti was trying to pass Lauda's Ferrari. As the Austrian moved across to close the door, the Parnelli hit the back of the Ferrari, which in turn was shunted into Clay Regazzoni's sister car and thence into

THE STARS ALIGN 165

ABOVE For a brief moment, the Ferraris of Niki and Clay Regazzoni headed the field at the start of the Spanish Grand Prix. Seconds later, both were eliminated in a multiple shunt.

OPPOSITE In a dominant performance, Niki gave the Ferrari team its first victory at Monaco in 20 years.

the guardrail, before sliding sideways down the road in the middle of the pack. Lauda was out on the spot with the Ferrari's right front suspension broken.

The race ended in tragedy on the 25th of 75 laps. The rear wing of Rolf Stommelen's Hill became detached and in the ensuing crash the car leaped the barrier, killing five bystanders. The condition of the guardrail played no part in the incident.

167 Monaco Grand Prix

Monte Carlo, 11 May 1975, Formula 1
Ferrari 312T/023 • #12
Qualifying: 1st • Result: 1st

Lauda was quickest on both practice days, but only after a huge effort in the final session. In second practice with his race car he got his feet caught in the pedals by the swimming pool and clouted the barrier, damaging the front suspension. As Regazzoni was already using the spare car, the Austrian had little choice but to continue practice with his team-mate's usual car (021), which had a slightly bent right-hand suspension mounting. Despite this handicap, Lauda remained quickest but was happier when his own car was returned to him. Tom Pryce gave him a scare late in the day when the Shadow driver put in a faster lap, prompting Lauda to go out again, and with just 10 minutes of the session remaining he took an assertive pole position.

Fastest again in the warm-up, he opted for a cautious start on a wet track but this did not go quite to plan; his grid position was on a zebra crossing and he had too much wheelspin on the extra-slippery white lines. Staying just in front into *Ste Dévote*, he held the excitable Jean-Pierre Jarier (Shadow) at bay to lead by a narrow margin for the first few laps. After 14 laps the rain stopped, although it took him until lap 20 to break clear of his pursuers, headed by Ronnie

166 NIKI LAUDA

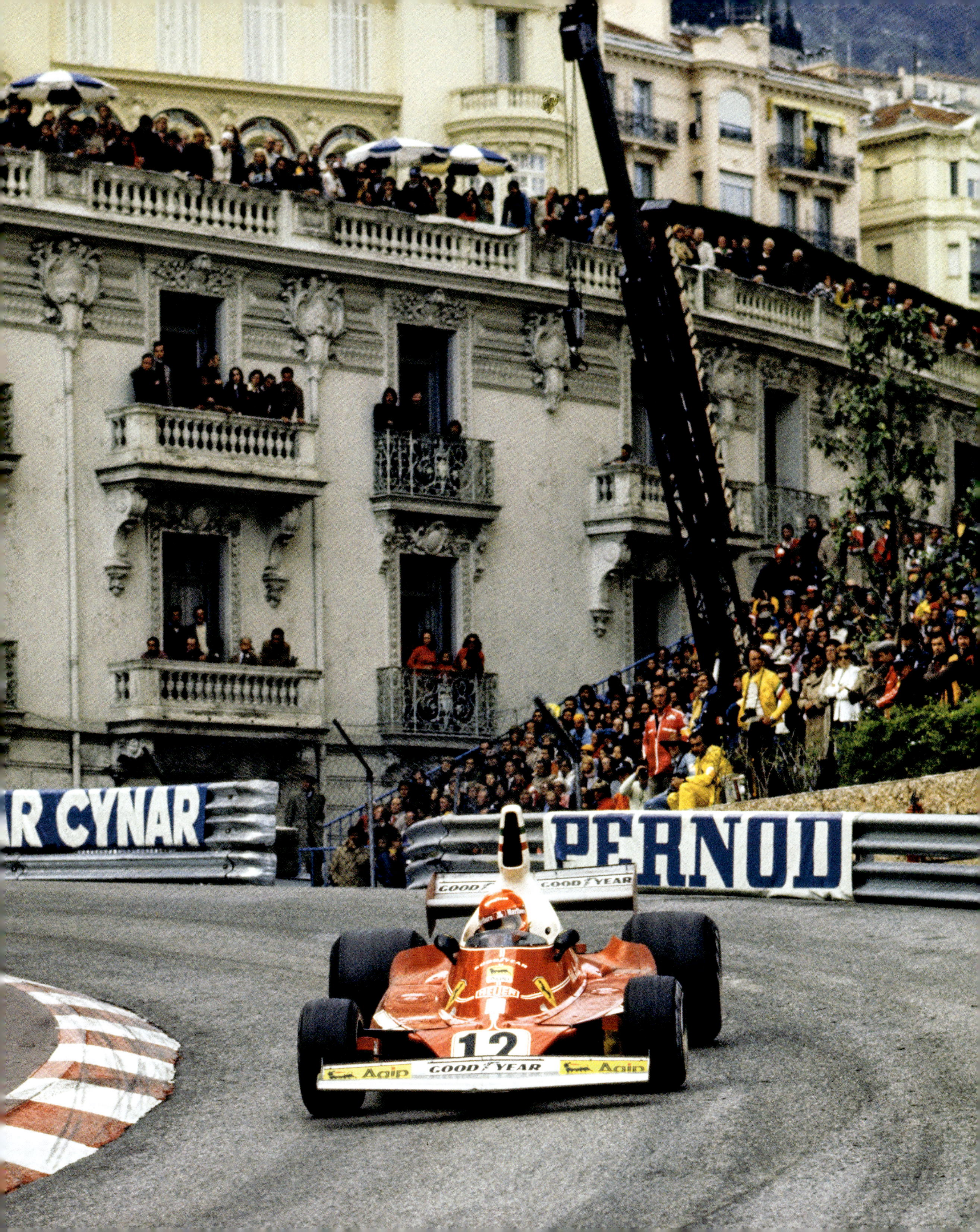
CYNAR
PERNOD
GOOD YEAR
Agip
12
GOOD YEAR
Agip

Peterson's Lotus. With the track now drying quickly, he pitted for slicks on lap 24 — leaving Peterson to assume the lead — and rapid work by his mechanics got him going again after only 33 seconds. On the following lap Peterson came in to change his tyres, so Lauda regained the lead and remained there when everyone else's stops were complete.

He enjoyed a determined, calculated run some 16 seconds clear of the field, although towards the end of the race his advantage dwindled as the flat-12's oil pressure flickered, especially in left-handers; a leaking pump seal had nearly emptied the system. He had to ease off, allowing Fittipaldi to close to within 2.75 seconds. Lauda was more relieved than most when the two-hour rule came into play and the chequered flag was shown after 75 of the scheduled 78 laps. This victory — Ferrari's first at Monaco since 1955 — was achieved thanks to the superior performance of the Austrian, who had remained error-free while others had not.

168 Belgian Grand Prix

Zolder, 25 May 1975, Formula 1
Ferrari 312T/023 • #12
Qualifying: 1st • Result: 1st

Other than a split in one of the Ferrari 312T's new titanium exhausts, which meant that the old system had to be put back on, practice went smoothly for Lauda. He was again fastest in the first session, and in the second, despite having oversteer in fast corners and an engine that was 300rpm down, he took pole position.

After deciding to start from the left-hand side of the grid, he was passed by Carlos Pace's Brabham in a wheel-to-wheel drag race into the first corner. He considered a challenge on the second lap but saw Vittorio Brambilla charging up behind and prudently moved over to let the March through, Brambilla nearly going off the track in the process. The Italian then took the lead and Lauda forced his way in front of the second-placed Brabham a lap later. As Brambilla

1975

grew more wayward in his excitement at leading a Grand Prix for the first time, Lauda patiently waited for his opportunity, overtaking the March with ease on lap 6 as its overworked brakes went off. Thereafter, the race was in effect over: Lauda was never threatened and had a trouble-free afternoon until 12 laps from the end his engine note became ragged. Another exhaust primary pipe had broken, costing him some 300rpm. Jody Scheckter, in second place, responded to signals from his pit to give chase but his Tyrrell was stuttering as it ran low on fuel and he was unable to close. Lauda's afternoon was almost ruined at the last gasp when the suspension of François Migault's Hill collapsed just as the Austrian was lapping him, but he remained over 40 seconds clear at the flag. It was the first time in two years that a driver had won successive races and the result put him top of the points standings.

169 Swedish Grand Prix

Anderstorp, 8 June 1975, Formula 1
Ferrari 312T/023 • #12
Qualifying: 5th • Result: 1st (fastest lap)

Although Ferrari had been quickest in the Goodyear tyre test that had taken place at Zandvoort immediately after the Belgian Grand Prix, no-one — Lauda included — really expected the 312Ts to show well at Anderstorp as the circuit's many third-gear corners seemed to favour the Ford-engined cars. Sure enough, he had to be content with fifth place on the grid.

Sixth at the start, he had to drive flat-out to keep up with swifter cars ahead of him, but was elevated to fifth place when Patrick Depailler's Tyrrell retired on lap 15, fourth as Vittorio Brambilla's understeering March slipped back, and third when the engine in Jean-Pierre Jarier's

ABOVE Through one of Zolder's plethora of chicanes, Niki's Ferrari 312T leads Vittorio Brambilla's March 751 and Jody Scheckter's Tyrrell 007 early in the Belgian Grand Prix.

OPPOSITE A smiling Niki in 1975, revelling in having a car at his disposal that was capable of winning consistently.

THE STARS ALIGN 169

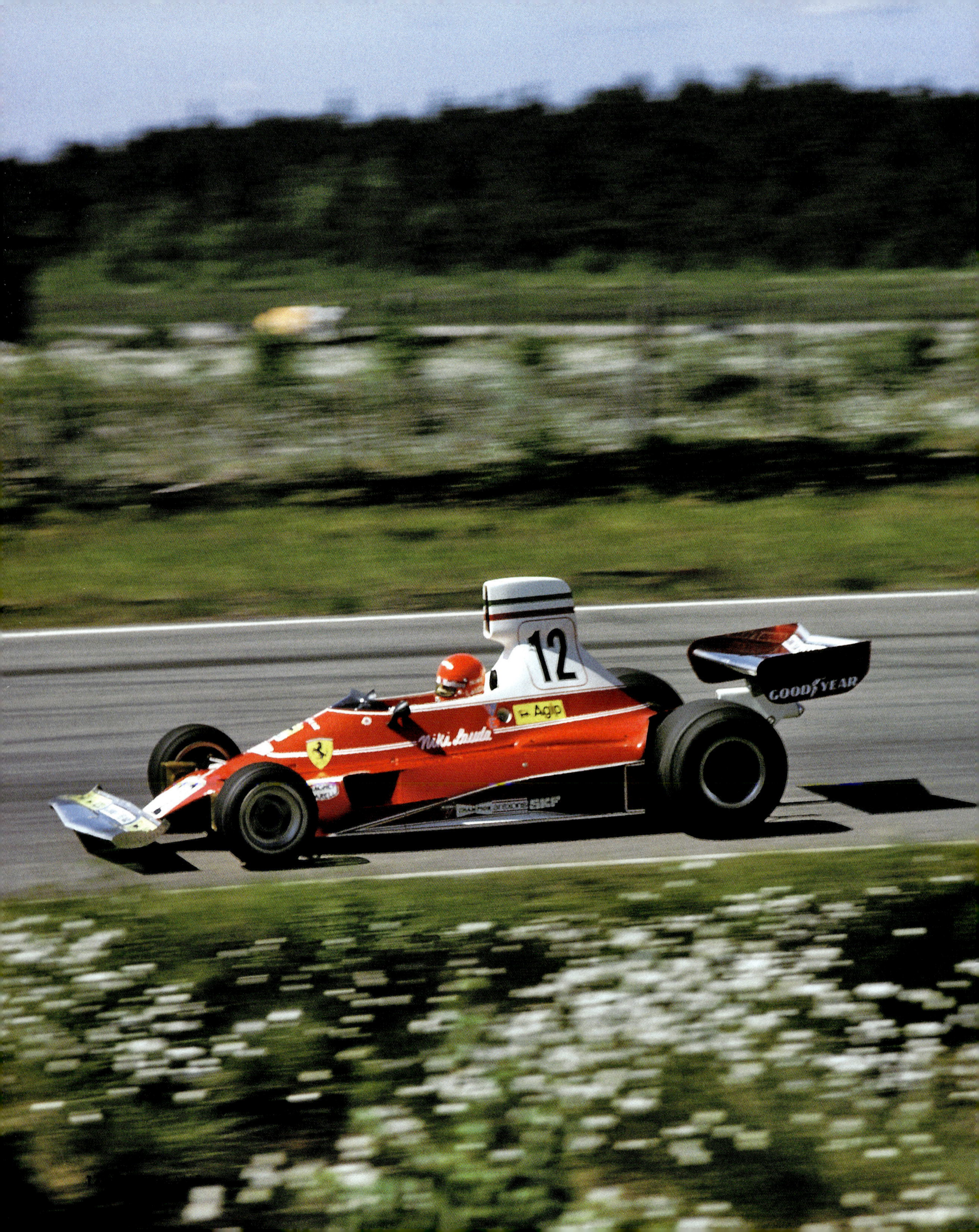
12
GOODYEAR
Agip
Niki Lauda
SKF

Shadow blew up on lap 39. This left just the Brabham pair in front of him. He pressured Carlos Pace into a spin coming onto the straight and dived through. Now he set off after the leader. His pursuit of Carlos Reutemann was the highlight of the race as he repeatedly set fastest lap, running an average of 0.7 second quicker than the Argentine driver. The Ferrari had been understeering initially but was now coming into its own as its fuel load lightened. With 10 laps remaining, Lauda took the lead, which he extended to six seconds by the time the chequered flag fell. It was a beautiful drive and his most satisfying victory to date. His hat-trick of victories was the first by any driver since 1971.

170 Dutch Grand Prix

Zandvoort, 22 June 1975, Formula 1
Ferrari 312T/022 • #12
Qualifying: 1st • Result: 2nd (fastest lap)

Most observers anticipated a repeat of the previous year's Ferrari benefit and right from the start of practice the 312Ts were quickest, Lauda securing pole position despite incidents on both the Friday and Saturday. He had a huge moment when a bolt pulled loose in the rear suspension subframe, pitching him over the kerb at the point where Roger Williamson had perished two years previously. The next day he was delayed again when the front aerofoil mounting collapsed as he pulled out of the slipstream from Bob Evans's BRM. He conceded philosophically that it was better to have these issues in practice rather than during the race.

Although concerned about using an untested engine after an overnight change had been necessary, he led from the start in the wet conditions. By lap 7 the rain had ceased, but the team failed to see Lauda signal his request for dry tyres so he was not able to stop for slicks until lap 13, when he screamed into the pits and rather alarmed his mechanics. He rejoined in second place but was overtaken by Jean-Pierre Jarier's Shadow while his new tyres warmed up. Meanwhile, James Hunt had made an inspired early tyre stop (on the lap when Lauda first tried to attract the attention of his crew) and his Hesketh now led. After a lengthy tussle that lasted for over 20 laps, Lauda repassed the

OPPOSITE On a beautiful Scandinavian afternoon at Anderstorp, Niki fought his way through to complete a hat trick of victories.

BELOW The best scrap of the year: Niki's Ferrari 312T hounds James Hunt's Hesketh 308 during the late stages of the Dutch Grand Prix in duel that lasted for over 20 laps.

THE STARS ALIGN 171

Frenchman under braking into the *Tarzan* hairpin on lap 43, but the Ferrari's compromised wet/dry settings somewhat handicapped his challenge to the Hesketh, which was on a fully dry set-up. He quickly closed the gap and for the next 20 laps it was then a two-horse race to the flag, the cars running nose-to-tail around the circuit. Lauda exerted huge pressure, making repeated efforts to get on terms, but Hunt resisted manfully and held on to take his first victory by just 1.06 seconds. It had been the race of the season, a magnificent duel.

171 French Grand Prix

Paul Ricard, 7 July 1975, Formula 1
Ferrari 312T/018 (practice only) • #12T
Ferrari 312T/022 • #12
Qualifying: 1st • Result: 1st

Continuing its development programme during untimed practice, Ferrari tried out further revisions to the 312T that involved moving the front suspension rocker arms forward to extend the wheelbase by five inches, an adaptation first seen at Monaco. After only a brief trial run on Friday, Lauda decided there was no time at a race meeting to test such a major modification properly and the car was put back to standard format in case it was needed as a spare. The team also assessed several front wings where the normal endplates were replaced by rocket-shaped versions, with inconclusive results. By now, Lauda's rivals were rather ruefully referring to him as 'World Champion of Testing'.

The Austrian shook off the lingering effects of 'flu and set to work on qualifying. Declaring that it was impossible to set up the car properly for the circuit, he was 7mph off the pace through the speed trap on the *Mistral* straight. Having sandbagged through the first timed session, he set his quickest time late on the second day and it was good enough for pole position, the only man below 1m 48s, four tenths clear of Jody Scheckter's Tyrrell.

He made a storming getaway at the start, braving it out with Scheckter through the first turn. When he crossed the line at the end of the first lap he was almost two seconds in front. By the time James Hunt's rapidly driven Hesketh had got through into second place on lap 8, Lauda had built his advantage to 12 seconds. It was a dominant exhibition and he remained unchallenged throughout the race, although later the Ferrari began to understeer as its front tyres wore down. He drove the 312T only as hard as he needed to, allowing his lead to shrink slowly but controllably as the race reached its conclusion. He crossed the line 1.6 seconds ahead of Hunt, having led all the way.

172 British Grand Prix

Silverstone, 19 July 1975, Formula 1
Ferrari 312T/023 • #12
Qualifying: 3rd • Result: 8th

After spending considerable time trying out different aerofoils during the dry early qualifying sessions, Lauda was caught out when a rainstorm fixed the grid, leaving him third. The Ferraris had not handled well on Silverstone's fast, open sweeps but overnight work by the mechanics helped and he found his car much-improved on full tanks during the warm-up.

The weather was changeable for race day. He

BELOW During first practice at Paul Ricard, Niki tried out several modifications to the 312T, including these unusual rocket-shaped appendages to the front wing.

1975

LEFT Niki utterly dominated the French Grand Prix, his Ferrari 312T comfortably the class of the field despite excessive front tyre wear later in the race.

BELOW The 'Silverstone Aquashow'. In a rain-affected British Grand Prix, Niki kept his car on the road while many others did not.

THE STARS ALIGN 173

held fourth place behind Clay Regazzoni off the start but soon a heavy shower brought a flurry of tyre changes, starting on the 12th lap, and the pack was shuffled. Lauda pitted on lap 23, after his team-mate's pit stop, a troubled one, and found the Ferrari mechanics in disarray. The Austrian's stop was shambolic. A wheel had not been fastened when he was released and fell off within 20 metres, resulting in a scramble to reattach it. He stopped again a lap later for the nut to be tightened properly and rejoined the race a lap down, having lost a precious minute.

Showing stunning speed as the track dried, he was four seconds a lap faster than the rest but then came another deluge and the field was decimated by a series of aquaplaning shunts. The race was red-flagged. Behind Vittorio Brambilla (March) and Emerson Fittipaldi (McLaren), only the two Ferraris and Mario Andretti (Parnelli) actually finished the lap, the last three — all on dry tyres — tiptoeing round in first gear at 10mph. But the official results announced shortly afterwards were based on a count-back lap, which meant that Lauda was classified eighth despite being third across the line, and Fittipaldi was named the winner. Ferrari protested that the stewards had issued the wrong results but to no avail.

173 German Grand Prix

Nürburgring, 3 August 1975, Formula 1
Ferrari 312T/022 • #12
Qualifying: 1st • Result: 3rd

A plague of punctures afflicted the whole weekend but the big story of practice was Lauda becoming the first man to officially lap the 'Ring in under seven minutes, with a 122mph lap right at the end of qualifying. Rain in the first practice session had stopped him from going for the accolade, but with sparks flying from the undertray as the Ferrari landed after the notorious jumps, he completed his record lap to frantic waving from his pit crew and cheers from the grandstands.

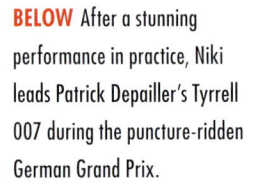

BELOW After a stunning performance in practice, Niki leads Patrick Depailler's Tyrrell 007 during the puncture-ridden German Grand Prix.

1975

He got away perfectly at the start and although troubled by slight understeer he led confidently, well clear of the rest and pushing no harder than necessary. Having carefully avoided debris for several laps from accidents that befell Jochen Mass's McLaren and Jody Scheckter's Tyrrell, he was unlucky when a stone punctured his left-front tyre at *Bergwerk* on lap 10, at about two-thirds distance. With eight miles to travel back to the pits, he drove at 60mph in second gear and had got as far as *Kesselchen* when the tyre delaminated, the flailing rubber destroying the front wing. Struggling to hold the steering wheel because the car was shaking so hard, he could offer no defence as Carlos Reutemann (Brabham), Tom Pryce (Shadow) and Jacques Laffite (Williams) swept by.

He limped into the pits for new tyres and a replacement nose, blasting away after a 19-second stop during which James Hunt (Hesketh) passed as well. One of the McLaren crew suggested that nine mechanics had worked on Lauda's car, which was more than the rules allowed, but no protest was lodged. Hunt's retirement on lap 11 gifted Lauda a place and on lap 13 he passed Pryce, whose car was leaking fuel into its cockpit, for third position. At the flag he was still headed by Reutemann and Laffite, the only drivers not to suffer a puncture that afternoon.

174 Austrian Grand Prix

Österreichring, 17 August 1975, Formula 1
Ferrari 312T/022 • #12
Qualifying: 1st • Result: 6th

Practice began with Lauda renewing his acquaintance with his old employer Kurt Bergmann, who had had the idea of filming his protégé's Ferrari lapping the circuit via a camera mounted to the rear of a Kaimann Formula Super Vee racer driven by Hans Royer. With a chance of clinching the World Championship on home ground, Lauda pushed from the outset and broke his 1974 pole record on the first day of practice.

Race day was wet and the Österreichring was

ABOVE Ahead of the Austrian Grand Prix, Niki and Luca di Montezemolo discuss tactics and what will be needed to secure the World Championship title.

THE STARS ALIGN 175

ABOVE With compromised wet/dry settings on his Ferrari, Niki grapples with the conditions while holding station ahead of team-mate Clay Regazzoni during the rain-shortened Austrian Grand Prix.

gloomy, the more so when Mark Donohue and a track marshal lost their lives after his Penske-entered March suffered a tyre failure. At the start Lauda out-dragged the rest of the grid and was a second clear of everyone at the end of the first lap. He traded fastest laps with James Hunt (Hesketh), but as the weather deteriorated and the track got wetter the Ferrari's handling on semi-wet settings was just not good enough to keep him in front. With his Hesketh carrying more wing, Hunt slipped past on lap 15 and shortly afterwards, in a hair-raising maneouvre, Vittorio Brambilla (March) overtook Niki just as an ambulance took to the track. Next to pass were Jochen Mass (McLaren) on lap 23 and Tom Pryce (Shadow) a lap later after Lauda slid onto the grass at the super-fast *Hella-Licht* curve. The Austrian was not overly concerned: his focus was on Emerson Fittipaldi (McLaren) and Carlos Reutemann (Brabham), his only mathematical rivals for the championship, and he was circulating a second a lap faster than they were. With the rain intensifying and spray reducing visibility almost to fog-like conditions, the race was stopped after 29 laps of the scheduled 54 had been run, with Brambilla the winner. Ronnie Peterson (Lotus) squeezed past the ill-handling Ferrari on lap 29 to leave Lauda sixth, for which he received half a point as the race had not reached two-thirds distance. Had the race been stopped a lap earlier, he would have been crowned World Champion on home ground. As it was, he still needed half a point to be sure.

175 Italian Grand Prix

Monza, 7 September 1975, Formula 1
Ferrari 312T/023 • #12
Qualifying: 1st • Result: 3rd

The 312Ts had revised engines for Monza and from the outset the red cars proved perfectly suited to their home track. Lauda had a trouble-free practice, setting a pole time 0.9 second faster than the previous year's before sitting out most of the short final session. Mindful that Ferrari had not won since France, having failed in Britain, Germany and Austria, he was not complacent. A huge overnight thunderstorm flooded the track and for a while it appeared as if the race might be cancelled, but after the start was postponed until late afternoon it was able to go ahead.

The Ferraris screamed into the lead with Clay Regazzoni in front, just as the two drivers had agreed between themselves before the race, although Lauda had bogged down with wheelspin in any case. Niki had told his pit crew to inform him only of the gap to Carlos Reutemann, the Brabham driver his last remaining championship rival. After only two laps, the Ferraris were 6.5 seconds clear of the pack, drawing away steadily with Lauda content to run second, already with a 16-second advantage over Reutemann. At half distance, though, Lauda started to fall back as a rear damper slowly failed and increasingly severe oversteer gradually set in. An inspired Emerson Fittipaldi steadily reeled in the 10-second gap that had built up and he met with little resistance when he pushed his McLaren past the Austrian at the first chicane with six laps to go. Nevertheless,

176 NIKI LAUDA

ABOVE Championship clinched. Niki steers his Ferrari 312T to a prudent third place in the Italian Grand Prix to take the points needed to assure him of his first World Championship title.

LEFT The victorious Clay Regazzoni and runner-up Emerson Fittipaldi celebrate with the new World Champion and the Ferrari crew on the Monza podium.

THE STARS ALIGN 177

ABOVE Even without his team-mate's intervention, Niki's Ferrari 312T dominated the US Grand Prix at Watkins Glen. Here he tackles the uphill section at the back of the circuit.

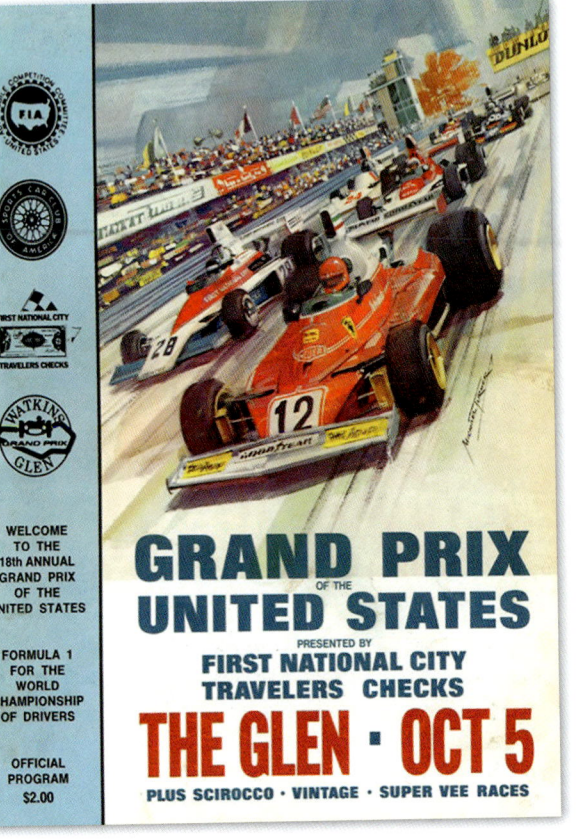

Lauda's third place was enough to secure the World Championship title, with Regazzoni taking the win and Ferrari claiming the Constructors' Championship. It was a day of unbounded joy for the *Tifosi*.

176 United States Grand Prix

Watkins Glen, 5 October 1975, Formula 1
Ferrari 312T/023 • #12
Qualifying: 1st • Result: 1st

For this last round of the World Championship trail, Lauda set the pace in first practice some 1.6 seconds quicker than he had gone in pre-race testing a week earlier even though the engine in his race car was not running properly. Any suggestions that he was receiving preferential equipment were dispelled when he took over the T-car (022) and still lapped quicker than anyone else, and when Clay Regazzoni was also obliged

1975

to use the spare he could not get within a second of Lauda's time in it. Lauda's pole position was his ninth of the year (there were 14 races).

At the start he out-dragged a determined Emerson Fittipaldi into the first corner and the pair ended the opening lap well clear of the pack. However, with his Ferrari heavy on fuel for the long race, the Austrian could not shake off the McLaren driver. On the fifth lap Regazzoni pitted for a new nose and, after he resumed, Lauda and Fittipaldi, still less than a second apart and dicing hard, caught up with him. On lap 18 the Ferrari number two let his team-mate past but then baulked the McLaren blatantly and repeatedly, even though Lauda needed no such assistance because he had the race pretty much under control. Regazzoni's tactics caused the gap between the leading pair to grow to 12 seconds in only four laps and, not surprisingly, the Swiss driver was black-flagged by the stewards. Lauda backed off visibly in the final laps to win by five seconds. It was the Ferrari team's first-ever success in the US Grand Prix, rounding off a satisfying season with the biggest purse of the year.

SUMMARY

The 1975 season had brought fulfilment of the goal that Niki Lauda had set out to achieve once he had recognised he had the necessary talent and commitment.

Having patched up the lapses that had damaged his title challenge the previous year, he had been the best driver in the best car in 1975. Nine pole positions, equalling his 1974 achievement, left no-one in any doubt about the speed of the Lauda/Ferrari combination. Nevertheless, he was not complacent for the forthcoming season.

The decision of his friend and collaborator Luca di Montezemolo to pursue other opportunities within the Fiat group, having completed his job in reorganising the Formula 1 team into a winning outfit, caused Lauda great concern. Earlier in the season he had been able to persuade the aristocratic administrator and Fiat boss Gianni Agnelli that Montezemolo should stay on in his role, only travelling to the races that he enjoyed, but a new regime would be in place for 1976. It would be a different dynamic in many ways.

FIORANO
16 OCTOBER 1975

The new-for-1976 Ferrari 312T2 was formally unveiled to the motoring press at Ferrari's Fiorano test track and a week later Lauda gave the car an initial shakedown test there. The revised car was designed to comply with changed regulations that would come into force at the forthcoming Spanish Grand Prix, including a ban on tall engine airboxes and the use of 'safety structures' around dashboard and pedals.

THE STARS ALIGN 179

1976
THE MORAL VICTORY

The new-for-1976 Ferrari 312T2 had been formally unveiled to the motoring media at Fiorano on 16 October 1975 and a week later Lauda gave the car an initial shakedown test at the factory circuit. Over the winter, Mauro Forghieri tried a number of variants on both the 1975 and 1976 cars in anticipation of forthcoming rule changes, but by January Lauda found that the 312T2 was not showing the same kind of step forward that the 312T had achieved, although he had racked up thousands of miles in it at Fiorano, Mugello and Vallelunga. Forghieri's efforts to wrap the 312T2's mechanicals in a slightly longer but much narrower envelope had disturbed the neutral handling that had characterised the previous car and its lightened monocoque proved counter-effective in getting the tyres to work. Already the Austrian was concerned that the opposition was catching up, prescience that proved to be correct.

The changes in the Ferrari team's management structure were also less than ideal from Lauda's perspective. New team chief Danielle Audetto was a very different personality from Luca di Montezemolo, who as well as being an excellent organiser and motivator had been a friend and ally to Lauda in Ferrari's politically complex world. Lauda later described Audetto as a rather fraught individual, more concerned with his ultimate career ambitions than the detail of a Formula 1 World Championship campaign. The relationship between driver and manager would deteriorate throughout the year, although his working ties with Forghieri remained strong.

1976

177 Brazilian Grand Prix

Interlagos, 25 January 1976, Formula 1
Ferrari 312T/023 • #1
Qualifying: 2nd • Result: 1st

The new Ferrari 312T2s were not taken to the two 'fly-away' races at the start of the season, the team's management agreeing with its lead driver that relying on the proven 312Ts was a more prudent option. Fastest on Friday, Lauda was pipped to pole position on Saturday by just 0.02 second by James Hunt, now firmly installed at McLaren and with his tried and tested M23 entering its fourth season. Niki had been seeking to save his engine and tyres for the race, but was slowed on his hot laps at the end of the session by oil spilled from Ian Ashley's exploded BRM V12 engine.

Come the race, the traditional practice of waving the national flag as the signal to start was replaced by lights changing from red to green, and the inexperienced officials flicked the lights too early. At that moment, many of the drivers towards the back of the grid were still moving, effectively benefiting from a rolling start. From a more conventional getaway, Lauda was passed by team-mate Clay Regazzoni into the first turn, putting the Ferraris 1–2. Niki held second place until lap 9 when, concerned that 'Regga' was not going quickly enough to distance himself from the pursuing Jean-Pierre Jarier (Shadow) and Hunt, he pressured the Swiss driver into running wide

PAUL RICARD AND VALLELUNGA
FEBRUARY 1976

An extended series of tests at Paul Ricard ended on the weekend of 14–15 February with a session exclusively for Ferrari and Goodyear to which a group of French Ferrari enthusiasts had been invited to watch. The work included evaluation of a version of the 312T2 with de Dion rear suspension but Lauda found that the existing suspension gave better stability in fast corners although the new set-up provided a small traction advantage. His keen radar had also noted that McLaren seemed to be developing a closer relationship with Goodyear, a strategy that would pay dividends later in the year, while Ferrari's leverage with the tyre manufacturer appeared to be diminishing. During the season Goodyear would alter its tyres so often that Ferrari was usually having to play catch-up rather than setting the pace by specifying the constructions and compounds it wanted.

After the Paul Ricard sessions, Lauda also completed a comprehensive programme of tests at Vallelunga on revised airbox systems (pictured) for the 312T2. Already it seemed that a huge number of avenues were being explored as the team struggled to find a breakthrough in performance.

LEFT Once in the lead at Interlagos, Niki dominated the race in his Ferrari 312T, starting the new season in much the same way as he had ended the old one, with a resounding victory.

THE MORAL VICTORY

and took the lead, which he soon extended to five seconds. Shortly afterwards, the second Ferrari pitted with a puncture and Lauda was left with a comfortable margin.

As the race progressed in searing heat, Niki slackened off his pace, allowing Jarier's Shadow to close up, but when Hunt's engine blew after 33 laps oil was dropped onto the track at *Curva do Sargento*. The quick-reacting Austrian saw the slick but Jarier did not and slid off into the barriers. Now unchallenged, Lauda reeled off the remaining laps to win from Patrick Depailler's Tyrrell by just over 20 seconds. It was the best possible start to his defence of his World Championship title.

BELOW Niki's Ferrari 312T is readied for qualifying as he waits for the Kyalami pitlane to open. He would secure a position on the front row of the grid.

178 South African Grand Prix

Kyalami, 6 March 1976, Formula 1
Ferrari 312T/023 • #1
Qualifying: 2nd • Result: 1st (fastest lap)

At Kyalami James Hunt again secured pole while Lauda had to settle for second spot, unable to reproduce the times he had achieved when dominant in testing at the circuit a week earlier. He spent much of practice with his 312T trying out the experimental de Dion rear end — as developed for the 312T2 — and found it unstable, but his car was little better in standard format, although a narrower rear track made it slightly quicker in a straight line. He was also delayed when mismatched qualifying tyres were fitted to his car and this no doubt played its part in a row with team manager Daniele Audetto. During race-day warm-up he was troubled by a misfire that necessitated a new distributor.

However, the race brought a hard-won victory. Beating Hunt off the line, he was soon 2.5 seconds clear and thereafter was never headed, despite picking up a slow puncture in the left rear tyre on the 20th lap that caused the car to pull to that side. With 12 laps to go his lead started to shrink dramatically as his brake balance went awry, such that it seemed Hunt would catch him on the last lap and quite probably pass. Luckily, Niki just managed to lap John Watson's Penske and used it as a buffer to keep Hunt 1.3 seconds behind at the flag, but his car was all over the place, with the offending tyre found to have only 2psi pressure left in it when examined post-race.

179 Race of Champions (GB)

Brands Hatch, 14 March 1976, Formula 1
Ferrari 312T2/025 • #1
Qualifying: 2nd • Result: Retired (brake line)

This non-championship race at a mildly revised Brands Hatch — changes included a realignment of the challenging Paddock Hill

182 NIKI LAUDA

ABOVE Jody Scheckter's pole-sitting Tyrrell 007 is swamped as Gunnar Nilsson's Lotus 77 jumps the start of the Race of Champions. Niki's new-for-1976 Ferrari 312T2 leads the pursuit, flanked by the Surtees TS19 of Alan Jones and Jacky Ickx's Williams FW05, the latter for once near the front of the grid.

LONG BEACH
27 MARCH 1976

As part of the pre-race build up at Long Beach, Juan-Manuel Fangio drove his 1955 World Championship-winning Mercedes-Benz W196 (chassis 008-54) in a historic car race that featured a number of other retired Grand Prix drivers reunited with old mounts. Earlier in the day, Lauda also had a try-out in the car, doing a few demonstration laps for the benefit of the Californian spectators. Niki is seen checking the cockpit for size while the maestro himself points out the controls.

THE MORAL VICTORY 183

Bend — provided a pressure-free opportunity for Ferrari to give the new 312T2 its race début, although the team decided against running the much-tested de Dion rear suspension. On the single day of practice, Lauda was third fastest in the morning but improved to second spot in the quicker afternoon session, two seconds adrift of Jody Scheckter's rather suspect pole time in his 1975-specification Tyrrell.

Niki was second at the off behind the fast-starting Lotus of Gunnar Nilsson, who was later penalised 60 seconds for jumping the start. On the first lap he was passed first by the impressive Alan Jones's Surtees and then briefly by a recovering Scheckter, who promptly crashed at Dingle Dell, while Hunt overtook him on lap 2. When Nilsson stopped on lap 8, the leading trio — with Lauda third — circulated close together until lap 17, when the Austrian came into the pits with failing brakes, the result of a fractured rear brake pipe, and had to retire. However, he had been able to race competitively and was now happier about the 312T2's potential.

BELOW Long Beach displays a different kind of street architecture from Monaco as Niki's Ferrari 312T sweeps past *en route* to second place, in his final outing in the championship-winning design.

180 United States Grand Prix (West)

Long Beach, 28 March 1976, Formula 1
Ferrari 312T/023 • #1
Qualifying: 4th • Result: 2nd

Lauda's prediction that the bumpy Long Beach street circuit would be a car-breaker proved accurate. Quickest on the first morning of practice, he lost an engine early on when a cylinder liner failed. A switch to the T-car (022) was soon abandoned when its on-board fire extinguisher exploded and as a result he did not post any significant times for the rest of the day. Come Saturday, he was second fastest in unofficial practice, but wheel-alignment issues and a driveshaft breakage in the crucial final qualifying session left him a somewhat disappointed fourth on the grid, over half a second adrift of team-mate Clay Regazzoni's pole time.

He got away fourth at the start but soon gained two places when James Hunt's McLaren

FIORANO
APRIL 1976

Niki and Enzo Ferrari smile for the camera as Clay Regazzoni takes his turn at the wheel for development testing at a rather cold and wet Fiorano, the revised 312T2 featuring a variation on the large front 'spats' that had been seen on the car at the press launch six months earlier and were also subsequently tried in pre-race testing at Jarama.

collided with Patrick Depailler's Tyrrell at the hairpin on the third lap, putting the Ferraris 1–2. He followed in Regazzoni's wheel tracks as they pulled away from the pack until he flat-spotted his front tyres, creating a strong front-end vibration that caused him to slip back, the gap stabilising at about 12 seconds. With 15 laps to go, he began to fall back further as a very noisy whine from the crown-wheel and pinion presaged its impending failure. He nursed the transmission carefully, holding on to take second place, 42 seconds behind Regazzoni, on a day when finishing at all was an achievement.

181 Spanish Grand Prix

Jarama, 2 May 1976, Formula 1
Ferrari 312T2/025 • #1
Qualifying: 2nd • Result: 2nd

Ferrari finally débuted the 312T2 in a World Championship race, bringing the new cars to Jarama for both Lauda and Clay Regazzoni. Following a tractor accident at his Salzburg home, Niki arrived nursing two broken ribs and there was doubt about his fitness to race. Intensive therapy from Austrian ski coach Willi Dungl and heavy strapping to support his chest enabled him to participate, although whether he could endure a race distance was another matter. He firmly rejected suggestions in the Italian media that he should make way for Formula 2 driver Maurizio Flammini.

Further to work at Fiorano, more tweaks to the new car tried in practice included low-set air scoops ahead of the rear axle. There was also further evaluation of the de Dion rear suspension, which Lauda described as 'good, but not better'; despite extensive testing of it, he was never convinced that this suspension system brought any worthwhile benefit over the conventional version. His injured ribs did not stop him putting in a lot of laps and he managed a very quick time in the first session; to help reduce his discomfort, a new seat was made up

ABOVE The Spanish Grand Prix at Jarama distilled into a Hunt/Lauda duel for the first 30 laps, until Niki's broken ribs took one blow too many from the high kerbs and he was forced to concede to the Englishman.

OPPOSITE A forest of catch fencing surrounds the Zolder circuit as Niki's heavily modified Ferrari 312T, wearing 312T2 bodywork and an unusual cockpit surround, picks its way through a chicane during practice for the Belgian Grand Prix.

for that afternoon's practice but it did not help much. He did very well to qualify on the front row, 0.32 second behind James Hunt's pole-sitting McLaren.

As at Kyalami, he got a better start than Hunt and won the drag race to the first corner. Although he led for 30 laps, he was plainly beginning to tire from his injuries. When Hunt finally pulled alongside on lap 32 he was forced to run over a kerb, jarring his damaged ribs, and he slowed noticeably. This allowed Jochen Mass's McLaren to get ahead three laps later, but when the German's Cosworth engine blew up 10 laps from the end Lauda regained second place and remained there.

After the race, looking paler than usual, he had already left the circuit when the stewards announced Hunt's disqualification as his McLaren was found to be 18mm too wide, so the Austrian was declared the winner. The decision was overturned by an FIA tribunal some two months later and Hunt's victory was reinstated.

182 Belgian Grand Prix

Zolder, 14 May 1976, Formula 1
Ferrari 312T2/026 • #1
Qualifying: 1st • Result: 1st (fastest lap)

Hoping that the combination of pain-killing injections, electric-shock treatment and a surgical corset would get his broken ribs through the weekend, Lauda was quietly confident, declaring himself 90 per cent fit and brushing aside Daniele Audetto's suggestion that he should let Clay Regazzoni win for a change. After the engine in his race car (026) swallowed the wire mesh covering of an inlet trumpet in first practice, for the rest of this session and the whole of the second he had to switch to the spare (023), a 312T, strikes in Italy having put production of the third 312T2 two races behind schedule. Nevertheless, this 312T had been uprated to new specifications — as required by rule changes — and wore

1976

FIORANO
MAY 1976

Motivated by a Ferrari 308 GT4 that the North American Racing Team (NART) had unsuccessfuly attempted to qualify for the Le Mans 24 Hours in 1975, engineer Gaetano Florini obtained Enzo Ferrari's approval to build a Group 4 version of the new 308 GTB production model to contest high-profile international events including the Targa Florio and Le Mans. With Ferrari's racing department focused on Formula 1 and too busy for such a project, a prototype 308 GTB4 LM (chassis 22711) was instead built at Ferrari's Assistenza Clienti customer operation and testing was undertaken at Fiorano.

Some of this testing was conducted by Lauda to take advantage of his sports and touring car experience in developing the car's set-up. However, the 308 GTB4 LM was ultimately never raced, probably because of restrictions by Fiat on Ferrari's competition activity. The car reappeared briefly in September 1976 in Group 5 'silhouette' guise, amid uncertainty created by Enzo Ferrari's threat that his team was going to quit Formula 1.

the recently modified 312T2 bodywork that featured a small but distinctive alteration to the cockpit surround-cum-airbox. He found that the old car suffered from understeer, which was put down to the difference in weight distribution between the 312T and 312T2 allied with the updated aerodynamics. Once back in the 312T2, with fresh engine installed, he was one of only two men to improve his time on Saturday, putting himself smoothly and calmly on pole again.

He won a frantic, four-abreast start and after a settling-in lap he started to draw away from James Hunt's McLaren at 1.5 seconds a lap in a demonstration that seasoned journalist Denis Jenkinson observed was reminiscent of Alberto Ascari in the 1950s. Regazzoni got though into second place after six laps and thereafter they ran about six seconds apart, well clear of the rest. It was another Ferrari benefit: other than a brief moment on lap 50, when his car suddenly stepped sideways on unseen oil, Niki cruised

THE MORAL VICTORY 187

ABOVE At the start of the Belgian Grand Prix, Niki's Ferrari 312T2 blasts into an immediate lead with the McLaren M23 of James Hunt tucked under his rear wing. Behind them the pursuing pack is headed by Clay Regazzoni's sister Ferrari, the Ligier JS5 of Jacques Laffite, Patrick Depailler's Tyrrell P34 and Vittorio Brambilla's March 761.

OPPOSITE TOP Niki's Ferrari 312T2 sweeps along the Monaco harbour front on the way to a dominant victory.

untroubled to the finish. Fastest lap completed a flawless performance for his fourth win of the year, with any lingering doubts as to whether he was fit enough and could stand the pace now comprehensively dispelled.

183 Monaco Grand Prix

Monte Carlo, 30 May 1976, Formula 1
Ferrari 312T2/026 • #1
Qualifying: 1st • Result: 1st

After being out-paced by the six-wheeled Tyrrells of Jody Scheckter and Patrick Depailler on the first day and switching to Clay Regazzoni's former chassis after his allocated 025 broke its engine in practice, Lauda was in a class of his own on Saturday. He finished qualifying a good half-hour early to watch the others trying unsuccessfully to challenge his pole time. Determined to be on his best form for the race, he attended the traditional drivers' party on Saturday evening only briefly, leaving after eight minutes.

After another superb start, he led away and drove forcefully while remaining neat and tidy, pulling away from Ronnie Peterson's second-placed March by a second a lap. While others — including Regazzoni and Peterson — fell foul of the oil slick that James Hunt's exploding engine dropped on lap 24 between the chicane and *Tabac*, he negotiated the hazard with barely a lift. He was also unaffected by a brief rain shower just after half distance. Even his passage through the backmarkers was a breeze, in contrast to that of his pursuers who had to scrabble their way past. Although he gave himself a brief scare when he missed a gear going through Casino Square with 15 laps remaining, he was otherwise untroubled on his way to victory. It was as dominant a win as any the Austrian would have in his career, with the Tyrrells of Scheckter and Depailler the only cars on the same lap at the finish.

Six races into the season, Lauda had

produced a series of stunning performances to achieve five wins and one second place, although one of those wins — Jarama — was soon to be handed back to Hunt. In the World Championship standings, he now led his nearest challenger, Hunt, by the enormous margin of 48 points to 15, figures that include the Jarama adjustments.

184 'Race for Friuli' (I)

Varano, 2 June 1976, Group 1
Fiat 131 Abarth (with Giancarlo Martini) • #2
Qualifying: 1st • Result: 4th (Race 1, 2nd; Race 2, 4th)

After a catastrophic earthquake struck Friuli in north-east Italy on 6 May 1976, causing the deaths of over 1,000 people, the weekly magazine *Autosprint* organised a charity 'Race for Friuli' day at the little Varano circuit. Involving various Formula 1 drivers, the exercise had the specific aim of raising funds to rebuild the school in the village of Lusevera, and Enzo

FIORANO
MAY 1976

Lauda experimented with a 312T2 (either 025 or 027) equipped with a 'dead' front axle akin to the rear-end de Dion arrangement that he had tried several times since the car's inception, but the set-up — seen in this fuzzy 'spy shot' — was soon discarded as it gave no steering feel. The development chassis was also fitted with modified bodywork that had been seen in practice at Zolder and would appear again at the Nürburgring, although this does not seem to have been the principal focus of the test.

ABOVE Niki's Fiat 131 Mirafiori (nearest the camera) lines up at the little Varano circuit for his event at the 'Race for Friuli' charity meeting, which raised funds to rebuild a village school following a devastating earthquake in north-east Italy.

Ferrari, who very rarely left Maranello, was in attendance. Among a number of contests, Lauda competed with Giancarlo Martini in a two-part race involving four driver pairings in identical Abarth-tuned Fiat 131 Mirafiori saloon cars. After his engine expired during practice, Lauda decided that he preferred Clay Regazzoni's car, so swapped mounts with his Formula 1 team-mate. It made little difference.

On lap 2 of the first race, Regazzoni passed Lauda for second place at the *Parabolica*, and then the Austrian lost further ground two laps later with a spin at the same corner. Mr Ferrari was reportedly unimpressed. When an inspired Roberto Cambiaghi forced his way past Regazzoni to take the lead, Lauda followed him through and kept his second place to the flag. Martini took over for the second race and challenged Giorgio Pianta for the lead — and the possibility of victory on aggregate. However, a deflating tyre caused Martini to spin at the Esses and he dropped to fourth place. Instead of winning outright on aggregate, the pair finished fourth and last.

185 Swedish Grand Prix

Anderstorp, 13 June 1976, Formula 1
Ferrari 312T2/026 • #1
Qualifying: 5th • Result: 3rd

This time Anderstorp did not suit the Ferraris, Mauro Forghieri blaming the lack of form on the truncation of a Mugello test session by his drivers' attendance at the Varano charity day. The team tried bulbous-shaped wing endplates in first practice in an attempt to improve handling. Although fastest in the first session, Lauda then found that the available tyre options gave either excessive oversteer or excessive understeer, and he had a tired engine that was due to be changed for the race. After a frantic final hour of qualifying, he ended up on the third row of the grid.

Out-dragged off the line by Gunnar Nilsson's Lotus, he completed the first lap in sixth place and held that position until the Swede crashed out on lap 4. Driving as hard as he could, he circulated alone but gained places when Chris

Amon's Ensign spun out (lap 39) and the engine in race leader Mario Andretti's Lotus blew up (lap 46). That left him third behind the on-form six-wheeled Tyrrells of Jody Scheckter and Patrick Depailler, but, try as he might, he was unable to make any impression on them, troubled by inconsistent handling and low tyre temperatures. He finished a lonely 33 seconds behind Scheckter and 14 adrift of Depailler.

186 French Grand Prix

Paul Ricard, 4 July 1976, Formula 1
Ferrari 312T2/026 • #1
Qualifying: 2nd • Result: Retired (engine) (fastest lap)

Recovering from the 'flu, Lauda struggled to achieve a satisfactory balance in first practice. During that session the three Ferraris

ABOVE In 1976 Anderstorp was not a happy hunting ground for Niki, seen passing light aircraft lined up along the landing strip that doubled as the circuit's back straight. His third place owed as much to the retirements of others as it did to his own progress.

LEFT Air-deflecting spats moulded with the front brake ducts, as seen at the Maranello launch of the Ferrari 312T2 the previous autumn, appeared on the cars in first practice at Paul Ricard but were then banned on the grounds that they were 'movable aerodynamic devices'.

were fitted with glass-fibre deflectors ahead of the front wheels, very similar to those seen at the original press launch. Moulded with integral air scoops for the front brakes, they turned with the wheels and therefore the scrutineers deemed them to be 'movable aerodynamic devices', so they had to be removed before the second practice session and the normal brake ducts put back — and the Ferrari times set in the first session were disallowed. Niki also briefly tried the de Dion rear suspension again on the spare (025) but had the car returned to the conventional set-up in case it was needed later. Second practice was run in faster conditions and despite an engine failure he duly lined up second on the grid alongside James Hunt's McLaren, although his new engine was emitting oil that left worrying streaks on the cowling.

Lauda got away first at the start and was the clear leader at the end of the opening lap, but despite pulling away at a second a lap the Ferrari was already leaving a slight vapour trail. While holding an eight-second lead as he blasted down the *Mistral* straight at full speed on lap 9, the crankshaft broke without warning and the engine seized, locking the rear wheels. He managed to disengage the clutch and keep the car on the road, but it was a scary moment. He coasted to a halt to record his first retirement of the year — and, in fact, his first non-finish in 18 Grands Prix.

The following morning, Hunt's Jarama disqualification was overturned by the FIA — Lauda had lost two races in as many days. Nevertheless, his lead in the World Championship remained considerable, for Hunt's score, 26 points, was only half of Lauda's 52.

187 British Grand Prix

Brands Hatch, 18 July 1976, Formula 1
Ferrari 312T2/028 • #1
Qualifying: 1st • Result: 1st (fastest lap)

Lauda spent first practice sorting out new-car niggles on the latest chassis (028) and tried the spare (026) during the untimed session on Saturday morning, but found no great difference.

BELOW A haze of smoke and dust rises from the grid as Niki's Ferrari powers away at the start of the French Grand Prix with James Hunt's McLaren M23 tucked behind him, while Ronnie Peterson's March 761 takes a wide line. Lauda was holding a commanding lead when his engine failed dramatically.

ABOVE Paddock Hill Bend, British Grand Prix, lap 1; Clay Regazzoni's Ferrari has just tangled with Niki's sister car and is about to tip James Hunt's McLaren onto two wheels, breaking its steering. Mario Andretti's Lotus 77 and Chris Amon's Ensign N176 take avoiding action, while the Tyrrell P34s of Patrick Depailler and Jody Scheckter, Ronnie Peterson's March 761, Jacques Laffite's Ligier JS5 and John Watson's Penske PC3 are looking for a way through the carnage.

LEFT Lauda v Hunt again; Niki led for 45 laps this time until gear-selection difficulties allowed the McLaren to get ahead.

THE MORAL VICTORY 193

ÖSTERREICHRING
LATE JULY 1976

Testing for Ferrari between races was even more intense during the 1976 season than in previous years. Here during a private session at the Österreichring a week before the German Grand Prix, his Ferrari 312T2 wears experimental bodywork and the illegal air-deflector brake ducts as it sweeps around the *Texaco Schikane* section of Niki's home circuit. In the second photo, Niki looks unusually hot and dishevelled, while in the background Mauro Forghieri intently studies his set-up sheets.

He waited patiently for a clear slot in the afternoon and comfortably claimed pole position.

Choosing to start from the left (the 'uphill' side of the grid) and this time being allowed to do so, Lauda made a superb getaway as James Hunt was slow off the line, but when Clay Regazzoni braked too late while trying to tuck inside at Paddock Hill Bend, the two Ferraris collided. The Swiss spun into the path of Hunt's McLaren, pitching it onto two wheels and leaving them both *hors de combat*, the McLaren with a broken steering arm, while Lauda continued unhindered. An over-cautious RAC official ordered that the race should be red-flagged at the end of the lap because of debris on the track.

Spectators voiced their discontent noisily when they learned that, according to the rules, those not running when the red flag was shown could not restart in their spare cars. Worried, the officials relented and the race was restarted with all the original runners on the grid, leaving the arguments for later; as it turned out, the McLaren mechanics were in any case able to repair Hunt's car during the long interval.

Within 10 laps of the restart, Lauda and Hunt were clear of the rest, the Austrian edging away as they traded fastest laps. But by half distance he was losing ground, his gearshift starting to seize, so he stayed in fourth gear and relied on the Ferrari's torque and his own ability to keep his lap times competitive. This was exhausting for him as his broken ribs were still not fully healed, but he maintained his lead until he started to lap backmarkers, whereupon the troublesome gearshift made overtaking very difficult. Within two laps Hunt was able to close up again and, on lap 45, the McLaren squeezed past under braking at Druids and pulled away comfortably. Unable to respond, Lauda was well ahead of third-placed Jody Scheckter's Tyrrell so he eased off and nursed the car (and himself) to the finish.

Protests were lodged by the Ferrari, Tyrrell and Fittipaldi teams almost as soon as the chequered flag fell. These were initially rejected by the British stewards but when an appeal was heard by an FIA tribunal, in September, Hunt was disqualified and Lauda was awarded victory.

188 German Grand Prix

Nürburgring, 1 August 1976, Formula 1
Ferrari 312T2/028 • #1
Qualifying: 2nd • Result: Retired (accident)

Despite publicly opposing the dangers of the *Nordschleife* in common with most other drivers, Lauda rose above personal feelings about the Nürburgring, where he had produced so many stirring drives in the past. He showed his character by setting fastest time in first practice but during the afternoon Hunt was slightly quicker. Reporting that his car was oversteering and difficult to drive on its supposedly puncture-resistant tyres, Lauda again tried the new bodywork on his race chassis but found no noticeable benefit, while revised camber and damper settings for the second session actually made things worse. Heavy rain during final practice meant the grid was decided on Friday's

ABOVE Whatever his misgivings about the Nürburgring circuit's safety standards, no-one could question Niki's commitment. Here in qualifying his Ferrari 312T2 is fully airborne at *Brünnchen* as he powers his way towards second place on the grid.

THE MORAL VICTORY

ABOVE The wreckage of Niki's Ferrari 312T2/028 is returned to the pits after his huge accident on lap 2 of the German Grand Prix. The Austrian had described the consequences of a major crash at the Nürburgring as 'one hundred per cent death' — he was so nearly correct.

times and made it impossible to test the set-up changes he had made, so he had to start the race in what was effectively a strange car.

In changeable conditions on race day, Lauda started on rain tyres, like everyone else except for Jochen Mass (McLaren). With too much wheelspin leaving the grid, he was swamped by the pack at the start, holding ninth place into the *Südkehre* but improving to seventh during the first lap. When he pitted for slicks at the end of the lap, he was delayed by a queue in the pitlane and his stop was slow.

On Niki's second lap, grappling with slow backmarkers still on wet tyres and troubled by handling deficiencies on his cold Goodyears, the Ferrari snapped out of control — probably because of a suspension failure — at the flat-in-fifth curve before *Bergwerk*. It plunged through two layers of catch fencing into the earth bank and exploded in flames as it rebounded onto the track. Guy Edwards (Hesketh) managed to avoid the burning car but Brett Lunger (Surtees) and Harald Ertl (Hesketh) hit it, and Arturo Merzario (Wolf Williams) quickly arrived at the scene. These four drivers were Lauda's saviours.

Merzario climbed onto the blazing Ferrari and managed to unfasten its stricken driver's belts and pull him clear. Lauda's helmet and fireproof balaclava had been ripped off by a catch-fencing pole and it was obvious to his rescuers that he had been badly burned.

Worse became apparent when he arrived at Mannheim hospital. He had inhaled toxic fumes from the car's burning bodywork and his chances of survival appeared slim. He remained in the hospital's intensive-care unit for four days, his life hanging in the balance.

His home race, the Austrian Grand Prix on 15 August, came and went without him. Ferrari withdrew its entries in the absence of its lead driver, using the political bickering that had

FIORANO
7 SEPTEMBER 1976

Just over five weeks after the crash, Lauda climbed back into a Ferrari cockpit at Fiorano to find out if he could, as he bluntly put it, 'still drive an F1 car'. Although he had asked for this first test to be completely private so that he could acclimatise in peace and quiet, the media had stirred up a frenzy and the reality could not have been more different, the police having difficulty controlling the thousands of fans who turned up the Fiorano gates. Although Lauda's smile for the camera in this photo belies it, he was irritated by the media circus and the atmosphere was joyless as he prepared for the test.

Willi Dungl had made a special surgical fitting that allowed him to wear a helmet over his bandaged wounds and after he completed a sequence of laps, each progressively nearer to the record, he made a longer run of 20 laps. Although the car was the old testing chassis (026) with a tired engine, it was clear to the Austrian that his ability to drive was still there and the speed had come naturally.

pervaded Formula 1 throughout the year as the excuse. Team manager Daniele Audetto even encouraged several Austrian journalists to lobby the Österreichring organisers to cancel the race, which John Watson won for Penske. A few days later the remarkable Lauda discharged himself from hospital to recuperate at home in Salzburg with his wife Marlene, whom he had married earlier in the year. By now he was talking about making his return at the Canadian Grand Prix.

For the Dutch Grand Prix at Zandvoort on 29 August, a single Ferrari appeared for Clay Regazzoni in an effort to protect Niki's position in the World Championship, although several well-informed observers noted that the consistent half-second advantage that Lauda had displayed over his team-mate during the season, coupled with the stronger performance of the 312T2 at Zandvoort, meant that the Austrian would probably have prevailed over Hunt's winning but hobbled McLaren.

189 Italian Grand Prix

Monza, 12 September 1976, Formula 1
Ferrari 312T2/026 • #1
Qualifying: 5th • Result: 4th

Having missed only two Grands Prix, Lauda returned, incredibly, at Monza — one race earlier than his stated target — ready to go racing. He would later admit to feeling fear in the wet conditions of first practice but, having thought things through that evening, he rationalised that he was trying too hard and simply needed to get back in the car and drive without looking at his lap times or those of his competitors.

Busying himself trying out a new tri-plane rear wing, he took things more steadily, going progressively faster and faster. His qualifying performance, fifth on the grid and fastest of three Ferrari entries, astounded his team and his rivals. As much as anything, he had been motivated by

THE MORAL VICTORY

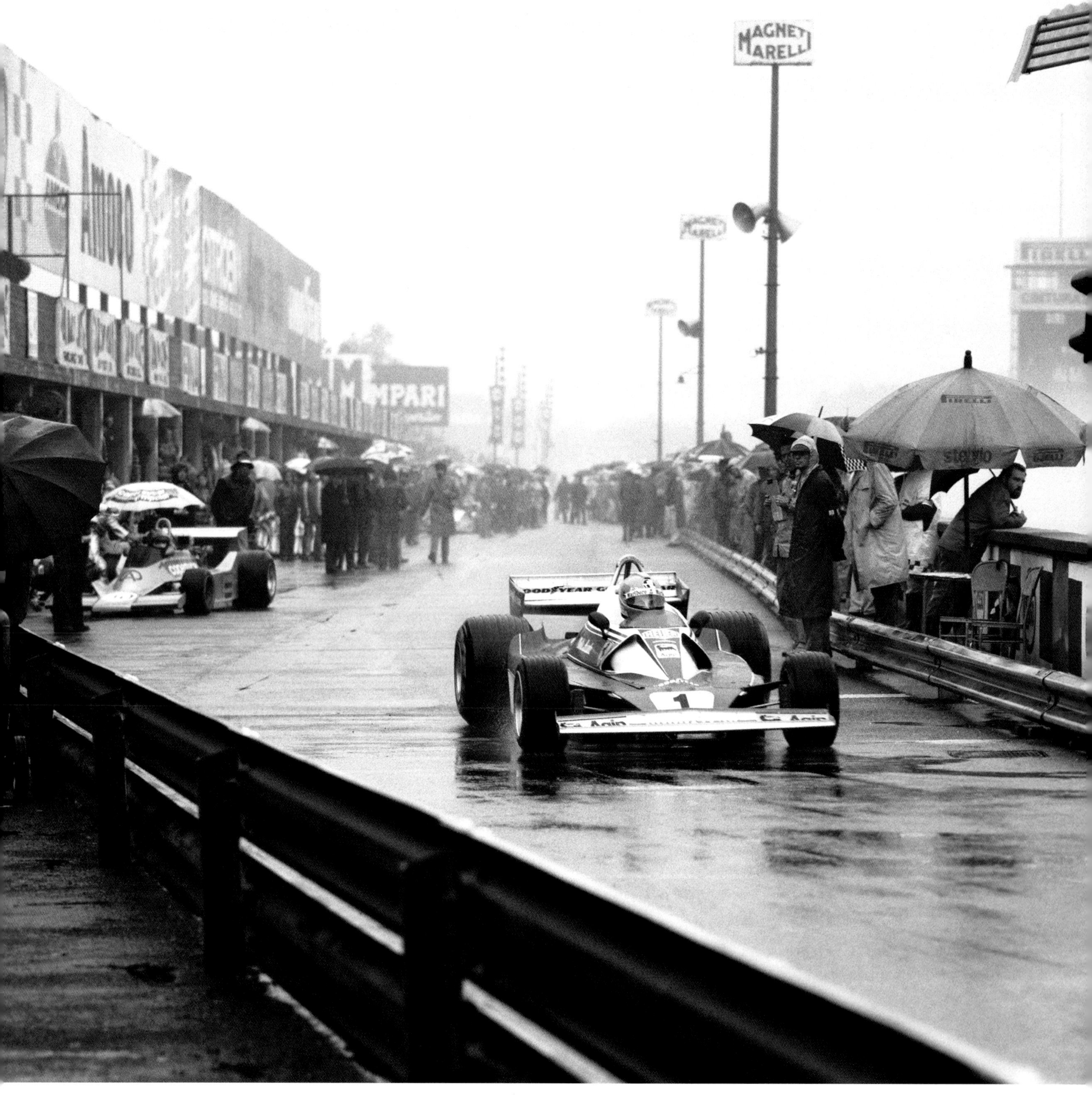
MAGNETI
MARELLI
Amoco
MPARI
GOODYEAR

1976

LEFT It is easy to see why Niki said he was terrified in first practice at Monza as he heads out for his initial exploratory laps; the pitlane is blanketed in dankness and gloom while the track disappears in a wall of spray.

anger at Enzo Ferrari's suggestion that he should become team manager rather than drive again and by the arrival of Carlos Reutemann from Brabham as supposed number one. He was just 0.74 second adrift of pole position, claimed by Jacques Laffite (Ligier), and quicker than his team-mates, seventh-placed Reutemann and ninth-placed Regazzoni, respectively by 0.29 second and 0.87 second.

Like several others, he was caught out at the start, with the car still in neutral when the green light flashed while he was watching the 10-second board; the team had forgotten to tell him that for this race the traditional flag had been replaced by an electronic system. As a result, he completed the first lap 12th, but then gradually worked his way forwards, deposing 'replacement' Reutemann on lap 8. His relentless progress took him past Vittorio Brambilla's March for sixth place on lap 14, to roars from the crowd. He kept up the pressure and by lap 42 he had caught and passed Jody Scheckter's down-on-power Tyrrell for fifth, which became fourth as Patrick Depailler's sister car fell back. Despite flickering oil pressure, he held fastest lap until three laps from the end,

ABOVE Absorbed in thought, Lauda put in a remarkable effort to out-qualify both of his Ferrari team-mates on his return to racing at the Italian Grand Prix.

THE MORAL VICTORY

ABOVE Niki gets a push-start from the Ferrari crew as he heads out to the Monza grid for his comeback race. The packed spectators on the pit roof are about to witness a great moment in sporting history.

when Ronnie Peterson (March) finally bettered it. On the last lap Scheckter closed up as Lauda's engine faltered coming out of the *Vialone* chicane, but his fourth place was secure and he led the South African over the finish line by 0.1 second.

His stunning and courageous drive would go down in history as one of the greatest-ever sporting comebacks. Afterwards, as he removed his helmet and blood-stained balaclava in the pits, the enormity of his achievement was still more inspiring.

190 Canadian Grand Prix

Mosport, 3 October 1976, Formula 1
Ferrari 312T2/026 • #1
Qualifying: 6th • Result: 8th

Lauda was forced to recuperate after his exertions at Monza, so with no pre-race testing at Mosport he spent Friday practice somewhat under his limit. Struggling to sort out the car over the track's bumps and ripples, he admitted that he was not driving well. His car's oil cooler had to be repositioned after the stewards ruled that it was mounted too far back. Despite reservations about the circuit's poor safety arrangements, in Saturday qualifying he hurled the 312T2 round, improving sufficiently to take sixth position on the grid even though the Ferrari lacked traction in the bitterly cold conditions, understeered in slow corners and locked its suspension over the bumps.

At the start of the race he got away seventh and eased past the Marches of Vittorio Brambilla and Hans Stuck in the early laps to gain fifth, but this was as high as he got. Running alone from half distance, he gradually lost ground; one of the new top links in the rear suspension had failed on the right-hand side and the car began to oversteer very badly. Understandably cautious of any potential chassis fault after his still-unexplained Nürburgring accident, he eased off markedly and fell back to eighth. Although he had driven a perfectly clean race, he scored no points.

191 United States Grand Prix (East)

Watkins Glen, 10 October 1976, Formula 1
Ferrari 312T2/026 • #1
Qualifying: 5th • Result: 3rd

At Watkins Glen, Lauda was worried about just how much Ferrari's development programme had lagged during his absence, and with some justification. Having initially traded fastest laps with James Hunt in the damp first practice, Lauda qualified a disgruntled fifth; the Italian team's lack of tyre testing showed up starkly as the 312T2 was just not suited to the stiffer constructions that Goodyear had introduced at Brands Hatch and provided since then. He was far from happy with the behaviour of his car and could be seen in agitated discussion with both engineer Mauro Forghieri and team manager Daniele Audetto.

When the race started, he put aside his frustrations, holding his grid position at the head of a queue to quickly dispose of Ronnie Peterson's March on lap 4. Forcing his way past Vittorio Brambilla's untidily driven March a lap later, he took third place with a clear track in front of him, but that was as good as it got. The gap to second-placed Hunt remained around three seconds for the first half of the race, but then began to widen. With the Ferrari held back by terrible oversteer as its fuel load lightened and the tyres cooled, Niki could do nothing but watch from a distance as his World Championship points margin dwindled, especially after Hunt passed Jody Scheckter's Tyrrell to take the lead. Almost a minute behind Scheckter by the end, he even had to make a resolute defence against Jochen Mass's McLaren to retain third place in the final laps.

Before the fateful German Grand Prix, Lauda had been 35 points ahead in the World

ABOVE His Ferrari 312T2 handling poorly, Niki traverses the patched and bumpy Mosport Park track as he heads for eighth place (and no points) in the Canadian Grand Prix.

BELOW A solid third place was the most that Niki could wring from the Ferrari 312T2 at Watkins Glen. Lack of chassis development and tyre evolution that favoured his rivals meant the car that had dominated the first half of the season was now very much second best.

THE MORAL VICTORY **201**

Championship standings, but Hunt had eaten away at that massive advantage with four wins — at the Nürburgring, Zandvoort, Mosport Park and here at Watkins Glen — plus fourth place at the Österriechring. Now, going into the final race, in Japan, Lauda's points lead was just three.

192 Japanese Grand Prix

Fuji, 24 October 1976, Formula 1
Ferrari 312T2/023 • #1
Qualifying: 3rd • Result: Retired (withdrew)

Had this been a 'normal' season, the World Championship would have ended in the United States, but an extra race had been awarded to Japan, where national hopes for a quiet initiation into Formula 1 were far from fulfilled. Practice started under a bad-tempered cloud when Ferrari accused McLaren of reneging on a pre-race agreement not to test at Fuji ahead of the race, although Lauda distanced himself from the politicking. Using a revised front suspension set-up that changed his car's behaviour, if not its speed, he was second to James Hunt in first practice, both benefiting from new sticky tyres provided by Goodyear in response to the super-soft Dunlops fitted to

ABOVE Debating whether or not the Fuji race should go ahead in torrential rain, James Hunt appears calm and confident, Niki pensive and calculating. With them, Ronnie Peterson (back to the camera) makes an animated point to FOCA (and Brabham) boss Bernie Ecclestone, who is keen to get things underway to satisfy the television schedules.

BELOW In the monsoon conditions of the race at Fuji, Lauda's Ferrari throws up spray as he heads down the straight. Two laps into the race he had seen enough and withdrew.

202 NIKI LAUDA

1976

Masahiro Hasemi's Kojima. When Mario Andretti (Lotus) snatched a late pole position, Lauda ended up third on the grid, with worsening understeer caused by tyre issues that led him to spin uncharacteristically in the second session.

Sunday brought an unrelenting deluge and after a long-running argument over whether the race should be run or abandoned — with the drivers split 50/50 on the matter — it started one and a half hours late in swirling mist and darkening conditions. Lost in the ball of spray as he fluffed his start, Lauda quickly dropped back to 10th by the end of the first lap. A lap later he pulled into the pits and climbed out of the car to retire. He made no excuses, simply declaring that the conditions were murderous and he was not prepared to race. Years later it was revealed that he was unable to blink his burned eyelids, so was driving blind. It was possibly the most courageous decision he ever made.

SUMMARY

Until the Nürburgring accident, Lauda had dominated the year, taking five wins from the nine races that preceded the German Grand Prix and looking almost certain to become World Champion again. But his withdrawal from the Japanese Grand Prix handed the initiative to Hunt, who needed four points to become World Champion and duly finished in the third place required to do that.

But Lauda's greatest achievement in 1976, of course, had been to survive.

Enzo Ferrari was unhappy with his driver's decision to return and attempt to defend his title, believing that an honourable defeat as an injured warrior would have been preferable. As ever in motor racing, a team soon moves on and, while Lauda was hospitalised, Daniele Audetto had approached both Emerson Fittipaldi and Ronnie Peterson to enquire if they were interested in taking his seat, before turning to Carlos Reutemann. Forghieri later maintained that Reutemann had been hired to take points off Lauda's rivals and help protect his championship lead, although it seems that this motive had not been communicated to the Austrian. Nevertheless, Niki denied German radio reports of a rift with the *Commendatore* and confirmed that he was staying with Ferrari for 1977.

ABOVE Brushing aside suggestions from his crew that a mechanical reason for his retirement could be fabricated, Niki explains his decision to withdraw. For him, the conditions were unacceptably dangerous and his life was worth more than the World Championship.

THE MORAL VICTORY

1977
THE PHOENIX RISES

Having roundly dismissed Enzo Ferrari's suggestion that he should become team manager rather than return to the cockpit after the Nürburgring accident, Lauda was faced with another change in the Scuderia's hierarchy when Daniele Audetto was replaced by Roberto Nosetto as team manager. Nosetto was a long-serving Ferrari administrator with an intensely superstitious nature and in consequence the pragmatic Austrian had little time for him. Fortunately for Lauda, the practical and reliable Sante Ghedini remained as team co-ordinator, giving him at least one friend in the camp.

There was also a change of team-mate, with Carlos Reutemann confirmed for the year and Clay Regazzoni, who had become increasingly outclassed by Lauda, moving on to Ensign.

Initial tests of the Ferrari 312T2 in its 1977 configuration failed to fill Lauda with confidence as the car was already displaying the handling vagaries that would bedevil it throughout the season ahead. The main issue was tyres: Goodyear was focusing on developing constructions to suit the new ground-effect Lotus 78 and, with Ferrari widely known to be courting Michelin (the team would make the switch for 1978), it was no surprise that the Akron manufacturer was looking to the future.

Niki also found himself pointedly left out of Ferrari's winter testing programme. This was a snub from Enzo Ferrari for going against his wishes, and entirely typical of his Machiavellian 'divide and rule' philosophy, but it was totally counter-productive as far as development of the cars was concerned. Gifted though Reutemann was on his day, he was not in Lauda's class as a development driver and his driving style favoured rather different set-ups from the Austrian's preferences. The result of all this was that the 312T2s appeared at Buenos Aires in virtually the same trim as at the end of the previous season.

1977

193 Argentine Grand Prix

Buenos Aires, 9 January 1977, Formula 1
Ferrari 312T2/026 • #11
Qualifying: 4th • Result: Retired (fuel metering unit)

Visibly struggling in practice to wring a decent time out of the Ferrari, Lauda was having to run so much wing to get improved rear adhesion that the car's straight-line speed was only middling. He tried the spare (027) but found this no better. The misfiring, vibrating 312T2 was destroying soft tyres and sliding on hard ones; on Friday he slithered off after an uncharacteristic spin at the tight left-hander behind the paddock. A frantic final effort saw him drag the car up to fourth on the grid, settling the first round of the intra-team rivalry with Carlos Reutemann in his favour as the Argentine driver was two rows further back.

Forcing his way between the front-row starters, James Hunt's McLaren and John Watson's Brabham, he almost overtook Hunt for second place at the first corner but had to settle for third. Gradually he slipped behind first Jochen Mass's McLaren and then Carlos Pace's Brabham, the Brazilian passing him with ease. It was obvious that the Ferrari's misfiring engine was in bad shape and by lap 20 the whole car was vibrating so badly that he pitted to see if anything could be done. The problem was traced to the fuel metering unit, which could not be repaired or replaced, so he retired.

194 Brazilian Grand Prix

Interlagos, 23 January 1977, Formula 1
Ferrari 312T2/026 • #11
Qualifying: 13th • Result: 3rd

Lauda continued to fight with the recalcitrant 312T2, winding up eighth fastest at the end of the first day after dashing in and out of the pits for numerous adjustments to the front and rear suspension settings. More disgruntled on

ABOVE The Ferraris were nowhere near the pace at Buenos Aires and Niki's unhappy weekend ended in retirement after only 20 laps. For the 1977 season the cars now carried Fiat identity.

THE PHOENIX RISES

the second day as he did not get to try out a new rear wing that his new team-mate Carlos Reutemann had used (and was later found to be 4cm too high), he was relegated to the spare car (027) when a fuel bag leaked into the cockpit during the crucial final session. Whereas Reutemann qualified second, Niki was only 13th, having failed to improve on his Friday time; this was his worst qualifying position since his BRM days.

Discovering that his car's ride height had been changed without his knowledge, he used the warm-up to get the Ferrari into more balanced trim and things were better for the race. He made up places in the early laps after Vittorio Brambilla (March) and Carlos Pace (Brabham) both spun off at the double left-hander at the bottom of the hill after the pits, a corner that had been resurfaced and was now like black ice for those who strayed off-line. He avoided the wreckage and set about Emerson Fittipaldi's eponymous car, pressuring the Brazilian double champion into an error and getting past on lap 11. Recognising that there was no point in having a futile battle with James Hunt, who had taken on new tyres on lap 25, he waved the Englishman's McLaren by and continued at his own pace. He gained more places when John Watson's Brabham hit the wall at Turn 3 and when the perennially unlucky Tom Pryce retired with a blown engine with seven laps to go. He finished a distant third, almost two minutes behind the winner — his team-mate.

Frustrated at the team's lack of progress in the first two races and in particular by its evident favouritism towards Reutemann, Lauda seized control of the development programme during the six-week break before the next race and personally tried out every individual 312T2 chassis. During one session at Fiorano, he had a very big crash after braking too late.

195 South African Grand Prix

Kyalami, 5 March 1977, Formula 1
Ferrari 312T2/030 • #11
Qualifying: 3rd • Result: 1st

After the extensive testing undertaken by Lauda, including pre-race sessions at Kyalami, the cars that appeared for practice in South Africa were heavily revised. With a new chassis (030), Lauda was second quickest on the grey, drizzly opening day, and he also used the spare (029) while further modifications were tried on his race car. In the end, hampered by unusual tyre-pressure problems caused by condensation within the carcasses, he was disappointed with third spot on the grid, although this time he was five places higher than Carlos Reutemann.

From the start he got away well and settled into second place behind pole-sitter James Hunt as the pair pulled away from the pack. Going into lap 7, he slipstreamed past the McLaren down the straight and was well ahead by the time they reached Crowthorne, drawing away imperiously thereafter.

A horrific accident occurred on lap 23 when two fire marshals ran across the track halfway down the main straight to put out an engine fire

BELOW Lauda's Ferrari 312T2 leads James Hunt's McLaren M23 at Interlagos. Third place flattered the Italian car, which had progressed little since the end of the previous season.

1977

on Renzo Zorzi's stranded Shadow. The other Shadow, driven by Tom Pryce, hit one of the men at top speed and both driver and marshal died instantly, Pryce from the impact of the marshal's fire extinguisher on his head. The race continued and on the following lap Lauda's Ferrari ran over part of the wrecked Shadow's roll-over bar, which, unknown to the Austrian, became jammed under his car and caused a slow leak from one of the water radiators. As he could feel something scraping the road in right-hand corners and could see his engine temperature rising, he nursed the car for the next 10 laps while Jody Scheckter's Wolf closed in.

Having got the situation under control, Lauda speeded up again and lapped slower cars with ease. His opponents, unaware of the Ferrari's overheating engine and fading oil pressure, gave up the chase. As the race approached its conclusion, his margin was big enough to allow him to ease off and try to get the ailing car home with its oil pressure warning light

ABOVE Niki's uprated Ferrari 312T2 heads Jody Scheckter's Wolf WR1 and James Hunt's McLaren M23 out of Leeukop during the South African Grand Prix.

BELOW No smiles from Niki on the Kyalami podium; although he has scored his first victory since the Nürburgring accident, he has just been informed of the deaths of Tom Pryce and a marshal during the race.

THE PHOENIX RISES 207

FIORANO AND NARDÒ
MARCH 1977

Following some eye-catching performances by Tyrrell's six-wheeled P34, notably in winning the 1976 Swedish Grand Prix, Ferrari had announced its own six-wheeler project in December, generating a huge wave of publicity. The two extra wheels were attached to a single back axle, a configuration that had been popular with hillclimb cars in earlier decades. Mauro Forghieri had apparently conceived the project to assess whether the smaller tyres, which were more rigid than the regular ones, would deform less under cornering loads and provide more grip.

All then went quiet until March 1977 when the Ferrari '312T6' (a semi-official designation) broke cover in tests at Fiorano. Lauda gave no statement afterwards, but Carlos Reutemann had a big accident after the failure of a rear upright and he was vociferous in his dislike of the car.

Although testing was undertaken principally at Fiorano, on 13 March Lauda also drove the 'T6', which was adapted from 312T2/025, at top speed for several laps of the 7.8-mile (12.5km) circular bowl at the Fiat-owned Nardò testing facility in the heel of Italy (pictured below right). The tests were carried out secretly so nothing is known about the performance of the 'T6' compared with the standard 312T2, which had been used by the Austrian the previous day to establish a baseline. Soon after, in May, the project was shelved, Enzo Ferrari stating the reason as the need for Goodyear to provide special tyres, although in fact the tyres used were regular fronts. In any case, the extended rear axle meant that the car was wider than the legal maximum and therefore would never have been allowed to start a Grand Prix — so the entire exercise was rather pointless.

flickering. Heading towards the chequered flag, he switched off the engine to avoid a last-minute seizure, causing astonished spectators to think he had run out of fuel. When Ferrari's mechanics examined the hobbled car afterwards, only a third of its coolant and a tenth of its oil remained.

It was a landmark victory for Lauda, his first since the Nürburgring accident. His mechanical sensitivity and resilience in adversity combined with the flat-12 engine's robustness had kept it all together.

196 United States Grand Prix (West)

Long Beach, 3 April 1977, Formula 1
Ferrari 312T2/030 • #11
Qualifying: 1st • Result: 2nd (fastest lap)

Carrying a larger rear wing for this high-downforce track, Lauda took pole position — his first since the 1976 British Grand Prix — 10 minutes before qualifying ended, after a frantic three-way fight with Jody Scheckter's Wolf and the otherwise dominant Lotus of Mario Andretti. Although he had been delayed by a broken rear anti-roll bar earlier and still had oversteer problems, his car at last looked in good shape.

The starting gantry was set too high for him to see both the lights and his rev counter at the same time and he got away badly. When Scheckter dived ahead of him at the first corner, Ferrari team-mate Carlos Reutemann tried optimistically to follow and only managed to slide up the escape road, but Andretti did slip through and Niki lay third. After briefly getting ahead of Andretti on lap 3, he made an error trying to outbrake him at the hairpin next time around, flat-spotting a front tyre and causing a bad vibration that lasted for the rest of the race. He held on grimly, hounding the second-placed Lotus for 73 laps in an absorbing and closely matched battle until, with four laps to go, they both moved ahead of Scheckter's Wolf, which was suffering a slow puncture. Andretti won with Lauda just one second behind. Had he achieved a better start, Niki might well have won

208 | NIKI LAUDA

1977

RIGHT His Ferrari 312T2 much more competitive on the streets of Long Beach, Niki set fastest lap during a race-long battle with Jody Scheckter's Wolf WR1 and Mario Andretti's Lotus 78 on his way to second place.

FIORANO
APRIL 1977

In a quest to find improved downforce for the increasingly gripless 312T2, Lauda tested Mauro Forghieri's twin-wing concept on the original 312T development car (019), which was kept at Fiorano. While questions remained as to the potential legality of the extra centrally mounted wing (upper picture), the tests in any case showed that there was no significant gain and it was not seen again.

Attention was also paid to identifying a more aerodynamically efficient cooling solution for the 312T2. A much-revised cockpit surround incorporating larger air intakes and a revised profile was tried out, but the new developments did little to address the car's underlying mechanical shortcomings. Niki slogged around Fiorano in a 312T2 test chassis with makeshift revisions to the bodywork and cooling inlets (lower picture), the car's tatty appearance reflecting the desperation of the search for aerodynamic solutions to the car's lack of performance.

The veil of secrecy that was maintained around tests at Fiorano meant that photographers resorted to long-lens 'spy shots' to satisfy the voracious appetite of the Italian press for Ferrari news.

THE PHOENIX RISES 209

ABOVE Niki hangs out the rear of his oversteering Ferrari 312T2 during practice for the Spanish Grand Prix. A recurrence of his rib injury during the race-morning warm-up meant that he did not take the start.

the race given the difficulties in overtaking on the streets of Long Beach and the closeness of the leading trio.

197 Spanish Grand Prix

Jarama, 8 May 1977, Formula 1
Ferrari 312T2/030 • #11
Qualifying: 3rd • Did not start

After the first four practice sessions Lauda was pretty unhappy, having endured myriad mechanical problems including mismatched brake pads. By the end of practice he had systematically solved most of them and, despite obvious understeer through the fast corners, he posted third-fastest time by running on the ragged edge, 0.04 second ahead of team-mate Carlos Reutemann and 0.06 second behind Jacques Laffite's Ligier.

On his third lap during warm-up on race morning, he suddenly felt acute pain in his chest when changing down a gear for a fast corner. Medical checks revealed that one of the ribs he had broken in his Nürburgring accident had not healed properly and had simply snapped under the g-force. He could not take part in the race and his grid slot remained empty. His withdrawal allowed the first reserve, Brett Lunger (March), one of his Nürburgring rescuers, to get into the race. The situation also helped Carlos Reutemann, whose car was fitted with Lauda's front wing when his own was found to be 25mm too wide.

198 Monaco Grand Prix

Monte Carlo, 22 May 1977, Formula 1
Ferrari 312T2/030 • #11
Qualifying: 6th • Result: 2nd

Lauda was sufficiently recovered from his rib injury to take part in Monaco, helped by his seat having been remoulded to give him better body support. In first practice on Thursday he seldom completed more than two laps without calling into the pits because his car was oversteering so badly, but he drove with smoothness and precision to record the day's fourth fastest time. Unable to make the Ferrari handle to his liking, he changed his approach in Saturday's session and threw the car round the circuit in opposite-lock slides, bullying it to sixth place on the grid. Considering that he had started from pole here in 1974, 1975 and 1976, it was a very disappointing outcome. A driveshaft failure forced him briefly to use the spare (027) but he was back in his regular car for the race.

Holding sixth place at the start, he passed Ronnie Peterson's Tyrrell at *Mirabeau* and hassled Hans Stuck until the German's Brabham coasted through Casino Square with an electrical fire. He was waved through into third place by team-mate Carlos Reutemann, who had overworked his tyres and was unable to challenge for the lead. He closed on John Watson's Brabham and took second place when the Ulsterman went down the escape road at the harbour-front chicane. That left only Jody Scheckter's Wolf ahead of him: charging hard, he reduced a 15-second deficit to less than one second at the finish after an inspired drive.

1977

LEFT Lauda is wheel-to-wheel with Ronnie Peterson's Tyrrell P34 into *Mirabeau* during the Monaco Grand Prix, while the McLaren M23s of James Hunt and Jochen Mass — separated by Mario Andretti's Lotus 78 — are poised to take advantage of any mishaps.

FIORANO
14 MAY 1977

The Italian weekly newspaper *Oggi* ('Today') organised a private road-test-cum-race with the newly updated Fiat 127, hiring Ferrari's Fiorano test track for the purpose. Seeking opinions on the little hatchback, it brought together seven Formula 1 drivers to take part in a demonstration 'race' in identical 1050 Lusso models, numbered and liveried to mirror the sponsorship of their drivers' usual mounts. The participants were the two Ferrari men, Lauda and Carlos Reutemann, Italian drivers Vittorio Brambilla, Renzo Zorzi and Lella Lombardi, and the ever-popular Ronnie Peterson and Jacques Laffite.

Over three laps they engaged in the anticipated hooliganism, involving lurid slides and side impacts. Lauda indulged in his share of robust driving when he passed Peterson on the outside of a turn, creating havoc in the pack, which he said was an intended test of the car's stability. The 'Gran Premio 127' ended in a friendly photo finish, with Lauda and Reutemann leading the pack over the line in a dead heat.

THE PHOENIX RISES 211

BELOW Ferrari mechanics swarm around Niki's 312T2 as he pits for dry tyres during the Belgian Grand Prix. His stop was significantly quicker than anyone else's and would have won him the race, had Gunnar Nilsson's ground-effect Lotus 78 not enjoyed a huge performance advantage towards the end.

199 Belgian Grand Prix

Zolder, 5 June 1977, Formula 1
Ferrari 312T2/030 • #11
Qualifying: 11th • Result: 2nd

Although Lauda was clearly trying hard in practice, arriving at the pits chicane with smoke pouring from locked-up front tyres and piling on opposite lock everywhere else around the circuit, it was equally obvious that the Ferrari was still plagued by excessive oversteer. He was fined 1,000 Swiss francs for ignoring the pit-exit signal and wound up an angry 11th on the grid.

Pre-race rain ceased as the start approached but the track was wet enough for most runners to choose wet tyres. Seventh at the end of an eventful first lap, Lauda was one of the first to pit for slicks, on lap 15. His mechanics did the job very quickly, getting him out again within 16 seconds. He was ninth when he rejoined and when all the pit stops had been completed he led comfortably. Driving smoothly and consistently, he lost a little time — although not the lead — with a spin on lap 32 during a drizzly spell while lapping David Purley's Lec; there was a suggestion that the cars had touched, but when the two drivers 'had words' after the race the Englishman was unrepentant.

The next challenge came from an inspired Jochen Mass chasing him down, but the German spun his McLaren on lap 40 and it appeared for a while that Lauda could relax a little. However, as the track dried again, Gunnar Nilsson took over the pursuit, his ground-effect Lotus clearly the best car in the race, vastly superior to the rest. The Swede, who had been delayed at his tyre stop by a sticking wheel nut, reduced the gap at an astonishing rate and on lap 50 he out-braked the ill-handling Ferrari into the chicane behind the pits as if lapping a backmarker. Lauda could do nothing about it and instead nursed his car home to take second place while Nilsson cruised to his only Grand Prix win.

ZANDVOORT
6 JUNE 1977

Goodyear arranged a tyre-testing session at Zandvoort directly after the Belgian Grand Prix. Lauda was present only on the Monday and completed 15 laps with the car he had raced at Zolder (030), after which he did one lap in the spare (027) in experimental long-wheelbase form before rain intervened.

During the wet weather at this somewhat relaxed day, Lauda rather surprisingly tried out a Ligier JS7 (upper picture), a car that was showing promise. Gérard Ducarouge and his engineers were more than happy to hear the Austrian's feedback, as the Ligier was well off the pace on the day and its regular pilot, Jacques Laffite, was never regarded as a good test driver. Niki did 15 laps in the Ligier before encountering front-suspension problems and reported that its Matra V12 engine was as good as Ferrari's flat-12.

On returning to the pits, he casually slipped into the cockpit of Emerson Fittipaldi's new Fittipaldi F5 (lower picture) and was enthusiastic about the design and build quality of the car that ex-Ensign engineer Dave Baldwin had created for the Brazilian double World Champion; he also provided helpful feedback by identifying a steering problem.

Whether or not Niki's interest in these rival machines was meant to be any sort of message to Ferrari is unclear, but he was certainly beginning to feel disgruntled with the team and making noises about the need to build a completely new car rather than persevere with the 312T2.

As Goodyear continued to develop its tyres with increasingly stiff sidewalls to suit the ground-effect Lotus 78, which had won three of the season's first seven races, Ferrari was finding it more and more difficult to generate satisfactory tyre temperatures. After the Zandvoort tests, Lauda tried Michelin tyres at Fiorano and reported a marked improvement.

FIORANO
JUNE 1977

Between the Zolder and Anderstorp races, Lauda and Carlos Reutemann both tested the experimental long-wheelbase 312T2 (027) extensively at Fiorano. Contrary to the graphic shown on the cover of *Autosprint* magazine, the increase was effected by a 20cm spacer between the monocoque and the engine, rather than the more conventional arrangement between engine and gearbox — which the transverse gearbox precluded. Although Reutemann found the long-wheelbase car slightly better than the conventional one, Lauda was unenthusiastic, completing 70 laps without setting any particularly quick times.

The car was taken to Anderstorp unchanged for use as the spare and Lauda had to resort to it, fruitlessly, in the final practice session. Back at base, it was then returned to standard specification for continued use as the spare.

PARMA–POGGIO DI BERCETO HILLCLIMB
11 JUNE 1977

The Parma–Poggio di Berceto hillclimb was inaugurated in 1913 to commemorate the centenary of the birth of the composer Giuseppe Verdi and in 1919 it was the scene of Enzo Ferrari's début as a racing driver. By the 1970s it had become a nostalgia event for historic racing cars but still attracted huge crowds. As Lauda's personal sponsor, Parmalat, was backing the 1977 event, he was persuaded to take part in a 1934 Fiat 508 Balilla Coppa d'Oro, but to the disappointment of the many fans who were waiting at the finish to greet him he did not complete the twisty 32.8-mile (52.8km) course. Instead, after driving the first three miles (5km) he pulled over to hand the Fiat back to its owner, Fausto Renaudo. With that, he headed back to Fiorano in his Ferrari 308 GTB to continue an extended test programme ahead of the Swedish Grand Prix, judging that his time was better spent on the future rather than the past.

1977

200 Swedish Grand Prix

Anderstorp, 19 June 1977, Formula 1
Ferrari 312T2/030 • #11
Qualifying: 15th • Result: Retired (handling)

There was now every indication that Ferrari had lost its sense of direction. Although the cars from Maranello had seldom shone at Anderstorp, they were again woefully short of grip despite trying all tyre combinations, and even having old 1976-specification rubber flown in. Lauda could only manage 15th on the grid, while Carlos Reutemann was 12th.

Lauda had a torrid time in the race, the Ferrari's terrible traction out of slow corners an embarrassment to its driver. Lying 10th and looking unlikely to improve, he was being harried by Jean-Pierre Jarier's ATS-run Penske when he spun at the left-hander before the pits, losing a further three places. It took him 12 laps to scrabble past Jackie Oliver (Shadow) after a number of unsuccessful attempts to outbrake him. Lauda finally abandoned the struggle after 47 laps when running 19th, having made two pit stops for fresh tyres and a further one for a new front spoiler in the hope of improving the aerodynamics (rather than as the result of any damage).

201 French Grand Prix

Dijon-Prenois, 3 July 1977, Formula 1
Ferrari 312T2/031 • #11
Qualifying: 9th • Result: 5th

After a day's pre-race testing at Dijon, Lauda spent a lot of time setting up his new chassis (031), which had a revised nose and oil cooler, but despite trying a wider front track he was plagued by understeer and worked hard for little reward, qualifying ninth.

ABOVE Anderstorp in 1977 was an even more troubled experience than it had been a year earlier. Niki qualified only 15th and gave up the unequal struggle when running 19th.

LEFT The fast swoops of the Dijon-Prenois circuit were far from ideal for the Ferrari 312T2's troublesome handling and poor traction, but Niki wrestled the car home for two more World Championship points.

THE PHOENIX RISES

BELOW Niki's dissatisfaction with the Ferrari 312T2 and the need for a new design is very apparent as he surveys his car in the Silverstone pitlane.

He managed to get the Ferrari going better in the early stages of the race, driving splendidly to pass Alan Jones's Shadow, Vittorio Brambilla's March and Jody Scheckter's struggling Wolf. Unable to progress any further, he spent the rest of the race in an intense dice with Gunnar Nilsson (Lotus) and Jacques Laffite (Ligier). The three of them were held up for 16 laps trying to lap Hans Stuck (Brabham), who managed to ram Laffite's car, allowing Lauda to gain a place. He stayed very close to Nilsson but the Swede withstood the pressure and Niki had to accept fifth place, still dissatisfied with his car's handling and traction, but at least in the points.

In fact his two points here put him at the top of the World Championship table for the first time in this very open season, which had seen six different winners in the first eight races. He had 33 points to Mario Andretti's 32, the American now looking like a class act in his ground-effect Lotus 78 after winning at Dijon, his third victory of the year.

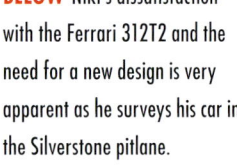

202 British Grand Prix

Silverstone, 16 July 1977, Formula 1
Ferrari 312T2/031 • #11
Qualifying: 3rd • Result: 2nd

The Ferrari 312T2s arrived at Silverstone with revised front suspension and looked steadier than they had for a long time. Despite a lurid spin at Becketts when pushing hard, Lauda qualified third and was very much happier, no doubt in part because he was much higher up the grid than Carlos Reutemann, who had out-qualified him in the previous four races.

Niki got a screamer of a start and held second place behind John Watson's Brabham, driving aggressively to keep Jody Scheckter's Wolf at bay. Watson and Lauda pulled away steadily and had built up quite a gap by lap 7, when the slow-starting James Hunt got his pole-sitting McLaren into third place and set off in pursuit. By one-third distance Lauda was embroiled in a scrap with the McLaren until Hunt finally overtook at the Woodcote chicane at the end of lap 23. Having been bothered for some time by poor braking and having to use the gearbox to help slow his car, Lauda dropped away and circulated on his own, content with third place and more points. When Watson pitted on lap 49 with a fuel pick-up problem, Niki was promoted to second but was unable to challenge for the lead, eventually coming home 20 seconds behind Hunt. His brakeless Ferrari was almost caught on the line by the hard-charging Gunnar Nilsson, but he just held the Lotus at bay.

1977

LEFT The class of 1977 strung out along Silverstone's Hangar Straight: Niki's Ferrari 312T2 leads Jody Scheckter's Wolf WR1, James Hunt's winning McLaren M26, the Lotus 78 twins of Gunnar Nilsson and Mario Andretti, new boy Gilles Villeneuve's McLaren M23, Jochen Mass's McLaren M26, Vittorio Brambilla's Surtees TS19, Jacques Laffite's Ligier JS7, Carlos Reutemann's Ferrari 312T2 and the rest; John Watson's leading Brabham BT45B is already out of shot.

203 German Grand Prix

Hockenheim, 31 July 1977, Formula 1
Ferrari 312T2/031 • #11
Qualifying: 3rd • Result: 1st (fastest lap)

Very encouragingly, Lauda was quickest in pre-race testing at Hockenheim. During second practice he took the opportunity to try out an experimental two-tier rear wing with streamlining pods at either end of the lower part, a configuration that was supposed to reduce air turbulence behind the rear wheels. The Ferrari's handling was still deficient, but in final qualifying — after insisting on an engine change — he claimed third spot on the grid and was fastest through the speed trap.

The German crowd gave him a great welcome on the anniversary of his accident and there was much cheering and banner-waving from the packed grandstands as he took his place on the grid. The start, however, was shambolic: it was signalled by a flag as the lighting gantry had been damaged by a service vehicle and in mid-grid the inattentive Patrick Depailler (Tyrrell) hesitated, causing a chain reaction that eliminated Clay Regazzoni's Ensign and Alan Jones's Shadow. Lauda, meanwhile, ran third behind John Watson until the Brabham's Alfa

BELOW Niki poses with the experimental two-tier rear-wing arrangement during practice for the German Grand Prix at Hockenheim.

THE PHOENIX RISES **217**

ABOVE A year after his life-threatening crash at the Nürburgring, Lauda scored a resounding and popular victory in the German Grand Prix at Hockenheim.

Romeo engine expired after seven laps, leaving Lauda with only Jody Scheckter's Wolf ahead of him. Stalking Scheckter remorselessly, on lap 13 he pushed the South African into a minor error exiting the *Östkurve* that allowed him to outbrake the Wolf in a superb move at the second chicane.

He opened up a small gap but had to work hard for several laps to maintain his lead in a close-running four-car group. Once he had established his position, he drove smoothly and confidently, appearing in complete command as he steadily pulled out a six-second advantage that he held to the chequered flag. His dominant drive, one year on from the accident that had almost killed him, earned a huge ovation from the crowd.

This success gave him more victories than any previous Ferrari driver, putting him ahead of Alberto Ascari's tally of 13 during the period 1951–53. It also consolidated his position in the World Championship, 10 points ahead of his closest challenger, who was now Scheckter.

204 Austrian Grand Prix

Österreichring, 14 August 1977, Formula 1
Ferrari 312T2/031 • #11
Qualifying: 1st • Result: 2nd

In a four-day test session at the Österreichring during the week after the German Grand Prix, Lauda proved fastest over the first three days, when Goodyear confined everyone to hard tyre compounds, and then departed before the last day. The circuit was now appreciably slower due to the introduction of a chicane before the very fast *Hella-Licht* curve after the pits and many of the drivers thought this an improvement.

A week later, Lauda applied the lessons from the test in front of a huge partisan crowd. Driving in an economical and apparently effortless manner, his practice times fell steadily and he always looked in command. Although briefly relegated to the spare car (030) when a throttle-linkage bearing seized, he remained

1977

quickest, and then set his best time in his race car after it had been repaired, securing a serene pole position. After that, he stood on the pit wall to watch the others trying to get near his time.

Prolonged heavy rain on race morning left the track damp for the start. Like most, Lauda selected slick tyres but he was far from happy with his car's behaviour on dry settings in these conditions. Although he led away, third-placed Mario Andretti (Lotus) made a daring move into the *Boschkurve* and passed not only second-placed James Hunt (McLaren) but Lauda too. To the crowd's dismay, Hunt also got through before the end of the first lap, and within another lap Jody Scheckter (Wolf) and Gunnar Nilsson (Lotus) overtook as well. With the Ferrari oversteering viciously, Lauda's slump continued and by lap 9 he lay 10th. But now the track was dry and he came back into the picture, driving flat out. Within four more laps he was back up to fifth, then picked off Hans Stuck (Brabham) and Scheckter to occupy third place by lap 38. Soon after, with 11 laps to go, he was promoted to second place when Hunt retired from the lead with a blown engine, leaving Alan Jones to take over at the front and score Shadow's first Formula 1 victory, some 20 seconds clear of Lauda.

BELOW The pack piles into the new *Hella-Licht* chicane on the opening lap of the Austrian Grand Prix. Niki's Ferrari 312T2 heads the charge as James Hunt's McLaren M26 takes the outside line and Mario Andretti's Lotus 78 looks for a gap between them. Partly obscured are Carlos Reutemann in the second Ferrari 312T2, Hans Stuck's Brabham BT45B and Jody Scheckter's Wolf WR3 as the Ensign N177 pair of Patrick Tambay and Clay Regazzoni crest the hill behind them.

THE PHOENIX RISES

ABOVE Lauda's Ferrari 312T2 has just overtaken Jacques Laffite's Ligier JS7 20 laps into the Dutch Grand Prix to take the lead that he would hold until the finish.

205 Dutch Grand Prix

Zandvoort, 28 August 1977, Formula 1
Ferrari 312T2/031 • #11
Qualifying: 4th • Result: 1st (fastest lap)

Lauda's endless set-up adjustments during practice made little difference to his 312T2's persistent lack of grip, with such bad wheelspin out of the hairpin before *Hunzerug* that at times the car appeared to be on ice. He also tried the spare (030) for a few laps but found it no better. So he concluded that he would just have to attack the circuit and hope for the best — and he qualified fourth.

Off the start he ran in fourth place, which became second on lap 5 when Mario Andretti (Lotus) tried to overtake James Hunt (McLaren) on the outside at *Tarzan* and the pair collided. While Hunt was eliminated, the American recovered and when he caught up with Lauda's Ferrari on lap 11, the Austrian wisely allowed the ground-effect Lotus just enough room at *Tarzan* to pull off a similar move, this time without incident. When Andretti's Cosworth engine failed two laps later, Lauda hunted down Jacques Laffite's leading Ligier and, after a brief but entertaining scrap, slipstreamed past with relative ease at the end of the main straight on lap 20, just after quarter distance. The Frenchman was unable to respond and Lauda quickly opened up a five-second advantage, controlling the rest of the race comfortably. As he reeled off the remaining laps, he was badly held up when lapping Emerson Fittipaldi, allowing Laffite to close again. This time his Ferrari had the legs of the powerful Matra-engined Ligier and he paced himself home to take a copybook win by two seconds.

This victory meant that a second World Championship title was now looking highly probable, his 63 points putting him far ahead of Scheckter (42), Reutemann (35) and Andretti (32). But Lauda's dissatisfaction with Ferrari

1977

had been intensifying and the following day he went to Maranello for a meeting with Enzo Ferrari, his son Piero Lardi, Luca di Montezemolo and financial manager Ermanno della Casa. They parted on amicable terms, but Lauda had made it clear that nothing would persuade him to stay with the team, and he had made no technical or financial demands during the meeting. He had, in fact, secretly signed for another team that very weekend.

Some weeks earlier he had made up his mind to leave Ferrari at the end of the season. He had talked extensively with both Team Lotus and Wolf Racing, the latter having a particular attraction because Walter Wolf's family background was Austrian and the two men had become firm friends. Lauda also had preliminary talks with Formula 1 newcomers Renault, who could certainly afford his salary expectations and had offered the enticing prospects of a team built around him, the challenge of developing its turbocharged car, and exclusive use of Michelin tyres.

But Lauda finally opted for Brabham.

206 Italian Grand Prix

Monza, 11 September 1977, Formula 1
Ferrari 312T2/031 • #11
Qualifying: 5th • Result: 2nd

Ten days before the Italian Grand Prix, and with perfect timing in light of his record number of wins for the Scuderia and his comfortable lead in the World Championship, Lauda provided further proof of his bravery (if any was still needed) by announcing his departure from Ferrari — lesser men would have chosen to keep the news quiet until *after* the Monza race. So it was that at the circuit's traditional pre-race test session he was met by jeers and taunts from spectators, although such behaviour was no longer evident by the time official practice started.

Answering partisan displeasure in the best possible manner, he was fastest on Friday, although when trying out a set of special Goodyear tyres in the following day's untimed practice he spun into the guardrail at *Parabolica*

BELOW The trees at Monza cast dappled shadows in the late-afternoon sun as Niki drags his recalcitrant Ferrari 312T2 towards second place — and another six points towards the title.

THE PHOENIX RISES 221

while attempting to pass Gunnar Nilsson's Lotus on the outside. With the rear suspension of 030 grafted onto the back of his regular 031 for the final session, he qualified fifth before running out of fuel, disappointed to be adrift of team-mate Carlos Reutemann, who was on the front row.

Sixth at the end of the first lap of the race, Lauda passed Clay Regazzoni's fast-starting Ensign on lap 2 for fifth place, which became fourth 10 laps later when pole-sitter James Hunt spun his McLaren and lost places. When Jody Scheckter's Wolf blew its engine on lap 24, the Austrian moved up to third, behind Reutemann. Another 11 laps later the sister Ferrari lost some ground when part of its exhaust broke and Lauda slipped past his team-mate for second place. Shortly after, while the two Ferraris were closing in to lap Bruno Giacomelli's McLaren, the Italian driver's engine blew up and deposited an oil slick right in front of them; Lauda's fast reflexes allowed him to steer around it but Reutemann, unsighted, spun off into retirement. Thereafter, the Austrian's down-on-power engine prevented him from making any impression on Mario Andretti's lead and he duly finished 17 seconds adrift of the Lotus.

BELOW At a damp and miserable Watkins Glen, Niki completes his last race as a Ferrari driver and clinches his second World Championship.

207 United States Grand Prix (East)

Watkins Glen, 2 October 1977, Formula 1
Ferrari 312T2/031 • #11
Qualifying: 7th • Result: 4th

By now, Lauda's move to Brabham had been officially confirmed. As with so many departing Ferrari drivers in the past, Lauda found himself out of favour and the sympathetic relationship between driver and team had vanished. He was no longer allowed to go to Fiorano so whatever development work he had hoped to complete before the two North American races was impossible and at Watkins Glen he simply ran out of time before he had finished trying all the combinations of tyres

222 NIKI LAUDA

1977

and aerodynamics he had planned. Out of the picture for most of practice, he ended the final session early with an engine failure caused by a cracked cylinder liner and had to settle for seventh on the grid.

In cold, wet weather, he got away sixth but was elbowed wide on the long turn in the Anvil section and several cars got by. He forced his way back into contention and a brief tussle with team-mate Carlos Reutemann was decided in Lauda's favour when the Argentine driver spun on lap 11, letting Lauda through into a comfortable fourth place. Taking no chances thereafter, he drove a tactical race, preserving his wet tyres in drying conditions to collect the three points he needed to make sure of his second World Championship title.

Lauda then decided to opt out of the Canadian Grand Prix the following weekend. Ferrari announced on the morning of Friday practice that he was unable to race for medical reasons, but in reality he was not prepared to drive given the toxic political climate at the Italian team, a fact he admitted with typical candour when asked. There were three things that particularly irked him: he was dismayed by the sacking of his faithful mechanic Ermanno Cuoghi; he was annoyed about the decision to run a third car for Gilles Villeneuve in the French-Canadian's home race because he thought this would stretch the team's resources too far; and he had had enough of Mauro Forghieri's histrionics at races, considering that they detracted from focusing on the job in hand.

Mindful that fans were being denied the presence of the new World Champion, Bernie Ecclestone — his new employer at Brabham as well as Formula 1's emerging commercial supremo — tried to persuade the Austrian to change his mind but without success. Lauda carried out his contractual promotional duties before the race, collected his fee and headed off to buy a Learjet.

Lauda's entry for the Japanese Grand Prix on 23 October was scratched and Villeneuve instead drove his car. The 312T2s handled abominably at Fuji, lacking both grip and traction, and Villeneuve later commented that his car was 'unbelievably bad'. In the race the young hotshoe rammed the back of Ronnie Peterson's Tyrrell at the end of the main straight, supposedly because of brake failure, and cartwheeled off the track, killing a marshal and a photographer.

SUMMARY

The 1977 season was not necessarily one of classic confrontation. It was the reliability of the Ferrari 312T2 rather than its performance that underpinned Lauda's second World Championship title, allowing him to focus on amassing more points than his opponents in the certain knowledge that his car could not match them on speed. The top five in the standings were Lauda (72 points), Jody Scheckter (55), Mario Andretti (47), Carlos Reutemann (42) and James Hunt (40). Niki did well to complete the third-greatest distance in the lead at 558 miles, behind Mario Andretti's 729 and James Hunt's 711, despite three fewer starts.

It is easy to overlook just how poor the 312T2 was at times. At three Grands Prix Niki qualified outside the top 10, unheard of for a World Champion, and more often than not the car was simply uncompetitive. The fact that his main rivals suffered bad luck and poor mechanical reliability certainly aided his cause. It could be argued that Lauda salvaged the championship in his final year with Ferrari rather than won it, but it remains the case that his is the name in the record books; he had won the title under the rules as they stood, and that was good enough.

Ferrari also collected its third successive constructors' cup, by the considerable margin of 95 points to Lotus's 62.

ABOVE The programme for the Japanese Grand Prix carried Niki's photograph prominently on the front cover but he failed to turn up at Fuji after walking out on Ferrari ahead of the Canadian Grand Prix.

THE PHOENIX RISES 223

FROM VALLELUNGA TO JACAREPAGUÁ
NOVEMBER AND DECEMBER 1977

With the new season again due to kick off early, in Argentina on the second weekend of January, November and December were packed with testing commitments for Brabham at an array of circuits.

Lauda's first run in a Brabham — a 1977-specification BT45B — came at a private four-day test at Vallelunga in mid-November and he put in a huge number of laps. He set the best time ever recorded at the circuit, over a second quicker than he had achieved in a Ferrari, and described the chassis as 'fantastic'.

It was the promise of developing Gordon Murray's technically advanced new BT46 that had really sparked Lauda's interest and, along with a hefty pay cheque, sealed his move to Brabham. The BT46's main novelty was 'surface cooling', by means of flat heat exchangers on the bodywork flanks rather than the usual water and oil radiators. However, during earlier testing by John Watson at Donington and Silverstone in the cool weather of early November, the car boiled its water after only a few laps, although the oil cooling system worked satisfactorily. A comprehensive rethink was needed, much to the Austrian's chagrin.

The team was left with little choice in the short term but to persevere with the BT45B, uprated to 'C' specification. An early opportunity to put in extensive lappery with the revised car came on 6–8 December in Brazil at a private Goodyear tyre test, organised by the Brabham team under the auspices of an official evaluation on behalf of FOCA of the new Jacarepeguá circuit outside Rio de Janeiro. With building work temporarily

LEFT First time in a Brabham: Niki prepares for his initial exploratory laps of Rome's Vallelunga circuit in the BT45B. He was enthusiastic about the car's handling in comparison with the Ferrari 312T2 with which he had wrestled all year.

1977

RIGHT It is easy to see how Niki's head was turned by Gordon Murray's dart-shaped, technically advanced Brabham BT46 in its original configuration as it sits here in the Silverstone pitlane. The various angular shapes on the flanks are the heat exchangers for the car's 'surface cooling' but this system did not work well enough and the car never raced in this guise.

LOWER RIGHT Seen testing at Paul Ricard in December, Niki's Brabham BT45C wears both a new nose design and a very briefly seen variant of its Parmalat livery.

suspended for the occasion, Lauda set his best time on the second day after completing 64 laps with a new nose and rear wing fitted, but the nose then fell off on the ascending section after the pits. On the third day the engine blew up after only two laps and he lost three hours while it was changed. In the afternoon, with soft tyres fitted, he set his best time of the test but was then forced to stop as the promised new Goodyear tyres had not arrived in Brazil. Murray was satisfied with the progress that had been made and Lauda was happy at having learned the new track, although he thought it was unacceptably bumpy. He then left immediately for Europe to continue the testing programme.

Having grown accustomed to Ferrari having its own test track at Fiorano, Lauda was pleased that Brabham's deal to use the Alfa Romeo flat-12 engine meant that he continued to have access to an exclusive facility, the company's test track at Balocco, between Turin and Milan. In addition to testing there, he put in many miles at Paul Ricard and Vallelunga.

During this period Murray developed a revised slimline nose for the BT45C. It still contained two water radiators, one on either side, but it was shallower in depth and the air intake now took the form of a thin slot across the full width. In this guise the car was seen at Paul Ricard on 13 December, where Lauda began the day wearing new team-mate John Watson's helmet because he had left his own at his hotel. Although conditions were cold and it was difficult to get heat into the tyres, during the afternoon Lauda tried some special softer Goodyears and got to within 0.15 second of the official lap record.

He and the Brabham team went into the 1978 season in confident mood.

THE PHOENIX RISES

1978
CHANGING HORSES

Lauda's enthusiasm had been sapped during 1977. Despite his certainty that Ferrari would get it right again in 1978, his overwhelming desire was to be in a team that provided a more sympathetic climate. Acknowledging that he was a difficult person to work with and that he expected others to have the same work ethic as he demanded of himself, he wanted a team that would be moulded around him. Brabham, free of the political squabbling that took up so much time at Ferrari, was a natural choice.

There was also the other side of the equation. Brabham offered a complicated car with an engine that had proved very quick but also unreliable. Many observers questioned the logic of Lauda's decision, but they failed to consider the Austrian's need for a fresh challenge, coupled with his overt admiration for Gordon Murray's design pedigree.

A big development task lay ahead in ironing out reliability shortcomings and finding marginal gains — all of which was right up Lauda's street. Other teams may have presented an easier option and a proven winning car, but the appeal of turning a front-running but under-performing team into regular winners was irresistible.

1978

ABOVE The Brabham BT45C flattered to deceive in Argentina: Niki's second place at Buenos Aires gave the team cause for optimism, but the circuit's unusual characteristics masked wider issues with the revised interim design.

208 Argentine Grand Prix

Buenos Aires, 15 January 1978, Formula 1
Brabham BT45C/7 • #1
Qualifying: 5th • Result: 2nd

The Brabhams were at the right end of the time sheets in Buenos Aires. After a good start on Friday, Lauda's race car was affected by failures to both the ignition unit and the fuel pump, stranding him out on the circuit. This obliged him to use the spare car (BT45C/6) for the few remaining laps and also prevented him from trying any of the myriad different tyre choices available. As neither Brabham driver improved his times on Saturday, the previous day's efforts put Lauda fifth on the grid with team-mate John Watson fourth, 0.28 second quicker. For the race, the Austrian elected to run softer Goodyears that had been earmarked for practice rather than the advised race rubber.

He got away fourth at the start but was passed by his team-mate on lap 3. Having initially watched how his rivals' tyres were behaving, he overtook Ronnie Peterson's Lotus for fourth place on lap 8 but then took another 14 laps to find his way past the Ferrari of Carlos Reutemann for third. By half distance things were looking good with the Brabhams running strongly in second and third places, although Lauda was having to watch his mirrors as Patrick Depailler (Tyrrell) was closing menacingly. With 14 laps to go, Watson's BT45C slowed with a water leak and Lauda moved up into second place behind Mario Andretti's Lotus. Although he was pushed hard in the closing laps by Depailler's understeering car, he had everything well under control and was able to resist. He had driven a carefully judged first race for Brabham.

209 Brazilian Grand Prix

Jacarepaguá, 29 January 1978, Formula 1
Brabham BT45C/7 • #1
Qualifying: 10th • Result: 3rd

Despite setting the eighth-quickest time during the Thursday acclimatisation session, the Brabhams were in trouble in practice as they suffered from poor handling, so Lauda tried his car with the old nose/radiator set-up of

CHANGING HORSES 227

RIGHT Reverting to the 1977-specification nose, Niki's Brabham BT45C sits in the Jacarepaguá pits before the second qualifying session for the Brazilian Grand Prix.

BELOW Happy crew: Brabham designer Gordon Murray (centre) enjoyed Niki's respect and the two had a similarly intense work ethic; John Watson (right) had effectively been supplanted as number one driver by the Austrian's arrival but he was confident in his own abilities and had a good relationship with the double champion.

228 NIKI LAUDA

1978

the BT45B and immediately went a second a lap quicker. Much later, designer Gordon Murray admitted that the issue was the new-for-1978 full-width nose, which was mounted very low and — unbeknown at the time — was generating ground effect, causing a huge imbalance in front/rear grip. In the final session Lauda got down to a time good enough for the fifth row and then gallantly allowed the struggling John Watson to use his chassis in the last 10 minutes to try to improve his lowly grid position. The Ulsterman could only qualify 21st but at least he would have an old-style nose for the race as one was flown out for his car.

After his troubled practice, Lauda found his BT45C more to his liking in the warm-up and was more confident. Ninth after the first lap, he played his usual waiting game in the early stages, saving his tyres and his energy, although he came within inches of injury when, tucked in behind Hans Stuck's Shadow, a balance weight flew off one of the German's wheels and smashed through his screen, burying itself in the rear wing. He moved up to fourth when Stuck retired and on lap 57 passed Mario Andretti's Lotus, which had stuck in fourth gear. He took the final podium position just under a minute behind Carlos Reutemann's winning Ferrari. The irony of his former team's resurgence was not lost on the Austrian.

210 South African Grand Prix

Kyalami, 4 March 1978, Formula 1
Brabham BT46/1 • #1
Qualifying: 1st • Result: Retired (engine)

Extensive pre-race testing had paid off and the revamped BT46 was immediately among the pace-setters. Armed with the latest Goodyears and despite a broken rev counter, Lauda took a resounding pole position although he expressed doubts as to whether the tyres would last the race distance. In an error of judgement for which he apologised, later in

BELOW The new BT46 was quick 'out of the box' at Kyalami and after extensive pre-race testing Niki put it on pole. His strong showing in the race was ended by engine failure.

CHANGING HORSES 229

practice he ran into the back of Jean-Pierre Jarier's ATS at Leeukop but neither car was seriously damaged. Saturday qualifying was affected by a headwind along the main straight, so with 10 minutes still remaining Lauda sat back in the pits knowing that his pole time was beyond reach.

After causing a brief fracas by choosing to start from the opposite site of the track from the usual pole slot, which resulted in half of the grid being switched, he fumbled a gear change at the off and was swamped by the pack on the run up to Crowthorne, ending the lap in third place. Mario Andretti's leading Lotus ran into tyre problems after 16 laps and the American was closed down by a tremendous scrap between Jody Scheckter (Wolf), Lauda and Riccardo Patrese (in the brand-new Arrows). They all got past the ailing Lotus on lap 21 but by now the Brabham's engine was trailing an oil haze and was becoming more gutless as the race progressed. Although both Scheckter and Lauda were passed by Patrick Depailler (Tyrrell) within three laps, the Austrian managed to get ahead of the Wolf for third place, which he retained until his engine finally expired on lap 53.

BELOW Pictured in practice for the Silverstone International Trophy, Niki did not make the start of the race after spinning off in monsoon conditions during the warm-up.

211 Daily Express International Trophy (GB)

Silverstone, 19 March 1978, Formula 1
Brabham BT45C/8 • #1
Qualifying: 2nd • Result: Did not start (accident)

Back in a BT45C, Lauda qualified second and was optimistic about his chances in this non-championship race, but torrential rain fell just before the race was due to start, causing a delay. A brief acclimatisation session was organised for the drivers to assess the worst of the puddles, during which both Lauda and Ronnie Peterson (Lotus) spun off, the Brabham getting stuck in a quagmire that had formed between Becketts and Chapel. A willing marshal came to Niki's aid and carried him across the mud so he could keep his racing boots clean. By the time he arrived back at the pits in a course vehicle, the spare Brabham (BT45C/7) had been set up ready for him. Lauda took it out for a few reconnaissance laps but returned rather briskly to inform the team that it had a sticking throttle. It was tempting fate to run with this fault in such hazardous conditions, so the team decided to withdraw.

212 United States Grand Prix (West)

Long Beach, 2 April 1978, Formula 1
Brabham BT46/4 • #1
Qualifying: 3rd • Result: Retired (ignition)

Although Lauda and Carlos Reutemann (Ferrari) seemed to be setting the pace, the timing arrangements for Friday qualifying were shambolic and the overall placings were agreed among the teams on the basis of times collated by Ligier, Brabham and Ferrari. Matters were resolved on the second day and Lauda put his car third on the grid, having been consistently the fastest through the speed trap.

At the start, the Ferraris of Reutemann and Gilles Villeneuve and the Brabhams of John Watson and Lauda funnelled into the tight Queen Mary Hairpin and somehow all got through intact, the Austrian hanging on in third place. After 10 laps Watson retired from second place with oil leaking from his engine and Lauda took over the challenge for the lead, albeit some way behind Villeneuve. A procession developed, the Austrian running in close company with Reutemann, but this only lasted until lap 27 as his engine suddenly cut out on the top straight. The ignition unit had failed and he coasted up the escape road to retire.

213 Monaco Grand Prix

Monte Carlo, 7 May 1978, Formula 1
Brabham BT46/4 • #1
Qualifying: 3rd • Result: 2nd (fastest lap)

Having taken a tough line with the Brabham team over what he felt was an under-resourced test session at Jarama, for most of practice Lauda looked in splendid form. Second fastest on Thursday, he qualified a strong

ABOVE Niki takes a wide line into Queen's Hairpin on the opening lap at Long Beach, taking care to avoid any potential tangles between the Ferrari 312T3s of Carlos Reutemann and Gilles Villeneuve, while John Watson keeps to the inside in his sister Brabham.

CHANGING HORSES 231

ABOVE Brabham boss Bernie Ecclestone and Niki chat in the pitlane ahead of the Monaco Grand Prix. Formula 1's ringmaster maintained that the Austrian was the hardest negotiator he ever encountered among his drivers.

third, finishing the Saturday session early after deciding he could go no quicker — but he was then surprised to be leapfrogged by team-mate John Watson late in the day.

Indulging in some pushing and shoving with James Hunt (McLaren) and Carlos Reutemann (Ferrari) at the start, he nudged the Argentine driver at the first corner, *Ste Dévote*, puncturing the Ferrari's rear tyre but sustaining no damage to his Brabham. For half of the race he ran behind Watson, the leader, and Patrick Depailler (Tyrrell), at first staying far enough back to keep out of harm's way if the squabbling pair tangled, but then, as one-third distance approached, he closed right up on the French driver. On lap 38, Watson, his brakes fading, lost the lead when he went up the escape road at the chicane, leaving Depailler in front with Lauda all over him for the next seven laps. On lap 45 the Brabham picked up a rear puncture and Niki dived into the pits for a rapid tyre change. Leaving the pits like a dragster, he rejoined sixth and began a stirring drive through the field, gaining a place when Ronnie Peterson (Lotus) retired and pulling back eight seconds on Gilles Villeneuve (Ferrari) within five laps. By lap 63 he was tucked under the Ferrari's rear wing, swarming all over the red car as they approached *Mirabeau* and getting past when the French-Canadian crashed in the tunnel following a puncture.

Now Lauda had his sights on his team-mate in third place and the Brabhams swapped positions right in front of the pits. Closing down second-placed Jody Scheckter (Wolf) with three laps to go, Niki recorded an incredible new lap record, 0.23 second faster than he had gone in practice and an amazing 1.9 seconds faster than anyone else managed in the race. Immediately afterwards, Scheckter's gearbox stripped its second gear coming out of *Rascasse* and Lauda stormed past to take a superb second place behind Depailler, the Frenchman scoring an impressive maiden victory.

For Lauda, it had been perhaps the best drive of his career.

214 Belgian Grand Prix

Zolder, 21 May 1978, Formula 1
Brabham BT46/4 • #1
Qualifying: 3rd • Result: Retired (accident)

Announcing that the Brabham was good on its preferential Goodyear tyres but that other cars were better, Lauda missed the front row by 0.01 second after a long-running qualifying battle with the Ferraris of Carlos Reutemann and Gilles Villeneuve, although none of them could get near the times set by Mario Andretti, his eye-catching new Lotus 79 making its début.

There was chaos at the start. Jody Scheckter (Wolf) decided to drive for some distance along the grass to give himself a clear run past Reutemann's slow-shifting Ferrari, but only succeeded in ramming the back of Lauda's Brabham, pushing the Austrian into the barrier and out of the race before he had even got going. This was only one of a number of separate incidents that decimated the field on the first lap.

ABOVE In what was possibly the best drive of his career, Niki hurls the Brabham BT46 around the Loews hairpin in Monte Carlo during his stunning recovery drive to second place after being forced to pit with a puncture.

LEFT On the parade lap of the Belgian Grand Prix, Carlos Reutemann (Ferrari 312T3) and Mario Andretti (Lotus 79) lead away from Niki, Gilles Villeneuve (Ferrari 312T3), James Hunt (McLaren M26) and Jody Scheckter (Wolf WR5). Minutes later, the Argentine driver fluffed his start and, in the ensuing mêlée, Scheckter's over-ambitious driving put Lauda out of the race.

CHANGING HORSES 233

BRANDS HATCH
MAY AND JUNE 1978

In an effort to challenge the ground-effect Lotuses, Brabham's Gordon Murray devised a refinement of the Chaparral 'sucker' concept of 1970, with a large fan fitted to the back of the BT46 ostensibly for cooling purposes but in reality to extract air from under the car. His design also involved sealing the engine bay and underbody as well as adding the clutch system and fan behind the final drive. Chassis BT46/4 and BT46/6 were modified and tested in secret at Alfa Romeo's private Balocco test track, with encouraging initial results.

On 26 May, Lauda completed a second brief run in the fan-equipped BT46/4 amid tight security on the Brands Hatch short circuit, unofficially beating the lap record by two seconds. After experimenting with skirt configurations, fan speeds and radiator sizes, the revised car had a semi-public airing in Lauda's hands at the mid-week Goodyear tyre test at Brands Hatch in June. His times were not especially impressive, being some two to three seconds off the pace of the quickest runners, and the tests highlighted a weakness with fan blades. He had completed only a few laps when the plastic blades disintegrated and the same happened to subsequent glass-fibre versions, so new blades were cast in magnesium just in time for the Swedish Grand Prix. When the Austrian's second run at Brands Hatch during the morning session ended with an engine failure, the BT46B was loaded onto a truck and taken away; significantly, Brabham had brought no other cars to the test.

BELOW Niki's Brabham BT46 is wheeled out of the way and the two ATS HS1s of Jochen Mass and Alberto Colombo are told to wait as Riccardo Patrese's Arrows FA1 trundles down the Jarama pitlane during practice for the Spanish Grand Prix.

215 Spanish Grand Prix

Jarama, 4 June 1978, Formula 1
Brabham BT46/6 • #1
Qualifying: 6th • Result: Retired (engine)

Equipped with a brand-new chassis because his regular one had been damaged in the start-line shunt in Belgium, Lauda qualified on the third row, as ever driving the Brabham as hard as it would go and stating he had nothing left to give; the Lotuses and Ferraris ahead of him on the grid were just better cars. When conditions got hotter, he was one of only two drivers to improve his times.

He made a dreadful start and completed the first lap in 10th place. After passing Jody Scheckter's Wolf on lap 9, he caught up with the leading group by lap 16. For much of the race he was then involved in a battle with John Watson (Brabham), Jacques Laffite (Ligier) and Ronnie Peterson (Lotus) that developed into something of a stalemate. Watson was finding it difficult to select fourth gear and was holding up his challengers, but as they worked their way through the backmarkers Lauda got past his team-mate on lap 38 and moved forwards as attrition reduced the front runners. He was closing on the leaders and had just passed James Hunt's McLaren for fourth place when his race was ended by another blown Alfa Romeo engine, 20 laps from the finish.

216 Swedish Grand Prix

Anderstorp, 17 June 1978, Formula 1
Brabham BT46B/6 • #1
Qualifying: 3rd • Result: 1st (fastest lap)

Brabham revealed its famous 'fan car' at Anderstorp, initially to a certain amount of amusement among the other teams but that soon turned to dismay. Once the Brabham mechanics had sorted out the skirt system, the two BT46Bs were first and second on the opening day, Lauda having also briefly used the conventional spare car (BT46/5) in the morning session for comparison purposes. There was some sand-bagging by the two Brabham drivers on the second day — including qualifying with full fuel loads — to try to disguise the speed of their new cars and they allowed Mario Andretti's Lotus to take pole, Lauda ending up 0.46 second behind his team-mate for third place on the grid.

Niki slotted into second place behind Andretti at the start and stayed glued to the back of the Lotus, piling on the pressure as the pair streaked away from the pack. When, on lap 38, the American was late on the throttle exiting the last corner and slid wide, Lauda ducked inside the black car and moved effortlessly ahead on the main straight. As he blasted clear, his advantage was magnified by the fact that his was the only car that did not need to slow for oil dumped at the far side of the circuit by a backmarker, his level of grip such that he only had to keep in a higher gear through the affected section. Eight laps later the Lotus's engine let go, so Lauda — almost a full lap ahead of second-placed Riccardo Patrese's Arrows

ABOVE Niki dominated the Swedish Grand Prix in the Brabham BT46B, winning pretty much as he pleased with the 'fan car' giving hitherto unseen levels of grip and traction.

RIGHT This was pretty much the only view that Lauda's rivals, other than Mario Andretti, had of his Brabham BT46B 'fan car' at Anderstorp.

BELOW The sealed engine bay and side panels from the BT46B 'fan car' were fitted to Niki's conventional BT46 for the first day of practice at Paul Ricard.

— backed off and coasted to a dominant victory, by 34 seconds. Watson did not finish, having spun off on lap 19. It was the first Grand Prix win by an Alfa Romeo engine since 1951.

After the race, protests from five teams about the Brabham's legality were thrown out by the local stewards, so the dissenters took their greivance to an FIA tribunal in Paris.

Recognising that the unity of the constructors was more important to his wider ambitions that some short-term wins, Bernie Ecclestone voluntarily withdrew the BT46B and it never competed again.

217 French Grand Prix

Paul Ricard, 1 July 1978, Formula 1
Brabham BT46/6 • #1
Qualifying: 3rd • Result: Retired (engine)

Having been easily quickest in pre-race testing, unofficially breaking the lap record by a full second, in practice Lauda ran some of Gordon Murray's new ideas on the spare car (BT46/5), which retained the BT46B's rear suspension and engine cover with infill panels behind the rear wheels. The car was lightly used as Lauda found it no better than his normal mount, so he stuck with the standard set-up. Despite a bent monocoque, he was fastest in the first practice session, although he lacked straight-line speed and was even slower through the speed trap, by some 5mph, than also-ran Vittorio

236 NIKI LAUDA

1978

Brambilla's Surtees. After a helping tow from team-mate John Watson, he was quickest in final practice, one of only three drivers to improve their times, but the rain-disrupted session meant he lined up third on the grid.

He ran in the leading quartet at the start, slipping past Patrick Tambay's McLaren for third place on lap 3 to press Watson for second. His Brabham colleague let him through at the end of the straight on lap 8 to see if he could do any better in challenging Mario Andretti's Lotus for the lead, but inadvertently the Ulsterman also let Ronnie Peterson's Lotus overtake as well. With Peterson threatening, Lauda only managed two more laps before his engine dropped a valve and he crawled into the pits to retire.

ABOVE Back in normal configuration, Niki's BT46 powers through the Esses at Paul Ricard ahead of James Hunt's McLaren M26, Alan Jones's Williams FW06, Jacques Laffite's Ligier JS7/9 and Jody Scheckter's Wolf WR5.

GOODWOOD
JULY 1978

Ahead of the British Grand Prix, Brabham gave the 'fan car' a low-key outing at Goodwood, with Lauda at the helm and a new sucker arrangement linked to the exhaust system this time. The intention was to test the resilience of Goodyear's softer rubber under the higher-downforce loadings generated by the BT46B, no doubt to provide useful data for Gordon Murray's next effort in the quest for ground-effect advantage.

By now several observant reporters had commented that Lauda was a notable absentee from the chorus of complainants protesting the Lotus 79's ground-effect 'unfair advantage', but this was no surprise to those who knew his belief in the benefits of developing a car to a point where it was significantly better than the competition. By the end of the year, although his mantra of 'testing, testing, testing' would make the Brabham the best-handling, Goodyear-shod, non-Cosworth package, it still could not overcome the inherent unreliability of the Alfa Romeo flat-12 engine.

CHANGING HORSES 237

ABOVE Niki's Brabham BT46 leads Jody Scheckter's Wolf WR5, Riccardo Patrese's Arrows FA1 and the Ferrari 312T3 of eventual winner Carlos Reutemann through Druids during the British Grand Prix.

218 British Grand Prix

Brands Hatch, 16 July 1978, Formula 1
Brabham BT46/6 • #1
Qualifying: 4th • Result: 2nd (fastest lap)

Lauda's Brabham was bottoming badly in first practice over Brands Hatch's notorious bumps, enough to damage the suspension and force him into the spare car (BT46/5) on Friday afternoon, although the trait was virtually eliminated by Saturday, when he qualified on the second row.

He was passed by Alan Jones's nimble Williams at the start, running fifth for six laps until promoted by the retirement of Ronnie Peterson's Lotus. This became third place on lap 24 when Mario Andretti (Lotus) pitted and then second just three laps later when Jones retired.

He hounded Jody Scheckter's leading Wolf and got past the South African rather easily on lap 33, holding the lead for the next 25 laps while Carlos Reutemann's Ferrari closed steadily, the Argentine driver's Michelin tyres in better shape than the Brabham's Goodyears.

Lauda appeared to have things under control until he was inadvertently baulked at Clearways on lap 60 by the McLaren of Bruno Giacomelli when lining up to lap it and this allowed the opportunistic Reutemann to squeeze through the resulting gap. Temporarily rattled by the incident, Niki took a few laps to lap Hans Stuck's Shadow and during that time Reutemann built up a margin of four seconds, but the Austrian came back with everything he could, shattering the lap record four laps from the finish. His spirited pursuit left him just 1.3 seconds adrift of the winning Ferrari at the flag.

1978

219 German Grand Prix

Hockenheim, 30 July 1978, Formula 1
Brabham BT46/6 • #1
Qualifying: 3rd • Result: Retired (engine)

During the first practice session, Lauda spent some time in the spare car (BT46C/3), which was fitted with relocated water radiators faired into the sides of the monocoque so as to sit flush to the bodywork just behind the front wheels, enabling Gordon Murray to employ the 'needle-nose' concept he had envisaged in his original 'surface-cooling' design for the BT46. Lauda was unconvinced by the new layout and when a water leak developed after only a few laps he returned to his usual car, which remained in standard configuration, to complete qualifying.

He was the only driver to stay in touch with the dominant ground-effect Lotus 79s of Mario Andretti and Ronnie Peterson during practice, showing breathtaking precision in particular through the quick right-hander into the stadium. He also tried out a cockpit-adjustable anti-roll bar in practice — just the sort of technical innovation he relished — and used it in the race, but it seemed to be of little benefit.

He held third position from the start but was passed by Alan Jones's quicker Williams in an impressive move on lap 3. Running on his own in fourth place, the Brabham slowed as he came past the pits to start his 12th lap and he pulled onto the infield to retire with another engine failure. In fact a water leak had been discovered on the grid and the Austrian had gone into the race with little confidence that his car would last the distance.

ABOVE During first practice at Hockenheim, Lauda tried the modified Brabham BT46C with water radiators mounted flush on the car's flanks and the chisel nose from the withdrawn BT46B.

BELOW Speeding past empty grandstands, Niki qualified third at Hockenheim.

CHANGING HORSES 239

BELOW Cresting the hill at the top of the start/finish straight, Niki's Brabham BT46 turns into the *Hella-Licht* chicane during practice for the Austrian Grand Prix.

220 Austrian Grand Prix

Österreichring, 11 August 1978, Formula 1
Brabham BT46/6 • #1
Qualifying: 12th • Result: Retired (accident)

Lauda and John Watson were among the first out on track in the initial practice session, both Brabhams having been converted to the C-specification side-radiator arrangement seen at Hockenheim. Although the revised configuration produced better weight distribution, bigger front wings were needed to balance the car's aerodynamics and Lauda found the handling to be worse than with the front-radiator set-up on the spare car (BT46/3). As well as consuming tyres at an alarming rate, the C-specification cars also lacked straight-line speed. After an hour of abortive attempts to find a decent set-up, over the lunch interval the cars were switched back to front-radiator

1978

PAUL RICARD
23 AUGUST 1978

Autodelta, the sporting arm of Alfa Romeo, had been running a sports car programme in the World Championship for Makes for many years but intended to curtail it at the end of 1977. The company's mercurial chief engineer, Carlo Chiti, turned his attention instead to developing an in-house Formula 1 project, amid much hype in the Italian media. There was a long gestation period before a running prototype was produced and then, after weeks of lobbying, the team managed to persuade Lauda to try out the long-awaited T177.

The first test session was carried out at Alfa's own Balocco track with Vittorio Brambilla. Lauda took part in a second session at Paul Ricard, completing 40 laps of the short circuit, but the car suffered persistent overheating and he could not get within two seconds of his Brabham time. For contractual reasons, he was obliged to run the car on Goodyear tyres while Brambilla used the experimental Pirellis for which the car had been designed; as a result, the Italian was slightly faster than Lauda. Anonymous eye-witnesses reported that the engine overheated after three laps, that the car's nose collapsed shortly afterwards and that the exercise ended with an engine failure.

The partisan Italian press reported widely — but incorrectly — that Lauda was unwilling to help and that he had strongly criticised the T177 to Alfa Romeo management, wrongly putting him in a bad light.

CHANGING HORSES 241

ABOVE Niki gave the Brabham BT46C its second and final public airing during first practice at the Österreichring. By the afternoon the car was back in its conventional configuration.

OPPOSITE Carlos Reutemann's Ferrari 312T3 follows Niki's Brabham BT46 through Zandvoort's *Panorama-Bocht*. The Austrian finished third and set fastest lap.

specification for the second session and the C-specification layout was not tried again.

Lauda then quickly lowered his times but had a big moment when a rear wheel came loose. His race car then broke its transmission and he abandoned it out on the circuit, switching to the spare until the engine in that blew up a few minutes later. He wound up 12th on the grid, two places behind his team-mate.

The race started in gentle drizzle, with everyone on slick tyres. When the rain became heavier, there were numerous incidents and proceedings had to be halted after seven laps, by which time Lauda had worked his way up to sixth place. The restart came an hour later with everyone on wet tyres and the grid organised according to positions at the stoppage.

Lauda capitalised and lay third at the end of the first lap and then fought his way past Patrick Depailler's Tyrrell to take second place on lap 5. After running faster than Ronnie Peterson's leading Lotus, he pitted on lap 11 with his wet tyres deteriorating, having been passed by the Michelin-shod Ferrari of Carlos Reutemann. His race came to an abrupt end on lap 21 when, trying too hard to catch up again, he got off the dry line at the *Rindtkurve* and spun backwards into the barrier. He was able to restart, but the rear suspension had been badly bent by the impact and he was forced to park in the pitlane. With typical candour, he admitted responsibility for the error.

221 Dutch Grand Prix

Zandvoort, 27 August 1978, Formula 1
Brabham BT46/7 • #1
Qualifying: 3rd • Result: 3rd (fastest lap)

Lauda now had a new race car (BT46/7) but while it was being readied on Friday morning he tried his old one (BT46/6), which was now the spare. Driving with tremendous verve and precision, despite being baulked by Arturo Merzario's self-built car, he qualified third behind the now almost unbeatable Lotus duo, Mario Andretti and Ronnie Peterson, who locked out the front row for the fourth consecutive race.

After encountering a strong headwind on Zandvoort's main straight during the warm-up, he went to the grid with a shorter fifth gear installed. On the second lap he passed the fast-starting Ligier of Jacques Laffite for third place under braking for *Tarzan* and a few corners afterwards squeezed safely through a blockage created by a first-lap tangle between Riccardo Patrese's Arrows and Didier Pironi's Tyrrell. Although his BT46 was not in the same class as the Lotuses, he drove forcefully and relentlessly to keep the leading pair under pressure, giving the all-conquering black cars their first real challenge in four races.

It almost seemed that the Lotus drivers were playing with him. When Lauda began to attack, Peterson fulfilled his contractual role in protecting Andretti and it was clear that the American was matching his pace exactly to Niki's. Towards the end, Andretti's engine sounded increasingly harsh due to an exhaust breakage and the fact that it was set rather 'lean' to make sure the car did not run out of fuel. Meanwhile, Lauda's engine started to sound like it was misfiring, but the explanation was simple: its rev limiter had suddenly reset itself to 11,800rpm instead of the normal 12,300rpm and Niki decided to put up with a few horsepower less rather than risk another engine failure. Just after he had set fastest lap while closing to within two seconds of the Lotus pair, the Brabham also lost a balance weight from a rear wheel, causing considerable vibration, so Lauda backed off for the last 12 laps and focused on finishing.

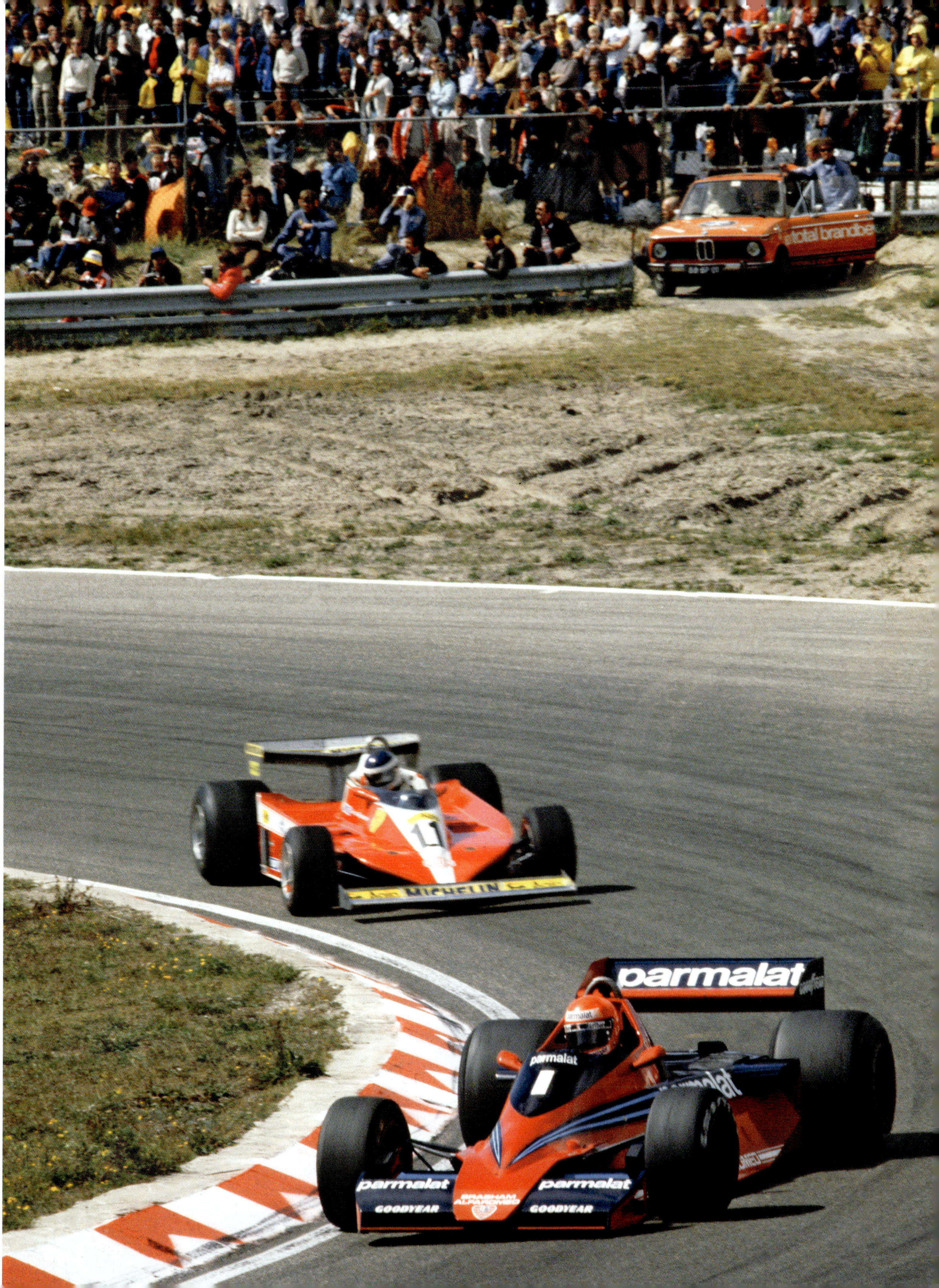
parmalat
MICHELIN
GOODYEAR

ABOVE Holding a drift through Monza's famous *Parabolica*, Niki heads for victory in the shortened Italian Grand Prix; he was third on the road but the two men ahead of him — Mario Andretti and Gilles Villeneuve — were penalised for jumping the start.

222 Italian Grand Prix

Monza, 10 September 1978, Formula 1
Brabham BT46/7 • #1
Qualifying: 4th • Result: 1st

Second fastest through the speed traps at Monza, Lauda was much more pleased with his car's performance if not the Alfa Romeo engine's reliability, as he suffered a camshaft failure in first practice and a blow-up at the end of the untimed session on Saturday morning. Both setbacks forced him to use the spare BT46/6, although an engine change saw him back in his allocated chassis for the race.

As the grid raced away, mayhem involving 10 cars broke loose in midfield. The first that the front runners, including Lauda, knew of the carnage was when, led by Gilles Villeneuve's Ferrari and Mario Andretti's Lotus, they were shown the red flag at the start/finish line as they completed their first lap. As the gravity of the incident became clear — it later claimed the life of Ronnie Peterson and left Vittorio Brambilla seriously injured — Lauda was a leading voice among those who called for the race to be cancelled, but it eventually went ahead, shortened to 40 laps from the original 52.

When the remaining cars reformed for the restart in gathering gloom, Villeneuve and Andretti began to creep forward and eventually the French-Canadian's Ferrari set off long before the green light appeared, with Andretti's Lotus in pursuit. The rest of the field waited for the signal to go and Lauda made an excellent getaway to run fourth behind Jean-Pierre Jabouille, pressuring the Renault driver until he retired after only five laps. After several laps

244 NIKI LAUDA

1978

the organisers announced that Villeneuve and Andretti were to receive a one-minute penalty for jumping the start, so Lauda — third on the road — was in fact the leader, even if the big electronic scoreboard did not register this for the duration of the race. Having held off a fast-closing John Watson in the latter stages, Lauda was declared the winner, although there was little for anyone to celebrate and the Austrian did not participate in the podium ceremony.

223 United States Grand Prix (East)

Watkins Glen, 1 October 1978, Formula 1
Brabham BT46/7 • #1
Qualifying: 5th • Result: Retired (engine)

Following their 1–2 in Italy, much was expected of the Brabham-Alfas on the fast Watkins Glen circuit, but they did not shine as anticipated. A new engine was fitted to Lauda's car between practice sessions, but the Austrian was not certain that it was any better than the original and he failed to improve on his Friday time. He had the engine changed again for the race, starting from fifth position on the grid.

Minutes before the start, his mechanics spotted oil leaking from a porous casting so it looked doubtful that the car would last the distance. For once the Lotuses did not escape from the rest of the field and in the pursuing pack Lauda ran fifth. He improved to fourth on lap 22 when Gilles Villeneuve's Ferrari blew its engine and had just passed Mario Andretti's Lotus for third when the American suffered a similar fate on lap 25. Three laps later he was out himself, the Alfa Romeo flat-12 also having expired after losing all its oil, just as had been expected.

224 Canadian Grand Prix

Montréal, 8 October 1978, Formula 1
Brabham BT46/7 • #1
Qualifying: 7th • Result: Retired (brakes)

The Canadian Grand Prix took place on Montréal's new 2.7-mile (4.4km) Île Notre-Dame circuit but Lauda was unimpressed with it and his 100th Grand Prix gave him little cause for celebration. Along with most drivers, he sat in the pits on Saturday morning waiting for the wet and windy conditions to improve, so he had

BELOW Another engine failure eliminated Lauda's Brabham BT46 while lying third at Watkins Glen.

CHANGING HORSES

ABOVE The futuristic Expo architecture of the Île Notre-Dame forms a strange backdrop as Niki splashes around the Montréal circuit during qualifying for the Canadian Grand Prix.

little track time. With its tight configuration, the circuit made high demands on brakes and the Brabham struggled, Lauda complaining of inadequate stopping power and turn-in difficulties into the slow corners. He was seventh when qualifying ended and there seemed to be a distinct lack of interest from the Brabham team in solving the problem, Gordon Murray having returned to base to work on the 1979 car.

Come the race, Lauda just avoided a collision at the first chicane between Hans Stuck (Shadow) and Emerson Fittipaldi (Fittipaldi) that caused chaos in the pack. Running in a tight nose-to-tail group, he stayed in his seventh position for the scant five laps he completed before his unsatisfactory brakes led him to clip a kerb at one of the chicanes. When he pitted to have the car checked, it was found that the incident had also deranged the steering, so he called it a day.

225 International Race of Champions (USA)

Riverside, 14 October 1978
Chevrolet Camaro Z28 • #14
Qualifying: 4th • Result: Retired (clutch)

The International Race of Champions (IROC) had established itself as a light-hearted but lucrative season-ending series of three fixtures in the United States, with rounds on the speedways at Michigan and Daytona sandwiching a pair of road races at Riverside in California. Given its use of matching NASCAR-style Chevrolet Camaros, IROC was of greater interest to American audiences, but nevertheless it was an opportunity for drivers from different disciplines to race in ostensibly equal machinery. The organisers had been trying to secure Lauda's participation for four years, but a clause in his

1978

Ferrari contract had prevented him from racing other cars (with the specific exception of Fords in touring car racing during 1974).

This was Lauda's first visit to Riverside and, when not besieged by fans, he spent a lot of time studying the circuit and the sector times of his rivals. However, his clutch failed at the start of the first of the two 30-lap races (some cynics thought this may not have been unintentional) and he dropped down the field before retiring at the end of the first lap. His non-finish ruled him out of any meaningful participation in the rest of the IROC series, so he collected his appearance money and went home.

SUMMARY

It had been a disappointing year that yielded only two wins, both of which were somewhat controversial. The season had been tarnished above all by appalling engine reliability — there were 11 failures for the team during the year — but too many other setbacks also intervened and Lauda finished only seven of the year's 16 Grands Prix, while team-mate John Watson completed 10. On the other hand, Niki had gained in speed and aggression, such that *Autocourse* — the highly respected motor racing annual — rated him as its driver of the year, ahead of World Champion Mario Andretti.

Former team-mate Clay Regazzoni drily observed that if Lauda had remained at Ferrari, he would have won the five races in which Carlos Reutemann and Gilles Villeneuve had been victorious and probably Monaco as well, all of which collectively might have been sufficient for him to prevail over Andretti's Lotus. Ifs and buts maybe, but there were others who agreed with Regazzoni.

For a while, Brabham's shortcomings had led Lauda to consider his options and ahead of the Italian Grand Prix he had discussed a possible move to the new Renault team. He was attracted by the development potential of the French team's new turbo engine technology and Michelin radials for the 1979 season, but the lure of Gordon Murray's radical new ground-effect BT48 prevailed.

ABOVE Niki manhandles the bulky Chevrolet Camaro Z28 around the sandy expanses of Riverside during practice for the IROC race — which for him lasted just one lap.

PAUL RICARD
OCTOBER 1978

Lauda was coaxed back by Autodelta to test slight modifications to the T177's bodywork and a new air intake over the front wing. After initially answering 'no comment' to questions regarding the car's performance, leading to speculation that he had been gagged as the project was an expensive failure, when pressed further he was uncomplimentary, reporting that the car was too heavy and handled poorly. He received another backlash from the Italian press for his trouble, although Alfa Romeo's contracted driver, Bruno Giacomelli, subsequently confirmed Lauda's misgivings. After this outing, he had no further involvement with this works project and he was undoubtedly lukewarm about the whole affair as he wanted Alfa Romeo to focus on developing the new V12 engines it was contracted to supply to Brabham for 1979.

CHANGING HORSES

1979
ALSO-RAN...
AND CHAMPION

Early in December 1978 while testing one of the Brabham BT46s at Interlagos in Brazil, Lauda had a huge accident after brake failure at 160mph. The impact tore off the front of the car and Niki suffered concussion after taking a blow to the helmet from a catch-fencing pole and also hurt his wrist. His car had looked unstable through fast turns and its times were never close to those of McLaren, Lotus or even Fittipaldi.

Despite this chastening experience, Lauda was optimistic about the new season, as he had been at the start of 1978, and was keen to get his hands on Gordon Murray's latest creation with its new Alfa Romeo V12 engine — reportedly the most expensive Formula 1 car ever built. The comment that he made when joining Brabham a year earlier — 'the more complicated, the better' — would come back to haunt him: the ground-effect BT48 was nothing if not complicated, but not in a positive way. A great deal of development work would be needed to make it competitive. There were also problems with the Alfa Romeo V12s, the performance of which varied alarmingly from engine to engine, with inconsistent revs and oil scavenging, and they soon proved to be very unreliable.

The scene was set for Lauda's most frustrating season in Formula 1. He would also have to contend with a new, young team-mate, Nelson Piquet, who was clearly very quick and soon showed great potential.

1979

BRANDS HATCH
23 DECEMBER 1978

Lauda's first drive in the lowline Brabham BT48 came just before Christmas in very cold conditions at Brands Hatch, the team's local circuit, but it achieved little. Soon after the seasonal festivities, a more serious session at Paul Ricard was abandoned amid torrential rain and snow, so the team hurriedly decamped to Jarama. With virtually no time available until the cars left for South America, even the Spanish sojourn allowed little more than a basic shakedown for the BT48. However, it was immediately apparent that with the combination of very long venturi, ineffective skirts and overly soft springs, the car's centre of aerodynamic pressure was moving half a metre or more in each direction while out on track.

226 Argentine Grand Prix

Buenos Aires, 21 January 1979, Formula 1
Brabham BT48/2 • #5
Qualifying: 22nd • Result: Retired (fuel pressure)

The largely untested Brabham BT48 proved troublesome, needing a complete revision of the Alfa Romeo V12's fuel system after first practice on Thursday. Seldom completing more than four consecutive laps, Lauda spent most of his time trying to get the sliding skirts to work; they were not sealing properly to the ground, causing the car to generate lift when they stuck in an 'up' position, and at one point he even felt the front wheels leave the road as he powered down the main straight. As conceived, the BT48 had a low-line rear flap rather than a conventional wing and this exacerbated the car's porpoising tendencies, so a makeshift wing was

LEFT Desperate measures: after myriad 'new-car' problems during practice, Brabham was forced to press the previous year's BT46 into service so that Niki could qualify for the Argentine Grand Prix.

ALSO-RAN… AND CHAMPION 249

ABOVE Despite appearances, the Brabham BT48 was a dog of a car at the start of the season. Lauda only managed a handful of racing laps at Buenos Aires before retiring with fuel pick-up problems.

built up for later practice and the race.

After these endless dramas left him at the very bottom of the timekeepers' sheets, late on Saturday afternoon Lauda took out the old BT46/7, which had been brought along as the spare, in a last-ditch attempt to qualify. Even then he just managed to scrape a place on the grid, 23rd, before the scavenge pump broke after only five laps and the car lost all its oil. His best time was over six seconds adrift of Jacques Laffite's Ligier on pole position.

Despite the problems, Lauda decided to continue with the BT48 'test' programme for as long as the new car would run in the race. After stuttering off the line with low fuel pressure, he encountered a first-corner mêlée that caused the race to be red-flagged. Triggered when John Watson (McLaren) and Jody Scheckter (Ferrari) collided, it involved four other cars, one of which was Nelson Piquet's BT48; Niki went to his new team-mate's aid and helped to pull him from his wrecked car.

The restart went more smoothly and Lauda made up three places in the first few laps, only to pit on lap 6 with the Alfa V12 again suffering serious fuel-pressure problems. A long stop dropped him to last place, but he tried another couple of laps before finally giving up. To compound his frustration, a planned private test session after the Grand Prix had to be abandoned because no fire crew could be found to attend the proceedings.

227 Brazilian Grand Prix

Interlagos, 4 February 1979, Formula 1
Brabham BT48/1 • #5
Qualifying: 12th • Result: Retired (gear linkage)

At Interlagos things looked up a little for the BT48 development programme and Lauda got the car onto the sixth row of the grid. New skirt material and a revised fuel system had cured two of the car's biggest problems, so he could now focus on fine tuning of aerodynamics and suspension. He was also more positive about Alfa Romeo's new V12, which this time did not break, although technical niggles meant he was unable to record a single flying lap on Saturday. Gordon Murray was impressed and relieved by the way Lauda worked steadily to resolve

1979

the problems rather than throw up his hands in despair and give up.

Tenth at the end of the first lap, Lauda then dropped well down the field after his promising start as gear-selection difficulties set in. Often unable to select fourth or fifth gears, he lost places hand over fist. After being passed by team-mate Nelson Piquet and struggling on for another few laps, he parked in the pits for good on lap 5 after the gear linkage was found to be flexing.

228 South African Grand Prix

Kyalami, 3 March 1979, Formula 1
Brabham BT48/2 • #5
Qualifying: 4th • Result: 6th

Recognising one of Kyalami's unpredictable 'fast' days, Lauda quickly set about practice

ABOVE Niki's Brabham BT48 dives through Interlagos's *Ferradura* corner *en route* to another early retirement, this time with gear-selection problems.

BELOW A blend of youth and experience, although neither looks particularly happy — Brabham team-mates Nelson Piquet and Niki in the pits before the South African Grand Prix.

ALSO-RAN... AND CHAMPION **251**

with the softest qualifying tyres and used three sets before the favourable conditions faded. Running without fins on its nose, the new Brabham now looked more promising and he was a surprising fourth quickest, the fastest Goodyear runner. After briefly trying the spare car (BT48/1) he spent the rest of the day running on full tanks and race rubber in preparation for Sunday.

The race was stopped after only two laps when the far side of the circuit became drenched by heavy rain. When it restarted, he opted for wet tyres, like most of the field. Passed by the Tyrrell of Jean-Pierre Jarier on the second lap, he dropped briefly to sixth before becoming one of the first to pit for dry tyres, on lap 9, but his stop was slow and he fell to the back. After five chaotic laps of pit stops, the order settled and he found himself seventh, where he ran for a long time, slowed by a loose rear wing mounting and a down-on-power engine. He dropped behind the Renaults of Jean-Pierre Jabouille and René Arnoux until they both retired but eased his way back to sixth, finishing a length ahead of Nelson Piquet after the Brabhams swapped places with four laps remaining.

BELOW Kyalami, lap 1: Niki's Brabham BT48 narrowly leads Jacques Laffite's Ligier JS11, the two Tyrrell 009s of Didier Pironi and Jean-Pierre Jarier, René Arnoux's Renault RS01, Mario Andretti's Lotus 79 and the rest.

229 United States Grand Prix (West)

Long Beach, 8 April 1979, Formula 1
Brabham BT48/2 • #5
Qualifying: 11th • Result: Retired (collision)

A raft of problems denied Lauda any participation in the quickest practice session: a slow engine change on his race car forced him to use the spare (BT48/1), which was also troublesome, so for a while he was left sitting in the pits with nothing to drive. With only 30 minutes of the final session left, he was hampered by a loose wing mounting, which had been bent when marshals pushed the car away earlier in the afternoon. This upset the car's handling so he had the nose fins remounted to improve balance, with little effect. Despite all the problems, his 11th place on the grid was better than that of his new team-mate, who lined up right behind him.

After an initial false start, there was a long wait for the race to restart, and when it did there was a first-corner shunt. Behind the leaders, the field arrived at the hairpin in one great bunch: Patrick Tambay darted out to the side but, off the racing line, locked his McLaren's front wheels on the sand-covered track, mounted the back of Jan Lammers's Shadow and landed on top of Lauda's Brabham, removing its rear wing and flattening the exhaust pipes. The Austrian retired immediately.

SALZBURGRING
10 APRIL 1979

Needing a way to show off BMW's new mid-engined M1 coupé, the company's motorsport supremo, Jochen Neerpasch, came up with the idea for the Procar series, to be run as support races at selected Grands Prix. Lauda was one of the first to sign up for the championship, with an eye on both the cash bonuses available and the prize of an M1 for the champion, and he was keen to explore the car's potential.

He was asked to undertake a detailed test at the Salzburgring of the Group 4 silhouette version, potentially destined for Group 5 although production problems meant that the homologated version of the car in the bigger class was unlikely to be ready before the beginning of 1980. When the rear bodywork flew off on his first lap, the test had to be abandoned.

ABOVE Niki's Brabham BT48 is assaulted by Patrick Tambay's McLaren M28 at Queen's Hairpin just after the start of the United States Grand Prix (West). The rear wing of Jan Lammers's Shadow DN9 has also been damaged by the errant McLaren, although Clay Regazzoni seems unaware of what is happening to the right of his Williams FW06.

ALSO-RAN... AND CHAMPION 253

230 Race of Champions (GB)

Brands Hatch, 14 April 1979, Formula 1
Brabham BT48/2 • #5
Qualifying: 2nd • Result: 5th

This long-time non-championship fixture was back after a break in 1978. Originally scheduled for 18 March, it had had to be abandoned at 24 hours' notice because of heavy snow, and was rescheduled for Easter weekend. It was contested by seven World Championship regulars and 12 participants from Britain's Aurora AFX Formula 1 Championship, the latter starting from a separate grid.

In morning practice, Lauda's BT48 sported heavily revised bodywork and radiators but the Austrian ran only briefly before a constant-velocity driveshaft joint broke, stranding him out on the circuit and bringing the session to a halt while the car was recovered. He returned to the pits with instructions for the BT48 to be

ABOVE Niki pulls out of the Brands Hatch pits in an unusual-looking Brabham BT48, with a configuration of bodywork that was only ever seen during first practice for the Race of Champions.

BELOW With his Brabham BT48 restored to its conventional layout, Niki made a more positive impression, leading early in the Race of Champions at Brands Hatch.

1979

ABOVE Niki produced a forceful drive in the Spanish Grand Prix at Jarama but engine failure brought yet another retirement.

converted back to normal specification for the afternoon runs, when he looked consistently stronger. Quickest for most of the second session, he was pipped for pole in the dying minutes by Mario Andretti's Lotus when he encountered gear-selection problems.

The American opted to start from the left-hand side of the grid, taking the outside line into Paddock Hill Bend, but as the green light flashed Lauda lit up the Brabham's super-soft Goodyears and blasted away into the lead. He was two seconds to the good at the end of the first lap and looked to be running away with the race as his lead extended, but by lap 6 Gilles Villeneuve's Ferrari had halved the gap. On lap 8 Niki pitted to replace blistered tyres and rejoined fifth. Thanks to mild weather and a compromised suspension set-up, he had to stop for more fresh tyres on lap 20, rejoining sixth. When Rupert Keegan's Arrows retired with five laps to go, Niki moved up to fifth place, albeit a lap behind.

The Brabham team stayed put for further tests on 16 April, when Lauda completed 90 laps of the short course, now known as the 'Indy' circuit in honour of the previous year's Indycar race here. With subtle changes to skirts and sidepods, he set the fastest time recorded on this 1.2-mile (1.9km) bowl, much quicker than the more powerful Indycars had achieved, and better even than the BT46B 'fan car'.

231 Spanish Grand Prix

Jarama, 29 April 1979, Formula 1
Brabham BT48/2 • #5
Qualifying: 6th • Result: Retired (engine)

Initially well down the order on Friday, Lauda was unhappy with his car's handling and asked for nose fins — not seen since Brazil — to be refitted, and a weak engine was also replaced on Friday night. The following day he used the last of the available qualifying tyres early and took sixth position on the grid.

Using a different race strategy from everyone else, he started on Goodyear's softest tyres and drove with restraint to spare them until the last third of the race. Seventh initially, he moved forward when Gilles Villeneuve's Ferrari and Jacques Laffite's Ligier quit, respectively on laps 4 and 16, before pressuring Mario Andretti for 27 laps, eventually forcing his way past the unbalanced Lotus. Suitably encouraged, he reined in Jody Scheckter, who was also fighting handling problems with his Ferrari, and after a 14-lap tussle found a way past when the South African made a mistake while tearing off a visor strip. He was now third but his forceful drive ended just 12 laps from home when, thanks to a leaking water union, water temperature disappeared off the clock and the Alfa Romeo V12 all but seized.

ALSO-RAN... AND CHAMPION **255**

232 Procar race (B)

Zolder, 12 May 1979, Procar Championship
BMW M1 (WBS59910004301028) • #5
Qualifying: 4th • Result: Retired (flywheel damper)

New for 1979, the Procar Championship was devised as a series for Formula 1 and touring car drivers in BMW M1s at eight European rounds of the World Championship, each race to be run on the day preceding the Grand Prix. Five M1s were prepared and entered by BMW Motorsport for the Friday morning session's five fastest Formula 1 drivers, who automatically received the top five grid slots, although their practice times in the M1s were not divulged. The rest of the grid — a further 14 entries for this inaugural event — came from privateer teams with their own regular drivers.

At Zolder, Lauda's Friday performance in his Brabham BT48 put him in the top five and made him eligible for one of the 'works' Procars, but in fact he was entered for the race anyway. Rather shrewdly, he had organised a seat for the season in the Marlboro-backed car run by Ron Dennis's Project Four organisation and had tested it for the first time at Silverstone a week earlier. He drove this in place of his allocated factory car, which remained unused, but he was nevertheless allowed to start fourth on the grid as allotted by his Formula 1 time.

During Procar practice in wet conditions, Lauda was visibly the neatest — and quickest — of the five Grand Prix participants, the others being Mario Andretti, Jacques Laffite, Nelson Piquet and Clay Regazzoni; in fact Ferrari's Gilles Villeneuve and Renault's Jean-Pierre Jabouille should have been involved by virtue of their practice times, but their teams used Michelin tyres and contractually they were not allowed to participate in the Goodyear-supported series. Revelling in the relaxed atmosphere, Lauda proclaimed of the M1s, 'They're quick, and they oversteer.'

In the 20-lap race, he made a superb start and lay second to Regazzoni at the end of the opening lap. He hounded the leader until lap 6, when his engine broke its crankshaft damper and lost all of its water.

BELOW The Project Four crew complete their final pre-race discussions with Niki, who is strapped into the BMW M1 in the Zolder pitlane in readiness for the inaugural event of the Procar series.

233 Belgian Grand Prix

Zolder, 13 May 1979, Formula 1
Brabham BT48/4 • #5
Qualifying: 13th • Result: Retired (engine)

Lauda looked his usual efficient self in practice but he was overshadowed by team-mate Nelson Piquet, whose best time was 1.5 seconds better and put him 10 places further up the grid, in third spot. Using a new chassis with a slightly lighter monocoque and other detail changes, in Friday morning practice he was six positions slower than the bulky Alfa Romeo T177, which was making its début in the hands of Bruno Giacomelli. This spurred his resolve and in the timed session he was the first to use his qualifying tyres and after 11 minutes he was the quickest man in the field, but then many others went faster while he did not. Complaining that the engine in his new car was weak, he transferred to the spare (BT48/2) for Saturday's final session but handling problems meant that he completed only a few laps. The warm-up was no better and the electrics were changed after the Alfa engine lapsed onto 11 cylinders.

After a poor start, he was overtaken by Jochen Mass, whose Arrows had got a flyer from the penultimate row. Niki struggled to repass his old touring car partner but finally got in front, only to come under attack from another German driver, Hans Stuck, whose ATS overtook on lap 19 as Lauda struggled increasingly with falling oil pressure caused by a leak. On lap 23 his engine expired with a release of oil, which caused some scary moments for the rest of the pack.

This was Lauda's fifth non-finish in six races and his dissatisfaction with Brabham and its ineffective and unreliable ground-effect car was growing.

234 Procar race (MC)

Monte Carlo, 26 May 1979, Procar Championship
BMW M1 (WBS59910004301028) • #5
Qualifying: 1st • Result: 1st

Despite knowing what they had signed up for, some of the drivers of privateer Procar entries were already complaining about the fact that the five 'guest' Formula 1 drivers, who were reportedly receiving $6,000 each for taking part in a race, occupied the top five grid positions regardless of practice times. This time the Grand Prix participants joining Lauda were Jean-Pierre Jarier, Patrick Depailler, Emerson Fittipaldi and Clay Regazzoni, but it was the Austrian who stood out with his smooth, fast progress, rarely hitting the BMW-imposed rev limiter, unlike most.

Come the 15-lap race, Regazzoni just pipped Lauda into *Ste Dévote*. Niki stayed in touch as the pair broke away from the rest of the field, with Jarier holding third place until he had to pit on

ABOVE Finally making a race start, the Alfa Romeo T177 of Bruno Giacomelli noses out alongside Niki's Brabham BT48 before the Belgian Grand Prix. Queuing up behind the Austrian in the Zolder pitlane are the Arrows A1 of Jochen Mass and Nelson Piquet's sister Brabham BT48.

ALSO-RAN... AND CHAMPION 257

ABOVE Niki's BMW M1 takes the chequered flag to win a popular victory in the Monaco Procar race, with Clay Regazzoni's second-placed factory entry in pursuit.

lap 7 for a new tyre. By lap 9 Lauda was right up with Regazzoni, harrying his old BRM and Ferrari team-mate, only inches from his rear bumper, and eventually pressuring him into missing a gear at *Rascasse* with two laps to go. Lauda elbowed his way through a tight gap amid smoking tyres and flying fragments of glass-fibre from damaged wheel arches and took the win.

This was the high spot of his season so far and confounded cynics who said that it was impossible to pass on the confined street circuit in equally matched cars. It was reported that the spectacle resulted in dozens of sales of BMW M1s after the race.

235 Monaco Grand Prix

Monte Carlo, 27 May 1979, Formula 1
Brabham BT48/4 • #5
Qualifying: 4th • Result: Retired (collision)

Lauda was back to prominence in Monaco, a track at which he invariably performed well thanks to his precision and consistency. This time those traits in no way concealed an underlying aggression as he delivered exactly the same lap time with all three sets of qualifying tyres, tapping the barrier quite hard at *Mirabeau* in his efforts to set a good time just before qualifying ended. Although still troubled by understeer, he was certainly happier with his car and fourth place on the grid was probably less than his due.

He made a superb start and outdragged both Gilles Villeneuve (Ferrari) and Patrick Depailler (Ligier) into *Ste Dévote*, leaving only Jody Scheckter's pole-winning Ferrari in front of him. Two laps later, though, he was circumspect when Villeneuve made an audacious move at the same corner, bouncing over the kerbs, and he allowed the wild French-Canadian through. By lap 20 he was still third, now nine seconds down on the Ferrari pair and with a gaggle of cars behind, led by Didier Pironi's Tyrrell. One lap later Pironi left his braking far too late on the downhill approach to *Mirabeau* and rammed the back of the Brabham, removing its rear wing as he went over the top of the car and narrowly missing Lauda's head. The Tyrrell was destroyed against the barrier while Lauda limped back to the pits to retire.

1979

LEFT In the Monaco paddock, Niki discusses the BT48's lack of progress with Brabham boss Bernie Ecclestone.

BELOW Plunging into *Mirabeau*, Niki's Brabham BT48 leads Gilles Villeneuve's Ferrari 312T4, the Ligier JS11s of Patrick Depailler and Jacques Laffite, Didier Pironi's Tyrrell 009 (shortly to play a significant role for all the wrong reasons), Alan Jones's Williams FW07, Jochen Mass's Arrows A1 (largely obscured) and the second Tyrrell 009 of Jean-Pierre Jarier.

ABOVE An impetuous attempt by Didier Pironi to overtake Niki into *Mirabeau* saw the Tyrrell 009 ride over the back of the Brabham BT48, forcing both cars into retirement.

ALSO-RAN... AND CHAMPION 259

236 200 Meilen von Nürnberg (D)

Norisring, 24 June 1979, Group 4
BMW M1 (WBS59910004301028) • #82
Qualifying: 11th • Result: Retired (engine)

Along with five other Procar teams, Project Four decided to enter its M1 in Germany's premier event for sports cars and touring cars, even though these Group 4 machines were unlikely to be a match for the many Group 5 Porsche 935s taking part. This big-money event — the prize fund totalled 105,000 DM — was a round of the Deutsche Rennsport Meisterschaft and was organised as two 44-lap heats (for cars above and below 2 litres) and a 70-lap final for the top seven finishers from each heat.

Qualifying 11th for his heat, Lauda was second quickest of the M1 drivers, a mere 0.01 second slower than Hans Stuck. The 'race within a race' for the M1s was a hotly contested dice between Lauda, Stuck and Clay Regazzoni, Lauda starting cautiously while Stuck drove with his usual extravagance. Gradually the dogged Austrian fought back and he was soon nibbling at Stuck's stern, only for his engine's crankshaft damper to fail again, after only 10 laps.

237 Procar race (F)

Dijon-Prenois, 30 June 1979, Procar Championship
BMW M1 (WBS59910004301028) • #5
Qualifying: 3rd • Result: 8th

By now the Procar Championship had become mired in controversy thanks to Jean-Marie Balestre, who was president not only of the FISA (Fédération Internationale du Sport Automobile), which governed international motorsport, but also of the FFSA (Fédération Française du Sport Automobile), France's national sporting authority, which administered the French Grand Prix. After the first Procar

BELOW Lauda's Project Four Racing BMW M1 leads Wolfgang Schütz into the Norisring's *Grundig* hairpin during the team's one-off foray in Germany's Deutsche Rennsport Meisterschaft.

race at Zolder, Balestre had issued a statement describing it as a 'publicity demonstration' and announcing that no such event would be held at 'his' French Grand Prix. At the root of this bloody-minded stance lay the fact that the Procar Championship was promoted by the FOCA (Formula One Constructors' Association), which, led by Bernie Ecclestone, represented the commercial interests of Formula 1 teams. This was an early skirmish in the 'FISA-FOCA war' that would engulf Formula 1 in the early 1980s.

Ecclestone said that Procar was part of the package and, without it, the French Grand Prix could not take place. So the Procar race happened, grudgingly. Described as a 'Show Procar' event, it had no support from the track organisation, which meant that no fuel was provided for the M1s in the paddock and no official timekeeping occurred in practice or the race, leaving FOCA and BMW to organise this.

Most of the M1s ran up against their rev limiters on the long start/finish straight, so BMW agreed to raise the cut-off by 700rpm. There were also moans from privateer teams that the BMW-prepared 'works' cars for the fastest Formula 1 drivers were more powerful. Lauda started third in his Project Four entry but at the first corner he had to take avoiding action when Clay Regazzoni 'outbraked' himself and cut across the pack, leaving the Austrian eighth. Thereafter, the 20-lap race really did become a 'demonstration', with just a single overtaking manoeuvre in the top 10 — Balestre must have been pleased. Despite repeated challenges on Hans Stuck, Lauda could not make any of them stick and remained eighth at the finish, while Brabham team-mate Nelson Piquet won.

238 French Grand Prix

Dijon-Prenois, 1 July 1979, Formula 1
Brabham BT48/2 • #5
Qualifying: 6th • Result: Retired (spin)

Two weeks before the French Grand Prix, Lauda had been the sensation of Goodyear's tyre test at Silverstone; although he was

ABOVE In the rather processional Procar race at Dijon, Niki's BMW M1 makes its solitary way through the swooping 'S' de la Sablières.

ALSO-RAN... AND CHAMPION 261

ABOVE The tighter line that Niki is taking through this sweeping right-hander (note the tyre marks left by the other drivers) bears witness to the persistent understeer that plagued his Brabham BT48 during the early part of the weekend at Dijon.

present only on the first day (Tuesday), he was three seconds faster than the rest, putting in a lap at 143mph. In an effort to cure the BT48's porpoising, the sidepods had been shortened by six inches, which in turn allowed the rear wing to be very 'flat', and this had made a huge difference to the car's behaviour.

Buoyed by this progress, Lauda was frustrated to find that his designated car (BT48/4) for Dijon had persistent understeer on Friday so he took over the spare (BT48/2) for Saturday, feeling much happier with it. He qualified sixth after pinching an extra front qualifying tyre from Hans Stuck, whose bad-tempered team boss, Günther Schmidt, then withdrew his ATS after an argument with Goodyear. During warm-up, Lauda found that a new engine installed overnight was down on power and it was changed again for the race.

His race was lacklustre from the outset. Within five laps he had slipped to eighth place, passed in turn by René Arnoux's Renault (lap 4) and Alan Jones's Williams (lap 5), and then Clay Regazzoni (Williams) overtook on lap 17. Seven laps later he disappeared from the lap charts altogether after a spin at the exit from the ultra-quick right-hander before the pits. Although the car was undamaged, he was unable to restart the hot Alfa engine. This race famously culminated in a wheel-banging battle for second place between Gilles Villeneuve's Ferrari and René Arnoux's Renault, while ahead of them Jean-Pierre Jabouille achieved Renault's first win — and, significantly, the first Formula 1 victory for a turbocharged engine.

As Lauda's dissatisfaction with Brabham deepened, he reopened negotiations with several other teams. After further abortive talks with Wolf (whose owner was losing interest in Formula 1) and Williams (where Jones was established as the number one), draft contracts were agreed for a move to McLaren in 1980 using BMW turbo engines. With turbocharging in the ascendancy, this certainly looked a neat arrangement as Lauda had a strong relationship with not only the team's sponsor, Marlboro,

262 NIKI LAUDA

1979

ABOVE Niki's Project Four BMW M1 blasts past the Silverstone pits en route to his second Procar win of the year.

but also with BMW, and McLaren's Detroit-based subsidiary was already running the BMW 320i Turbo in North America's IMSA GT Championship. However, BMW's competitions director, Jochen Neerpasch, made an error of judgement in presenting the Lauda deal to the BMW board as a *fait accompli* — and it was rejected.

239 Procar race (GB)

Silverstone, 13 July 1979, Procar Championship
BMW M1 (WBS599100004301028) • #5
Qualifying: 3rd • Result: 1st

Following an average performance in the 'Show Procar' at Dijon, where Lauda admitted that he had simply not driven well, he dominated the 20-lap Procar race at Silverstone. Having tested the Project Four BMW M1 extensively at the circuit earlier in the year, he had found an optimum set-up that gave him an advantage. Although fastest in practice by over a second, he lined up third on the grid by virtue of his Formula 1 qualifying performance.

Alan Jones led away from Nelson Piquet and Lauda at the start, but the Australian made a mistake at the first corner and dropped behind. Niki pressured Piquet into running wide at Abbey on lap 5 and seized the lead, thereafter drawing away steadily from his young Formula 1 team-mate. Maintaining a commanding advantage, he had an untroubled run to the flag, winning by over seven seconds despite visibly easing off in the last five laps.

240 British Grand Prix

Silverstone, 14 July 1979, Formula 1
Brabham BT48/4 • #5
Qualifying: 6th • Result: Retired (brakes)

In the two years since the Grand Prix circus had last visited Silverstone, the advent of

ALSO-RAN… AND CHAMPION **263**

unscathed while the reigning World Champion retired on the following lap. Gradually Lauda slipped back: he lost two places to the Dijon duellists, René Arnoux (Renault) and Gilles Villeneuve (Ferrari), on lap 3 and Jacques Laffite's Ligier overtook him on lap 8. Four laps later he was heading for the pits, his brakes gone. The steel discs had been transferred from the spare car before the race and somehow the team had failed to refit the rear cooling ducts, so the hydraulic fluid boiled away.

241 Procar race (D)

Hockenheim, 28 July 1979, Procar Championship
BMW M1 (WBS59910004301028) • #5
Qualifying: 4th • Result: 1st

Lauda was happy with the well-prepared Project Four BMW M1 at Hockenheim, although the engine initially suffered a misfire in practice (cured by a change of spark plugs) and a problem with the car's new exhaust system caused a minor fire (all Procars now had a new type of exhaust system to make them sound better). With the grid positions of the participating Grand Prix drivers as usual determined by their performance in Formula 1 first practice, Niki lined up fourth.

Four cars were eliminated in a spectacular multiple shunt within seconds of the start, but Lauda avoided the carnage and lay third at the end of lap 1. Next time round he was clearly on a charge and almost squeezed past the leading pair, Didier Pironi and Jacques Laffite, at the stadium hairpin. Soon after, Laffite dropped out of the battle, leaving Lauda and Pironi to dispute the lead. Niki got in front briefly as they started lap 3 but their battle remained intense and the Frenchman retook the lead on lap 4. When they entered the stadium on lap 6, Lauda was ahead again and this time he was able to break away when Pironi was slowed by a wild challenge from Hans Stuck. From half distance he led comfortably to the finish to take a relatively easy victory ahead of Stuck.

ABOVE His Brabham BT48 shorn of its bodywork in the Silverstone pits, the driver's exposed position at the front of the car is very evident as the mechanics make adjustments during qualifying.

ground-effect cars meant that speeds through the airfield circuit's fast curves had increased enormously. Lauda pointed out that the drivers were largely passengers in the fastest corners and that the g-forces were almost unbearable. Brabham was one of the three quickest teams in practice, although on Thursday morning Lauda's engine blew up in a very big way on Hangar Straight, bringing out the oil flags and forcing him to use the spare car (BT48/2), which was fitted with steel brake discs rather than the newly developed carbon ones used on the race cars. He had no major problems thereafter but was unable to improve significantly on the impressive times he had set in testing a month earlier and sat sixth on the grid. For the third time in four races, Nelson Piquet was quicker, qualifying third. One reporter noted that when the Brabham-Alfas broke, which happened rather regularly, the team closed the garage doors to create a veil of secrecy.

Back in the newer car for the race, on the first lap Niki, lying fifth, had a minor bump with Mario Andretti's Lotus when the American tried to dive inside at Abbey, but he continued

264 NIKI LAUDA

1979

LEFT In deference to German advertising restrictions, all traces of tobacco sponsorship have been removed from Niki's BMW M1 at the Hockenheim Procar race, but a logo for Lauda Air is evident. Here he passes through the second chicane out in the 'forest' section as he heads to his third win in the Procar Championship.

BELOW The Brabham BT48s of Niki and Nelson Piquet chase through the Hockenheim stadium during the German Grand Prix.

242 German Grand Prix

Hockenheim, 29 July 1979, Formula 1
Brabham BT48/4 • #5
Qualifying: 7th • Result: Retired (engine)

By now it looked certain that Lauda would be leaving Brabham at the end of the year and the press was speculating about his destination. There had now been nine World Championship rounds and he had finished only one, scoring just a single point. The unreliability of the Alfa Romeo V12 was a particular issue and he had little confidence in its durability over Hockenheim's long flat-out sections, even if Alfa's temporary withdrawal of its own works contender after two appearances (at Zolder and Dijon) did at least give hope that the company might pay more attention to its Brabham obligations.

Having waited for the cooler conditions late in practice, Lauda's last-minute efforts went unrewarded as a blown engine and cracked titanium exhausts left him struggling. He was on his way back to take out the spare car and,

ALSO-RAN… AND CHAMPION 265

en route, waved to team-mate Nelson Piquet, who was watching the action because he had to sit out the last practice session; the Brazilian sprinted back to the pits and, by the time the Austrian arrived, was already out on track in the spare, over which Lauda had first call. While Piquet catapulted up to the second row in the replacement car, Lauda was left seventh on the grid, shocked at the way he had been treated. Reliability issues persisted and he then needed a new gearbox after the warm-up.

Still annoyed about Piquet's commandeering of the spare car the day before, he overtook the Brazilian on the second lap of the race and ran sixth for a while. Four laps later he had just been passed by the more powerful Renault of René Arnoux and Gilles Villeneuve's Ferrari when the French car's right rear tyre exploded, handing him back a place. Niki was able to hang on to the rear of the Ferrari, although he was being closed down by Jacky Ickx's Ligier until the Belgian retired. On lap 28, having just repassed Villeneuve, Lauda cruised silently down the escape road at the *Onkokurve* into the stadium and into the dead car park; the Alfa V12 had expired on the long drag down from the *Ostkurve*.

BELOW Lauda's Procar winning streak ended at the Österreichring, clutch failure putting him out after just one lap.

243 Procar race (A)

Österreichring, 11 August 1979, Procar Championship
BMW M1 (WBS59910004301028) • #5
Qualifying: 3rd • Result: Retired (clutch)

Having enjoyed a trouble-free practice, during which he requested just a slight adjustment to the rear wing and a change in the fuel mixture before completing six flying laps, Lauda damaged his BMW M1 during warm-up. Having won the two previous Procar races, his winning streak ended when he suffered a badly slipping clutch on the first lap, crawling slowly to the pits to retire.

With three wins from the six rounds held so far, he still retained a decisive championship lead and dismissed accusations that this was because he had a better car than his rivals. He claimed that after Silverstone the only attention his Marlboro-sponsored Project Four car had received before departure to Hockenheim had been to have its windows cleaned. He added, however, that during testing he had found that some of the Goodyear-supplied standard tyres were better than others.

244 Austrian Grand Prix

Österreichring, 12 August 1979, Formula 1
Brabham BT48/4 • #5
Qualifying: 4th • Result: Retired (engine)

The word was that Lauda had agreed to join McLaren for 1980 and when he arrived at his home circuit he found that the spare Brabham was set up for Nelson Piquet. This snub drew the best from him and he was on magnificent form in practice, quicker than the Brazilian in both sessions. He was delayed on Friday with a broken oil scavenge pump and ran his car briefly with nose fins, but decided these were unnecessary and his car was back to its normal specification on Saturday, although he was still more than two seconds behind the Williamses and Renaults.

Determined to perform well in front of his Austrian fans, he got away strongly at the start and lay third at the end of the opening lap. However, one of the Brabham's sliding skirts was getting jammed and on the second lap René Arnoux's Renault overtook him. Over the next few laps he slipped to eighth, passed successively by Clay Regazzoni (Williams), Jody Scheckter (Ferrari) and Jacques Laffite (Ligier), but then he was able to dig in ahead of his team-mate. Piquet overtook on lap 16 with a rather desperate manoeuvre at *Hella-Licht*, causing Niki to run wide and hit a bump, but this had the helpful outcome of freeing the jammed skirt. Retaliating, he diced wheel-to-wheel with Piquet for a long time, getting ahead between laps 21 and 28, but the duel ended when the Brazilian's engine blew up on lap 32. Lauda's V12 lasted until nine laps from home, when it lost oil pressure and he came into the pits to retire.

ABOVE While his home race at the Österreichring brought yet another retirement in a season of woeful unreliability, his modified Brabham BT48 — now with much-improved handling — did at least qualify strongly, in fourth place. At the start he got away well, third behind Gilles Villeneuve's Ferrari and Alan Jones's Williams.

ALSO-RAN... AND CHAMPION

RIGHT Niki readies himself in the Zandvoort pitlane in preparation for the Procar race. After hurting his right hand in an accident during warm-up for this event, he is having to use his left hand to fasten the collar of his overalls; the painful injury would force his retirement from both the Procar contest and the following day's Dutch Grand Prix.

245 Procar race (NL)

Zandvoort, 25 August 1979, Procar Championship
BMW M1 (WBS59910004301028) • #5
Qualifying: 4th • Result: Retired (injury)

At this penultimate round of the Procar series, Lauda damaged his Project Four M1 in a spectacular accident during the warm-up, but it was repaired in time for the start.

Third at the off, he was passed by Hans Stuck before the first corner and found Manfred Winkelhock tight on his tail but held off the challenge. He was running fourth when a heavy shower caused the race to be halted after five laps. When it resumed after a 45-minute break, Lauda was missing. He had been sidelined reportedly by a broken timing chain but in fact he pulled out because his earlier shunt had left his right hand slightly injured.

In an amusing aside, at the start of the Procar series FOCA's Bernie Ecclestone and Max Mosley had decided that the drivers should be paid in cash as an incentive to make the series more exciting — and to attract more entries. This was generally done away from prying eyes, but at Zandvoort Mosley managed to get himself photographed behind the pits paying Lauda with a wad of dollars.

246 Dutch Grand Prix

Zandvoort, 26 August 1979, Formula 1
Brabham BT48/4 • #5
Qualifying: 9th • Result: Retired (injury)

Growing concerns about the speed of Formula 1 cars through Zandvoort's high-speed back section came to a head when Jody Scheckter and Lauda — senior members of the Grand Prix Drivers' Association (GPDA) —

1979

announced in Austria that the race would not take place unless changes were made. Despite the short notice, the organisers agreed to install a chicane and asked the two drivers for guidance about its configuration. However, the hastily conceived obstacle was considered by many of the other drivers to be more hazardous than the fast sweeper it replaced.

Both Brabhams were way off the pace in practice, although Lauda again out-qualified Nelson Piquet and improved further on Saturday despite his Procar hand injury. Unhappy with his understeering car, he parked it when his allotted qualifying tyres were used up.

His race did not last long; analgesic injections in his injured right hand had not worked and the pain was severe. Although he made a good start and had moved up to sixth place after the first lap, largely thanks to a collision between René Arnoux's Renault and Clay Regazzoni's Williams, he then lost a place on each of the next two laps before stopping for good on lap 4.

Ironically, this was all because of the chicane he had helped design, as that was where he had misjudged his line in the Procar and crashed it.

247 Procar race (I)

Monza, 8 September 1979, Procar Championship
BMW M1 (WBS59910004301028) • #5
Qualifying: 3rd • Result: 2nd

Going into this final round of the Procar Championship, Lauda headed the points standings but Clay Regazzoni and Hans Stuck both had a chance of toppling him. This time,

ABOVE A dull, miserable day at Zandvoort was rounded off by early retirement from the Dutch Grand Prix.

BELOW Niki charges past the Monza grandstands in his BMW M1 on his way to second place in the race and the title of Procar Champion.

ALSO-RAN... AND CHAMPION **269**

just to be safe, Project Four brought along a spare car, but it was not needed; nevertheless, Lauda's practice was not trouble-free as his car had a sticking starter motor and damaged clutch. With the first five grid places handed as usual to the Formula 1 participants, Regazzoni and Lauda lined up second and third respectively; Stuck was always going to be at a disadvantage under this system but he maximised his chances by being 'best of the rest' for sixth place on the grid.

At the start of the 18-lap race, Stuck very impressively catapulted into third place ahead of Lauda, Mario Andretti and Nelson Piquet under braking for the first chicane, while Regazzoni led from Alan Jones. On lap 2 Stuck passed Jones and on lap 3 he pounced when Regazzoni missed a gear in the *Curva Grande*. With a clear track in front of him, Stuck quickly extended his advantage to a remarkable 20 seconds as he reeled off a sequence of quick laps, helped by the fact that Regazzoni's engine blew on lap 5. This left Jones and Lauda battling for second place: when Lauda tried a pass at the first chicane they both half-spun, the Austrian having to take to the escape road and narrowly missing Andretti as he rejoined. After Jones retired on lap 14, Lauda finished a distant runner-up, but this was enough to make him Procar Champion.

He was almost as delighted as his Formula 1 team boss Bernie Ecclestone, who claimed a new BMW M1 as 'his' driver had taken the crown, albeit with the benefit of equipment provided by another entrant.

248 Italian Grand Prix

Monza, 9 September 1979, Formula 1
Brabham BT48/4 • #5
Qualifying: 9th • Result: 4th

Despite pressure from Parmalat, the Italian manufacturer of dairy products and Brabham's lead sponsor, to bring the new Cosworth-engined Brabham BT49 to the company's 'home' race, Gordon Murray's latest design was not ready and the drivers had to persevere with the unloved BT48. Lauda was quicker than Nelson Piquet on Friday but found his V12 down on revs in the last session, with

BELOW Into the first chicane at Monza, Niki's Brabham has just lapped Jochen Mass's Arrows A1 *en route* to fourth place and — for once — a points-paying finish.

Alfa Romeo showing little desire to solve the problem. Deciding that there was no point in continuing with the car, he turned to the spare (BT48/2) but its engine had no fuel pressure and refused to run, so his Friday time determined his qualifying position, ninth, while Piquet elevated himself to eighth.

After putting two wheels on the grass at the start, Lauda was only 13th at the end of the first lap, but he quickly moved up the field, breezing past Mario Andretti's Lotus on lap 9 in a way that suggested the Alfa engine had plenty of power when it was working properly. By lap 12 he had systematically worked his way up to an isolated seventh place, which became sixth when René Arnoux retired his Renault. This was the race at which Alfa Romeo débuted its own new car, the T179, and Bruno Giacomelli, who had qualified 18th, did well with it to close up on Lauda, but the Austrian increased his pace and on lap 28 Giacomelli spun off trying to keep up.

The problems of others elevated Lauda two more places, when Jacques Laffite's Ligier pitted (lap 42) and Jean-Pierre Jabouille's Renault engine let go (lap 46).

Niki came home a heartening and for once trouble-free fourth. It was the first time he had been in the points since South Africa, although he was almost a minute behind Ferrari's 1–2 finishers, Jody Scheckter and Gilles Villeneuve, a result that not only delighted the Italian fans but also confirmed Scheckter as World Champion.

249 Gran Premio Dino Ferrari (I)

Imola, 16 September 1979, Formula 1
Brabham BT48/2 • #5
Qualifying: 4th • Result: 1st

In preparation for Imola becoming host to the Italian Grand Prix in 1980, a 40-lap

ABOVE In the non-championship Formula 1 race at Imola, the front wing of Gilles Villeneuve's Ferrari 312T4 is bent askew following his coming-together with Niki's Brabham BT48 at *Tosa*. Lauda went on to win what turned out to be the final race of the first phase of his career.

ALSO-RAN... AND CHAMPION **271**

non-championship Formula 1 race was staged at the circuit. The event was treated somewhat casually by most of the teams, only Ferrari supplying two cars, for its regular pair of drivers. The rest mostly sent single cars and second-string drivers, resulting in only 15 entries. The track was still basic and drivers were faced with brick walls, loose barriers and inadequate catch fencing, all of which would probably have seen them refuse to race in normal circumstances.

Lauda, Brabham's sole representative, suffered a blown engine in the morning session, but the mechanics got him out 20 minutes before practice ended to qualify a solid fourth, while the Ferraris of pole-sitting Gilles Villeneuve and Jody Scheckter dominated.

Fired up for the race, Niki got away third, but briefly slipped to fourth behind Carlos Reutemann before regaining the place on lap 10 when the Argentine driver's Lotus lost a wheel-balance weight. Lauda closed on the leading Ferraris as their Michelin tyres went off and the track became more slippery. Scheckter offered little resistance, but Villeneuve was less easy to deal with and Lauda tailed him closely for six laps before slipping by at *Tamburello* to take the lead on lap 21.

Villeneuve came straight back and repassed at *Tosa*, then on the next lap Lauda was through again on the straight. He kept to the left under braking for *Tosa* to avoid the Ferrari getting alongside, but Villeneuve misjudged his intentions and slid into the back of the Brabham, knocking his Ferrari's front wing wildly askew. Lauda, his car undamaged, was left to take an unchallenged win, and although he later slowed with a broken exhaust, the pursuing Reutemann had a similar problem and was unable to capitalise.

He promptly dedicated his victory to Enzo Ferrari, with whom he was now reconciled after his acrimonious departure two years previously, but otherwise he seemed not to care very much, arriving on the podium late and in his regular clothes ready for a quick departure by helicopter.

250 Canadian Grand Prix

Montréal, 28 September 1979, Formula 1
Brabham BT49/3 • #5
Qualifying: Untimed practice only • Result: Did not start

Now the Cosworth-powered BT49 was ready and Brabham took three examples to Canada. They looked good and worked well too. Untimed first practice on Friday was the first time Lauda had sat in a BT49, partly because Bernie Ecclestone, in full knowledge of Lauda's negotiations with McLaren, wanted to prevent his lead driver from learning the new car's secrets too soon. With a few teething problems, Lauda completed 10 laps in that first session, featuring midway down the field.

Just before first qualifying was due to start, he took his boss to one side and told him that he was retiring from the sport immediately. When the news got out, it came as a complete shock to everyone and even the journalists who were closest to him, Helmut Zwickl and Heinz Prüller, had no inkling. The decision had been coming a long time, Niki said, but he knew for certain when he arrived in Canada. Ecclestone, to his credit, did not try to dissuade him.

With good prospects for 1980, Lauda should have been excited about the future, but he was not. Instead, his heart was set on establishing his new airline and he headed off to Los Angeles to acquire a Learjet for that very purpose. His helmet and overalls were left behind at the track, where they would be used by last-minute stand-in Ricardo Zunino.

AFTERMATH

The surprise at Lauda's sudden retirement quickly subsided. Having clarified to journalists any misunderstanding concerning his comments about being 'tired of driving round in circles', he got on with sourcing finance for Lauda Air. The justifiable frustration of the Brabham mechanics, who had built three new BT49s in just 55 days only for the man with the best chance of achieving a good result to turn his back on the team, also receded quickly as tests of the new car went well with Nelson Piquet at the wheel. Revisions to Lauda's advertising contract with Parmalat suggested he would be present at several Grands Prix in 1980 (Brazil, Monaco and Britain were specifically cited), although there was scepticism as to whether this would happen.

Some English insiders suspected that Lauda had retired to avoid legal entanglements, fuelling rumours that he had signed contracts with both Brabham and McLaren for 1980. He went on record with the journalist Helmut Zwickl to insist that this was not true and that, although he had held extensive talks with McLaren, he had only agreed a contract with Brabham, which was finalised but not yet signed.

Either way, Lauda's unexpected retirement created serious problems in Formula 1 circles, as his widely anticipated move from Brabham to McLaren affected a number of other interests, including those of major sponsors Marlboro and Parmalat as well as the two teams concerned.

Marlboro had agreed to increase its contribution to McLaren's budget by 50 per cent if Lauda signed for 1980, while Parmalat — looking to capitalise on the association it had built up with the Austrian over the previous two years — was prepared to underwrite two-thirds of his reported $2 million salary. After he quit, however, McLaren was left depleted, short of funding, lacking a competitive car and with some of its key technical people having departed. According to press rumours, it looked as if McLaren might be forced to close.

Ironically, these unintended but potentially seismic consequences of Lauda's decision to walk away from Formula 1 were the catalyst for McLaren's soon-to-be announced merger with Ron Dennis's Project Four organisation, which had run Niki's successful Procar campaign. Two years later the wheel would come full circle, with the revitalised team providing the platform for the Austrian's return.

ABOVE Lauda's first — and only — run in the new Cosworth-engined BT49 came during first practice session at Montréal. When he got out of the car, he informed Brabham boss Bernie Ecclestone that he was retiring from the sport with immediate effect.

ALSO-RAN... AND CHAMPION 273

INTERLUDE
SCRATCHING THE ITCH

In an interview with Herbert Völker for *Rallye Racing* in November 1979, Lauda was asked if he would completely exclude the possibility of a comeback. He replied, 'You cannot rule out anything in life. God knows, maybe I'll go crazy and drive at Indy. But again, I do not believe it, cannot imagine it.' These words were to be repeated to him many times during the autumn of 1981 as news broke of his return to racing.

Other than dropping in to see the new McLaren MP4 while on a free day in England in April 1981, Lauda had taken no interest in the sport since he had quit, but a visit to the Austrian Grand Prix on 16 August 1981 as a TV summariser with his old journalist friend Heinz Prüller rekindled a desire to race. A month later at Monza he asked McLaren's Ron Dennis, via his old friend John Hogan, Marlboro's sponsorship guru, to arrange a test, which duly confirmed that the speed and ability were still there. Despite persistent pressure from Calisto Tanzi, boss of his personal sponsor Parmalat, Lauda resisted a return to Brabham, but he did have extended talks with Williams following the Caesar's Palace Grand Prix at Las Vegas. Finally, he decided upon McLaren and the deal was announced on 12 November.

Lauda was joining a team in the ascendancy. During his last pre-retirement season, 1979, McLaren had become also-rans. While he was away, Marlboro had brokered the amalgamation of Ron Dennis's Project Four team with McLaren and gradually Dennis had taken over the show, thanks in part to the brilliance of a new Cosworth-powered Formula 1 car — the first with a monocoque made entirely of carbon fibre — that his designer, John Barnard, had on the drawing board at the time of the merger. This saw light of day as the McLaren MP4 ('P4' stood for Project Four) and achieved its first win in John Watson's hands at the 1981 British Grand Prix. Lauda saw for himself the safety of the MP4's chassis during the Italian Grand Prix when Watson walked away unscathed after a huge accident.

INTERLUDE

SALZBURGRING
30 AUGUST 1981

The Oldtimer Grand Prix for historic motorcycles and automobiles was the brainchild of Professor Dr Helmut Krackowizer, a journalist and ex-motorcycle racer, and was held at the Salzburgring nine times between 1974 and 1987. For the 1981 event, Krackowizer successfully tempted Lauda back to the track for the first time with the opportunity to drive a 500bhp Grand Prix Mercedes-Benz W154, the very car in which Hermann Lang won the European Championship in 1939. Lauda was able to stretch this legendary machine's legs on the fast sweeps of the Salzburgring and both he and the spectators — attracted in bigger numbers than usual — loved it.

DONINGTON PARK
16 SEPTEMBER 1981

Once Lauda had decided to consider a return, his first outing was in a McLaren MP4 at Donington Park, a circuit that was new to him. Despite the passage of time and the unfamiliarity of the car with its radial tyres, he completed 48 laps and posted a time only 0.1 second slower than John Watson's benchmark. He later admitted that he found the physicality of the ground-effect car unexpectedly challenging and made numerous pit stops to ask for unnecessary adjustments, just so he could have a rest.

PAUL RICARD
NOVEMBER AND DECEMBER 1981

After Lauda had signed for McLaren, private testing on 16–17 November at Michelin's Ladoux test track, where he matched John Watson's times immediately, again showed that he had lost none of his skill.

Moving on to Paul Ricard, an enormous accident on 16 December, caused by a steering arm breakage as he exited the daunting *Signes* corner at 160mph, also showed that he had lost none of his ice-cool nerve. Although he was unhurt, the car was badly damaged and out of action for two days.

A bigger surprise after a day and a half of testing was that he was in even better physical shape than John Watson to handle the exhausting demands of ground-effect aerodynamics. What his new team had not realised was that Niki had begun a training programme under the direction of his long-time fitness instructor, Willi Dungl, a long time before he had talked seriously about getting back into a racing car.

SCRATCHING THE ITCH 275

1982
THE SECOND CAREER

Formula 1 had moved on considerably during Lauda's two-year absence. There had been a leap in turbocharging technology, which meant that engines — for those teams equipped with turbos — now delivered significantly more power than they had in 1979, although for the 1982 season McLaren remained one of the teams still equipped with the trusty Cosworth DFV. Even more significantly, designers had gained a much better understanding of ground effect, resulting in stiffly suspended cars that cornered faster but were more physically punishing to drive. Before the season started, Lauda worked hard on his personal fitness with trainer Willi Dungl and completed thousands of miles of testing to make sure he was as well prepared as possible.

During discussions about remuneration with Marlboro, McLaren's main sponsor, Lauda had cleverly pointed out that his PR value alone outweighed any question marks about his ability to return to top form on the track — and the global media attention surrounding the announcement of his comeback proved it. While a deal was eventually concluded, lingering doubts about the Austrian's ability to sustain his performance and commitment ensured that McLaren had the option to drop him if things did not work out. Confident that all would be well, Lauda signed. Ironically, the issue of driver contracts would dominate the first race of the new season.

1982

251 South African Grand Prix

Kyalami, 23 January 1982, Formula 1
McLaren MP4/1B-04 • #8
Qualifying: 13th • Result: 4th

Lauda quickly made his presence felt at Kyalami as his McLaren MP4/1B was the quickest non-turbo in private testing before the race. The first day of practice was lost as the FISA's new requirement for drivers to have 'superlicences', with certain obligations attached, led to a drivers' strike, with Lauda one of the prime movers as he, more than most, realised that this unnecessary piece of bureaucracy had some unwelcome implications regarding driver contracts. When the action did get underway, a mistake under braking put him into the catch fencing at Crowthorne and bent a lower front wishbone, but he promptly reversed out and continued with the car unrepaired to set a time that put him 13th, mid-grid, before rain fell and ended any chance of further progress.

He made a cautious start, but any doubts as to whether he could get back in the racing groove were soon dispelled. Fourteenth at the end of the first lap, he was 10th by lap 7 and settled in behind Jacques Laffite's Talbot-Ligier and Michele Alboreto's Tyrrell. By lap 19 he had passed both of them and now lay behind teammate John Watson, with whom he remained in close contact until Didier Pironi (Ferrari) barged past on lap 37. He briefly duelled with the rapid Renault of Alain Prost, who had lost the lead after a tyre flew off its rim and was now carving through the field in a superb recovery that ended with victory. In the closing stages Niki put on a late charge to chase down Watson, who was now mixing it with Keke Rosberg's Williams, passing them on laps 65 and 67 respectively. That took him up to fifth place, which became a respectable fourth when Pironi pitted with eight laps remaining. It had been a solid comeback performance.

The subsequent threat by the FISA of a lifetime suspension for his role as ringleader of the drivers' strike was treated with the contempt it deserved.

ABOVE The comeback: Lauda's McLaren MP4/1B exits Clubhouse during the South African Grand Prix on his way to fourth place.

THE SECOND CAREER 277

ABOVE Rio de Janeiro's hinterland looks rather dramatic as Niki speeds along in front of a huge Jacarepaguá grandstand during the Brazilian Grand Prix.

252 Brazilian Grand Prix

Jacarepaguá, 21 March 1982, Formula 1
McLaren MP4/1B-04 • #8
Qualifying: 5th • Result: Retired (collision)

In oppressive heat, Lauda was the fastest Michelin runner — there were four tyre companies in Formula 1 now — and shrewdly completed only 12 timed laps throughout the two days of practice. On Friday engine problems kept him down the order and a replacement Cosworth unit was needed; on Saturday he was baulked on his first fast lap and his second set of qualifying tyres caused too much oversteer. Nevertheless, he claimed a very impressive fifth place on the grid, getting on for two seconds better than team-mate John Watson's best time. The night before the race, he set out his strategy: take the first 30 laps slowly and carefully, push for the next 20 and only attack fully in the final 10.

After a poor start the plan seemed to be working as he paced himself, although his team-mate almost hit him when chopped by Andrea de Cesaris's wildly driven Alfa Romeo. Having shadowed the Italian cautiously for a few laps, Niki passed the Alfa for seventh place and by lap 19 he had also scythed past Carlos Reutemann (Williams) and Alain Prost (Renault). He was poised to move further up the order when the Argentine driver made a mistake under braking for the last corner and ran into him. Although Lauda kept his car on the road and was able to continue, the McLaren's right rear suspension had been bent in the collision and a lap later he was in the pits for good.

253 United States Grand Prix (West)

Long Beach, 4 April 1982, Formula 1
McLaren MP4/1B-04 • #8
Qualifying: 2nd • Result: 1st

Quick to realise that qualifying tyres were a waste of time in Long Beach, Lauda parked his McLaren during the final practice session after just seven deceptively smooth and accurate laps, announcing that it was unlikely to go much faster. Although he was quickest at that point, he was beaten to pole by a late effort from Andrea de Cesaris (Alfa Romeo). First practice had been less smooth, when he had spun and wiped off the car's nose, but thereafter he was serene.

Fishtailing off the line, he was outdragged by the Renault of René Arnoux before the first turn and lay third at the end of lap 1. When Bruno Giacomelli decided to make a rather desperate overtaking move at the Turn 11 hairpin on lap 6, Lauda did not try to block him and the Italian's Alfa Romeo locked up and slid into Arnoux's Renault, putting the Frenchman out of the race. Applying his precise driving to the crumbling track conditions, he relentlessly pursued de Cesaris, the leader, closing up with clinical precision before boxing in the young Italian behind backmarker Raul Boesel's March at the chicane on lap 15. While de Cesaris shook his

ABOVE Lauda's McLaren MP4/1B drops over the crest into the downhill Linden Avenue at Long Beach.

LEFT Three races into his comeback, Niki returned to the top step of the podium with victory in the United States Grand Prix (West). Keke Rosberg (in Goodyear cap) and Gilles Villeneuve (later disqualified when his Ferrari's rear wing was declared illegal) join in the celebrations.

THE SECOND CAREER 279

fist at the Brazilian when he should have been changing gear, Lauda slipped through to take the lead.

He eased away steadily — both the fastest and neatest man on the circuit — and by working the traffic effectively he had built up a huge 50-second advantage when de Cesaris crashed out 20 laps later. His decision to run on harder Michelins than his team-mate proved to be a wise one, as his tyres remained in excellent condition while Watson had to pit for new rubber five laps before de Cesaris's demise. Some of Lauda's handsome lead, with Keke Rosberg's Williams now his pursuer, was lost due to a couple of anxious moments: when he rounded a blind corner (one of several on the circuit) he encountered a tow truck trundling down the middle of the track after recovering Piquet's crashed Brabham and was almost forced into the wall while getting around it; then late in the race an untypical slide when he missed his braking point at the top of Linden Avenue cost him nine seconds. Although he slowed towards the end and allowed Riccardo Patrese (Brabham) and Michele Alboreto (Tyrrell) to unlap themselves, he remained 14 seconds clear of Rosberg at the end to take a superb win.

Afterwards he revealed that his contract contained a performance clause allowing McLaren to drop him if the team was not completely convinced of his ability and motivation after three races. Victory in the third race of his comeback emphatically answered that question.

254 Belgian Grand Prix

Zolder, 9 May 1982, Formula 1
McLaren MP4/1B-06 • #8
Qualifying: 4th • Result: Disqualified

In Lauda's two-year absence the 'FISA-FOCA war' had escalated into such an intense conflict that now there were essentially two camps in the Grand Prix paddock — the FISA-

BELOW With a new set of qualifying tyres mounted for the start of the afternoon session, Niki waits expectantly in the rather relaxed atmosphere of the Zolder pitlane.

1982

aligned 'manufacturer' teams and the FOCA-supporting 'constructors'. In the build-up to the San Marino Grand Prix at Imola on 25 April, an FIA decision to disqualify two FOCA entrants, Nelson Piquet's Brabham and Keke Rosberg's Williams, from their first and second places in the Brazilian Grand Prix led FOCA to boycott the race. This meant that only 14 cars turned out at Imola and the McLarens were not among them. Ferrari dominated, with Didier Pironi controversially beating Gilles Villeneuve.

Two weeks later, Villeneuve fatally crashed during practice for the Belgian Grand Prix when he hit Jochen Mass's slower March while on an all-out qualifying lap, leading to a spotlight being shone on the dangers of qualifying tyres that were usable only for one or two laps. Their risks were illustrated again when the BMW turbo engine in Riccardo Patrese's Brabham suddenly expired just as Lauda — on a hot lap — was right behind him going into the chicane. With his foot firmly planted, the Austrian managed to get through an almost non-existent gap in a perilous-looking move. Having improved his Friday time by over a second, he decided he could do no better and was content with fourth spot on the grid. Significantly, his McLaren was second fastest in the warm-up.

Early in the race he was soon in front of the two Renaults that had locked out the front row, passing Alain Prost's on lap 3 and gaining another place when Arnoux's suffered a turbo failure two laps later. This put him in second place, three seconds behind leader Keke Rosberg, who was lucky to find that when he damaged a skirt on a kerb it actually improved the handling of his Williams. Lauda was fending off a strong challenge from Andrea de Cesaris's Alfa Romeo when Chico Serra's Fittipaldi spun in front of him, forcing him to brake almost to a standstill and allowing the Italian to pass. Although the McLaren's soft Michelins were not working well, he regained second place when de Cesaris retired on lap 35, but now he was being forced to conserve his tyres and his fading brakes, so he did not resist when team-mate John Watson outbraked him 12 laps later. Having shrewdly calculated that a stop for new rubber would give him no advantage in the remaining time, he settled for a gentle run to the finish in third place, with all those behind him now lapped.

His tenacious drive, however, came to nothing when his McLaren was found to be 1.8kg under weight in post-race scrutineering, the team having miscalculated the weight loss from brake and tyre wear. He learned of his disqualification only when on his flight home.

255 Monaco Grand Prix

Monte Carlo, 23 May 1982, Formula 1
McLaren MP4/1B-06 • #8
Qualifying: 12th • Result: Retired (engine)

Having won at Long Beach, Lauda was a pre-race favourite at Monaco but McLaren was baffled to find that its cars lacked traction,

BELOW Through the swimming pool section of Monaco's harbourside, Niki's McLaren MP4/1B leads Nelson Piquet's Brabham BT50, Manfred Winkelhock's ATS D5, Elio de Angelis's Lotus 91 and Eddie Cheever's Ligier JS19.

THE SECOND CAREER **281**

ABOVE Concrete and guardrails abound at Detroit as Lauda forces his way up from 10th place on the grid; a rare error saw him spin out when leading the restarted race on aggregate.

the team's drivers spending much of practice circulating but making little impression. Lauda blew an engine on Thursday afternoon and then worked hard on adjustment of skirts and ride height to suit the circuit's bumps, possibly leading to an excessively stiff set-up.

Forced to change his race strategy because of his lowly grid position, 12th of only 20 starters, Lauda settled in behind Manfred Winkelhock's ATS but found a way past on lap 15 to move up to 10th place, with teammate John Watson ahead of him. Suffering a down-on-power engine and running in a four-car midfield pack, he gained a couple more positions with Watson's retirement (lap 36) and a pit stop for Nigel Mansell's Lotus (lap 47) before being lapped by the leader, Alain Prost (Renault), on lap 49. He lost eighth place to the Lotus of Elio de Angelis on lap 53 and four laps later he felt his engine tighten and saw it lose oil pressure; it had been weakening all afternoon and he retired.

256 Detroit Grand Prix

Detroit, 6 June 1982, Formula 1
McLaren MP4/1B-04 • #8
Qualifying: 10th • Result: Retired (accident)

All of Thursday and most of Friday practice was lost as the temporary street track was still being constructed when the teams arrived. Lauda took 10th place on the grid, his McLaren troubled by ineffective aerodynamics and a tendency to understeer. These traits did not stop him from setting the fastest time on a soaking wet track in the afternoon session, albeit 18 seconds slower than he had been in the morning, commenting that the opportunity to race Formula 1 cars on public streets in the 1980s was something to be grasped.

He had moved up from ninth to seventh place when the race was stopped after only six laps, the organisers overreacting to a minor incident that partly blocked the track. The restart saw the grid formed in the finishing order after the six laps, with the overall result to be determined from the aggregate of the two parts of the race. His progress continued as he passed René Arnoux's Renault (lap 6), the struggling Bruno Giacomelli's Alfa Romeo (lap 20) and Alain Prost's Renault (lap 22) to reach fourth place, but now he had charging team-mate John Watson behind him and was hampered by a gearbox that was reluctant to select third gear. After Watson overtook him, he seemed to become spurred into action and the two McLarens quickly slipped past Eddie Cheever's Talbot-Ligier and Didier Pironi's Ferrari to close up on the leader, Keke Rosberg's Williams. Watson took the lead on lap 31, leaving Lauda looking for a way past Rosberg as well. It all went wrong four laps later when, in a rare error of judgement, he attempted to outbrake the Finn at the first left-hander beyond the pits, lost control and spun into the wall.

As Watson cruised to victory, Lauda was left to rue the fact that he could have followed him home and still won overall, thanks to his time advantage over his team-mate in the first part of the race.

257 Canadian Grand Prix

Montréal, 13 June 1982, Formula 1
McLaren MP4/1B-04 • #8
Qualifying: 11th • Result: Retired (clutch)

Returning to the scene of his sudden retirement from racing in 1979, Lauda stated that he would be pushing hard from the outset and he certainly appeared committed in qualifying. Perplexed by the handling of the McLaren after an experiment with a different set-up failed to yield an improvement, he was frustrated to be back on the sixth row of the grid. The fact that his car was 20mph slower through the speed trap than the turbocharged Brabham-BMWs of Nelson Piquet and Riccardo Patrese had more than a little to do with this.

As one of the drivers on the right-hand side of the grid, he was able to see Didier Pironi's stalled Ferrari at the start and managed to avoid the carnage of the ensuing first-lap shunt that claimed the life of Osella driver Ricardo Paletti, but he burned out his clutch in the process.

BELOW Once again Montréal brought no joy for Niki, with a mid-field qualifying position and early retirement from the race with clutch failure.

When the race restarted at 6.15pm, he was never in serious contention and was passed by several cars early on. Clearly in trouble, he finally called it a day on lap 17, by which time he had slipped to 15th place; he had been making clutchless gear changes since the restart and this had proved too much for the transmission, making any meaningful progress impossible.

258 Dutch Grand Prix

Zandvoort, 3 July 1982, Formula 1
McLaren MP4/1B-06 • #8
Qualifying: 5th • Result: 4th

After three rather nondescript races, Lauda, driving with deceptive smoothness and speed, was the fastest Cosworth runner in practice, one of only two to get among the phalanx of turbo cars in the top 10. McLaren had been pursuing an intensive development programme for the upcoming fast circuits and the MP4/1B's improved underbody aerodynamics showed in higher straight-line speed. An engine change was needed after his proposed race DFV was found to be using too much oil.

Although he got ahead of the slow-starting Nelson Piquet, he was easily repassed by the Brazilian's Brabham on the second lap and lost a further place to Keke Rosberg's Williams on lap 8. He ran seventh for the first third of the race until the retirements of the Renaults promoted him to sixth on lap 22 and fifth on lap 33. He duelled with Patrick Tambay, whose Ferrari was much quicker under acceleration, finally passing the Frenchman for fourth place with an assertive move down the inside into *Tarzan* at the start of lap 38. By this time Rosberg was some 30 seconds up the road in third place and Lauda, finding that he had made the right tyre choice with his Michelins now coming into their own, set off in pursuit. It was a vain chase, however, as the top four positions remained unchanged for the second half of the race and Lauda — briefly blocked by Eliseo Salazar's recalcitrant ATS — ran out the last unlapped finisher, more than a minute behind Rosberg.

RIGHT Zandvoort in bloom: Niki powers through one of the seaside circuit's gently banked corners on his way to fourth place in the Dutch Grand Prix.

259 British Grand Prix

Brands Hatch, 18 July 1982, Formula 1
McLaren MP4/1B-06 • #8
Qualifying: 5th • Result: 1st

McLaren's Michelin tyres suffered vibration issues in practice and were no match for Goodyear's rubber in the warm conditions, but late in practice Lauda drove what he termed a 'chaos lap' to jump from ninth to fifth on the grid. He told designer John Barnard that the car was perfect and was not to be touched.

Come the race, things improved further for Lauda when two of the cars ahead of him on the grid had problems. Keke Rosberg's pole-position Williams was reluctant to fire for the parade lap and got away late, forcing the Finn to start at the back, then Riccardo Patrese's Brabham in second spot failed to move when the lights went green, having slipped out of gear. From the opposite side of the grid, Niki avoided the ensuing mêlée and took an immediate second place behind Nelson Piquet's Brabham, which was starting with half a tank of fuel because his team's technical wizard, Gordon Murray, had worked out that a mid-race refuelling stop could be the best strategy.

The Brabham pulled away as expected at a second per lap but Lauda's patience was quickly rewarded when, on lap 10, Piquet pulled off the track behind the pits, handing the Austrian the lead. Already Niki was 15 seconds ahead of his nearest challenger, Didier Pironi's Ferrari, and thereafter he was never at risk, driving masterfully and looking after his tyres. Behind, Derek Warwick caused lots of excitement for his home crowd as he charged up from 11th on the first lap to second place in his Toleman, but he was 25 seconds adrift of the serene Lauda when a driveshaft joint broke. In the last few laps, Niki eased back from his 40-second advantage and

ABOVE Niki acknowledges the strong support from fans at Brands Hatch after taking victory in the British Grand Prix.

BELOW The long straights and hot temperatures at Paul Ricard were always going to place the normally aspirated cars at a disadvantage to the turbos, and sure enough the Renaults and Ferraris dominated. Niki's McLaren MP4/1B came home a rather breathless eighth.

cruised home to a convincing win ahead of the Ferraris of Pironi and Patrick Tambay without ever having been seriously challenged.

After the race McLaren's Teddy Mayer philosophised, 'To win in the future, you need one of two things; either a turbo engine or Niki Lauda. Both are very expensive.'

260 French Grand Prix

Paul Ricard, 25 July 1982, Formula 1
McLaren MP4/1B-06 • #8
Qualifying: 9th • Result: 8th

As at Brands Hatch, Lauda had no major complaints other than a shortage of horsepower on the long back straight. Again the fastest Cosworth runner, he set his time on Friday; an engine change for the final session after a blow-up made no difference.

At the start he was passed by Derek Daly's Williams (the Irishman having decided to use the grass rather than the tarmac) but soon got ahead of the Alfa Romeos of Andrea de Cesaris and Bruno Giacomelli to run seventh, and gained another place when Daly made an early stop for fresh tyres. Lauda needed tyres too and came into the pits at the end of lap 15 to find that his team-mate was already there having a broken battery connection fixed. He drove on through the pitlane and completed another lap before halting again for his new rubber, the resulting double delay dropping him to a lapped 12th. Charging back into the fray, he quickly overtook Brian Henton's Tyrrell and Manfred Winkelhock's ATS on successive laps, and then gained further places when Nelson Piquet (Brabham) retired from the lead and Giacomelli made a late pit stop. He finished a rather frustrated eighth.

261 German Grand Prix

Hockenheim, 8 August 1982, Formula 1
McLaren MP4/1B-06 • #8
Qualifying: 8th • Result: Did not start (injured)

With typical efficiency, Lauda set his best time on his first flying lap on Friday afternoon; it would have been good enough for eighth place on the grid had he been able to start the race.

Two laps later he spun off into the catch fencing at the corner after the pits, putting the cause down to dirt on his sticky tyres after a grassy moment avoiding Rupert Keegan's March at the previous turn. He walked back to the pits and continued in the spare car, but after practice he began to feel pain in his left wrist, kickback from the steering wheel having torn some ligaments. Annoyed with himself that he had not let go of the wheel during the incident, he sat out the wet Saturday practice sessions — one of which was halted by Didier Pironi's career-ending crash — in the hope that all would be well for race day. However, he and the team decided that he should skip the race and aim to be fit in time for his home Grand Prix the following weekend

ABOVE At the German Grand Prix, Niki appeared only on the first day of practice, his weekend curtailed early by a wrist injury after he was forced into catch fencing.

THE SECOND CAREER 287

ABOVE Niki's decision to reverse his retirement brought a big increase in ticket sales for his home race. The holiday atmosphere at the Österreichring is clearly evident from the massed spectators encamped on the hillside.

262 Austrian Grand Prix

Österreichring, 15 August 1982, Formula 1
McLaren MP4/1B-06 • #8
Qualifying: 10th • Result: 5th

The Austrian Grand Prix had been in doubt a year earlier due to financial difficulties, but ticket sales were boosted significantly by Lauda's return. However, all the non-turbo runners at the super-fast Österreichring were disgruntled and off the pace, Lauda among them. He had an engine failure on Friday and managed only 10th fastest time on Saturday, unable to overcome nagging understeer and restricted by Michelin qualifiers that were good for only one lap. His injured wrist had not fully healed but the attentions of Willi Dungl meant that he was able to race.

McLaren's choice of rubber for the race was too conservative, offering little grip. After dropping a place at the start and narrowly avoiding a collision with Andrea de Cesaris's Alfa Romeo, he slowly moved up the field, passing Nigel Mansell's Lotus and benefiting from the simultaneous retirements of the Tolemans of Teo Fabi and Derek Warwick on lap 7. Two laps later he lost a place to Brian Henton's Tyrrell but he continued to gain ground through attrition, which accounted for René Arnoux's Renault and Riccardo Patrese's Brabham. He slipped back to seventh when Patrick Tambay's Ferrari overtook at the chicane but rose further when Nelson Piquet retired his Brabham on lap 32 and Henton pitted a lap later. He finished fifth, a lap down on winner Elio de Angelis's Lotus.

288 NIKI LAUDA

1982

263 Swiss Grand Prix

Dijon-Prenois, 29 August 1982, Formula 1
McLaren MP4/1B-07 • #8
Qualifying: 4th • Result: 3rd

Outstandingly quick in first qualifying on Friday, Lauda produced a smooth, effortless lap when he found the track free of traffic and was so satisfied with it — beaten only by the two Renaults — that he did not appear at all on Saturday, although Riccardo Patrese (Brabham) made a late charge that day and bumped him to fourth spot on the grid.

On race day, however, his car was disappointing: fourth at the end of lap 1, he was passed by Nelson Piquet's Brabham on lap 2 and Keke Rosberg's Williams three laps later. This left him in a battle with Patrese, the powerful Brabham slow and awkward in corners but so fast on the straights that it was difficult to find an overtaking opportunity, but Niki managed it on lap 10 and set off after Rosberg, who was now seven seconds to the good. Gradually he caught up with the Finn and was within sight of the Williams by lap 40. The pair moved ahead of Piquet when he pitted for Brabham's now-regular mid-race fuel stop, leaving them in pursuit of the dominant Renaults, but they were badly and persistently baulked when they came up to lap Andrea de Cesaris's Alfa Romeo. Rosberg eventually passed the Italian and picked up pace, such that he was a long way up the road again by the time Lauda got through, with a very forceful move. In the closing stages a vibration from the front wheels caused the McLaren to fall back further, although Lauda gained a place on lap 74 when the engine in René Arnoux's Renault expired. While Rosberg staged a dramatic finish by taking the lead from Alain Prost's Renault two laps from the end, Niki brought his hobbled McLaren home for a well-earned podium finish, over a minute behind and the only other finisher to complete the distance.

264 Italian Grand Prix

Monza, 12 September 1982, Formula 1
McLaren MP4/1B-07 • #8
Qualifying: 10th • Result: Retired (handling/brakes)

Insolubly poor handling and a general lack of grip from Michelin's qualifying tyres, particularly out of the chicanes, left the McLarens on the sixth row of the grid when practice ended.

LEFT Swiss by name, French by nature — Dijon played host to the revived Swiss Grand Prix. Niki powers his McLaren through the esses on his way to third place.

THE SECOND CAREER 289

ABOVE As his McLaren MP4 exits the *Parabolica* onto Monza's pit straight during the Italian Grand Prix, the 'TAG' logo on the chin bar of Niki's helmet indicates the future — a Porsche-developed TAG turbo engine.

Saturday had been the better day for the team as changes to springs, ride height and skirts improved the cars' behaviour in readiness for the race, although these set-up tweaks meant little in the context of an 80bhp deficit to the turbos at this circuit where power counted for a great deal. The fact that Niki's helmet now bore a TAG motif drew plenty of attention: it was a secret at the time but Techniques d'Avant Garde, owned by McLaren director Mansour Ojjeh, had commissioned Porsche to design and build a turbo engine for use in the new MP4/2 being designed by John Barnard for the 1984 season.

Although Niki progressed as far as ninth place by lap 21, this was only a consequence of attrition in front of him and for the duration he was stuck behind Michele Alboreto's Tyrrell. A lacklustre outing ended on lap 22 when Lauda stopped at the pits to complain that the combination of acute understeer, poor handling (the result of a sticking skirt) and grabbing front brakes was making competitive driving impossible; his decision not to continue went almost unnoticed.

265 Caesar's Palace Grand Prix (USA)

Las Vegas, 25 September 1982, Formula 1
McLaren MP4/1B-07 • #8
Qualifying: 13th • Result: Retired (engine)

Formula 1's trip to the temporary circuit laid out in the parking lot of the Caesar's Palace Hotel in Las Vegas was billed as a World Championship showdown between Keke Rosberg of Williams and McLaren's John Watson, although the Ulsterman had it all to do as he was nine points behind and therefore had to win with the Finn scoring nothing.

But even Lauda, sitting three points adrift of his team-mate, still had the slimmest of chances because McLaren's outstanding appeal against his Belgian Grand Prix disqualification was due to be heard the day after the race. Should Niki win in Las Vegas and get his four points from Zolder reinstated, he could become World Champion if things went wrong for Rosberg and Watson.

290 NIKI LAUDA

1982

The tight, bumpy street circuit should have suited McLaren and the MP4/1B was good on race rubber, but it took a while to set it up on qualifiers. When his car was finally sorted, Lauda's Cosworth engine tightened in the final session and he was unable to improve his existing time, a mere 13th on the grid compared with Watson's ninth.

In the first half of the race he had a frustrating spell trying to get past the Alfa Romeo of Andrea de Cesaris, who was again applying questionable tactics to keep in front and clearly holding Lauda up. After a prolonged struggle, the Austrian finally forced his way through at the end of the pit straight on lap 34, banging wheels with the Italian car as he passed. Then showing the same sort of pace that had taken Watson up to third, Lauda rapidly caught Derek Daly (Williams), who resisted only briefly before conceding sixth place. However, overheating brought about by his battle with de Cesaris had taken its toll and after 53 laps, with his oil pressure warning light flickering and the engine showing signs of seizure, he was forced to retire.

Watson finished a game second behind Michele Alboreto's Tyrrell, but it was not enough to deny fifth-placed Rosberg the title at the end of a very open season that had seen 11 different winners in 16 races.

SUMMARY

Although McLaren had been the most successful team of 1982 with four victories, a well-balanced car and experienced drivers, form had been inconsistent. When competitive, the McLarens were very good; when off-form, they were nowhere. The extremes of Lauda's year were winning convincingly at Long Beach and Brands Hatch but trailing around with the also-rans at Monaco and Monza.

With his usual curt summary of the position, he noted that the failings at Monaco and Monza were down to the team because the car could not be made to perform, but that there were two races — Detroit and Hockenheim — in which he had messed up himself. He added rather ruefully that in his first career he had had 100 per cent mastery of his car, but that in the current technical environment he was only 90 per cent in charge, with the remaining 10 per cent in the lap of the Gods.

In part, the inconsistency in McLaren's performance was due to the wide range of tyre compounds available from Michelin. The only Cosworth team running on the French rubber, McLaren found that the tyres that suited the MP4/1Bs best were often in short supply and in the first half of the season the quality of the qualifying tyres was variable. John Watson's victory at Detroit was the result of a gamble that worked.

Even without his two victories, Lauda's comeback was in itself an achievement. For him to return to Formula 1 in the solid-sprung cars of the period and immediately put himself among the front runners surprised some, but not him. He usually out-qualified Watson, sometimes by a considerable margin, and his two victories were as dominant as any he had achieved in the previous decade.

ABOVE There is barely a spectator in sight at Las Vegas as Niki's McLaren MP4/1B passes the casinos on his way around the concrete wasteland of the Caesar's Palace circuit laid out in a parking lot.

THE SECOND CAREER

1983
MARKING TIME

New technical regulations for 1983 banished the excesses of ground-effect aerodynamics by requiring cars to be flat-bottomed, which meant that rock-hard suspension — which Lauda disliked and made no secret of it — was a thing of the past, at least for now. Formula 1 cars became much more progressive and pleasurable to handle, with characteristics that would have favoured a smooth, precise driver like Lauda had it not been for the small matter of the power deficiency of his normally aspirated Cosworth-engined McLaren MP4/1C compared with the proliferation of 1.5-litre turbos, now used by Alfa Romeo, ATS (BMW), Brabham (BMW), Ferrari, Lotus (Renault), Renault and Toleman (Hart).

However, McLaren had a turbo on the way in the form of the Porsche-developed TAG V6 engine, but it was far from ready and the plan was to introduce it with an all-new MP4/2 car for the 1984 season. At the end of 1982, Lauda met Hans Mezger, the Porsche engineer in charge of the project, to discuss how the new engine could be delivered in the most successful manner. The Austrian agreed to keep the engineer informed about pitlane politics (rather than technical details) and visited Porsche for the first time in December 1982, when a prototype engine shoehorned into a 911 chassis had its track début at the company's Weissach test facility.

Lauda was excited by the Porsche association. The German manufacturer was way ahead of the competition in terms of turbo experience, having begun its development of the technology over 10 years earlier in the all-conquering Can-Am 917/10 and 917/30 cars, and gone on to win the Le Mans 24 Hours and the World Sports Car Championship multiple times with turbo machinery.

1983

266 Brazilian Grand Prix

Jacarepaguá, 13 March 1983, Formula 1
McLaren MP4/1C-7 • #8
Qualifying: 9th • Result: 3rd

In pre-race testing at Rio, Lauda's revised McLaren MP4/1C was the fastest Cosworth-powered runner — both over a lap and through the speed trap — despite Niki still recovering from eye surgery, a residual consequence of the Nürburgring accident. Come practice, he found his Michelins useless in qualifying and spent most of his time working on a decent race set-up. Instead the astonishing Keke Rosberg was the fastest Cosworth-equipped driver, qualifying his Williams on pole ahead of seven turbos and then Lauda.

After the searing heat of practice and qualifying, Lauda was pleased that Sunday dawned slightly cooler and overcast and at the start he led a tight knot of midfield runners. Having been easily passed by team-mate John Watson on lap 2, he spent several laps stuck behind the Toleman of Derek Warwick, who in turn was struggling to pass Mauro Baldi's Alfa Romeo. On lap 20 Niki made an optimistic move on Warwick that met with little resistance and two laps later he also got past Baldi, who promptly collided with the Toleman and spun. Next in Lauda's sights was Patrick Tambay's fifth-placed Ferrari, which he overtook on lap 34. A lap later he gained another position with Watson's retirement and on lap 42 he caught Alain Prost's Renault to take second place, but he was unable to make any impression on the 55-second lead that Nelson Piquet had built up in his Brabham.

With 10 laps to, Niki had to surrender his second place to a charging Rosberg, whose Williams team was now copying Brabham's race strategy by having a mid-race pit stop for fuel and new tyres. Although the Finn was subsequently disqualified for receiving a push start during his pit stop, an unusual ruling by the stewards meant that the drivers who finished behind him were not promoted.

LEFT In this rather posed photograph, the contrast between the cutting-edge technology of Niki's McLaren MP4/1C and the rudimentary surroundings of the Jacarepaguá pits is particularly marked.

MARKING TIME 293

ABOVE Lauda's charge through the field at Long Beach from 23rd on the grid to second place at the flag was one of the highlights of his year.

267 United States Grand Prix (West)

Long Beach, 27 March 1983, Formula 1
McLaren MP4/1C-7 • #8
Qualifying: 23rd • Result: 2nd (fastest lap)

Despite trying a new three-element rear wing, the McLarens were also-rans in practice, afflicted with persistent understeer and so far off the pace that they could only qualify 22nd (John Watson) and 23rd (Lauda). They struggled to get heat into their Michelin qualifiers on the Friday, when everyone was affected by a very severe bump on a new section of the track, so that evening the mechanics did a complete set-up change that included lowered ride height. The changes made little difference, even with the overnight removal of the bump. As Michelin's race tyres gave more grip, Lauda concentrated on optimising his race settings.

On race day, the tyre picture was completely reversed. Those drivers on Goodyears either wore out their rubber or ran into each other. From the start the McLarens progressed through the field in tandem, Lauda ahead of Watson, and few people noticed they were lapping as quickly as the leaders. Their passage was eased from time to time as others hit trouble. On lap 10 they lay 18th and 19th; on lap 20 they were 12th and 13th; and by lap 28, a little over one-third distance, they had reached third and fourth, thanks in part to tangles that took out three of the top four within a few seconds. Now only Jacques Laffite's Williams and Riccardo Patrese's Brabham remained to be hauled in. By this stage, Watson, having chosen a harder tyre compound, was quicker than Lauda and outbraked the Austrian on lap 33. They continued to circulate in close company and were just five seconds behind the leading pair when, on lap 43, Patrese tried an over-ambitious outbraking move on Laffite at the end of Shoreline Drive and took to the escape road, allowing the McLarens to sail past before he could resume. Just a lap later, Laffite, struggling on ailing Goodyears, had to give best as well.

Everything held together and Watson and Lauda were able to take an astonishing 1–2 victory, with the Austrian — who had to slow down briefly late on when hampered by cramp in his right leg — also setting a new lap record. Another record, which has stood to this day, went to Watson as the winner of a Grand Prix from the lowest starting position.

268 French Grand Prix

Paul Ricard, 17 April 1983, Formula 1
McLaren MP4/1C-7 • #8
Qualifying: 12th • Result: Retired (wheel bearing)

On the Saturday Lauda was the first driver to use the new Cosworth DFY engine, which had revised cylinder heads, but he reported that it seemed little different from the old DFV apart from a slight improvement in mid-range power. Nevertheless, he was easily quickest of the non-turbo runners, albeit down in 12th place despite taking the curves after the pits flat out.

Out-dragged by Andrea de Cesaris's Alfa Romeo at the start, he grimly worked his way up through the field, passing Michele Alboreto's Tyrrell and Bruno Giacomelli's Toleman in short order, pressing on to get ahead of Elio de Angelis's Lotus on lap 19. He jumped two places on the next lap when both Riccardo Patrese (Brabham) and de Cesaris pitted, and further progress came over the next six laps as the leaders made their pit stops for fuel and tyres. It all came to an abrupt end on lap 29 when a rear wheel bearing seized, spinning him out of sixth place and into retirement.

269 San Marino Grand Prix

Imola, 1 May 1983, Formula 1
McLaren MP4/1C-7 • #8
Qualifying: 18th • Result: Retired (accident)

Despite having new Cosworth DFY engines, which Lauda still maintained were little

BELOW Although Niki came to the French Grand Prix as championship leader, retirement in the race did little to help his cause. Here he leads Elio de Angelis's Lotus 93T and Andrea de Cesaris's Alfa Romeo 183T out of *Virage du Pont* and onto Paul Ricard's start/finish straight.

ABOVE Three abreast into *Tosa*: Niki's McLaren MP4/1B is flanked by Nigel Mansell's Lotus 92 and Michele Alboreto's Tyrrell 011, with the Williams FW08C of Jacques Laffite tucked in tightly behind them. Marc Surer in his Arrows A6 watches from a distance.

better than a good DFV, McLaren's technical people were mystified by a sudden decline in qualifying performance. There was nothing particularly wrong with the MP4/1Cs, but after two days in which both drivers struggled for grip on qualifying tyres (of relatively hard compound for a non-turbo car) a combination of rubber on the track and increased ambient temperature left Lauda 18th and John Watson 24th. However, Niki was eighth quickest in the warm-up and another charge from the back of the grid was expected.

After climbing quickly through the field to ninth place, he was caught out on lap 11 by the track surface breaking up at *Acque Minerale*. In a rare error, he left his braking slightly too late, clipped the kerb and slid on the crumbling tarmac into the tyre barrier, damaging the car's front end too heavily to continue.

WEISSACH
1 MAY 1983

Without McLaren's knowledge and much to Ron Dennis's annoyance when he found out, Porsche installed an early example of the new TAG turbo engine in one of its Group C 956 sports cars (chassis 107) for use as a mobile test bed on the company's private track at Weissach. Engine designer Hans Mezger had observed that for the first 5,000km (about 3,000 miles) a 'taxi driver' would be enough as the purpose of this exercise was simply evaluation of functions, but Lauda was insistent that he and no-one else would carry out the initial runs.

He completed some 300km (about 190 miles) and reportedly drove very hard, unconcerned by the track's meagre safety features and its undulating surface. He revelled in the engine's smoothness and reliability but conceded that little else could be learned from the experience, particularly because the 956 was over 250kg heavier than a Formula 1 car.

In this photograph engineers Hans Mezger (third from left) and Alwin Springer (black polo shirt) discuss progress with Porsche test driver Roland Kussmaul (in Rothmans overalls) and Niki.

1983

270 Monaco Grand Prix

Monte Carlo, 15 May 1983, Formula 1
McLaren MP4/1C-7 • #8
Qualifying: Did not qualify

This was a race in which Lauda and John Watson would certainly have scored points had they been able to qualify. As it was, they were in trouble from first practice and once again it was a question of getting enough heat into their Michelin qualifying tyres, mainly due to the fact that these had been designed for turbo cars with more power and downforce. The suspension of the MP4/1Cs had been softened as much as possible and Lauda drove as neatly as ever around the notorious kerbs, but it made no difference; on the first day the cars were five seconds away from Alain Prost's provisional pole time in his Renault.

A bespoke batch of Michelins was delivered on Saturday morning and Lauda immediately went two seconds faster, setting a time that would have given him a midfield position had he been able to repeat it in the afternoon, but rain washed out the qualifying session. Although he was fourth quickest in the wet, his chance of a place on the grid had vanished. Had this been anywhere other than Monaco, with its 20-car limit, his misery in recording a time that was only good enough for 22nd place would have been just bearable.

271 Belgian Grand Prix

Spa-Francorchamps, 22 May 1983, Formula 1
McLaren MP4/1C-7 • #8
Qualifying: 15th • Result: Retired (engine)

The Belgian Grand Prix returned to its traditional home, Spa-Francorchamps, after a 13-year absence. Much of the old 8.76-mile (14.10km) circuit, which had been run on public roads at very high speed, was now replaced by a shorter but still quite fast purpose-built section to give a 4.33-mile (6.97km) lap with proper safety provision. As with all the Cosworth runners, the McLarens were nowhere in practice.

In one of several attempts to find a cure for the tyre problems, Lauda tried a revised rear suspension arrangement (with new uprights) and

BELOW Despite new Michelin tyres that had been specially flown in to get the McLarens back on terms, rain during the final qualifying session washed out any chance that Niki had of making the grid for the Monaco Grand Prix.

MARKING TIME 297

ABOVE Niki's normally aspirated McLaren MP4/1C leads Bruno Giacomelli's turbo-powered Toleman TG183B into Spa's Bus-Stop chicane during the Belgian Grand Prix. He retired when his engine dropped a valve.

OPPOSITE Debris fencing and steel barriers give the Detroit street circuit a prison-like feel as Niki battles with his badly handling McLaren MP4/1C.

rear wing (with modified endplates) on the spare car (MP4/1C-5) in Friday morning free practice, but the changes brought no advantage and were not seen again. Using the revised Michelins introduced at Monaco, he managed only 15th quickest time on Friday, and after rain washed out Saturday qualifying his starting place was fixed, almost five seconds off Alain Prost's pole time in his Renault.

One of the few drivers who had experienced the old Spa, Lauda voiced concerns about the rain that fell on race day and left rivers running across the track, but — like his colleagues — he was delighted to be back at a 'proper' circuit. After a false start delayed proceedings, when the race finally got going he rapidly dispatched Michele Alboreto (Tyrrell) on lap 2 and, after a brief battle, passed Roberto Guerrero (Theodore) on lap 10. By 20 laps — half distance — he was on the tail of Jacques Laffite's Williams and harried the Frenchman remorselessly, well clear of the pursuing pack. Racing without stopping while the front runners pitted, he had progressed to seventh place when he crawled into the pits on lap 34 to retire after a broken valve destroyed an inlet trumpet.

272 Detroit Grand Prix

5 June 1983, Formula 1
McLaren MP4/1C-7 • #8
Qualifying: 18th • Result: Retired (shock absorber)

On a circuit that was modified and slightly quicker than the configuration used in 1982, the McLaren drivers were the first out when qualifying began in very wet conditions, Lauda setting the eighth quickest time. Saturday was dry, but the usual lack of traction from the Michelins persisted and Lauda saved his qualifiers for late in the session, only to find that

298 NIKI LAUDA

1983

WEISSACH
JUNE/JULY 1983

With Porsche having successfully tested the robustness of the TAG turbo engine in different chassis of its own, McLaren's Ron Dennis and John Barnard bowed to pressure to try the engine straight away in an existing McLaren rather than wait for completion of the first MP4/2, which was specifically designed around the new V6 and would use the engine as a stressed member. The prototype MP4/1C-1, therefore, was modified using hacked-about MP4/1B bodywork and this 'compromise' car was designated MP4/1D-1.

John Watson made the first runs at Weissach on 30 June because Lauda had other commitments, but the Austrian arrived a few days later to complete a large number of laps, watched by Ferry Porsche and under the supervision of engineer Hans Mezger (seen in the photograph leaning forward with hands on knees). While Barnard and Dennis still believed that the MP4/1D-1 'hack' was a distraction, Lauda wanted to get on-track experience of the new power unit as soon as possible. Compared with his previous experience of the engine in a Porsche 956, in the much lighter Formula 1 car he immediately identified excessive throttle lag and an alarming oil-breathing problem, both issues that race-proving would help to resolve. Other than this, Lauda completed over 500 miles around Weissach without encountering any major technical difficulties.

he had been quicker on race rubber and was left 18th on the grid.

In the race he soon progressed thanks to a flurry of retirements that accounted for Elio de Angelis (Lotus) and Marc Surer (Arrows) on lap 5 and Jacques Laffite's Williams on lap 7. That same lap he managed to find a way past Nigel Mansell's Lotus, but he was struggling for grip and made not one but two pit stops for fresh tyres, on laps 15 and 23, leaving him a lap behind in 18th place. Now he realised that the problem with his car, which was becoming virtually undriveable, was not just tyres. He ran near the tail of the field for much of the race before finally pulling into the pits on lap 50, having run at the very back for the previous 12 laps. The problem was traced to a seized shock absorber.

John Watson's race was rather different. Having started three places behind Lauda, he finished third, snapping at the heels of second-placed Keke Rosberg's Williams, and set fastest lap.

MARKING TIME 299

ABOVE Down among the tail enders, Niki perseveres with the reluctant McLaren MP4/1C in Montréal.

273 Canadian Grand Prix

Montréal, 12 June 1983, Formula 1
McLaren MP4/1C-7 • #8
Qualifying: 19th • Result: Retired (spin)

Still unable to generate heat in its tyres, Lauda's McLaren qualified a lowly 19th. As usual he made up several positions at the start and then found himself in a battle with Thierry Boutsen's Arrows for 14th place. On lap 12, a lap after Boutsen had outbraked Bruno Giacomelli's Toleman, Lauda tried a similar move on the Italian but uncharacteristically locked his brakes and spun. As he was unable to restart his stalled engine, he walked back to the pits, his retirement from the race largely unnoticed.

By now opinion was forming among observers that he seemed to be biding his time, appearing disinclined to scrap with the also-rans while awaiting McLaren's turbo-engined car.

274 British Grand Prix

Silverstone, 16 July 1983, Formula 1
McLaren MP4/1C-7 • #8
Qualifying: 15th • Result: 6th

A blown Cosworth engine in the first qualifying session was an unwelcome surprise and caused Lauda some delay, while oversteer on the second day of practice hampered his smooth style and prevented him from improving his time. Although only 15th on the grid, he was second fastest of the Cosworth runners (behind Keke Rosberg), some 7mph down on the turbos through the speed trap. With little hope of getting near the front at a circuit with an average lap speed of around

SILVERSTONE
20 JULY 1983

McLaren's new engine made its first public appearance in three days of tests during the week following the British Grand Prix. These showed immediate promise and Lauda lapped Silverstone with the MP4/1D-1 'hack' in a time that would have elevated him three places on the grid the previous weekend.

The progress being made convinced Lauda to push for the new engine to be used in races as soon as possible, but John Barnard and Ron Dennis — perfectionists both — continued to resist, believing this to be an unhelpful compromise when their plan all along had been to put the new V6, with its very narrow base, in a chassis designed around it. Lauda, however, persuaded the team's sponsor, Marlboro, to apply pressure and have the engine's race début brought forward, to Dennis's considerable displeasure. It was rumoured that Marlboro docked McLaren around $250,000 for not having the new turbo car running soon enough and some sources suggest that McLaren made a corresponding deduction from Lauda's retainer.

150mph, the normally aspirated cars were once again left to fight over the minor placings, but the introduction of a planned fuel stop into McLaren's race strategy seemed to revitalise Lauda's interest in using the Cosworth engine, at least for the time being.

Comfortably the fastest non-turbo driver in the race, he made up a place on each of the first five laps, his unobtrusively precise style gaining him time through Silverstone's fast sweepers. His pit stop, on lap 38 when running fifth, went surprisingly well considering that the team personnel had had no opportunity to practise their routine. Rejoining eighth, he spent the next 11 laps battling with Manfred Winkelhock's ATS before finally passing it on lap 47. His strong drive took him to sixth place at the finish to give him his first point since Long Beach.

275 German Grand Prix

Hockenheim, 7 August 1983, Formula 1
McLaren MP4/1C-7 • #8
Qualifying: 18th • Result: Disqualified

After blowing an engine on Friday morning, Lauda needed more than good luck — he needed a turbo as the Cosworth was nothing more than an also-ran on the long, flat-out blasts of Hockenheim.

Repeating the vigour he had shown at Silverstone, he made up eight places in the first 10 laps of the race to head a group running some way behind the leaders. Seventh when he stopped for fuel and tyres on lap 28, he did not lose a place but was lapped while stationary. Clearly on form, he drove impeccably to finish

ABOVE Late adjustments are made to Niki's McLaren MP4/1C in the Silverstone pits as he prepares to go to the grid for the British Grand Prix.

ABOVE Unable to keep up with the turbo cars along Hockenheim's flat-out blasts, the Cosworth-engined runners enjoyed their own 'race within a race'. Here, Lauda's McLaren MP4/1C holds off Keke Rosberg's Williams FW08C through the stadium while John Watson in the sister McLaren keeps a watching brief.

fifth on the road and completely outpaced all of his normally aspirated rivals.

His only mistake of the weekend was made in the pits and it was to prove costly. With locked front wheels, he overshot his garage and — according to varying reports — either reversed his car into position or was pushed back. Either way, it was an illegal move because a car must not move against the direction of the track. Although there was no formal protest, a member of the Williams team alerted the stewards by asking whether or not they intended to enforce the rule, resulting in Lauda's disqualification. In fact this was a 'tit-for-tat' situation: at the Brazilian Grand Prix a McLaren representative had similarly observed that Keke Rosberg's push start in the pits should not remain unpunished and the Williams driver had been disqualified after the race.

276 Austrian Grand Prix

Österreichring, 14 August 1983, Formula 1
McLaren MP4/1C-7 • #8
Qualifying: 14th • Result: 6th

Despite optimistic reports to the contrary, the new TAG turbo engine was not yet race-ready. Happy with the handling of his car, Lauda was again the fastest non-turbo driver, by almost a second, but he was 15mph slower than the turbos through the speed trap and wound up only 14th on the grid with his Friday time. This effort, he felt, was the best he could wring out of the McLaren/Cosworth/Michelin combination, so he did only two flying laps on Saturday to underline his opinion that there was no point in flogging round on qualifiers.

Although he made a poor start, he steered

1983

clear of the incidents that plagued the early part of the race and made up four places in the first 14 laps. After successfully wrestling with Michele Alboreto (Tyrrell) for the honour of being 'best Cosworth', he kept the advantage and was one of the last to pit, making his stop on lap 33 when running sixth and retaining position upon rejoining. There he remained, despite Stefan Johansson's efforts in the temperamental Spirit-Honda, but by the end he was two laps behind the winning Renault of Alain Prost. A single point was scant reward for a tough afternoon's work.

277 Dutch Grand Prix

Zandvoort, 28 August 1983, Formula 1
McLaren MP4/1E-6 • #8
Qualifying: 19th • Result: Retired (brakes)

Having finally convinced his team of the need to race-test the now-delivered TAG turbo engine, a new MP4/1E was built on the chassis of MP4/1C-6 in such a rush that the car was only completed while *en route* to Holland on a cross-channel ferry. After using the Cosworth-engined MP4/1C-7 for half of the first session, he finally got to drive the turbo car in anger. Featuring midway on the time sheets in Friday qualifying, the MP4/1E ran with impressive reliability until a turbo problem occurred on Saturday afternoon and left Lauda having to settle for 19th position on the grid, four places behind his Cosworth-powered team-mate. However, the fact that the car was fourth fastest through the speed trap gave its driver much cause for optimism.

ABOVE Leaning heavily on its left suspension through the *Hella-Licht* chicane, Niki's Cosworth-powered McLaren MP4/1C makes its final appearance in his hands at the Austrian Grand Prix.

LEFT The waiting is over: the TAG turbo V6 engine is installed in Niki's McLaren MP4/1E at Zandvoort ready for its first run in anger.

MARKING TIME 303

ABOVE For a hybrid car, the McLaren MP4/1E displays remarkably clean lines as Lauda finds himself short of brakes during the Dutch Grand Prix.

RIGHT The programme for the Dutch Grand Prix carried a rather unusual image of Niki in the McLaren MP4/1D test hack in the Silverstone pits, foreshadowing the race début of the TAG turbo engine at Zandvoort.

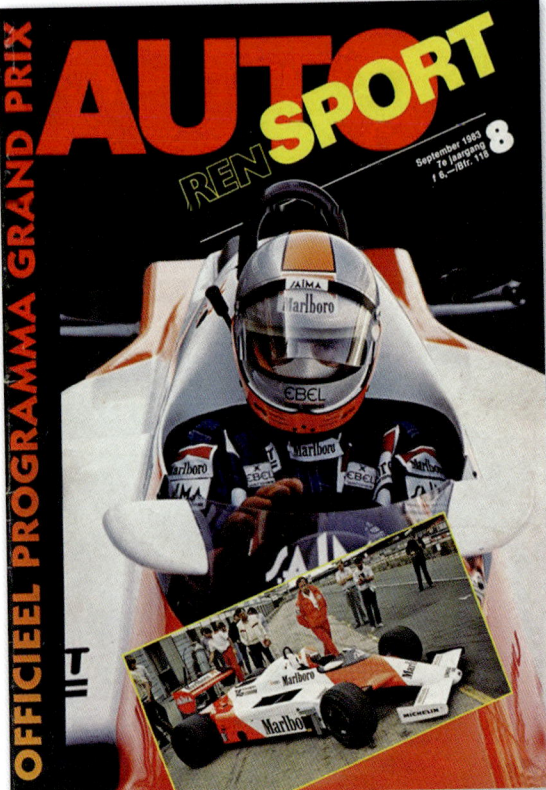

Lauda started quietly and had progressed to 12th place by lap 18 of the race, but on lap 25 he pitted with the brake fluid boiling. The engine had performed strongly — proving to be a match for the Ferraris, BMWs and Renaults in terms of straight line speed — but the carbon brakes had run hotter than usual owing to the new car's extra weight, higher top speed and inherent lack of engine braking. Nevertheless, it was a very promising début.

278 Italian Grand Prix

Monza, 11 September 1983, Formula 1
McLaren MP4/1E-6 • #8
Qualifying: 13th • Result: Retired (engine)

A lot had been learned at Zandvoort, including the need to revert temporarily to cast-iron brake discs instead of carbon ones,

304 NIKI LAUDA

1983

and Lauda moved up the grid at Monza to start 13th while team-mate John Watson, now with a turbo car as well, was two places behind him. Although the McLarens were second only to the Brabham-BMWs in speed on Monza's long straights, they still lacked the large wings and overall downforce of their turbo-engined rivals, leaving their drivers with plenty of work to do in the corners. Lauda's efforts were not helped by an infected insect bite on his left foot that made pressing the clutch pedal very painful.

An electrical problem that had shown up in practice caused a bad misfire from the start of the race and Lauda made a prolonged pit stop on lap 3, losing five laps. All the same, with the problem fixed he opted to get more race experience with the engine and ran at the back of the field. Coming in for his now-regular mid-race pit stop on lap 30, he stalled the engine — apparently an easy thing to do — in the pitlane and rolled to a halt in front of the Brabham pit, just as that team's mechanics were preparing to receive race leader Nelson Piquet. As Brabham men hastily pushed the McLaren away, its engine spluttered into life again but shortly afterwards Lauda stopped out on the circuit, feeling that the V6 was about to seize.

279 European Grand Prix

Brands Hatch, 25 September 1983, Formula 1
McLaren MP4/1E-6 • #8
Qualifying: 13th • Result: Retired (engine)

As New York had failed to meet its deadline to prepare for its scheduled Grand Prix, Brands Hatch stepped into the breach and the circus returned to England. A huge rear wing on each of the McLarens provided better rear-end grip while revisions to the turbos and radiators were a step forward. On Friday Lauda missed much of the first practice session while a replacement engine was installed after the original dropped a valve. On a damp and grey Saturday he had a spin at Druids in the tricky conditions on his final set of qualifiers, losing further time while the car was checked over.

BELOW Heading into the second *Lesmo* corner at Monza, Niki's McLaren-TAG MP4/1E leads John Watson's similar car, Bruno Giacomelli's Toleman-Hart TG183B, the Arrows-Cosworth A6 pair of Marc Surer and Thierry Boutsen, Roberto Guerrero's Theodore-Cosworth N183, Danny Sullivan's Tyrrell-Cosworth 011B and Stefan Johansson's Spirit-Honda 201.

MARKING TIME 305

ABOVE For the European Grand Prix at Brands Hatch, the McLaren MP4/1E wore a more fashionable over-sized rear wing in common with the more developed turbo cars.

Complaining of understeer, he was out-qualified by team-mate John Watson, 13th versus 10th.

In the early laps he slipped back as far as 15th but then worked his way up through the nose-to-tail midfield group to run in tandem with Watson. He passed the Ulsterman for 10th place on lap 22, but three laps later his progress was halted when the engine's camshaft drive train broke.

280 South African Grand Prix

Kyalami, 15 October 1983, Formula 1
McLaren MP4/1E-6 • #8
Qualifying: 12th • Result: 11th (not running at finish)

The TAG turbo's Bosch Motronic computer-controlled injection/ignition system was an area that needed plenty of development attention and at Kyalami Lauda tired of the endless fiddling required from Bosch's engineers, eventually telling them not to touch his car any more. After that, he reported few problems with the V6 engine, which now had revised intercooling. Following a low-key qualifying performance, he grabbed everyone's attention in the warm-up by topping the time sheets with his car in race trim.

Goodyear runners were at a disadvantage in the very hot weather and Lauda gambled on soft-compound Michelins for the race. Holding off Eddie Cheever's Renault at the start, he rocketed forward to 10th place at the end of the first lap and made remarkable progress as first Manfred Winkelhock's ATS dropped out (lap 2) and then in quick succession he passed Elio de Angelis's Lotus (lap 3), René Arnoux's Ferrari (lap 5) and Keke Rosberg's Williams (lap 6). Next in his sights was Patrick Tambay's

306 NIKI LAUDA

1983

Ferrari, which he despatched under braking at Crowthorne on lap 9. Driving with a level of aggression that had been missing for much of the year, three laps later he was past Andrea de Cesaris's Alfa Romeo and then within seven more laps he reeled in Alain Prost (Renault) to take third place with ease, much to the surprise of the Frenchman, who went into this race as the World Championship leader. Niki was closing on Riccardo Patrese's Brabham when he pitted for fuel and tyres on lap 33, only for a jammed nut on the right rear wheel to delay his stop — he spent 23 seconds up on the jacks — and leave him seventh.

Again he set about the task of climbing the order. In an impressive display, he clawed his way back into contention, reaching third place again by lap 46 after Prost's retirement and passing moves on Cheever, Tambay and de Cesaris. Now he put pressure on second-placed Nelson Piquet (Brabham), who, with Prost out of the race, only had to finish fourth to become World Champion. The Brazilian, backing off to save his car, let the McLaren through into second place on lap 69.

The possibility of a last-minute victory for Lauda was tantalisingly close, as Patrese was only four seconds ahead and there were eight laps left. But within three laps the TAG turbo fell silent and left Niki stranded at Clubhouse. The cause was electrical failure brought on by the combined effect of heat and vibration on a regulator. Although not running at the flag, he was classified 11th.

It was a bitterly disappointing outcome for him but at least there was consolation in the knowledge that he could expect to be a serious contender in 1984.

SUMMARY

It had been a patchy season, punctuated by a couple of lacklustre performances — his spin into retirement at Montréal was the nadir — among outstanding drives in the Cosworth-powered MP4/1C in Britain, Germany and Austria. McLaren had been the leading Cosworth team on these faster circuits through Lauda's ultra-smooth precision, which had kept the underpowered car competitive by avoiding scrubbing off speed.

Although the season ended on a high note with his strong performance at Kyalami and the promise of a highly competitive car for 1984, the goalposts moved unexpectedly for Lauda at the end of 1983. John Watson, his McLaren team-mate for two years and a trusted ally, had been holding out for a better pay deal after some impressive performances and had not yet signed a contract for the new season. When Renault summarily sacked Alain Prost on the Monday after Kyalami because of his criticism of the team's organisation and preparation, which the Frenchman believed had cost him the World Championship, suddenly Ron Dennis had the chance to sign a proven winner for a bargain-basement salary. The deal was done — and Watson was out of a drive.

Now Lauda now had a younger, faster team-mate ensconced in the middle of 'his' team. If he was to make the most of the effort he had put into developing the turbocharged McLaren, he would have to rise to the occasion.

ABOVE Declaration of intent: 12 laps into the South African Grand Prix at Kyalami, Niki's McLaren MP4/1E has just overtaken the Renault RE40 of Alain Prost, who was leading the World Championship. Although electrical failure denied him second place, the car's highly competitive showing in the last race of the year gave him confidence for the new season.

MARKING TIME 307

1984
AS CLOSE AS IT GETS

Testing during January and February with the interim MP4/1E was not a very happy experience for McLaren as Alain Prost and Lauda set only middling times after a lot of trouble with the Porsche-developed TAG turbo engine's Bosch Motronic engine management system. A number of different exhaust systems and turbo layouts were tried on the single development chassis, which Lauda — insisting on his absolute priority in testing as his contract dictated — drove initially before Prost took over. The Austrian was more reassured by the V6's excellent mechanical reliability and he put in a great many laps while the definitive 1984 car was being finalised. By the end of February he was fourth fastest around Paul Ricard's long circuit, exactly a second slower than the quickest runners testing there.

After plans to test the new MP4/2 at Brands Hatch had to be shelved, McLaren's drivers were very encouraged by its showing during its first tests at Paul Ricard early in March. The new car immediately went quicker than the older version had a month before, with both Lauda and Prost tackling the short circuit this time. Even with hard Michelin tyres and race boost, there were no apparent problems and the drivers were enthusiastic, although bad weather meant that they did not get in quite as much running as they would have liked.

Lauda went into the new season as fit as he had ever been. At the weigh-in before the first race, the Brazilian Grand Prix at Jacarepaguá, it was no surprise that he was one of the lightest drivers, even though at 35 he was now the second oldest, after Jacques Laffite.

1984

281 Copa Escort JPS Press Trophy (BR)

Jacarepaguá, 24 March 1984
Ford Escort XR3 (with Peter Windsor)
Qualifying: 9th (ballot) • Result: 4th

Before the serious matter of the new World Championship season started in earnest, there was a light-hearted sideshow in Brazil following final practice on Saturday. Sixteen pairs of journalists and Formula 1 drivers took part in a support race sharing 1.6-litre ethanol-fuelled Ford Escort XR3s, each taking turns as driver and passenger. In an entertaining if rather lurid competition run in 50-degree temperatures, the journalists drove two laps before pitting for a tyre valve-cap change and swapping seats with their partners, who then completed a further three laps.

Lauda had readily accepted Australian journalist Peter Windsor's request to co-drive and the reporter made a good start to hold second place within a close pack. Then the car driven by journalist Yorn Pugmeister, with Manfred Winkelhock alongside him, turned hard right at the *Vitoria* corner in front of Windsor, who was unable to avoid ploughing into the back of it. Pugmeister alleged that Winkelhock had grabbed the wheel to cause mayhem, cutting across cars behind, although Windsor suggested that the German writer himself might have been the guilty party — but Mike Doodson, who was sharing with Martin Brundle, later admitted that he had rammed the Germans' car, forcing it into a spin. Windsor got going again with battered bodywork and a damaged engine.

When Lauda took over at the stops, he quickly made up ground. Forcing his way through the pack, he overtook the Nigel Mansell/Jeff Hutchinson car but at the end of the long straight Mansell outbraked him again to take third. Lauda and Mansell then enjoyed a spirited battle to the flag, the Austrian finishing fourth. After the race it was reported that he had vowed never to get involved in such races again.

282 Brazilian Grand Prix

Jacarepaguá, 25 March 1984, Formula 1
McLaren MP4/2-1 • #8
Qualifying: 6th • Result: Retired (electrics)

After disastrous pre-race testing, despite a break of nearly five months since the end of the previous season, the McLarens were trouble-free in practice and in the warm-up they were quickest by a convincing margin — all of which proved to be an accurate barometer of what was to come. McLaren was much less worried than its rivals about the lower fuel limit of 220 litres (58.12 gallons) that had been introduced for the new season in order to rein in turbo power outputs, knowing that Porsche, with its wide experience of fuel restrictions in Group C sports car racing, had done a good job on the TAG V6's fuel consumption. As for intra-team rivalry in qualifying, Prost bettered Lauda by just over half a second, fourth to the Austrian's sixth.

Niki made a superb start, bursting through from the third row to end the first lap in fourth

ABOVE Journalist Peter Windsor concentrates intently as Niki straps himself into the bog-standard Ford Escort XR3 in which the pair is about to contest the JPS Press Trophy race ahead of the Brazilian Grand Prix.

AS CLOSE AS IT GETS 309

place, while Prost messed up his getaway and slipped to 10th. Charging hard, a lap later Lauda was third, with Derek Warwick's Renault ahead of him. On lap 10 he made a run on the Englishman from a long way behind on the back straight to outbrake him for second place, although just as he ducked through his McLaren was unsettled by a bump and its right rear wheel nudged the Renault's left front. When the leader, Michele Alboreto, spun his Ferrari wildly going into the last corner on lap 12, Lauda was gifted a commanding lead and quickly widened his advantage over Warwick.

By lap 29 the recovering Prost moved into second place, putting the McLarens 1–2. But when the Frenchman made his routine stop on lap 38, Lauda followed him in, clearly in trouble. As the McLaren mechanics could not attend to both cars at the same time, Lauda was waved on to complete another lap and on his return coasted to a standstill with a cracked plug connector in the electrical wiring loom, a problem that could not easily be fixed. Prost went on to win the race.

BELOW The new McLaren MP4/2 fulfilled its promise from the word go. Although Lauda retired from the Brazilian Grand Prix with electrical problems, he led the race with ease from the 12th lap onwards, and new team-mate Alain Prost won.

283 South African Grand Prix

Kyalami, 7 April 1984, Formula 1
McLaren MP4/2-1 • #8
Qualifying: 8th • Result: 1st

The McLarens were struggling in practice as the TAG engines refused to run cleanly at Kyalami's 5,300ft (1,600m) altitude, although fitting smaller turbos for the race improved matters. A delay to the warm-up session allowed Lauda's mechanics to fix a misfire and, with his car now running perfectly for the race, he devastated the opposition. From eighth on the grid, he was a strong fourth by the end of lap 1, then powered past the Williams of Keke Rosberg on lap 4. His McLaren handling beautifully, he harried the leading Brabhams of Nelson Piquet and Teo Fabi into overworking their tyres. Slipstreaming past Fabi in front of the pits on lap 10, he held his line into Crowthorne to fend off an attempted repass by the very fast Brabham, but his McLaren was so much quicker down the hill through Barbecue Bend and Jukskei Sweep that he was well clear by the end of the lap. He had closed right up on the other Brabham when Piquet pitted for new tyres on lap 21, handing him the lead and a 40-second advantage over Rosberg. By the time Niki made his own stop, on lap 34, Piquet had dropped out and he resumed with his lead intact.

Prost, meanwhile, had had to start from the pitlane in the spare car after the engine in his own had refused to fire up on the grid. By lap 43 he reached second place, half a minute behind Lauda. Despite exhortations to reduce his pace, Niki kept reeling off fast laps to be certain of the win, and perhaps to emphasise his authority over his younger team-mate. The McLaren duo lapped the entire field to achieve a convincing 1–2, with Lauda more than a minute ahead of Prost.

His 20th victory had been a long time coming — he had last won at Brands Hatch in 1982 — but he had certainly achieved it in style. Bizarrely, the organisers were unable to find the correct trophy and instead awarded him the Rand Grand Prix trophy, but it failed to dampen his joy.

284 Belgian Grand Prix

Zolder, 29 April 1984, Formula 1
McLaren MP4/2-1 • #8
Qualifying: 14th • Result: Retired (engine)

Unexpectedly the McLarens — with revised rear wings — were nowhere in practice, the peculiarities of the Zolder circuit suiting Goodyear rather than Michelin this time, so the entire weekend was a Ferrari benefit. Lauda got off to a bad start in practice when a fuel leak caused a sizeable fire and considerable bodywork damage, stranding his car out on the circuit. Before he could resume with the spare (MP4/2-3), he was forced to wait for the new rear wing from Alain Prost's race car to be transferred to it after the Frenchman had used up his soft tyres, and then he found that the spare car had a sticking fuel pressure-relief valve. When he got his race car back, he encountered further separate delays with a faulty coil and a pinion failure. Things

ABOVE Niki's McLaren MP4/2 swoops through Kyalami's Wesbank Corner (formerly Leeukop) *en route* to winning the South African Grand Prix.

AS CLOSE AS IT GETS **311**

were not improved when the new engine that had been installed overnight blew up as soon as it was started. All in all, Lauda's qualifying was severely compromised and he ended up only 14th on the grid to Prost's eighth.

In an unusual move, the FISA had decided that the leading title contenders would perform a handful of demonstration laps before the grid formed, so Lauda's McLaren duly appeared with Keke Rosberg's Williams, Elio de Angelis's Lotus and Derek Warwick's Renault. Warwick and de Angelis then stopped at the beginning of the main straight for a private drag race and had just set off when Lauda came through the final corner, nearly collecting them both.

Although he had been third quickest in the warm-up, when the race started the Austrian was never in contention, his car hampered by a cracked intercooler and consequent loss of boost pressure. He got no higher than seventh and a pit stop for new tyres on lap 30 dropped him to 12th. He was finally sidelined by water pump failure on lap 35, by which time he had been lapped.

BELOW Lauda barely featured in the Belgian Grand Prix, running no higher than seventh and retiring when his McLaren's water pump broke.

285 San Marino Grand Prix

Imola, 6 May 1984, Formula 1
McLaren MP4/2-1 • #8
Qualifying: 5th • Result: Retired (engine)

Lauda lost half of Friday practice with a water leak and a broken fifth gear, while incurable understeer on Saturday left him waiting for Alain Prost to finish with the spare car (MP4/2-3). When he finally got in the spare, he found that it had too much understeer for his liking but nevertheless he used it to reasonable effect to qualify fifth, albeit two seconds slower than his team-mate.

Unable to select first gear at the start due to a dragging clutch and boxed in right behind Keke Rosberg's stalled Williams, he completed the opening lap in 10th place. Relishing the challenge, he scythed his way back into contention, revelling in a competitive car and throwing it around the circuit with gusto. He lapped 0.7 second faster than Prost, who had taken the lead from his front-

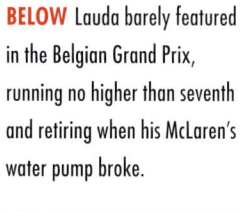

312 NIKI LAUDA

row grid position and was himself pulling away from Nelson Piquet's Brabham. On successive laps Niki dealt with the Ferraris of Michele Alboreto and René Arnoux over the crest into *Piratella*, and he passed Manfred Winkelhock's ATS with almost contemptuous ease. He was on the verge of depriving Derek Warwick's Renault of third place on lap 16 when a piston failed in the TAG engine on the approach to *Tosa*; a puff of smoke came from the back of the McLaren and he rolled to a halt at the side of the track.

286 Mercedes-Benz 'Race of Champions' (D)

Nürburgring, 13 May 1984
Mercedes-Benz 190E 2.3-16 • #20
Qualifying: 20th • Result: 2nd

A one-off demonstration race was organised in a joint venture with Mercedes-Benz as part of the official opening of the newly remodelled Nürburgring, with every living World Champion invited to join in with other Formula 1 drivers past and present. Jackie Stewart declined, honouring his pledge never to race again, and Juan-Manuel Fangio declared himself too old at 72; Nelson Piquet was the only active driver to refuse; and Mario Andretti and Emerson Fittipaldi were at Indianapolis 500 qualifying. A significant stand-in was Formula 3 sensation Ayrton Senna. Despite miserable conditions, 100,000 spectators turned out for the occasion.

Practice was competitive despite most of the contenders saying that they intended to take it easy in the race, but Lauda — who had missed qualifying due to TV commitments and had to start from the back of the grid — was not one of them. Problems in an untimed session just before the race meant that he had to switch cars at the last minute, so he had an unfamiliar machine to deal with.

Midway round the first lap Senna barged his way past Alain Prost to take the lead and make an early break, while Lauda charged up from the back. John Watson — keen to show McLaren that

ABOVE Into *Tosa* early in the San Marino Grand Prix, Niki's McLaren MP4/2 leads Riccardo Patrese's Alfa Romeo 184T, Elio de Angelis's Lotus 95T and Teo Fabi's Brabham BT53.

AS CLOSE AS IT GETS 313

the team should have retained him — tried to overtake Lauda in Turn 1 but was caught out by his car's anti-lock braking and half spun. In the closing stages of the 12-lap race, Lauda shook off Carlos Reutemann and Keke Rosberg to make a determined attempt to win, but Senna just held on for victory by 1.38 seconds.

287 French Grand Prix

Dijon-Prenois, 20 May 1984, Formula 1
McLaren MP4/2-3 • #8
Qualifying: 9th • Result: 1st

Fourth on Friday morning boded well, but Lauda's afternoon was blighted by engine failures in both his race car and the spare, leaving him ninth fastest to Alain Prost's fifth. A new engine was flown in from Weissach overnight but prolonged rain on Saturday meant that the day's qualifying session was a wash-out.

ABOVE At the inaugural Nürburgring event, problems with Niki's originally allocated Mercedes-Benz 190E 2.3-16 during practice forced him to switch from this car to an untried alternative for the race.

BELOW In the 'Race of Champions' feature to promote the opening of the new Nürburgring, Niki leads Carlos Reutemann, John Watson and Alain Prost in their identical Mercedes-Benz 190E 2.3-16s.

1984

LEFT Paying close attention to guidance from Porsche engineer Hans Mezger, Niki ponders his chances ahead of the French Grand Prix.

At the start, Lauda made up three positions in as many laps and was closing on sixth-placed Nelson Piquet when the Brazilian retired. After storming past Derek Warwick's Renault and the Lotuses of Nigel Mansell and Elio de Angelis in the space of six laps, he reached third place behind Prost by lap 21. For once he was faster than Prost and was slightly disappointed when the Frenchman was slowed by a loose wheel as he was sure that he would have overtaken him anyway. Either way, he moved up into second place and relentlessly pressured Patrick Tambay's Renault until the Frenchman eventually made a slight error at *Courbe de Gorgeolles* on lap 41, allowing Lauda to dive through into the lead.

He immediately tore away into the distance. Although he should have received a signal from the pit wall to indicate the halfway mark of the 79-lap race, it never came and he ended up making his tyre stop very late, on lap 56. It was hopelessly slow, converting his 30-second advantage over Tambay into an 11-second deficit. Angry that he was now forced to drive harder than necessary, he got back on terms with the Renault in only six laps. When Tambay's speed through *Courbe de Pouas* was compromised by Mauro Baldi's Spirit, it was all Niki needed. With a better exit, he breezed past the leader on the main straight and went on to take a win that was as commanding and determined as any of his previous 20.

BELOW On his way to a hard-won victory in the French Grand Prix, Niki's McLaren MP4/2 has just lapped Mauro Baldi's Spirit 101 as they crest the rise before the *Bretelle* left-hander.

AS CLOSE AS IT GETS **315**

288 Monaco Grand Prix

Monte Carlo, 3 June 1984, Formula 1
McLaren MP4/2-3 • #8
Qualifying: 8th • Result: Retired (spin)

McLaren claimed to have learned a lot from a three-day test at Michelin's Ladoux track immediately after the French Grand Prix and approached Monaco in confident mood. Lauda had an untroubled practice other than being baulked by Mauro Baldi's Spirit on his second set of qualifiers, meaning that he wound up a disappointed eighth on the grid although very happy with his car. In the wet warm-up session he was fastest by over a second.

Torrential rain made the conditions for the race the worst in memory and Alain Prost pointed out that the winner would be the driver who made the fewest mistakes. When the start eventually came, delayed by 45 minutes, Lauda drove smoothly and unobtrusively, catching Michele Alboreto napping in his Ferrari to pass him into Loews Hairpin on lap 4 and gunning past René Arnoux in a daring move up the hill out of *Ste Dévote* when the Ferrari's engine hesitated. He then ran more or less on his own for the rest of his race, inheriting second place behind team-mate Prost when Nigel Mansell (Lotus) crashed out at *Beau Rivage* on lap 16.

This was the race of Ayrton Senna's famous drive up the order in his Toleman and the Brazilian effortlessly passed Niki for second place at the end of the 18th lap. Six laps later Lauda lost the rear end at Casino Square and spun out, stalling the engine. He had been grappling with a locking rear brake for a few laps but took responsibility for the incident rather than blame the car. Seven laps later the race was halted in worsening rain with Prost declared the winner.

BELOW Monaco in appallingly wet conditions provided the opportunity for Ayrton Senna and Stefan Bellof to give virtuoso performances, but Lauda's afternoon was less satisfactory and ended with a spin at Casino Square. Here, Senna's Toleman TG184 is tucked in tight behind Niki's McLaren MP4/2 as they exit *Ste Dévote* and head up *Beau Rivage* in swirling rain.

289 Canadian Grand Prix

Montréal, 17 June 1984, Formula 1
McLaren MP4/2-1 • #8
Qualifying: 8th • Result: 2nd

Lauda used the spare car in practice and spent the first Saturday session running on race tyres. That proved to be a mistake when Alain Prost's engine deposited oil on the track and the Austrian had to settle for eighth position on the grid once again, having never looked like matching his team-mate.

Quickly into his stride after the start, he progressed rapidly through the field, passing Nigel Mansell (Lotus), Derek Warwick (Renault) and Elio de Angelis (Lotus) before the end of lap 5 to lie fifth with two Ferraris ahead of him. Within nine more laps the red cars were gone, Michele Alboreto's with fuel-pump failure and Rene Arnoux's because of an early pit stop for new tyres. Now Prost was next in line: although Niki was trying to conserve his tyres and brakes while his McLaren's fuel load was heavy, he closed inexorably on his second-placed team-

1984

mate and was right behind by lap 40, just after the halfway mark. The McLaren pair circulated in close company for several laps but it was clear that Lauda was the faster man and on lap 44 Prost waved him through.

That put Niki just four seconds behind the leader, Nelson Piquet's Brabham, with 26 laps to go. Straight away, however, the gap opened out to seven seconds, but not through any fault of Lauda's: Elio de Angelis, whom he had just lapped, nearly T-boned him under braking for a slow right-hander and he was forced to take to the grass. Gradually the Austrian clawed back the lost time, but he had increasing difficulty in selecting fourth gear and had to settle for second place, just 2.5 seconds behind the Brazilian.

290 Detroit Grand Prix

24 June 1984, Formula 1
McLaren MP4/2-1 • #8
Qualifying: 10th • Result: Retired (engine)

Lauda initially felt confident in his MP4/2's performance and was second quickest on Friday until his efforts were disallowed when his rear wing was found to be 1.5mm too wide, the result of heat distortion on a bond between the main aerofoil and the side plate. Concerned about the possibility of rain on Saturday morning, he was out on track as soon as the session began but he was baulked by traffic on both of his hot qualifying laps and ended up a disgruntled 10th on the grid. Despite public pronouncements that he wanted his team to stay together for 1985, Ron Dennis conspicuously disappeared from the sponsors' dinner on the eve of the race to meet Ayrton Senna, whom he described as 'the future', a fact that did little to improve Lauda's mood.

A start-line shunt halted the race at the first attempt. Eighth after the restart, Lauda duelled with Elio de Angelis (Lotus) for a dozen laps until the Italian broke away. Alain Prost, meanwhile, had slipped back from his second place at the start and now the McLaren men briefly ran sixth and seventh, both displeased

ABOVE No fan of the stop-start Île Notre-Dame track, Lauda steers his McLaren MP4/2 through one of the Montréal circuit's many chicanes.

BELOW Niki checks a slide in his McLaren MP4/2 as he picks his way through the asphalt and concrete of the temporary Detroit street circuit. This time his TAG engine let him down.

AS CLOSE AS IT GETS 317

with their Michelin tyres. When Prost stopped for a new set on lap 18, Niki gained a place, but he too halted for fresh rubber four laps later, dropping to 13th. He continued to toil away doggedly and was lying 10th when he returned to the pits on lap 33 with a rough-sounding engine. He resumed after a change of plugs but the engine was clearly on borrowed time and he retired a lap later before it blew up.

291 Dallas Grand Prix

Fair Park, 8 July 1984, Formula 1
McLaren MP4/2-1 • #8
Qualifying: 5th • Result: Retired (accident) (fastest lap)

Brushing aside concerns about Dallas's rough-and-ready temporary circuit with its inadequate run-off areas, Lauda was almost two seconds faster than the rest in untimed practice on Friday morning. This remained the quickest time set all weekend because the Texan heat intensified in the afternoon and the track surface began to break up. In that day's qualifying he hit the wall twice after sliding on the crumbling asphalt, damaging the suspension on both his race car and the spare, but still achieving the fourth quickest time, which became fifth place on the grid after one man, Derek Warwick (Renault), went far quicker than anyone else on the Saturday. For the first time this season, team-mate Alain Prost was further down the grid, in seventh spot.

A 50-lap Can-Am race planned for Saturday evening caused the already fragile tarmac to disintegrate completely and the following morning's Formula 1 warm-up was cancelled as frantic last-minute resurfacing work was carried out against the threat of a boycott, led by Lauda and Prost. The McLaren drivers pushed to have a 10-lap evaluation session before the race — a suggestion that Bernie Ecclestone initially seemed to support — but in the end TV schedules prevailed and the drivers went to the grid without knowing the vagaries of the track.

Despite the concerns, it turned out to be an enthralling race. After a clean start, Lauda passed Elio de Angelis (Lotus) on lap 7 for third place and briefly inherited second when Warwick misjudged his attempt to outbrake Nigel Mansell (Lotus) for the lead. For a while Niki slipped back, repassed by de Angelis and overtaken by an inspired Keke Rosberg (Williams). On lap 17 he let his team-mate through to pursue the leaders and settled into fifth place behind him. That became third as the two Lotus men slipped out of contention, Mansell because he had to surrender the lead to Rosberg with a stop for new tyres. By lap 49, McLaren's prospects looked very good when Prost took the lead from Rosberg, with Lauda still third, although that became fourth two laps later when René Arnoux (Ferrari) displaced him.

But then both McLaren men made driving errors and hit concrete retaining walls. Prost did it first, throwing away the lead on lap 57. Three laps later, and with only seven to go, Niki made his mistake, clipping the wall with his right rear wheel at the tight right-hander before the first hairpin.

BELOW Baking under the heat of the Texan sun, Niki and Alain Prost thread their McLaren MP4/2s around the makeshift Dallas Fair Park circuit with its patched-up track surface, industrial-looking concrete walls and generally messy infield.

1984

292 British Grand Prix

Brands Hatch, 22 July 1984, Formula 1
McLaren MP4/2-1 • #8
Qualifying: 3rd • Result: 1st (fastest lap)

Lauda had always found Brands Hatch very satisfying and his form reflected his liking for the track. Initially he was second fastest in qualifying to Alain Prost, but both McLaren drivers were later demoted by Nelson Piquet's Brabham. Niki reaffirmed his pace in the warm-up with second-fastest time.

While Piquet led off the line, he was soon in tyre trouble and first Prost and then Lauda passed him in quick succession, respectively at Clearways and Druids, to put the McLarens 1–2 at 12 laps. Moments later, the race was red-flagged after Jonathan Palmer's RAM crashed heavily, and while Piquet was in the pits for fresh tyres. There would now be a two-part race, with the overall result decided on aggregate. Because the grid order for the restart was determined by race positions at the end of the last full lap before the red flag was shown, Piquet — much to the dismay of Lauda and Prost — was able to start from pole again, now with the benefit of more favourable rubber.

When they got going again, Prost led from Piquet and Lauda, these three quickly pulling away from the rest in dominant style. After 19 laps Niki repeated his passing move on the Brazilian at Druids, by which time Prost was six seconds up the road. Gradually the gap between the McLarens stretched to 11 seconds, but suddenly, on lap 28, it came down to just 2.7. There was briefly the prospect of the straight battle between the McLarens that fans had been denied so far that year, but Prost's gearbox failed. So Lauda inherited the lead, with Piquet right on his tail.

By this time the other focus for the crowd's attention was a fierce dispute involving Andrea de Cesaris in his Ligier and the Ferraris of René

ABOVE At Brands Hatch, Niki looks thoughtful while Alain Prost appears merely amused as McLaren designer John Barnard makes his point to the men charged with driving his creation.

AS CLOSE AS IT GETS

ABOVE Niki rounds Druids during the British Grand Prix, having just lapped Riccardo Patrese's Alfa Romeo 184T.

BELOW Second-placed Derek Warwick applauds as Niki raises the winner's trophy after his victory in the British Grand Prix.

Arnoux and Michele Alboreto. Exhibiting the worst of his blocking tactics, sixth-placed de Cesaris held up the red cars for many laps and eventually the leaders bore down on this obstacle. Although Lauda made short work of the trio, using all his racecraft and judgement, Piquet had a slightly easier time getting through and closed up a little — but Lauda was always in control of the situation. Six laps from the end, the Brabham slowed with boost problems and Lauda was able to cruise home, taking victory by over 40 seconds on aggregate from Derek Warwick's Renault.

This was the best drive of his McLaren career so far. It also made him Formula 1's all-time top points scorer, the nine points he had earned taking him past Jackie Stewart's previous record of 360. He was also now very much in the title hunt, on 33 points to Prost's 35.5 (half points had been awarded in Monaco).

1984

293 German Grand Prix

Hockenheim, 5 August 1984, Formula 1
McLaren MP4/2-1 • #8
Qualifying: 7th • Result: 2nd

Lauda was fastest in the first unofficial session but slipped to fourth in the afternoon after taking off too much rear wing. On Saturday he made an uncharacteristic error, pushing too hard too soon and spinning on the pit straight. Thwarted by an old engine that was gradually losing power and showing signs of wear, he slipped to seventh position on the grid. A scary moment came on Sunday morning when, in pouring rain, his throttle stuck open and the ignition switch failed, so he arrived at the pits with the clutch out and the engine screaming.

Once the race was underway, he lay eighth at the end of the first lap but soon advanced, passing Michele Alboreto's Ferrari (lap 2), Patrick Tambay's Renault (lap 4) and Ayrton Senna's Toleman (lap 5). More gains came swiftly when Elio de Angelis's Lotus retired from the lead (lap 8) and Derek Warwick's Renault fell into the Austrian's clutches (lap 9), so now he lay third with Alain Prost second and Nelson Piquet's Brabham in the lead. Having steadily closed on his team-mate, the McLaren pair became first and second on lap 22 — just over half distance — when Piquet fell back with gearbox problems.

Niki pushed hard for the next seven laps but Prost responded to his challenge, holding the gap constant. Ever the realist, and with his rear tyres having suffered as a result of the pursuit, Lauda decided that six points would be an acceptable reward for his efforts and settled for second place.

294 Austrian Grand Prix

Österreichring, 19 August 1984, Formula 1
McLaren MP4/2-1 • #8
Qualifying: 4th • Result: 1st (fastest lap)

For his home race, Lauda was second fastest during first qualifying, despite a near miss with Derek Warwick's Renault when he was forced to put two wheels on the grass coming out of the *Boschkurve* on his fast lap. On Saturday he experienced bad oversteer on his first timed run and was late out for his second with a sticking throttle-return spring, all of this preventing him from bettering his Friday time, which put him fourth on the grid. Second fastest to Alain Prost in the warm-up left him feeling confident for the race.

After an aborted start, he got away badly but this was to be his only mistake of the afternoon. Sixth at the end of the first lap, he passed Elio de Angelis (Lotus) on lap 2 and Warwick on lap 3. Next came Patrick Tambay's Renault, which remained in his way for only six laps before he slipped through to take third. Now, just as at the previous race, those ahead of him were second-placed Prost and Nelson Piquet's Brabham in the lead. Again, he closed remorselessly, slicing past backmarkers and setting the race's fastest lap. After Prost, hampered by having to hold his car in gear, spun on oil on lap 29, Lauda aggressively chased down Piquet, who was struggling with worn rear tyres. On lap 39 Piquet got into a slide while lapping Michele Alboreto's Ferrari at the *Hella-Licht* chicane and Lauda snatched the lead. The Austrian fans erupted: this was the first time in seven years that their hero had led at the Österreichring.

ABOVE Lauda weaves his McLaren MP4/2 past the tyre wall of Hockenheim's second *Bremmschikane* on his way to second place in the German Grand Prix.

AS CLOSE AS IT GETS 321

Three laps later the spectators at the *Boschkurve* saw him raise his hand as he exited the corner. He had heard a bang behind him and, thinking the engine had blown, he slowed briefly before trying to change down to fourth gear — but in fact the problem was that fourth gear had broken. Despite this being a rather important gear at this circuit, he quickly adapted to the car's disability, giving no indication that anything was wrong and appearing instead just to have eased off to cruise home ahead of the struggling Brabham. Maintaining the gap sufficiently to fool Piquet into settling for second place, he nursed the McLaren through nine more laps to take a very fine victory. As he crossed the line, the gearbox internals collapsed and when he pulled into the pitlane after his slowing-down lap the clattering noise alerted the Brabham crew to their missed opportunity.

Not only had he won his home Grand Prix for the first time but his nine points also moved him to the top of the points standings. Ever since Prost's win at the opening round, the Frenchman had headed the table, but now Lauda did so on 48 points to his team-mate's 44.5.

BELOW A home win at last: Niki takes the chequered flag for his first and only Grand Prix victory at the Österreichring, having fooled second-placed Nelson Piquet into thinking he was simply cruising to the finish and had speed in reserve. Writing in *Motoring News*, Niki's friend Alan Henry started his report of the race with the headline 'Local Boy Shows Promise'.

295 Dutch Grand Prix

Zandvoort, 26 August 1984, Formula 1
McLaren MP4/2-1 • #8
Qualifying: 8th • Result: 2nd

Delayed by a faulty rev limiter in Friday practice and blocked on both of his fast laps in the final session, Lauda's disappointing grid position, eighth, may have cost him victory. Knowing from Hockenheim that he would need a different strategy to beat Alain Prost, who claimed pole position, he chose to gamble by running softer Michelins on the right side of his car for the race.

He arrived late on the starting grid after a turbo had to be replaced and a water leak fixed. He struggled off the line as his revs dropped, getting away ninth, but progressed quickly and impressively, making the most of his tyre advantage on the greasy track to reach fourth place by lap 9 after some assertive outbraking moves. On lap 10 Nelson Piquet's Brabham retired from the lead, Prost taking over, and a lap later at *Tarzan* Lauda forced his way past

Keke Rosberg's Williams. Now the McLarens were 1–2 again, Niki about 10 seconds behind his team-mate.

Gradually Lauda whittled away at Prost's lead. The closest he got was 2.1 seconds on lap 27, but by then his soft Michelins were going off and his team-mate's harder rubber was coming into its own. Thereafter Prost was able to widen the gap little by little, stretching it to five seconds by lap 40. Soon after, Niki lost more time picking his way through a gaggle of backmarkers and decided to settle for a secure runner-up position, 10 seconds behind Prost at the end.

This ninth victory of the season for McLaren — five for Prost, four for Lauda — secured the constructors' championship for the team with three rounds left. As for the drivers' title, that could hardly be closer, with Lauda now just half a point ahead of Prost and everyone else out of contention.

296 Italian Grand Prix

Monza, 9 September 1984, Formula 1
McLaren MP4/2-1 • #8
Qualifying: 4th • Result: 1st (fastest lap)

Friday's qualifying session was damp, so the grid was decided in Saturday's better conditions. That morning while negotiating one of the chicanes Lauda dislocated a lower thoracic vertebra that left him in excruciating pain. Nevertheless, during afternoon qualifying he achieved fourth on the grid — nearly two seconds adrift of team-mate Alain Prost in second spot — after his very last lap brought an improvement of over a second, but the agony had been so intense that he confessed that he had screamed through the long *Parabolica* right-hander.

It seemed doubtful that he could take any further part but Willi Dungl set to work on him.

ABOVE Strung out through Zandvoort's *Panorama* curves, the field completes its formation lap as Lauda heads for his fifth-place grid slot. Behind him are the Williams FW09Bs of Keke Rosberg and Jacques Laffite, Michele Alboreto's Ferrari 126C4, Teo Fabi's Brabham BT53, Thierry Boutsen's Arrows A7, Nigel Mansell's Lotus 95T, Ayrton Senna's Toleman TG184 and the rest.

AS CLOSE AS IT GETS 323

ABOVE The *Tifosi* pack the grandstands at Monza's *Rettifilio* chicane as Niki's McLaren MP4/2 heads for victory and fastest lap in the Italian Grand Prix.

Suitably massaged and corseted, and with a new seat, Niki declared himself fit to race. During Sunday's warm-up both MP4/2s suffered water leaks and fluctuating boost pressure, so Lauda persuaded the team to put a new engine in his own car and convinced Prost to race the spare.

Lauda made a terrible start, initially dropping to seventh place, but he moved up to sixth by the end of lap 1 and passed Elio de Angelis for fifth on lap 2. He gained another place — and a significant World Championship advantage — when Prost's engine failed on lap 4, while a spin by Brabham number two Teo Fabi on lap 8 elevated him to third. He was briefly second after the leader, Nelson Piquet's Brabham, retired on lap 16, but a lap later the recovering Fabi repassed him. Lauda shadowed the Italian for a long time until they got among the backmarkers, when the Austrian's racecraft and guile came into play and he forced his way through under braking for *Parabolica* on lap 40. Now he started to haul in Patrick Tambay's leading Renault, just a few seconds ahead, and within three laps his opportunity came when the French car hesitated due to a sticking throttle, allowing him to snatch the lead at the *Lesmos* with eight laps to go. Reducing his pace by some three seconds a lap, Lauda stroked home over 20 seconds clear of Michele Alboreto's Ferrari, the only other car on the same lap.

It was another superb but hard-earned victory. He had been in great pain from the fifth lap but had relied on his resilience, stamina and experience to see him through. The legendary five-times World Champion Juan-Manuel Fangio was present to watch the Austrian equal his tally of 24 wins, but this was less important to Lauda than the fact that, with Prost failing to score, he was now equal with the Frenchman on wins — five each — and led the World Championship by 10.5 points with just two rounds to go.

1984

297 European Grand Prix

Nürburgring, 7 October 1984, Formula 1
McLaren MP4/2-1 • #8
Qualifying: 15th • Result: 4th

Lauda was unfortunate in qualifying at the 'new' Nürburgring, ending up only 15th on the grid while Alain Prost lined up second. On Friday morning his race car's gearbox had an oil leak so he was forced to use the spare (MP4/2-3), but a misfire caused by a wiring-loom problem prevented him from doing more than four laps in it. Back in his own car for the afternoon, mixed weather with the threat of rain persuaded him to use his qualifying tyres too early and in fact he set his best lap at the very end of the session. Any hope of improving on Saturday was lost to wet weather but, putting in many laps, he was fastest in the untimed morning session and second fastest in the afternoon. He went into race day prepared for all eventualities, with his race car on a dry set-up and the spare with wet settings.

Avoiding a spate of first-lap incidents that eliminated five cars, Lauda was ninth by the end of lap 1. On each of the next two laps he despatched an Alfa Romeo, first Eddie Cheever's, then Riccardo Patrese's, to sit behind two more Italian cars, red ones this time. On lap 5 he passed René Arnoux's Ferrari, but the other one, Michele Alboreto's, was running so close behind Derek Warwick's Renault that he was obliged either to try to pass both cars in one go or stay behind them. The stalemate lasted until the end of lap 22, when the trio caught up with Mauro Baldi's Spirit at the final hairpin. Although the Ferrari and the Renault nipped through under braking, Lauda realised at the last minute that he was not going to make it and stood on the brakes. His McLaren spun in a cloud of tyre smoke — flat-spotting the rubber — and went off onto the grass on the outside of the corner, but he kept the engine running and resumed the chase without losing his sixth place, although Elio de Angelis (Lotus) was now close behind. In the remaining two-thirds of the race, he gained two places when the Renaults ahead of him retired, Patrick Tambay's on lap 44 and Warwick's on lap 55. Had the race been a lap longer he would have finished second, as both Nelson Piquet (Brabham) and

LEFT Ron Dennis (far left) keeps an eye on things as the McLaren crew prepare Lauda's MP4/2 in the pitlane ahead of the European Grand Prix at the brand-new Nürburgring circuit.

AS CLOSE AS IT GETS 325

ABOVE The grubby nose of the McLaren MP4/2 shows just how hard Niki has been obliged to fight his way through the field to second place as he acknowledges the chequered flag at Estoril — and secures his third World Championship title.

Alboreto ran out of fuel on the final run to the flag. Meanwhile, Prost led from start to finish to take the nine points. Going into the final round, the McLaren rivals were three and a half points apart, Lauda (66) from Prost (62.5).

298 Portuguese Grand Prix

Estoril, 21 October 1984, Formula 1
McLaren MP4/2-1 • #8
Qualifying: 11th • Result: 2nd (fastest lap)

Lauda had set the fourth-quickest time in the acclimatisation session that preceded official practice on Thursday at this new circuit on the Formula 1 calendar, but when qualifying started in earnest he was plagued by a series of minor niggles and was never able to get into a rhythm. His first qualifying run was interrupted by a trip up the escape road at one of the uphill right-handers, flat-spotting his tyres in the process. He had just embarked on his last set of qualifying tyres when his engine began to lose power, the result of faulty master switch.

Instead of starting from near the front of the grid, he faced an uphill struggle from only 11th spot in his battle with Alain Prost for the World Championship title. Suitably motivated, he was fastest in the warm-up, almost half a second quicker than his team-mate, but then things again started to go wrong and he was delayed by a jammed wheel nut and the need for the engine to be replaced after showing signs of losing water.

He made an extremely cautious start and ran 13th at the end of the first lap with what looked like an impossible challenge ahead of him. He gained a position when Derek Warwick spun his Renault on lap 13 and then easily passed Elio de Angelis's tyre-troubled Lotus, but a damaged turbo on the left-hand cylinder bank meant that his engine was under-performing, keeping him behind Stefan Johansson's Toleman for a long spell. Eventually he decided that he had wasted

1984

enough time and that his cautious approach would yield no results, so he wound up the boost pressure and went on the attack.

On lap 27 Johansson missed a gear into the left-hander at the back of the circuit and Lauda dived through the gap, removing the Toleman's front wing in the process but luckily emerging with his own car undamaged. Less than a lap later he outbraked Michele Alboreto's Ferrari at the end of the main straight and surged past Keke Rosberg's Williams on lap 31 at the same place. His momentum carried him up to Ayrton Senna's Toleman and, after two further laps, he overtook the Brazilian in a similar manoeuvre.

In less than 10 minutes he had progressed from ninth place to third. However, second-placed Nigel Mansell (Lotus) was 35 seconds ahead of him. Although he closed the gap at more than a second a lap, a group of squabbling backmarkers delayed him and he lost most of the time he had made up. Then Mansell, still half a minute ahead, suffered brake failure on lap 51 and spun, allowing Lauda to close to within a few seconds while setting the race's fastest lap with a better time than he had managed in qualifying. Next time around the McLaren went past the Lotus, which promptly spun again, but that was of no consequence to Niki as he now held the vital second place that he needed to win the World Championship.

Although he was 50 seconds behind Prost, he could finally ease off and he had a trouble-free run for the last 18 laps as he followed his teammate to the flag. He was World Champion for the third time after a race that he later described as the most difficult of his career.

299 Nissan Pulsar International Super Challenge (AUS)

Calder Park, 18 November 1984, Group 1
Nissan Pulsar Turbo • #5
Qualifying: 3rd • Result: 2nd

After the end of the Formula 1 season, Lauda went to Australia — his reason, he stated, was mainly for a holiday — and while there he

ABOVE Alain Prost's smile hides his disappointment as he embraces Niki on the Estoril podium. Having won the race, he has lost the World Championship by just half a point.

BELOW Niki rounds Calder Park's Gloweave Corner during the Nissan Pulsar Challenge race held in support of the Australian Grand Prix. He kept his car largely unscathed — quite an achievement considering the amount of contact that went on elsewhere in the field.

took up an invitation, as did Keke Rosberg, to take part in the Australian Grand Prix. Before the main event there was a six-lap promotional jamboree, with all the drivers aboard ostensibly identical Nissan Pulsar saloon cars.

Rosberg led away from the rolling start while Lauda settled into fifth place, but he soon passed two local drivers to take third position and then chased down New Zealander Jim Richards. By the halfway mark, Richards and Lauda had reeled in Rosberg and the impressive Kiwi mounted an increasingly physical challenge on the leader, with Lauda right on his tail. On the final lap, Richards tried an overly ambitious move in the esses that gave Lauda the chance to force his way through to take second place, four car lengths behind Rosberg.

300 Australian Grand Prix

Calder Park, 18 November 1984, Formula Pacific
Ralt RT4/85 • #5
Qualifying: 20th • Result: Retired (collision) (fastest lap)

Race promoter and circuit owner Bob Jane had big plans for the final Australian Grand Prix at his Calder Park Raceway before the event became a Formula 1 World Championship round in Adelaide the following year. With backing from Dunlop, Jane invited some big-name drivers from Europe to the tiny Melbourne track and a crowd of 20,000 turned up to watch the Formula Pacific cars — mostly Ralt RT4s — in action. It had been 12 years since Lauda had driven a 'junior' single-seater.

He found that his Goold Motorsport-run Ralt had a troublesome engine (with fuel-pressure and electrical problems) and snapped between understeer and oversteer, so he decided to give third practice a miss and instead visited the nearby Essendon Air Show with fellow Formula 1 star Keke Rosberg. In his absence, Roberto Moreno, winner of the previous year's race and the man on pole position, tried to sort out his car and reported that it was satisfactory. Lauda's best time put him near the back of the grid, 20th out of 24 starters, and he wryly remarked that at least he would not have to worry about all the local heroes trying to beat him into the first corner.

Come the start, his racing instincts took over and he lay 12th first time round, then eighth by the end of the third lap. He had a spirited dice with François Hesnault's Ralt for sixth place before continuing his progress, reaching fourth by lap 22 and third by lap 31. However, Niki got

BELOW Driving a Ralt RT4/85 in the Australian Grand Prix at Calder Park, Lauda holds off Keke Rosberg's similar car through the infield while Bob Creasy's older Ralt RT4 follows at a distance.

no higher because Rosberg was closing in behind him and 10 laps later the Finn got past.

After one more lap, Rosberg tangled with local rising star Terry Ryan when lapping him, pitching Ryan into the dirt at the esses. The Australian steered back onto the track right in front of Lauda, who could not avoid him on a section of track that was breaking up, the resulting collision mangling the nose and foot box of the Austrian's car. While Rosberg and Ryan were able to continue, Lauda limped back to the pits to retire, with only the consolation prize of having set fastest lap.

SUMMARY

The 1984 season had shown Lauda still to be the shrewdest racer on the grid. Despite rarely qualifying well — he bettered Alain Prost only once in 16 rounds — his sharpness and aggression still shone through, especially in his charges through the field at Dijon and Imola, and he won five races to Prost's seven. Spurred on by his French team-mate's performances, his smooth, fluent driving style remained to the fore and his determination was irrefutable. Any doubts as to how much he wanted to win the World Championship title were dispelled at Monza, where he treated his back injury as a technicality that just had to be dealt with when many others would have chosen not to race in such circumstances.

A third World Championship after coming back from retirement was a vindication of Lauda's enduring commitment and doggedness. Despite his success, however, Lauda's relationship with Ron Dennis remained difficult and he looked at other options before the season was over.

Since his return from retirement, Fiat boss Gianni Agnelli had met him every year at Monza and each time floated the idea of him coming back to Ferrari. A serious look at this prospect in 1984 ended when sporting dirctor Marco Piccinini blocked it on the grounds that Lauda was just too expensive.

Then there was Renault. He had considered a move to the French team in 1979, when he had held talks with managing director Bernard Hanon and François Guiter of Elf, and the possibility arose again for 1985. Competitions director Gérard Larrousse's deal with Lauda, however, was vetoed by trade unions — Renault was state-owned — because of the cost.

This Renault dalliance weakened Lauda's negotiating position at McLaren and, following awkward discussions with Dennis, he was obliged to stay where he was for half of his previous retainer. A one-year deal was announced on 4 October but Lauda's relationship with his boss was now even more strained.

In contrast, his relationship with Prost was harmonious and the Frenchman was happy about Lauda staying on for 1985. Prost could live with the fact that the Austrian had taken the title despite winning fewer races, having played the percentage game, and he valued the trust they shared. Recognising early on that Prost had almost exactly the same preferences in car set-up as his own, Niki took the pragmatic view that there was more to be gained than lost if his team-mate became involved in the development programme, so he waived the clause in his contract that had given him absolute priority in testing.

After Lauda retired, Prost's comment was telling: 'I didn't know Niki when I came to McLaren, but I believed him to be completely honest; by the end of the 1984 season I was certain of it.' Curiously, they rarely had to battle on the track, the nearest thing they came to a straight fight occurring in Canada, where Niki overhauled his team-mate as they pursued Nelson Piquet's winning Brabham.

On 11 November, Lauda was guest of honour at the British Racing Drivers' Club's annual dinner and dance, where he received a standing ovation and was awarded the BRDC's top award, the Gold Star, in recognition of becoming World Champion for the third time. He was visibly moved that the presentation was made by Graham Hill's widow, Bette. In contrast, when he got wind of the fact that he was to be the subject of the popular TV programme *This Is Your Life*, his negative response meant the episode had to be scrapped.

1985
THE LAST LAP

As was becoming usual under John Barnard's technical regime at McLaren, the new MP4/2B was completed at the last minute. In fact, other than a few shakedown laps at a cold, wet Brands Hatch a matter of days before the cars were shipped to South America, the first time that the World Champion and Alain Prost completed any proper time in the cockpit was in practice for the Brazilian Grand Prix.

When he finally got to drive the car, Lauda reported a slight handling imbalance; Michelin's withdrawal had obliged the team to switch back to Goodyear and straight away Lauda found that the Akron company's rear race tyres were much less durable than the equivalent French rubber, and also gave rather less grip than the fronts. However, Lauda's scepticism soon gave way to enthusiasm when he found that in race trim the car was an improvement over its predecessor, and tyre concerns would be solved with development.

Lauda's 1985 season was one in which everything that could go wrong did so. Technical setbacks seemed unfailingly to afflict only his car, while Prost enjoyed a generally solid run of reliability that underpinned the ascendancy he achieved within the team. Undoubtedly Niki's motivation started to wane as the season progressed and his attention turned to thoughts of life after Formula 1, although his commitment remained undiminished.

1985

301 Brazilian Grand Prix

Jacarepaguá, 7 April 1985, Formula 1
McLaren MP4/2B-1 • #1
Qualifying: 9th • Result: Retired (electrics)

Although Lauda found the new MP4/2B a distinct improvement over the 1984 chassis, the TAG engine would not run properly on qualifying boost and the car oversteered persistently. He qualified ninth, three places down on Alain Prost, but third fastest in the warm-up in race trim was encouraging.

He made a brisk start, reaching seventh place when Nelson Piquet's Brabham retired on lap 3, then catching and passing René Arnoux's Ferrari within five more laps. He gained a further position when Keke Rosberg's Williams slipped back and he easily dealt with Elio de Angelis's Lotus on lap 13 thanks to superior speed on the straights. Four laps later he took third place when he dived past Ayrton Senna's Lotus with an ultra-late braking move into the fast left-hander at the end of the main straight. Prost, meanwhile, had just deprived Michele Alboreto's Ferrari of the lead and now Lauda closed right up with the red car, looking to pounce, but on lap 23 his TAG engine faltered and he was forced into the pits. The on-board ECU was changed, which took 12 minutes, and he returned to the track with a view to race-testing the car, but managed only three more desultory laps as the problem remained. Meanwhile, Prost went on to win.

302 Portuguese Grand Prix

Estoril, 21 April 1985, Formula 1
McLaren MP4/2B-1 • #1
Qualifying: 7th • Result: Retired (engine)

Third quickest on Friday, Lauda stopped out on the circuit on Saturday morning with engine management problems and in the afternoon gearbox troubles forced him into the spare car (MP4/2B-3), which was not handling well.

Torrential rain prevailed on race day. Although Lauda overtook Derek Warwick's Renault for fifth place on lap 3, it was soon evident that he was not enjoying himself in the very wet conditions, even if he was driving as smoothly as ever. Soon both Renaults were in front of him, Patrick Tambay

ABOVE Carrying the World Champion's number 1 as he passes new apartment blocks adjoining the Rio circuit, Niki knows that team-mate Alain Prost will be doubly determined to challenge him during the season ahead.

THE LAST LAP **331**

ABOVE The rain in Portugal was torrential: Niki's McLaren MP4/2B splashes around the sodden Estoril course ahead of Derek Warwick's Renault RE60 early in the race, but for once neither he nor team-mate Alain Prost would reach the finish.

getting ahead on lap 16 and Warwick repassing a couple of laps later, only for the latter to pit after three more laps. Lauda was restored to fifth place 10 laps later when Alain Prost spun off but then his engine began to lose power and he was passed in quick succession by Tambay, Nigel Mansell (Williams) and Stefan Bellof (Tyrrell). On lap 49 he crept into the pits with piston failure. It was the first time that neither McLaren had finished — or won — a race since Dallas the previous July. The conditions were so bad that after his retirement he suggested to the stewards that the race should be stopped.

303 San Marino Grand Prix

Imola, 5 May 1985, Formula 1
McLaren MP4/2B-1 • #1
Qualifying: 8th • Result: 4th

Again the No. 1 McLaren had most of the problems in practice. Only seventh quickest on Friday, Lauda was halted by a deflating tyre early in Saturday morning's untimed session when a rear brake caliper scored through the adjoining wheel rim, so he took to the spare car (MP4/2B-3) and promptly set the fastest time. When it came to the afternoon's qualifying, however, a further engine change left him idle until the final 20 minutes, by which time the track was damp and greasy, but he nevertheless improved by a full second to qualify eighth, two positions back from Alain Prost.

Having been passed briefly by Nelson Piquet's Brabham when the lights changed, he soon reasserted himself and was in front of the Williams pair of Nigel Mansell and Keke Rosberg by lap 6, and Elio de Angelis (Lotus) on lap 17. He quickly pulled away and closed steadily on Prost, but his progress was interrupted by an uncharacteristic spin at *Variante Bassa* when the engine began to cut out. Although he quickly recovered, the problem was once again an electrical gremlin, which grew steadily worse. Hampered further by the loss of fifth gear and then having to hold the lever in place for fourth, he fell behind de Angelis again and finally finished a lapped fifth. This was upgraded to fourth place when Prost's winning car was declared underweight and disqualified.

304 Monaco Grand Prix

Monte Carlo, 19 May 1985, Formula 1
McLaren MP4/2B-1 • #1
Qualifying: 14th • Result: Retired (spin)

Angered at being baulked by Ayrton Senna in the swimming pool section while the Brazilian was trundling around for many laps in what could have been little other than a disturbance tactic, Lauda missed a gear during his best lap of Thursday practice and found his engine reluctant to accept qualifying boost. All of this conspired to keep him out of touch with the front runners, qualifying only 14th of 20 starters. Although he was far from the fastest, he was nevertheless outstanding to watch on the twisty section from Casino Square down to the sea front.

In the race he was bottled up in 11th place behind Riccardo Patrese's Alfa Romeo for several laps, finally freeing himself on lap 8 to advance to eighth on successive laps. His progress came to an abrupt halt on lap 17 when oil dropped following a collision between Patrese and

ABOVE That unforgiving concrete wall is perilously close to the track as Lauda powers along Imola's back straight on his way to an eventual fourth place in the San Marino Grand Prix.

BELOW Niki's McLaren MP4/2B leads Nelson Piquet's Brabham BT54 along the harbourside early in the Monaco Grand Prix. Neither car finished the race.

THE LAST LAP 333

Nelson Piquet's Brabham caused him to spin at *Ste Dévote*, where no oil flags were showing. Although he avoided hitting the barrier, the engine stalled and with no on-board starter he had to abandon a perfectly healthy car. Prost won the race.

305 Canadian Grand Prix

Montréal, 16 June 1985, Formula 1
McLaren MP4/2B-1 • #1
Qualifying: 17th • Result: Retired (engine)

BELOW Lauda leads Martin Brundle's Tyrrell 012 at the Île Notre-Dame circuit in Montréal. Engine failure meant that he failed to finish.

Never a fan of the stop-start Montréal circuit, Lauda had a dismal time in qualifying, unhappy with his car's braking and struggling to get heat into his tyres. He admitted that he found it difficult to screw himself up for a single quick lap and, when he did so, he was astounded to find his best effort spoiled by a beaver — yes! — on the track at the hairpin. By his own admission he made a mistake in thinking that qualifiers would be quicker and used two sets. As a consequence, his times were pretty tame and the team was rather unhappy with him, although he sprang back to set fastest time in the warm-up.

Starting gently, he made steady progress during the early stages of the race, even if he was less assertive than usual. After outbraking Derek Warwick's Renault at the hairpin before the pits (lap 11) and then passing Riccardo Patrese's Alfa Romeo (lap 17) and Thierry Boutsen's Arrows (lap 20), he ran eighth. He was challenging for sixth place when his engine began to overheat, losing water because a broken intercooler mounting had holed the cooling system. He had noticed the engine temperature start to rise as early as lap 5 and pulled into the pits for good at the end of lap 38.

306 Detroit Grand Prix

23 June 1985, Formula 1
McLaren MP4/2B-1 • #1
Qualifying: 12th • Result: Retired (brakes)

Lauda was disappointed not to improve on another lowly grid slot, 12th, this time

334 NIKI LAUDA

1985

because his car repeatedly jumped out of fifth gear during Friday qualifying. Saturday was a total loss, with such miserable wet and windy conditions that only seven drivers ventured out.

His race was nondescript. He ran 10th for the first eight laps, hounded by Martin Brundle's Tyrrell, and gained a place when Michele Alboreto's Ferrari retired ahead of him on lap 7. Three laps later he was out, just making it back to the pits to retire with his brakes completely gone. The street course was extremely hard on brakes and the McLaren's carbon discs were simply not up to the job.

307 French Grand Prix

Paul Ricard, 8 July 1985, Formula 1
McLaren MP4/2B-1 • #1
Qualifying: 6th • Result: Retired (gearbox)

With a new rear-axle arrangement that eliminated the McLaren's tendency to oversteer, Lauda was delighted with the way his car was handling, although again he was unable

ABOVE Those few spectators present in Detroit seem more concerned with the food concessions as Niki's McLaren MP4/2B rounds one of the street circuit's many 90-degree right-handers.

BELOW The grid forms for the French Grand Prix: Niki's McLaren MP4/2B sits behind Nelson Piquet's Brabham BT54 while Patrick Tambay's Renault RE60B draws alongside him. Behind are the Arrows A8s of Gerhard Berger and Thierry Boutsen, and further back are the second Brabham of Marc Surer and the older Renault RE60 of Derek Warwick.

THE LAST LAP 335

ABOVE Electrical failure at sunny Silverstone signalled yet another retirement.

to give the engine full qualifying boost. Despite being baulked on his quick lap, he qualified on the outside of the third row and was second quickest in the warm-up.

He got away cleanly at the start, moving up to fifth place when Michele Alboreto (Ferrari) dropped out on lap 5 and passing Elio de Angelis (Lotus) on lap 10. After inheriting third when Ayrton Senna's Lotus retired, he was nearly eliminated when Pierluigi Martini (Minardi) chopped him at *Verrerie* on lap 16 while being lapped, causing him to veer onto the inside kerb to avoid collision. With teammate Alain Prost right behind, he became locked in a thrilling battle for second place with Keke Rosberg's Williams, but, despite turning up the turbo boost to 3.6 bar every lap at the beginning of the long *Mistral* straight, he still could not get past the powerful Honda-engined car. He was tucked in tight behind the Williams when, on lap 31, his transmission failed as he powered out of the right-hander before the pits and he coasted to a halt opposite the timing line.

308 British Grand Prix

Silverstone, 21 July 1985, Formula 1
McLaren MP4/2B-1 • #1
Qualifying: 10th • Result: Retired (electrics)

After the French Grand Prix, it was a surprise that McLaren was the only team not to participate in test sessions at either the Nürburgring or the Österreichring. Lauda was heard to comment sarcastically, 'Probably because we are so good', reflecting his dissatisfaction with his own results. Having been seventh fastest in Friday's first session, he qualified 10th at Silverstone after being unable to run the larger and more favourable of the two KKK turbo options at this super-quick circuit, which saw Keke Rosberg (Williams) set a new record for the fastest ever qualifying lap in Formula 1, at 160.9mph (259.0kph). Lauda had no hope of improving in the final session as his engine was 1,000rpm down and on his hottest lap he was baulked by Riccardo Patrese's Alfa Romeo. Earlier concerns about the handling of his car in race trim were banished when the McLarens once again set the pace in the warm-up.

Lauda made a dreadful start and completed the first lap in 19th place, but he made rapid and largely unobtrusive progress through the field. With no assistance from retirements ahead, he was ninth by lap 5, fifth by lap 17 and third by lap 22, but then his run of bad luck struck again. Initially his gearbox refused to change cleanly between fourth and fifth, and then, to make matters worse, electronic gremlins set in and he was unable to keep up with the duelling leaders, team-mate Alain Prost and Ayrton Senna (Lotus). He slipped back such a long way, although without losing his third place, that by lap 57 the leaders arrived on his tail to lap him, and at precisely the wrong moment his engine coughed and forced Prost to lift. The cause was an electrical problem and he retired next time around, while Prost sailed onwards to take his third win of the year.

309 German Grand Prix

Nürburgring, 4 August 1985, Formula 1
McLaren MP4/2B-1 • #1
Qualifying: 12th • R2 5th

Despite setting second quickest time in the first session, Lauda qualified only 12th and was dismissive of his efforts. When it mattered, he messed up one set of sticky tyres and on his other set he was held up by Stefan Bellof's Tyrrell. However, he was happy with his car and hopeful for the race.

Initially running in a five-car 'train', he eased past the Ligier of Jacques Laffite for 11th place on lap 4 and advanced further with the retirements of Riccardo Patrese's Alfa Romeo (lap 8), Nelson Piquet's Brabham (lap 23), Ayrton Senna's Lotus (lap 27) and Teo Fabi's Toleman (lap 29), along the way also passing Thierry Boutsen's Arrows. Just as he reached sixth place, on lap 29, a chafing heat deflector from a rear brake caused the

BELOW Niki takes a keen interest from the cockpit as the front suspension set-up of his McLaren MP4/2B is adjusted during qualifying for the German Grand Prix.

affected wheel to work loose, which threw him onto the grass at the second chicane and forced him to pit for repairs two laps later. Angrily, he tore back into the fray in 12th place on fresh tyres, by far the fastest man on the track as he passed both Bellof and Gerhard Berger (Arrows) before unlapping himself on lap 61. Aided by retirements, he got back into the points, deposing Nigel Mansell's sick Williams for fifth place on the final lap.

This was his first finish in six races and only his second of the season.

310 'Challenge Lauda in the Uno Turbo' (I)

Misano, 11 August 1985
Fiat Uno Turbo • #8
Result: 2nd (x3)

Rather untypically, Lauda agreed to support a competition organised by the newspaper *Il Resto del Carlino* and the magazine *Rombo* in collaboration with Fiat. The idea was to give 100 participants drawn from the readers of those publications the chance to show their talents in a slalom event on a 200-metre course marked out on Misano's main straight. The field was reduced to two finalists by a series of eliminators and by the end of the day the fastest pair were Guido Bricarello (a car salesman from Biella) and Marino Silingardi (a *barista* from Modena).

The precise format came as something of a surprise to Lauda, who arrived by helicopter during the afternoon to be greeted by a vast crowd who had waited all day in the baking sun. By this time the two finalists had plenty of experience of the slalom, whereas Niki had none, so perhaps it was not surprising that both beat him, each by over half a second. A final challenge was laid on between Lauda and René Arnoux, who was now a redundant Formula 1 driver after his departure from Ferrari, and again things went badly for the Austrian as he lost by 0.07 second.

311 Austrian Grand Prix

Österreichring, 18 August 1985, Formula 1
McLaren MP4/2B-1 • #1
Qualifying: 3rd • Result: Retired (turbo)

The day before his home race Lauda announced his retirement from Formula 1 at a press conference that he personally had organised. When McLaren boss Ron Dennis took the microphone and used the occasion to eulogise the work of designer John Barnard without any mention of everything that the Austrian had done for the team, Niki was understandably incensed. Suitably fired up, he underlined his determination to go out on a high by setting fastest time on Saturday morning and taking third place on the grid.

He made a storming start, beating both Alain Prost and Nigel Mansell (Williams) to lead off the line, but a multi-car shunt behind caused the race to be red-flagged as he reached the *Rindt-Kurve* some four seconds ahead of his team-mate. At the restart his getaway was not so rapid and he was squeezed into third place behind Prost, the leader, and Keke Rosberg (Williams), although the Finn dropped out on lap 4 to leave the McLarens running 1–2. By half distance he had closed up on Prost, who had switched his choice of tyres to match Lauda's for the second start, and together they pulled out an 11-second

BELOW Slaloms were a new experience for Lauda, despite their popularity in his native Austria. Awaiting the start of one of his runs, he was perhaps regretting that he had agreed to take part in this promotional contest at Misano, as the rivals who beat him in the final had enjoyed a whole day of eliminator runs in which to perfect the required technique.

1985

LEFT Despite deep mutual respect, Lauda's relationship with McLaren boss Ron Dennis was never close and became more strained over time. This is the much-reported press conference in Austria at which Niki announced his retirement and Dennis failed to pay tribute to him.

BELOW Snaking through the *Hella-Licht* chicane at the start of the Austrian Grand Prix, the McLaren twins of Niki and Alain Prost in their MP4/2Bs have already pulled out a gap over Keke Rosberg's Williams FW10, Nelson Piquet's Brabham BT54, Patrick Tambay's Renault RE60B, Riccardo Patrese's Alfa Romeo 184TB and Michele Alboreto's Ferrari 156/85, with Nigel Mansell's Williams FW10 just coming into shot.

THE LAST LAP 339

ABOVE Holding his line through the *Hugenholzbocht* hairpin behind Zandvoort's pit complex, Lauda makes his McLaren difficult to pass during his epic battle with team-mate Alain Prost during the closing stages of the Dutch Grand Prix. It was to be his last Formula 1 win.

advantage over Nelson Piquet's Brabham.

When Prost pitted for tyres on lap 25, Lauda swept into the lead. At first his margin was 30 seconds but Prost pulled this back to 16, although the two McLarens traded fastest laps. It all ended on lap 40 when, without fuss or emotion, Niki coasted to a halt just past the pits having suffered yet another broken turbo shaft. Thousands of spectators began to stream away from the track; the home victory they had hoped for was not to be.

312 Dutch Grand Prix

Zandvoort, 25 August 1985, Formula 1
McLaren MP4/2B-1 • #1
Qualifying: 10th • Result: 1st

Refusing to defer to Alain Prost as he felt it was too early in the season to be playing a supporting role, Lauda was second quickest on Friday but lined up 10th on the grid after what seemed like a cautious qualifying effort. In fact he had been in trouble on Saturday morning with an engine that had lost compression in one cylinder and he had been able to do only six laps, while on his first quick lap in afternoon qualifying Teo Fabi's Toleman baulked him. However, he was fastest in the warm-up session and commented that anything other than victory was meaningless to him.

A little luck went his way at the start when both pole-sitter Nelson Piquet and eighth-placed Thierry Boutsen (Arrows) failed to move, allowing him to complete the first lap in a remarkable fifth place. He quickly dispensed with Fabi and on lap 14 he overtook Ayrton Senna's Lotus to take third place. Six laps later the Honda engine in Keke Rosberg's Williams exploded, handing him second place. Now the McLarens were 1–2.

On an abrasive track that necessitated tyre changes, Lauda calculated that it would be best to stop early and did so on lap 21. Although his pit crew gave him an incorrect left rear that caused his car to oversteer, his decision was absolutely right and within 11 laps he had worked his way back up to second place, while Prost still led.

Two laps later, on lap 33, the Frenchman made his pit stop — with some delay owing to a sticking wheel nut — and Lauda swept past the pits to take the lead. Prost soon caught up again and the final 10 laps were spellbinding, Lauda holding the Frenchman at bay by making his car as wide as possible in all the right places and by shrewdly managing the traffic as they lapped backmarkers. For the last three laps their duel was even more intense, Prost searching for an opportunity. On the last lap the Frenchman tried to dive through on the inside at the chicane after *Schievlak* but Lauda held his line and his team-mate was forced to put two wheels on the grass.

Niki scored his 25th and final Grand Prix victory by just 0.2 second with a vintage performance.

313 Italian Grand Prix

Monza, 8 September 1985, Formula 1
McLaren MP4/2B-1 • #1
Qualifying: 16th • Result: Retired (transmission)

Thinking that qualifying tyres would not even last a complete lap, Lauda instead tried soft race tyres when going for a time in Saturday's qualifying but regretted the decision, especially as he was also troubled by an intermittent electronic cut-out that prevented him from improving on his Friday time, leaving him only 16th on the grid to Alain Prost's fifth. However, he was second quickest in the warm-up, when his concerns about the condition of his car's clutch led to a new one being fitted during the lunch break.

Finishing the first lap in 18th place, the scene was set for another of his now-famous charges. He was seventh by lap 8, assisted by his choice of softer tyres and a harder left rear. Clearly driving on the limit, he passed Michele Alboreto's Ferrari on lap 12 just as Nelson Piquet retired his Brabham, then quickly caught and passed the

BELOW With a new nose and brand-new tyres fitted (a sticker is visible on the left-front Goodyear), Lauda's McLaren MP4/2 rejoins the fray at Monza; his race ended in yet another retirement through mechanical failure.

Lotuses of Ayrton Senna (lap 15) and Elio de Angelis (lap 16). Now he was third, with Prost not far ahead of him and running on harder tyres, but his advance was halted on lap 26 when severe vibration caused the front wing mounting beam to break (although some reports erroneously suggested that the damage was caused by riding over a high kerb).

He dropped to 10th while a new nose and tyres were fitted but the vibration remained when he rejoined, making the whole car shake. Struggling to see properly, he resolutely made up ground but was forced to retire when the transmission finally surrendered on lap 34.

314 Belgian Grand Prix

Spa-Francorchamps, 15 September 1985, Formula 1
McLaren MP4/2B-1 • #1
Qualifying: No time, did not start

BELOW Niki is pictured in practice at Spa shortly before a jammed throttle caused him to crash, the resulting injury preventing him from taking part in the Belgian Grand Prix. The earthworks in the background still have an unfinished look after the circuit's remodelling.

The Belgian Grand Prix should have taken place on 31 May but it had had to be postponed because the track broke up during the first practice session. Back then, Lauda had been unofficially 10th fastest, complaining of an engine that was 500rpm down.

When everyone reconvened in September, he played little part. At the end of the first untimed session on Friday morning he was cruising back to the pits when, without warning, his throttle stuck open at Post 16, a right-hander on the new section of the circuit. The car slid wide and speared off the road into the guardrail, the impact whipping the steering wheel round and wrenching his right wrist as it did so. The car was not badly damaged but an X-ray revealed that he had suffered tendon damage, although nothing was broken; for the third time in his career he was sidelined by a wrist injury.

He returned almost immediately to Vienna for treatment and was forced to miss the European Grand Prix at Brands Hatch on 6 October. Soon after, ironically, he was involved in another crash, this time in a Viennese taxi, but was not hurt. While he was absent, Alain Prost was confirmed as the new World Champion having won five races.

315 South African Grand Prix

Kyalami, 19 October 1985, Formula 1
McLaren MP4/2B-1 • #1
Qualifying: 8th • Result: Retired (turbo)

Marlboro tried to distance itself from the politically sensitive issue of racing in South Africa, a country that was increasingly an international pariah, by having its identity removed from the McLarens; Lauda himself commented about Formula 1's double standards given the regime's human-rights record. However, as was always the case, the racing went ahead.

When practice started at Kyalami, the Bosch Motronic systems on the TAG engines were still mapped for Brands Hatch, which put them some 50–80bhp down on power at this high-altitude track, so a new programme was quickly developed by the Porsche engineers at Weissach and instructions phoned through in an effort to resolve the issue. Now that Alain Prost was World Champion, Niki demanded priority use of the spare car, a request that Ron Dennis eventually accepted so as not — so he said — to give the Austrian any excuses. With the smaller turbos fitted to suit Kyalami's thin atmosphere, he used the spare to good effect and out-qualified Prost for only the second time in two seasons, lining up eighth, one place ahead of the Frenchman.

Sixth at the start, Lauda lost position to Prost on lap 4, although he gained places when Nelson Piquet (Brabham) and Ayrton Senna (Lotus) both retired in short order, and on lap 10 he followed his team-mate past Elio de Angelis's Lotus at the slippery Crowthorne corner. Pitting for tyres on lap 32, he endured a frustratingly long stop, but Prost was similarly afflicted and in fact Lauda emerged with a net advantage. He was poised to overtake Nigel Mansell's Williams for the lead when, on lap 36, one of his turbos blew, overloaded by the heat and thin air despite running at standard boost pressure.

316 Australian Grand Prix

Adelaide, 13 November 1985, Formula 1
McLaren MP4/2B-1 • #1
Qualifying: 15th • Result: Retired (brakes)

For his farewell race, Lauda qualified only 15th but he was surprisingly philosophical about it. He found his tyres reluctant to warm up on Friday and after encountering electrical problems on Saturday he took to the spare car (MP4/2B-3). The tight, demanding street circuit in Adelaide placed more emphasis on racecraft than speed, and on getting to the finish rather than leading into the first corner, so the circumstances seemed to be tailor-made for the 1985-specification Lauda.

After lying 16th for the first two laps, he began a brilliant drive through the field as others fell out, crashed or simply succumbed to his overtaking moves. He was 15th on lap 3, 13th on lap 6, 12th on lap 10, 10th on lap 12, eighth on lap 13, seventh on lap 14 and sixth on lap 15. His progress then eased slightly but he still gained two more places when Elio de Angelis was black-flagged (lap 18) and team-mate Alain Prost's engine blew up (lap 26). Now his race stabilised for a spell so that approaching half distance he was fourth, behind a battle for the lead between Keke Rosberg's Williams and Ayrton Senna's Lotus, with Marc Surer's Brabham third.

Two incidents on lap 42 changed the situation. First Surer ran into the back of Teo Fabi's Toleman and spun into retirement. Then Senna lost a front fin when he knocked the back of Rosberg's Williams as it slowed down to pit for tyres, forcing the Brazilian to stop two laps later for a new nose. So Niki was elevated to second place. Senna, on fresh rubber, soon got past him again but both drivers were promoted on lap 53 when Rosberg made another pit stop for tyres, this time a longer one because of a sticking wheel nut.

Lauda, still on his original Goodyears after carefully conserving them, neatly outbraked Senna at the end of Brabham Straight on lap 56 and took the lead in his last Grand Prix, amid cheers from the McLaren pit that were echoed in the stands around the circuit. It was a glorious moment but sadly the prospect of a fairy-tale

ABOVE At the politically controversial South African Grand Prix, the McLarens carried no title sponsorship and even the familiar Marlboro chevron shapes were altered. After a charge through the field, Lauda was denied the chance of victory by a turbo failure.

ABOVE Adelaide was an altogether different kind of street circuit and was universally popular with the drivers. Niki, in his last Grand Prix, made another of his impressive climbs through the field.

ending vanished shortly afterwards. Lauda had been experiencing brake trouble since lap 10, a consequence of the rate of pad wear on the McLaren's lightweight carbon brakes. By now, the pads were completely worn out and under braking at the end of the main straight on lap 58 his brake pedal went to the floor. The rear wheels locked up and the car speared gently into the wall, bending the suspension and putting him out of the race.

Niki climbed out of the McLaren, pulled off his helmet and began the long walk back to the pits as the crowd rose to applaud him. They had witnessed the end of a champion's career. As recorded by Peter Robinson of *Wheels* magazine, Lauda's final words to his mechanics as he left the McLaren pit for the last time were, 'Now I grow up and do something useful with the rest of my life.'

SUMMARY

Lauda's season followed the pattern of 1984, with fairly average showings in practice and strategically managed race performances, competing as strongly as possible but without harming his car or compromising its tyres. The difference from the previous year was that he suffered appalling reliability by any standards, let alone McLaren's. He finished only three races, in stark contrast to Alain Prost's record of just three retirements.

He lost at least two wins when poised to take control. When his car stayed in one piece, as at Zandvoort, he showed that his racecraft remained unrivalled. His final race, at Adelaide, encapsulated his year: a nondescript qualifying performance followed by a stunning drive through the field that ended with mechanical failure. His three finishes — a win, a fourth and a fifth — were a very poor reward for a season in which his commitment had remained undiminished despite all the tribulations and his later decision to retire. Other than in Monte Carlo, where he spun out on oil, his retirements were entirely due to technical failures.

1985

LEFT & BELOW Niki was leading the Australian Grand Prix at Adelaide when his brakes failed on lap 58, denying him a fairy-tale final victory. Walking back to the pits, he was now an ex-Formula 1 driver.

The year was punctuated by rumours that Lauda would change teams again for 1986 and even after the announcement of his retirement there was continued speculation that he would still be on the grid the following year. During the summer, the ambitious and well-funded Beatrice Lola team showed interest in signing a big-name driver and approached Lauda with a $4 million offer, but negotiations did not progress. Lotus also came calling, but Lauda cancelled a meeting planned for the day after the European Grand Prix. At the 11th hour, he almost reversed his decision to quit after receiving an unprecedented $6 million offer from Bernie Ecclestone to return to Brabham, where Gordon Murray was conceptualising his low-line BT55 design with the promise of bespoke tyres from Pirelli — an exciting prospect for the technical challenges it would provide. Lauda said later that his rapid departure from Adelaide after the Australian Grand Prix was to avoid succumbing to the temptation of the new car.

THE LAST LAP 345

LATER TESTS & DEMONSTRATIONS

Although the 1985 Australian Grand Prix marked the end of Lauda's career as a professional racing driver, it was not surprising that a man who had spent most of his life behind the wheel of competition machinery would subsequently appear back in the driving seat from time to time.

The close links he maintained with his former teams, notably his old touring car employers BMW and his long-standing relationship with Mercedes-Benz, may have been nurtured mainly for commercial reasons by the ever-entrepreneurial Lauda, but the love of driving racing cars stayed with him always. Mario Andretti, a man who was never happier than when he was at the wheel, said of his friend and rival after witnessing his comeback at Monza in 1976: 'I never thought anybody had the love that I had for driving. And then he was there fighting.' It was a passion Niki retained until the end of his life.

This final chapter covers some of his more noteworthy and interesting appearances following retirement, in all manner of machines. They range in age from a 1908 Benz 120 HP Grand Prix car to a 2011 Mercedes-Benz SLS AMG GT3.

Nürburgring (D)

July 1986
BMW M5 (M-UP 6098)

Lauda was appointed by BMW as an official adviser and brand ambassador in January 1986, brought in at great expense by BMW Motorsport boss Wolfgang-Peter Flohr with a contract requiring him to represent the company for 60 days a year. By this time BMW had provided some examples of its new M5 (the E28 version) for the Nürburgring's *Renntaxi* ('Race Taxi') project, which gave paying guests the chance to lap the *Nordschleife* with a professional racing driver. Lauda, who had accumulated enormous experience of the *Nordschleife* before his huge crash there, completed some laps for promotional purposes, accompanied by passengers.

ABOVE Recently appointed as a brand ambassador for BMW, Niki poses at the Nürburgring in 1986 after signing the bonnet of the M5 'Race Taxi' in which he has just acted as chauffeur.

BELOW At speed in a works BMW M3, trying out the car at Monza before practice begins for the opening round of the 1987 World Touring Car Championship.

Monza (I)

19 March 1987
BMW M3

BMW persuaded Lauda to try out a race-prepared M3, one of its 1987 World Touring Car Championship contenders, during unofficial testing on the Thursday before the opening round at Monza and even went so far as to put his name on the entry list for the 500km race. This exercise was part of his advisory role for BMW and the purpose was to familiarise himself with the car so that he could offer guidance to the team's drivers. All parties were at pains to stress that this was not a racing comeback.

For his handful of laps, he borrowed works driver Emanuele Pirro's race suit and a plain white helmet, but he wore his everyday Timberland boots. He made a few set-up changes before having new tyres fitted and then recorded a faster lap than any of the works men had achieved by that stage. He was briefly back at the wheel of a racing M3 ahead of the Nürburgring WTCC round on 12 July but this time there was no suggestion that he would compete.

LATER TESTS & DEMONSTRATIONS 347

RIGHT Lauda remained a huge draw for spectators, as evidenced by his prominence on the cover of the 1992 Oldtimer Festival programme.

Salzburgring (A)

20 September 1992, Oldtimer Grand Prix
Mercedes-Benz W196 (008/54)

Having attended the Salzburg Oldtimer Grand Prix at the Salzburgring in 1981, Lauda agreed to return in 1992 for what was expected to be the event's swansong, noise restrictions and increasing environmental opposition having led to its approaching demise. Inevitably he was a huge attraction and he featured prominently on the programme cover. After the lunch break he demonstrated a Mercedes-Benz W196 Grand Prix car from the Mercedes-Benz Museum; it was the same chassis that he had sampled at Long Beach before the United States Grand Prix (West) in 1976.

Ennstal Classic (A)

Gröbming, 2 September 1995
Ferrari 500 Testa Rossa

The Ennstal Classic rally was devised in 1992 by the Austrian journalist Helmut Zwickl and photographer Michael Glöckner as a reaction to the restrictions that spectators experienced in getting close to the cars at contemporary events. The town of Gröbming was chosen as the starting point as Glöckner was also CEO of its tourism office. Famous names offered their services for free and the event quickly became popular.

RIGHT Niki prepares to misbehave at the wheel of the Ferrari 500 Testa Rossa in Gröbming's market square.

348 NIKI LAUDA

Zwickl invited Lauda, his long-time friend, to take part in 1995. Thousands of spectators turned up to see him make his Ferrari comeback at the wheel of Ernst Schuster's beautiful 500 Testa Rossa sports racer from 1957. Niki took part in the final on Saturday on a 0.9-mile (1.4km) demonstration route through the streets of Gröbming, sharing the car with its owner on two runs. There was a competitive element in the form of a 'regularity' test, the aim being for the time on the second run to match that set on the first run, with every hundredth of a second difference being penalised. After the event, the tell-tale on the Testa Rossa's rev counter showed 7,500rpm — Lauda and Schuster had certainly stood on the accelerator.

LEFT Niki appears to be sitting low in the cockpit in this fuzzy image of him testing Ellen Lohr's Mercedes-Benz C-class racer at Hockenheim in 1996.

week outing was strictly a one-off and that he had no intention of racing again. Given that some former Formula 1 drivers were now competing in the series, this was a pre-emptive move to prevent any media speculation.

Hockenheim (D)

19 March 1996
Mercedes-Benz C-class

At Hockenheim, Lauda sampled a Mercedes-Benz C-class saloon as raced by Ellen Lohr in the previous season's Deutsche Tourenwagen Meisterschaft (DTM). While the Stuttgart company was keen to hear the Austrian's feedback about the car, it stressed that this mid-

Ennstal Classic (A)

Gröbming, 29 August 1996
Ferrari 312B3

Returning to the Ennstal Classic, Lauda was reunited with the Ferrari 312B3 that he had last driven 22 years earlier in the Race of Champions at Brands Hatch. As with the Ferrari

LEFT Lauda trundles through the streets of Gröbming in 1996 in a Ferrari 312B3 from 1974 during the closing parade for the Ennstal Classic.

LATER TESTS & DEMONSTRATIONS

500 Testa Rossa he had used in the previous year's event, the 312B3 was owned by Ernst Schuster. The course was now a 1.5-mile (2.5km) circuit marked out by straw bales and regularly traversed by local delivery vehicles.

Given the rather drizzly conditions, Niki took the wheel wearing a Burberry raincoat and with his cap turned round, prompting *Austro Motor* magazine to note that Enzo Ferrari would have turned in his grave at the thought. Niki took great pleasure in showing the car to his sons Lukas and Matthias.

For the first time, the winner was presented with the Alfred Neubauer Trophy, an award that had been made personally by the great Mercedes-Benz team chief during his lifetime to only five drivers — John Surtees, Jim Clark, Jackie Stewart, Jochen Rindt and Niki Lauda. As its last recipient, Lauda had presented his trophy to Mercedes-Benz Austria and it was fittingly restored for use at the historic event.

Journalists v Drivers Inkart Challenge (B)

Puurs, 29 August 1996

The Belgian branch of Lauda Air approached Mike van Hooydonk from Inkart with a proposal to allow journalists, local racing drivers and their customers to race against Niki in a short event of about 12 minutes' duration at Puurs, near Antwerp. There were some conditions attached to the deal, one being Lauda's demand that the drivers had to start at the back of the grid and the less experienced journalists at the front — although he was insistent that he, too, would start from the front!

Although some of the professional drivers objected, they soon got on with it and swiftly made their way to the fore, the quickest of them, Wim Eyckmans, soon finding himself battling with Lauda for the lead. However, anyone who thought the triple World Champion might have lost his competitive edge was proved wrong. Then van Hooydonk was forced to halt the race early, handing victory to Lauda, with singer and sometime racing driver Koen Wauters a close second. The race director sheepishly explained that his decision was comparable to what happened at Monaco in 1984, when, as he saw it, clerk of the course Jacky Ickx stopped the rain-soaked race early to benefit Alain Prost, who was about to lose the lead to Ayrton Senna.

A1-Ring (A)

20 September 1997
Mercedes-Benz W196

Five years after his previous outing in a Grand Prix Mercedes-Benz W196, Lauda was back at the wheel of a sister example from the Mercedes-Benz Museum for a display to mark the return of Formula 1 to the remodelled Österreichring, now renamed the A1-Ring. He did his laps in the 1955 car during the break between untimed practice and qualifying, with his familiar cap reversed to avoid losing it in the wind.

BELOW Mike van Hooydonk (left), owner of the Inkart karting facility at Puurs in Belgium, secured Niki's participation in a Journalists v Drivers Challenge, which Niki won from Koen Wauters (right).

A1-Ring (A)

24 July 1998
Mercedes-Benz 300SLR

Continuing his association with historic Mercedes-Benz racers, Lauda completed a handful of demonstration laps in a 300SLR ahead of the Friday qualifying session for the revived Austrian Grand Prix at the A1-Ring. The car was the famous '722', as raced to victory in the 1955 Mille Miglia by Stirling Moss with Denis Jenkinson as his navigator. At the same time, McLaren-Mercedes test driver Nick Heidfeld demonstrated the W196 Formula 1 car that Lauda had driven the previous year.

Catalunya (E)

7 February 1999
McLaren MP4/98T-1

Lauda had commented on a few occasions that he would be interested to try a modern Formula 1 car and he was surprised to receive an offer from his old boss Ron Dennis to drive the McLaren two-seater as a 50th birthday present. The McLaren-Mercedes MP4/98T was based on 1998's MP4/12, with a second seat positioned directly behind the driver but slightly elevated. Built to 1997 FIA safety standards, it was only ever used for demonstration purposes.

For his first runs in the car, Lauda took his sons Lukas and Matthias along as passengers and later chauffeured King Juan Carlos of Spain for a couple of laps. He described the car as an incredible experience, but easier to drive than he had expected.

ABOVE Niki edges out of the paddock at Austria's A1-Ring, formerly the Österreichring, in the 1955 Mille Miglia-winning Mercedes-Benz 300SLR.

LEFT The pioneering — and soon to be copied — McLaren MP4/98T two-seater is piloted by Niki around the Circuit de Catalunya in 1999, with his son Matthias as passenger on this occasion.

ABOVE Leading Jörg Haider during the early stages of the Cart Rennen '99 charity race.

RIGHT Niki leaves the start line at the 2001 Goodwood Festival of Speed in the ex-Gilles Villeneuve Ferrari 312T3.

Cart Rennen '99 (A)

Velden, 25 July 1999

Entrepreneur Hannes Jagerhofer managed to persuade the triple World Champion to attend a five-hour charity kart race that he had organised at the Kart City circuit in the Austrian town of Velden, the tourist centre of the Wörthersee district. Lauda's presence along with other well-known people, including the controversial Austrian politician Jörg Haider, inevitably attracted a large number of journalists and camera crews.

Hockenheim (D)

1 August 1999
McLaren MP4/98T-1

Lauda had another run in the McLaren two-seater Formula 1 car at Hockenheim ahead of the German Grand Prix, this time with Daimler-Benz CEO Jürgen Schrempp as his passenger.

Festival of Speed (GB)

Goodwood, 8 July 2001
Ferrari 312T3 (034)

Lauda drove Gilles Villeneuve's 1978 Ferrari 312T3, owned by Pink Floyd drummer Nick Mason, for a timed run up the Goodwood hill in Class 17 ('Gentlemen and Players'). It was the first time he had experienced the next development in the 312T series that he had demanded for much of his final season with Ferrari.

Wearing a contemporary Jaguar race suit and an unfamiliar black crash helmet, he relished the sound and feel of the flat-12 engine that had powered him to so many wins three decades earlier, although the limitations of the short, narrow track meant he was unable to offer much comment on how the newer car compared to the unloved 312T2-77.

The event programme indicated that Lauda was also to appear in a Jaguar D-type, either the ex-Ecurie Nationale Belge car entered by John Coombs for Mike MacDowel or a distinguished Ecurie Ecosse example — the Le Mans 24 Hours winner of 1957 — entered by the Dutch National Motor Museum for Robert Brooks.

Ennstal Classic (A)

Gröbming, 25 August 2001
Jaguar D-type

Lauda made a third visit to the Ennstal Classic in his capacity as race director at Jaguar's Formula 1 operation, this time taking part in the opening parade through the streets of Gröbming in, appropriately, a Jaguar D-type.

Valencia (E)

13 January 2002
Jaguar R2C

Following a dare from Gerhard Berger that came to the notice of an Austrian journalist, Lauda tried out one of his Jaguar Formula 1 team's cars. After two spins in his first three laps, he was towed back to the pits, but he later took the R2C around the track at speed, completing three flying laps before stopping on the grid and performing a practice start. His best lap was about 10 seconds off a good time at the track — not bad for a 52-year-old who had not driven a

ABOVE Back for the Ennstal Classic parade in 2001, Lauda — now race director at the Jaguar Formula 1 team — drove a Jaguar D-type this time.

BELOW Trying out a modern Formula 1 car at Valencia in 2002: Niki discovered that the technological innovations that had evolved in the 17 years since his retirement meant that the Jaguar R2C required a completely different driving style from what he was used to.

Formula 1 car at full throttle for almost 17 years.

In experiencing traction control, launch control, an automatic gearbox, left-foot braking, power steering and grooved tyres for the first time, he remarked that he had to use a completely different driving style to adapt to the new technology.

Superfund Kart Grand Prix (D)

Nürburgring, 28 June 2003

On the eve of the European Grand Prix at the Nürburgring, a pro-celebrity race was organised on the infield course to raise funds for charity. More than 60 karts took part, piloted by a variety of drivers, journalists, photographers and Formula 1 team members. Well-known drivers included Christian Danner, Vitantonio Liuzzi, Felipe Massa and Allan McNish, with Formula 3000 contender Matthias Lauda, Niki's son, also taking part.

Niki himself was persuaded to drive the official pace kart to lead the parade lap for the rolling start. He refused to wear either helmet or overalls and seemed keener on putting in a fast lap rather than keeping the pack bunched together.

Modena Motorsport Track Day (D)

Nürburgring, 23–24 July 2003
Ferrari 312PB (0892)

Lauda was invited to Modena Motorsport's 10th Ferrari track day, which also celebrated the 20th anniversary of the Langenfeld-based concern. Present were 240 Ferraris with technical support provided by five factory mechanics from Maranello. Niki demonstrated a 312PB 3-litre sports prototype, the car that won the World Championship for Makes in 1972. Somewhat ironically, a derivative of this design would have raced in 1974 had Lauda not been instrumental in the cancellation of Ferrari's sports car programme. He drove without a helmet, but the trademark red cap was always in place.

ABOVE A helmetless Lauda prepares to lead the Superfund Kart Grand Prix field on its parade lap. He did not wait for them to keep up.

BELOW In an earlier and rather more attractive variant of the Ferrari 312PB that he had briefly tested at the end of 1973, Niki ventures out onto the modern-day Nürburgring course at the Modena Motorsport track day in July 2003.

354 NIKI LAUDA

A1-Ring (A)

7 September 2003
Mercedes-Benz CLK

Mercedes-Benz Motorsport Director Norbert Haug invited Lauda to attend the eighth round of the 2003 Deutsche Tourenwagen Meisterschaft (DTM) series and he was impressed by the atmosphere and the action. After a few exploratory laps in Bernd Schneider's latest-generation AMG-Mercedes, he drove it as much as he could with obvious pleasure, completing a total of 17 laps during the afternoon chauffeuring guest passengers. Among those for whom he acted as 'taxi driver' were his eldest son Lukas and Austrian ski idol Toni Sailer.

He described the car as being a lot closer to a Formula 1 machine than the leviathans he had experienced in touring car racing. He added that the car was very well set up and balanced, which made it fun to drive, and that he could understand why some of his former Formula 1 colleagues enjoyed racing in the DTM.

Magny-Cours (F)

21 June 2008
Benz 120 HP

To celebrate the 100th anniversary of the Mercedes team's victory in the 1908 French Grand Prix at Dieppe, a demonstration of historic Mercedes-Benz cars was held before the 2008 French Grand Prix at Magny-Cours. As his connections with the three-pointed star were growing closer, Lauda was offered the chance to drive a Benz 120 HP, the car in which Victor Hémery had finished second at Dieppe in 1908. This fearsome beast had been specially prepared for the run by the Daimler-Mercedes Classic division and normally resided in the Mercedes-Benz Museum in Stuttgart. Later in the day, McLaren-Mercedes Formula 1 driver Heiki Kovalainen also demonstrated the car.

ABOVE When trying out Bernd Schneider's Mercedes-Benz CLK in 2003, Niki found that touring cars had become much more responsive, sophisticated devices than those he drove in the early 1970s.

BELOW At Magny-Cours in 2008, Niki sits on — rather than in — the Benz 120 HP that finished second in the French Grand Prix 100 years earlier.

ABOVE Procar revival: Niki jumped at the chance to take part in what was billed as a 'demonstration race' for the 1979-era BMW M1 behemoths at Hockenheim. For many of the participants, the urge to race properly was hard to resist.

BELOW Niki and the Daimler-Benz technicians warm up Fangio's 1955 title-winning Mercedes-Benz W196 in readiness for his run at Hockenheim in 2009.

Procar Revival Demonstration (D)

Hockenheim, 19 July 2008
BMW M1

Spectators at the German Grand Prix were treated to a revival of the Procar series that had originally supported the Formula 1 schedule in 1979 and 1980. Ten original BMW M1s featured in races on both Saturday and Sunday, piloted by several drivers — including Lauda — who had participated in the original series as well as a few names from the modern era. Each car included a guest passenger.

Lauda took part in Saturday's race at the wheel of a car that had been assembled by Schnitzer in 1982 from original 1979 components for Hans Stuck to contest the German championship before being sold to BMW for the company's collection. Although these were ostensibly demonstration events, they featured a starting grid — drawn by ballot — and the participants were allowed to drive as they wished. They duly responded, giving no quarter.

After Jochen Neerpasch in the 'Art Car' failed to get away properly at the start, Lauda took the lead early in his first Procar 'race' for 29 years. He tussled briefly with Christian Danner but held him off effectively, eventually pulling clear to take a comfortable win. Afterwards he enthused about the experience, saying he would have to seriously reconsider whether his racing career really was over.

Nürburgring (D)

12 July 2009
Mercedes-Benz W196 (008/54)

Ahead of the German Grand Prix, Lauda took part in a parade at the wheel of Juan-Manuel Fangio's 1955 title-winning Mercedes-Benz W196. This was the same chassis that he had tried at Long Beach before the United States Grand Prix (West) in 1976 and at the Salzburgring Oldtimer event in 1992. The only driver to sport a crash helmet, he clearly enjoyed the reunion.

Hockenheim (D)

25 October 2009
Mercedes-Benz W196 (008/54)

Lauda got back in the same Mercedes-Benz W196 again for a historic demonstration held before a round of the Deutsche Tourenwagen Masters — Germany's national touring car championship — at Hockenheim, a short distance 'up the road' from the car's normal home in the Mercedes-Benz Museum in Stuttgart.

Red Bull Ring (A)

14 May 2011

Mercedes-Benz SLS AMG GT3

The official reopening of the rebuilt former Österreichring, which had been acquired by Dieter Mateschitz's Red Bull organisation and renamed accordingly, was celebrated with a series of races and demonstrations that included a 'Legends Parade'. Heavy rain did not dampen the enthusiasm of the drivers or spectators and Lauda showed that he was still no slouch behind the wheel in the poor conditions, mixing it with the Duller Motorsport BMW Z4 M Coupé GT piloted by his old adversary and fellow Austrian Dieter Quester. Other combatants included Sebastian Vettel, Mark Webber, Gerhard Berger and Helmut Marko.

Red Bull Ring (A)

22 June 2014

Ferrari 312T2

To mark the return of the Austrian Grand Prix to the calendar, all nine living Austrian Formula 1 drivers were back in some of their most famous cars for a 'Legends Parade'. Lauda's car was a Ferrari 312T2 from 1976 and he was clearly pleased that one of his former Ferrari mechanics was in attendance.

When the pitlane finally opened, he and his compatriots delighted the 100,000 spectators with an emotional spectacle that included Helmut Marko aboard a BRM P180, Gerhard Berger in a Ferrari F1-87/88C and Dieter Quester driving a Surtees TS16. Niki took the opportunity to address the crowd, bowing to the stands to a tumultuous response. For many of those present, this demonstration was the highlight of the day, eclipsing the Formula 1 race that took place an hour later.

ABOVE Heavy rain did not dampen the enthusiasm of either the spectators or the drivers at the opening of the newly named Red Bull Ring, formerly the A1-Ring and before that, of course, the Österreichring. Here, Niki's Mercedes-Benz SLS AMG goes wheel-to-wheel with Dieter Quester's BMW Z4 M Coupé GT.

LEFT Reunited with a Ferrari 312T2, the car that brought him so close to the 1976 World Championship title, Niki sweeps round the Red Bull Ring before the Austrian Grand Prix in 2014.

RIGHT At the Red Bull Ring in 2015 Niki demonstrated a McLaren MP4/2, the car in which he had won his home Grand Prix at this very circuit back in 1984.

BELOW Something different: at the wheel of a rally car for once, Niki tackles the pursuit course inside Stuttgart's Mercedes-Benz Arena during his head-to-head race with Toto Wolff.

Red Bull Ring (A)

21 June 2015
McLaren MP4/2

Following the success of the previous year's 'Legends Parade', Lauda was one of three retired Formula 1 drivers from the turbo era — the others were Alain Prost and Jean Alesi — invited to demonstrate some of the 1,000+bhp machinery. He was reunited with his 1984 World Championship-winning McLaren MP4/2 and, after some good-natured banter with Prost, complained that he could not keep up with the Frenchman's newer MP4/2C as his boost pressure was set too weak at 1.8-bar. He demanded the 3-bar boost that the car had used in period and soon had the TAG engine spitting fire on the overrun to the delight of the capacity crowd. After completing his run, he stopped on the main straight and climbed from the car to salute the fans.

'Stars & Cars' Celebration Pursuit (D)

Stuttgart, 20 December 2015
Mercedes-Benz 500 SL Rallye

Billed as an opportunity to settle his alleged feud with Mercedes-Benz's Head of Motorsport Toto Wolff, Lauda competed in the off-season 'Stars & Cars' party at the German brand's Mercedes-Benz Arena. The organisers staged a pursuit race for them in Mercedes-Benz rally cars, but Lauda's 1970s 500 SL (formerly the mount of Polish driver Sobieslaw Zasada) was overcome by Wolff's newer 1980s 450 SLC. Wolff, who in his youth had tried to be a professional driver but with little success, made some capital out of his narrow win over his countryman.

LEFT Back in a BMW Procar, this time his original title-winning Project Four machine, Niki revelled in the opportunity to participate in another 'show' race at the Red Bull Ring before the Austrian Grand Prix of 2016.

Red Bull Ring (A)

3 July 2016
BMW M1

A feature of Red Bull's Friendly Motorsport Festival held in support of the revived Austrian Grand Prix, the 'Legends Parade' in 2016 provided another emotional highlight with the opportunity for drivers from the old Procar series to revisit the much-loved, thunderous, fire-spitting BMW M1s. Fourteen cars contested the demonstration race and Lauda drove one of them. He was in fighting mood, saying: 'These races are so much fun. It just goes click and then it's all like it was back then. If Berger is going to overtake me, then of course I'll try to take him back. I still don't like trailing behind.'

Red Bull Ring (A)

12 May 2018
BMW 3.0 CSL

Having missed the Le Mans-focused 'Legends Parade' of 2017, Lauda was back at his home circuit to take another trip down memory lane in his now-traditional appearance at the Red Bull Friendly Motorsport Festival. With the theme being the Deutsche Rennsport Meisterschaft, to the delight of 185,000 spectators he took the wheel of a replica of the Alpina BMW 3.0 CSL that he had raced in the Nürburgring Six Hours 45 years earlier. Despite his role as Mercedes AMG F1's non-executive chairman, his employer seemed not to mind his presence in a BMW.

He was not seen at the wheel of a competition car again.

BELOW Final turn at the wheel: Niki made his last appearance in a race car in the 'Legends Parade' before the 2018 Austrian Grand Prix, demonstrating a replica of the BMW 3.0 CSL coupé in which he had set a touring car lap record for the Nürburgring *Nordschleife* 45 years earlier.

LATER TESTS & DEMONSTRATIONS

LIFE BEYOND THE DRIVING SEAT

At the time of his second, permanent retirement from racing, Lauda Air was a small regional airline, but in typical style Niki doggedly pursued his goal of making the company an international operator. With his relentless determination, he battled against obstructive Austrian bureaucracy and eventually secured licences to fly his Boeings on routes to Australia, the Far East and South America. Showing the same attention to detail as he had demanded in the preparation of his race cars, he differentiated his small airline from the competition by offering superior service standards: 'Service is our Success' was the company's motto.

The lure of motor sport, however, was never far away. In 1991, Lauda accepted an invitation from his old friend Luca di Montezemolo — by now Director of Ferrari with a free hand to do whatever was necessary to reverse the famous team's fall from grace — to act as a special adviser purely for its Formula 1 activities. Niki still had a full-time job running his airline and could only offer part-time support, so it was always going to be a challenge. His role was not eased by the arrival of technical director John Barnard, with whom Lauda had had a rather prickly relationship at McLaren, and it began to look superfluous when Jean Todt, who had masterminded world titles for Peugeot in endurance racing and rallying, was appointed as team principal. However, Niki had one more major task to fulfil for his old team — persuading the then double World Champion Michael Schumacher to jump ship from Benetton to the Scuderia. With this achieved for 1996, he was gone.

German TV company RTL then hired him as a pundit and commentator, his insight and dry wit resonating with a legion of new fans, but this more peripheral involvement with the Formula 1 circus did not seem to be enough. Having resigned from the board of Lauda Air after its acquisition by Austrian Airlines, he accepted an offer from Ford Vice-President Wolfgang Reitzle, who was also Managing Director of Jaguar, to bring his experience as head of the blue oval's Premier Performance Division to stabilise the chaotic revolving-door management of the Jaguar race team. Despite the fanfares and new technical personnel, the marriage was not a happy one, resulting in a dud car for 2002 that failed to live up to expectations. This led to Reitzle's replacement, Richard Parry-Jones, firing Lauda and some other significant employees in November that year.

If nothing else, this ignominious departure allowed him to return to his TV work and to set up a new budget airline. FlyNiki was a commercial success and he eventually sold it to Air Berlin in 2011. Later, in 2016, he took over charter airline Amira Air to create LaudaMotion, which ironically absorbed FlyNiki again after Air Berlin's collapse in 2017.

He was appointed non-executive Chairman of the resurgent Mercedes-Benz Formula 1 operation in September 2012. At that time the team was probably the fourth best on the grid; Michael Schumacher's comeback had not been as fruitful as had been hoped, and certainly not as successful as Lauda's own return had been. But Lauda knew that Mercedes was well advanced with its hybrid engine programme and, in an echo of his time as a consultant to Ferrari, he was instrumental in convincing Lewis Hamilton to join the three-pointed star for 2013 with a three-year deal. Under Mercedes-Benz's control, the former Brawn F1 team was an altogether more accommodating environment than Jaguar had been and, freed from most of the restrictive constraints of corporate politics, he was allowed to focus on driver development and team motivation in his usual outspoken manner. Momentum was building at the team and when the hybrid power units arrived in 2014, Mercedes was ahead of the game. A string of drivers' and constructors' titles followed.

The legendary lack of sentimentality also mellowed as he aged, although when the garage owner to whom Lauda had famously given his trophies in return for free car washes died and the artefacts became neglected, Niki recovered them, had them cleaned and promptly sold them on eBay.

In his later years Lauda was plagued by health problems, most of which were a legacy of his Nürburgring accident. In 1997 he bounced back from successive kidney transplants, a second replacement kidney donated by wife-to-be Birgit (his second wife) having been required after one from his brother Florian did not take. In 2018 a serious infection saw his damaged lungs finally start to give out and he received a full lung transplant in August. After being discharged from hospital in October, he appeared to be making a good recovery but his renal problems persisted and he was hospitalised again in December. Sadly, this time his almost superhuman resilience was not enough and he died at the Zürich University Hospital on 20 May 2019.

After a municipal funeral at Vienna's Roman Catholic Cathedral — he was the first sportsman ever to receive such an honour — he was buried in the family cemetery plot, wearing the red racing overalls from his later years as a Ferrari driver. At the Ferrari Museum in Maranello, all the lights were turned

ABOVE Ahead of the 2019 Monaco Grand Prix, the first race after Niki's death, the drivers share a minute's silence in his memory. They are all wearing red caps in tribute to his trademark headgear.

BELOW Several teams carried tributes to Niki on their cars at the Monaco Grand Prix. This was the message that adorned the nose cones of the Mercedes-Benz entries.

LIFE BEYOND THE DRIVING SEAT   361

off except for the one that illuminated Niki's 312T.

The Monaco Grand Prix was held on the Sunday following Lauda's death and his trademark red cap, for so long famous in the paddock, was widely in evidence as the Formula 1 community honoured his life. All the current drivers along with dignitaries and a number of Lauda's contemporaries (as well as large sections of the crowd) wore red caps while a minute's silence was observed on the starting grid before the race. In a demonstration of the respect and affection in which he was held, several teams also displayed tributes on their cars while Sebastian Vettel and Lewis Hamilton both sported variations of his crash helmet designs from the 1970s and 1980s. A month later at the Red Bull Ring, where Turn 1 had been renamed the *Niki Lauda Kurve*, 80,000 red caps were distributed to the spectators at the Austrian Grand Prix in an unprecedented public display for a departed World Champion.

Many tributes were paid and testimonials written, but three particularly encapsulate the respect and affection that was felt for Lauda.

The erudite Pierre Fillon, President of the Automobile de l'Ouest (organisers of the Le Mans 24 Hours) wrote:

'Motorsport involves machines, but it is about human endeavour more than anything. Some drivers make their mark on their discipline, some achieve greatness beyond the sport itself. Niki was one such driver. His attention to detail and fighting spirit was matched by his outstanding talent and admirable personality. His record is witness to that. He was also a great ambassador for motorsport and the values we uphold. He was a guide, a leader.'

In his obituary for *Autosport*, Nigel Roebuck summed up his friend with the following words: 'Niki was a great driver and, more unusually, a great man. These things are self-evident. More than that, though, perhaps the greatest compliment I can pay a man of whom I was immensely fond is that I have never met anyone who reminded me of him. He was in all ways a true original.'

The final thought comes from Frank Orthey, writing in the journal of Historic Formula Vee Europe: 'So what did Niki Lauda think about death? "I'll think about it when it's really time. Even after the accident, when a priest in the clinic gave me the last rites, I knew that I would continue to live. Because I wanted it." On May 20, 2019 Niki Lauda did not want it any more.'

LEFT Farewell to a champion: Niki's helmet rests on his coffin during the Memorial Service at St Stephen's Cathedral in Vienna on 29 May 2019. Family members, friends and thousands of fans gathered to remember the man who was seen by many as Austria's greatest driver.

'NEARLY RACES'

In any driver's career there are races for which they appear on an entry list or are even listed in a programme, but then do not turn up. This section itemises Lauda's unfulfilled race entries.

European Cup & Brno Grand Prix (CZ)
Brno, 18 August 1968, Group 2
Porsche 911S • #89
Lauda's non-participation arose because he was having discussions with Kurt Bergmann about potential single-seater opportunities at Kaimann.

National & International State Championship meeting (A)
Zeltweg, 25 August 1968, Formula Vee
Kaimann Mk3 • #31
Although Lauda's name appears in the race programme self-entered in a Kaimann, he did not participate in the race. It may have been an optimistic entry in the belief that Kurt Bergmann would allow him his first start in a relatively local race, but the reality was that he would have to earn his spurs somewhat further afield.

Rossfeld hillclimb (D)
6 September 1968, Group 1
Mini Cooper S • #113
This entry had been made some time previously but by now Lauda had sold his Mini Cooper S and in any case he was otherwise engaged, driving the Kaimann team's Opel Blitz transporter *en route* to Keimola for his single-seater début.

Finnish Grand Prix
Ahvenisto, 15 September 1968, Formula Vee
Kaimann Mk3 (V680X)
After competing at Keimola, Lauda and Lothar Schörg drove across to Hämeenlinna to the newly opened Ahvenisto circuit, where they were due to race the following weekend. For reasons that were not reported, the Austrian pair did not like what they saw and decided to skip the race.

Preis der Nationen (D)
Hockenheim, 13 September 1969, Formula Vee
Kaimann Mk4
Lauda's entry was scratched from this prestigious and well-attended Formula Vee meeting as he was instead accompanying his team boss to the private junior formula comparison race at Monza.

Gran Premio de Barcelona (E)
Montjuïc, 25 April 1970, Formula 3
McNamara Mk3B • #3
'Vienna Race Management' entered a three-car team for Gerold Pankl, Helmut Marko and Lauda, but the Austrian contingent did not turn up.

XV Internationale Bernauer Schleife-Rennen (DDR)
Bernauer Autobahn-Schleife, 31 May 1970, Formula 3
McNamara Mk3B • #30
Lauda was part of a three-car entry with Werner Riedl and Gerold Pankl for this opening round of the East German DDR Meisterschaft series in East Berlin, but once again the Austrian trio did not arrive.

AMOC Martini International Trophy (GB)
Silverstone, 7 June 1970, Formula 3
McNamara Mk3B
Lauda had optimistically entered the fifth round of the British Formula 3 Championship, but after making the long trip to Silverstone from Vienna in the hope of finding his entry accepted, he was turned away by the organisers and failed to take the start.

Jock Leith Trophy (GB)
Croft, 11 July 1970, Interserie
Porsche 908/2 (008) • #19
Rather than attend this Interserie race in northern England, Lauda took up the offer of a BMW seat with the Alpina team in the more prestigious Nürburgring Six Hours, which took place the next day.

III Flügplatzrennen (D)
Diepholz, 19 July 1970, Formula 3
McNamara Mk3B • #38
Lauda's Bosch Racing Team entry appeared in the programme, but he could not take part because his McNamara had been too badly damaged in his crash at Brands Hatch two days earlier. Somewhat ironically, his erstwhile McNamara team-mate, Gerold Pankl, narrowly won the race.

Canadian Grand Prix
Mosport, 19 September 1971, Formula 1
March 711
Lauda was listed as a possible driver for either the Alfa Romeo-engined chassis 711-4 or the Cosworth-engined 711-1 in what would have been his second Formula 1 start. In the event, the respective drivers of these cars were Nanni Galli and Mike Beuttler as they were first to come up with the necessary money.

Pau Grand Prix (F)
25 April 1971, Formula 2
March 712M/9
In a surprise move, the works March 712M usually driven by Lauda was instead prepared for Jean-Pierre Beltoise at the last minute, the team believing that running a French driver in this historic event in south-west France would be a popular strategy and no doubt attract some much-needed additional revenue.

IV Preis von Baden-Württemberg und Hessen (D)
Hockenheim, 3 October 1971, Formula 2
March 712M/9B (entered as '9') • #8
A combination of the Albi event the week before and the clashing United States Grand Prix meant that this was a non-championship event. As Ronnie Peterson was in the running for the European Formula 2 Championship title, March decided to conserve its cars for the round at Vallelunga the following weekend, so the works entries did not go to Hockenheim.

Il Gran Premio Madunina (I)
Vallelunga, 17 October 1971, Formula 2
March 712M/9B (entered as '9') • #33

Strangely, Vallelunga hosted the last two European Formula 2 Championship rounds on consecutive weekends. The March works team did not attend this second race as Ronnie Peterson had clinched the title the week before and the cars were being readied for a planned trip to South America.

Torneio Brasiliero (BR)
Interlagos, 31 October 1971, Formula 2
March 712M

With modernisation of the old Interlagos track complete, a three-race series was organised for Formula 2 cars on successive weekends starting on 31 October. Over 40 applications were received, including works Marches for Lauda, Ronnie Peterson and Wilson Fittipaldi, but in the end Niki was not among the 20 driver/car combinations that made the trip, financial considerations scuppering the team's plans.

Buenos Aires 1,000km (RA)
9 January 1972, sports cars
Lola T210 • #18

Lauda was down to drive Ecurie Bonnier's Lola T210 with his former sports car rival Chris Craft in the opening round of the 1972 World Championship for Makes in Buenos Aires, where he was due to compete in the Argentine Grand Prix two weeks later. Instead local drivers Héctor Luis Gradassi and Enrico Bertolini raced the car.

Gran Premio Mediterranio (I)
Enna-Pergusa, 20 September 1972, Formula 2
March 722/5 • #16

The cash-strapped March team, recognising its fading performance in the 1972 European Formula 2 Championship, decided to give the Enna round a miss. The time and cost of getting to the Sicilian venue was probably a factor, together with the strains that the track's flat-out slipstreaming blasts would impose on the team's already parlous stock of serviceable engines.

Austria Trophy (A)
Salzburgring, 20 May 1973, Group 2
BMW 3.0 CSL • #21

This four-hour race, originally due to take place on 22 April, had to be abandoned because of heavy snowfall, Lauda having been quickest in the only practice session held. He was unable to contest the rescheduled event as it clashed with the Belgian Grand Prix.

Spa 24 Hours (B)
Spa-Francorchamps, 21 July 1973, Group 2
BMW 3.0 CSL • #21

A week earlier, while with BRM for a Formula 1 tyre test at Mosport in Canada, Lauda had gone off the circuit and hurt his wrist. The injury was relatively slight but with the acquiescence of BRM team manager Tim Parnell, who wanted to veto his driver's involvement in touring cars wherever possible, Lauda used it as an excuse to release himself from his commitment to race a BMW 3.0 CSL in the Spa 24 Hours. Initially Harald Menzel was nominated in his place but eventually Brian Muir was given the seat. During the race, Hans-Peter Joisten, Lauda's driving partner in the Nürburgring Six Hours two weeks earlier, was killed in a violent collision at night.

Zandvoort Four Hours (NL)
12 August 1973, Group 2
BMW 3.0 CSL • #12

Following his third place the previous year, Lauda was listed to drive the Malcolm Gartlan-entered Alpina BMW 3.0 CSL with Brian Muir but instead his seat was taken by James Hunt, the pair finishing second.

Paul Ricard Six Hours (F)
2 September 1973, Group 2
BMW 3.0 CSL

The wrist injury that Lauda incurred at the German Grand Prix had not fully healed and was certainly not up to lugging the heavy BMW 3.0 CSL around Paul Ricard's fast sweepers for a minimum of three hours. Instead the Alpina car was piloted by Jacky Ickx and James Hunt, who brought it home in second place.

Monza Four Hours (I)
24 March 1974, Group 2
Ford Capri RS 3100

There were no works Ford Capris at Monza as financial constraints and problems at Cosworth meant that new four-valve engines were not ready in time. The entries were withdrawn and Lauda's race début with the Cologne-run team was delayed until the following month.

International 7th ADAC-Flugplatzrennen (D)
Diepholz, 21 July 1974, Group 2
Ford Capri RS 3100

An entry for Lauda was filed for this traditional aerodrome race amid the usual huge field, but the Capri RS 3100 he was due to drive had been badly damaged in Jochen Mass's accident at the Nürburgring the previous weekend and could not be repaired in time.

Zandvoort Trophy (NL)
11 August 1974, Group 2
Ford Capri RS 3100 • #4

A week after the German Grand Prix, Lauda was slated to share a Capri RS 3100 as usual with Jochen Mass in this four-hour European Touring Car Championship round, but he picked up a severe case of food poisoning and needed medical attention. Lauda decided to prioritise his recovery for the following weekend's Austrian Grand Prix and subsequent Formula 1 test at Monza, so instead Mass shared the car with Rolf Stommelen. The German pairing won.

Graham Hill International Trophy (GB)
Silverstone, 11 April 1976, Formula 1
Ferrari 312T2

The programme for the non-championship International Trophy race (named this year in honour of Graham Hill following his death a few months earlier) included Lauda in a Ferrari 312T2 but the entry was withdrawn at the eleventh hour. Ferrari's excuse was that the return of its cars from the previous race, at Long Beach in California, had been delayed by an Alitalia freight handlers' strike in New York, leaving insufficient time to prepare them. As no 312T2s had been taken to America, this claim was treated with more than a degree of scepticism.

Tribute to James Hunt (GB)
Brands Hatch, 7 November 1976
McLaren M23

A reciprocal deal was agreed whereby Lauda would attend the celebrations for his friend James Hunt's World Championship win and Hunt would open the 'Niki Lauda Racing Car Show' in Austria. Lauda duly arrived in Kent in his helicopter, but the two drivers did not actually meet on the day and the rumoured spectacle of Lauda doing some laps in a McLaren M23 — after Hunt had entertained the crowds in it — did not materialise.

Austria-Trophäe (Preis der Firma Elan) (A)
Salzburgring, 24 April 1977, Group 2
BMW 3.0 CSL

Alpina-contracted touring car driver Dieter Quester asked Lauda, his old friend and rival, to share his BMW CSL in the Austrian round of the European Touring Car Championship. After Ferrari refused permission, Gunnar Nilsson stepped in and he and Quester duly took the win.

Gunnar Nilsson Memorial Trophy Race (GB)
Donington Park, 3 June 1979, Procar
BMW M1

Procar regular Lauda was entered in this charity event at Donington but he did not appear due to an old dispute between circuit owner Tom Wheatcroft and Marlboro. Five years earlier, ahead of the 1974 French Grand Prix at Dijon, Marlboro had sponsored a parade of historic Formula 1 cars, five of which had come from Wheatcroft's Donington Collection. A disagreement arose about payment of the Donington Collection's fee and when Marlboro asked to rent the cars again for the 1979 British Grand Prix, which the company was sponsoring, Wheatcroft refused. As the sponsor of Lauda's Project Four BMW M1, Marlboro then withdrew his entry from the Donington event. It seemed that politics still prevailed even at a charity event to honour Formula 1 driver Gunnar Nilsson, who had died of cancer the previous autumn and in whose memory the Gunnar Nilsson Cancer Treatment Trust Fund had been set up.

Wynns 1,000km (ZA)
Kyalami, 30 November 1979, Procar
BMW M1

BMW planned to run six Procars in their own class alongside the regular Group 2 contenders in this South African endurance event. One of the Procar entries was Lauda's Project Four car, in which he was to be joined by Brabham team-mate John Watson, but then came his decision to retire from the sport. Instead Jochen Mass partnered Watson.

San Marino Grand Prix
Imola, 25 April 1982, Formula 1
McLaren MP4/1B

Along with most of the FOCA teams, McLaren withdrew its entries from this race in protest against the FISA's ban on water-cooled brakes (an exploitation of a loophole that effectively allowed the non-turbo cars to run underweight). The team was divided on the matter: Ron Dennis and the sponsors wanted to race but Teddy Mayer, Dennis's 'co-boss' and a FOCA steward, was equally determined not to. Almost alone among the non-participating drivers, Lauda turned up at Imola anyway and trenchantly expressed his views on the whole affair. He said he supported McLaren's position because the team had been loyal to him three months earlier in the dispute at Kyalami about driver superlicences, but added that he did not agree with FOCA's actions in boycotting the race.

James Hardie 1000 (AUS)
Mount Panorama, 6 October 1985, touring cars
BMW 635 CSi • #21

Having established links with Lauda at the Australian Grand Prix in 1984, the Goold Motorsport team persuaded him to enter the famous Bathurst 1000, the annual endurance race for touring cars at the Mount Panorama circuit in New South Wales. He was to share a BMW 635 CSi with his Formula 1 ex-team-mate Nelson Piquet (a BMW-contracted driver) but their entry was scratched when the date of the European Grand Prix was changed by FISA/FOCA at short notice and clashed. The BMW was instead handled by Johnny Cecotto/Roberto Ravaglia, who finished second. As it turned out, Lauda could not take part in the European Grand Prix anyway.

European Grand Prix (GB)
Brands Hatch, 6 October 1985, Formula 1
McLaren MP4/2B

Lauda had to miss this race because of the wrist injury he had incurred at Spa three weeks earlier. His former team-mate John Watson was invited back to deputise after Renault refused to release McLaren's initial choice of replacement, Derek Warwick, from his contract. Unusually, Watson's car still carried the World Champion's number 1. Afterwards, Lauda admitted to some private satisfaction that the out-of-practice Watson was further adrift of Alain Prost's times than he himself had been during the year.

Australian Grand Prix
Melbourne, 1 April 2006, Formula 1
Red Bull RB3

After the end of qualifying at Melbourne on 1 April 2006, German broadcaster RTL and Red Bull produced an 'April Fool' joke bulletin announcing Lauda as the replacement driver for Christian Klien, who was said to have an upset stomach and could not drive. Lauda was filmed wearing racing overalls and sitting in the Red Bull RB3 while high-profile Formula 1 officials confirmed on camera that he would be permitted to start the race after a 45-minute private practice session to settle in. The likelihood of the 57-year-old being able to complete a full Grand Prix distance was not discussed…

RUMOURS & POSSIBILITIES

Over the years there were also some instances of 'what might have been' in Lauda's career, some obscure and perhaps far-fetched, others more realistic and intriguing.

BRM, September 1971
In a press report considered somewhat unlikely at the time, there were rumours of an Austrian BRM 'branch team' with Helmut Marko and Lauda as drivers. Former Porsche team manager Rico Steinemann was to be race director of this potential 'national' team, which turned out to be little more than hopeful speculation and undoubtedly would have been a strain too far on the already over-large BRM armada.

Scuderia Filipinetti, September 1972
Scuderia Filipinetti announced its intention to run a pair of BMW-powered March 73S sports cars in the 1973 2-litre European Championship for Lauda and Jacques Coulon alongside an ex-works Ferrari 312P. Discussions were held with Lauda and the proposed team manager was Vic Elford, who was retiring from competitive driving, but the plan foundered inconclusively, which was probably no bad thing as Geneva-based Filipinetti ceased operations during the year.

International Race of Champions (IROC), July 1974
Roger Penske attended the 1974 French Grand Prix at Dijon, not only gathering information for his nascent Formula 1 project but also looking to sign up Lauda, Clay Regazzoni, Ronnie Peterson and Jody Scheckter for the second 'International Race of Champions' series, which would feature NASCAR-style Chevrolet Camaro Z28s instead of the Porsche Carrera RSRs used in the inaugural series. Regazzoni joked that they would be there if the money was good, but that he and Lauda would be the most expensive given their superb Formula 1 form. Already irritated by Lauda's concurrent Ford contract to race Capris in the European Touring Car Championship, Ferrari refused to allow its drivers to compete for another manufacturer.

Shadow, Indianapolis 500, May 1975
During practice for the Austrian Grand Prix in 1974, the Shadow Formula 1 team approached Lauda with the offer of a car — a variant of the Formula 5000 Shadow DN6 — to contest the Indianapolis 500 the following year. There does not seem to have been any subsequent dialogue and in any case Ferrari would have vetoed it.

Spyder, Can-Am, October 1978
Ex-Formula 1 driver and Le Mans winner Masten Gregory ran the Newman-Freeman team, which was co-owned by Paul Newman, the actor and amateur racing driver. At the 1978 United States Grand Prix (East) at Watkins Glen, Gregory approached Lauda with an invitation to contest the 1979 Can-Am series at the wheel of one of the team's Lola-based Spyder NF11 chassis alongside either Mario Andretti or Newman. Gregory's offer included Concorde flights but Lauda had previously registered his lack of appetite for a transatlantic career and negotiations did not get far. Instead the ride went to Keke Rosberg.

BMW, Le Mans 24 Hours, June 1981
BMW's Dieter Stappert, a former journalist, had known Lauda from his earliest racing days and tried to persuade him to get back behind the wheel of a BMW M1, this time in Group 5 configuration, for an attempt at the Le Mans 24 Hours. His timing, in the spring if 1981, was somewhat premature as another six months would pass before the temptation to return to the cockpit really clicked for Lauda. As for Le Mans, it would remain a race in which he never participated.

McLaren, Indianapolis 500, May 1983
Leaks within McLaren suggested that the team was planning to build a chassis to contest the Indianapolis 500 as a works entry in 1984 with Lauda driving. John Barnard, who had already designed the Indy-winning Chaparral 2K for Johnny Rutherford, was known to be keen on the project but Lauda thought the 1984 target too early, preferring 1985. Clearly Lauda in a McLaren at Indianapolis would have been a big attraction for the team's sponsors, whose exposure in the American market had been diminished through Formula 1 losing its foothold there. While racing at Indianapolis interested Lauda, he had no desire to compete in the Indycar championship as a whole alongside Formula 1, as Mario Andretti had done in the 1970s, given the demanding transatlantic commuting that would have been required.

F1 v CART Challenge, June 1985
In response to repeated questions asked at every American Grand Prix as to whether Formula 1 or Indycars in the CART (Championship Auto Racing Teams) series were the faster, Bernie Ecclestone announced that he was planning a competition. There would be no championship, just a direct comparison between the European Formula 1 machinery and the American Indycars in a street race (possibly at Detroit) and on an oval course (possibly the Michigan Speedway). A huge prize fund of $10 million was suggested, with FOCA and CART providing $2.5 million each and the race organisers $5 million. Ecclestone suggested that this amount would attract the very best to the grid, pitting Lauda against Mario Andretti, Nelson Piquet against Danny Sullivan, and so on. Whether this was a genuine plan or just mischief-making by Formula 1's supremo is unknown, but either way nothing ever came of the proposal.

STATISTICS

Races contested (by venue)	
Nürburgring	22
Österreichring	19
Hockenheim	16
Monza	16
Brands Hatch	15
Zandvoort	13
Kyalami	13
Monte Carlo	13
Silverstone	10
Zolder	10
Buenos Aires	7
Jarama	7
Paul Ricard	7
Watkins Glen	7
Anderstorp	6
Dijon-Prenois	6
Imola	6
Interlagos	6
Jacarepaguá	6
Long Beach	6
Montréal	6
Salzburgring	5
Aspern	4
Detroit	4
Innsbruck	4
Mosport Park	4
Spa-Francorchamps	4
Tulln-Langenlebarn	4
Keimola	3
Mantorp Park	3
Norisring	3
Thruxton	3
Brno	2
Calder Park	2
Crystal Palace	2
Diepholz	2
Dopplerhütte	2
Estoril	2
Karlskoga	2
Mallory Park	2
Montjuïc	2
Munich-Neubiberg	2
Nivelles	2
Oulton Park	2
Rouen-les-Essarts	2
Vallelunga	2
Adelaide	1
Ahvenisto	1
Albi	1
Alpl	1
Bad-Mühllacken	1
Belgrade	1
Budapest	1
Clermont-Ferrand	1
Dallas	1
Dobratsch	1
Engelhartszell	1
Fuji	1
Kasten-Vichtenstein	1
Kinnekulle-Ring	1
Knutstorp	1
Koralpe	1
Las Vegas	1
Magny-Cours	1
Misano	1
Nogaro	1
Parma-Poggio	1
Pau	1
Riverside	1
Rossfeld	1
Sopron	1
Stainz	1
Tauplitz	1
Varabo	1
Walding	1
Zeltweg	1

Excludes testing venues

CAREER STATISTICS

The statistics in this table throw up some interesting observations. Retirements due to mechanical failure, very much a feature of the period during which Lauda raced, are by some distance the biggest single feature of his results. As a consequence, his win-to-start ratio across all classes of racing is somewhat skewed, whereas his win-to-finish ratio is in the top quartile.

His percentages of retirements from all the races he started due to collisions (1.3%) and accidents that were his own fault (3.6%) are extremely low, underlining the discipline of his driving and endorsing the view of his contemporaries that he was a driver with whom all were happy to go wheel-to-wheel, confident that he was not going to do anything stupid.

The high number of out-of-points finishes, while largely biased to the earlier days of his career, reflects his mechanical sympathy and his ability to get a car to the finish line at a time when such tenacity was less commonplace.

Result	Quantity	% of starts	% excluding mechanical retirements	% of all finishes
Wins	51	16.6%	22.9%	26.7%
2nd	34	11.0%	15.6%	18.3%
3rd	19	6.2%	8.5%	9.9%
4th	19	6.2%	8.5%	9.9%
5th	18	5.9%	8.1%	9.4%
6th	9	2.9%	15.1%	17.7%
Other placings	33	10.7%	16.6%	19.4%
Starts	308	(308)	(223)	(191)
Did not start	9	–	–	–
Did not qualify	1	–	–	–
Disqualified	3	–	–	–
Pole position*	30	9.7%	–	–
Fastest lap*	32	10.4%	–	–

RETIREMENTS

Mechanical failure	89	28.9%	–	–
Accident – own fault	11	3.6%	–	–
Accident – other reason	6	1.9%	–	–
Collision – own fault	4	1.3%	–	–
Collision – other's fault	9	2.9%	–	–

Excludes hillclimbs

DRIVER COMPARISONS

All of Lauda's Formula 1 team-mates were, or would become, Grand Prix winners; with the exception of Jean-Pierre Beltoise, all won more than one Grand Prix, and two — Nelson Piquet and Alain Prost — became multiple World Champions.

There were only two seasons in which Lauda completed more laps than any other driver, a fact that gives the lie to any allegations that much of his success was down to mechanical reliability. However, his mechanical sympathy was legendary, McLaren later revealing that it was so confident in the driving partnership he formed with Prost that the team stopped insuring their chassis. Throughout 1984 there were no wrecked McLarens and the team completed the entire season with just two race cars and one spare — unprecedented even then.

The number of laps Lauda completed in 1979 — the nadir of his career — was 40% fewer than his next-worst season and reflects the woeful reliability of the Brabham BT48.

In his qualifying performance compared with team-mates, Lauda was comprehensively outpaced by the experienced and super-quick Ronnie Peterson in 1972, although the gulf was magnified by the second-string equipment (notably engines and tyres) he was given. This imbalance continued for much of the 1973 season, flattering the qualifying performances of Beltoise and Clay Regazzoni, both of whom he generally outpaced in race conditions. Thereafter, until he was paired with Prost in 1984, he outdid his team-mates and the margin of his superiority over Regazzoni and John Watson in particular is notable. Lauda freely acknowledged that Prost was the quicker man in 1984 and 1985, so generally he spent practice working on a good race set-up, which is reflected in his qualifying positions in those years.

His statistics for his first three years with Ferrari are outstanding, with 18 Grand Prix pole positions in 1974–75. In 1976, before his accident at the Nürburgring, he was utterly dominant, his results being first, first, second, second, first, first, third, retired, first.

Overall, he led 1,590 of his 8,218 race laps in Formula 1, amounting to 4,393 miles out of the 23,314 miles that he competed. The important statistic, of course, is how many times he was in front on the last lap of a race.

Year	Races started (total in year)	Laps driven	Most laps completed (driver)	Laps led	Most laps led (driver)	Qualifying v team-mate	Average grid position	Team-mate's average grid position
1972	12	631	750 (Hulme)	0	320 (Stewart)	2:10 (Peterson)	22.0	11.8
1973	14 (15)	626	915 (Hulme)	17	387 (Peterson)	5:8 (Regazzoni)	11.8	9.5 (Regazzoni)
						4:10 (Beltoise)		10.2 (Beltoise)
1974	15	783	897 (Watson)	338	339 (Lauda)	13:2 (Regazzoni)	2.2	4.8
1975	14	733	733 (Lauda)	298	298 (Lauda)	14:0 (Regazzoni)	2.0	5.9
1976	14 (16)	770	907 (Scheckter)	341	351 (Hunt)	13:1 (Regazzoni)	2.8	6.2 (Regazzoni)
						1:0 (Reutemann)		7.0 (Reutemann)
1977	14 (17)	846	988 (Scheckter)	190	281 (Andretti)	7:7 (Reutemann)	6.1	6.6
1978	16	667	931 (Reutemann)	58	445 (Andretti)	11:5 (Watson)	4.7	7.8 (Watson)
						1:0 (Piquet)		14.0 (Piquet)
1979	15	358	914 (Villeneuve)	0	308 (Villeneuve)	8:7 (Piquet)	8.7	9.2
1982	14 (16)	764	872 (Alboreto)	128	298 (Prost)	10:4 (Watson)	8.1	11.3
1983	14 (15)	577	835 (Prost)	0	326 (Piquet)	11:3 (Watson)	15.5	18.2
1984	16	853	853 (Lauda & de Angelis)	168	345 (Prost)	1:15 (Prost)	7.7	3.0
1985	14 (16)	589	903 (Boutsen)	52	270 (Senna)	1:13 (Prost)	10.5	4.1

NIKI AND THE NÜRBURGRING

As a consequence of his career-defining accident, Lauda's name is inextricably linked with the Nürburgring. Largely because of his outspoken comments in 1976 about the dangers of the circuit in the weeks before his fiery accident there, the Austrian has a reputation in some quarters as a Nürburgring hater. Older-school journalists such as Denis Jenkinson in particular blamed him for the removal of the grand old *Nordschleife* from the Formula 1 calendar, much as they had vilified Jackie Stewart for the suppression of Spa as a Grand Prix venue. This is unfair: from the earliest days of his career right up until his 1976 accident, Lauda had competed at the Eifel circuit and was seen by many as a Nürburgring specialist. Examination of his performances there makes interesting reading.

Date	Race	Comment
7 Jul 1968	Six Hours, touring cars	Spent a week ahead of the race with co-driver Lambert Hofer, repeatedly lapping in a determined attempt to learn the 170 corners
29 Jun 1969	ADAC Hansa-Pokal, Formula Vee	Held on the *Sudschleife*, which was allegedly more dangerous than the *Nordschleife* by this time; finished fourth after duelling for the lead throughout
3 Aug 1969	Continental Preis, Formula Vee	Set the first-ever sub-10-minute lap for a Formula Vee car and finished a close second to Helmut Marko as they dominated the field
12 Oct 1969	Eifel Cup, Formula Vee	Back on the *Sudschleife*, qualified on the second row but trailed home lapped after mechanical problems
19 Apr 1970	ADAC 300 Km, Formula 3	Qualified 15th, tangled with his team-mate, got up to fifth place before inexplicably spinning off
12 Jul 1970	Six Hours, touring cars	Among the best of the BMW runners but retired before half distance with mechanical failure
18 Oct 1970	SCM-Rundstrecken-Rennen Aachen, Sports/GT	Held on the *Sudschleife*, qualified fourth and fished third in a strong field
2 May 1971	Eifelrennen, Formula 2	Qualified eighth and ran fourth for much of the race before being slowed by mechanical issues to finish sixth
11 Jul 1971	Six Hours, touring cars	Sharing with Günther Huber, qualified fourth and was the best BMW contender, finishing second in class and third overall
30 Jul 1972	German Grand Prix	Qualified 24th in the under-funded March and managed four laps, progressing to 18th before retiring with a split oil tank
25 May 1973	1,000km, sports prototypes/touring cars	Qualified in the top half of the grid ahead of several prototypes, but unable to start as the car was wrecked in practice by co-driver Brian Muir
23 Jun 1973	24 Hours, touring cars	Qualified second and won convincingly with co-driver Hans-Peter Joisten; set fastest lap and repeated the feat with exactly the same time on the following two laps
8 Jul 1973	Six Hours, touring cars	Took pole position and finished third after co-driver Hans-Peter Joisten crashed; made up a complete lap during his recovery drive and set fastest lap, a new touring car record
5 Aug 1973	German Grand Prix	Qualified fifth and was running fourth when tyre failure on the second lap pitched him into the barrier, breaking his wrist
19 May 1974	1,000km, sports prototypes/touring cars	Qualified 19th in a large field but failed to finish when co-driver Jochen Mass lost a wheel on lap 11
May 1974	Tyre testing, Formula 1	Became the first driver ever to (unofficially) lap the *Nordschleife* in under 7 minutes
14 Jul 1974	Six Hours, touring cars	Qualified second; took over the team's second car when co-driver Jochen Mass crashed out and made up for a 28-minute stop with a class win and second place overall
28 Jul 1974	German Grand Prix	Qualified on pole but retired after colliding with Jody Scheckter in an over-ambitious passing move on the first lap
3 Aug 1975	German Grand Prix	Qualified on pole with officially the first sub-7-minute lap of the *Nordschleife*, a record that still stands; dominated until a puncture forced him to pit; finished third
1 Aug 1976	German Grand Prix	Qualified second; after changing to dry tyres, he was running low down the order on lap 2 when he suffered his accident

Races contested (by marque)	
Ferrari	60
McLaren	59
March	43
Brabham	33
BMW	24
Kaimann	21
Porsche	20
BRM	16
McNamara	16
Ford	7
Austin Mini	5
Fiat	3
Opel	2
Chevrolet	1
Chevron	1
Mercedes-Benz	1
Nissan	1
Ralt	1

Races contested v team-mates	
Clay Regazzoni	59
John Watson	46
Alain Prost	31
Nelson Piquet	16
Carlos Reutemann	16
Jean-Pierre Beltoise	15
Ronnie Peterson	13
Peter Gethin	1

Awards	
1977	Alfred Neubauer Trophy
1977	BBC Sports Personality, World Sports Star of the Year
1984	Autosport International Racing Driver of the Year
1984	BRDC Gold Star
1993	Inducted into International Motorsport Hall of Fame (USA)
2013	Autosport Gregor Grant Award for Lifetime Achievement
2013	Formula One Management Bernie Ecclestone Award
2013	Inducted into Motor Sport Magazine Hall of Fame (UK)
2016	Laureus World Sports Award for Lifetime Achievement
2018	Grand Prix 247 Newsmaker of the Year Award
2018	FIA President's Award

ACKNOWLEDGEMENTS

My particular gratitude is due to Mark Hughes, Publishing Director at Evro Publishing, who has been a huge support in this undertaking and without whose guidance and advice it would have been a great deal harder to complete the project. Working with him on editing the manuscript was a delight.

John Watson spared me an entertaining hour of his time to discuss the Foreword and share his anecdotes. Some of these are unfortunately unprintable, but his candour is much appreciated and his first-person account of Niki's personal qualities is illuminating.

Doug Nye has been an enthusiastic supporter of my project from the start, and I am proud that he has contributed the Preface to this book. His advice — 'get it done, but don't **** it up!' — has been taken to heart.

It was humbling to receive the contribution of Kurt Bergmann, Niki's first mentor and influential supporter, and with the resonance of his words this has been placed as an Afterword to provide a fitting final thought on his long-time friend.

Special thanks go to Richard Parsons, both for his work on the layout and design of the book and for his restoration work on some very old and sometimes poor-quality photographs. Thanks also to Lucy Saltinstall for her skills in cleaning up some rather grainy black-and-white images.

I am especially grateful to Nick Forsythe, who alerted me to the existence of some of the most obscure races and for his help in locating photographs of them. I am also indebted to Wolfgang Thomas, who has also been a huge help with local research in Austria and tracking down rare magazine reports.

It is difficult to thank everyone enough, but my sincere appreciation is due to the following people who have helped me immensely over the past nine years in finding the answers to some of the more obscure queries and in sharing contacts and archives for text and images:

Kathy Ager; Simone Amaduzzi; Veit Arenz; Torgny Arvidsson; Augusto Baldoni; Ray Bell; Erich Breinsberg; Allen Brown; Michael Catsch (deceased); Gary Critcher; Ralph Colmar; Alan Cox; Dr Stefan Culen: Frank de Jong (deceased); Arjan de Roos; Pierre Devillers; André Dietzel; Mike Doodson; Marie Esplund-Lynn; Jutta Fausel; Michael Ferner; Michael Garbacz; Timo Gerlitz; Stephan Gremler; Michael Gruber; Bengt-Åce Gustavsson; Peter Hoffmann; Bengt Åson Holm; Karl Holzinger; Peter Houston; John Humphries; Esa Illoinen; Yuka Inamura; Roland Jakobs; Bernhard Kadow; Tomas Karlsson; Franz Köhler; Franz Klinger; Andreas Kolbabek; Paul Kooyman; Peter Krackowizer; Martin Krejci; Peter Láng; Tapani Lehtinen; Jürgen Lehmler; Vesa Liukkonen; Roberto Manfredini; Josef Mayrhofer; Erle Minhinnick; Peter Morley; Tim Murray; Aaron Noonan; Peter Nygaard; Frank Michael Orthey; Sonia Paitoni; David Pearson; Alberto Piccinini; Romano Poli; Juke Puurunen; Gavina Ruzittu; Julian Roberts; Rob Ryder; Christian Sandler; Elke Santin; Thomas Schmidt; Michael Scott; Rob Semmeling; Lars-Göran Sjöberg; Richard and Darren Smith; Alfons Stockinger; Art Tidesco; Jens Torner; Henk Vasmel; Dirk van Hooydonk; Bruno von Rotz; Bill Wagenblatt; Jerry Wallwork; Peter Windsor; John Winfield; Tim Wright; Helmut Zwickl.

I am also grateful to many pseudonymous members of *Autosport*'s 'The Nostalgia Forum' and the Ten Tenths Motorsport Forum whose true identities remain unknown to me. It is fair to say that without 'TNF' this book would not have happened, as this community of enthusiasts and historians has been fundamental to sourcing many of the contacts who have helped to inform the text and images. They also provided me with the stimulus and encouragement to finish it.

PHOTOGRAPH CREDITS

Actualfoto P58 T, P69, P79, P94 T, P99, P190, P224.
Alamy / Deniz Calagan P358 B.
Alpina Archive P89 T, P116 B, P122, P126 T, P126 B, P127 B, Back Cover TM.
AN1 Images / Graeme Neander P327 B.
APA Picturedesk.com / Gert Eggenberger P352 T.
APA Picturedesk.com / Franz Neumayr P353 T.
Archiv Ferdinand Lanner P17 TL.
Archiv Historische Formel-Vau Europa e.V. P24 T, P25, P28 B, P29 T, P30 T, P30 B, P33 B, P34 B, P36 C, P39 T, P41.
Archiv Michael Gruber P44B, P45 T, P52 TL.
Archiv Peter Láng P32 T.
Archiv Prof. Dr. Helmut Krackowizer P275 T.
Veit Arenz P29 B, P39 B.
Autosprint P155 T, P164, P187 T, P189 B, P208 B, P209 M, P209 B, P213 B, P214 T, P214 B.
Augusto Baldoni P137 M.
Kurt Bergmann P36 B, P61.
Staffan Bergrann P102 T.
BMW Motorsport P130 T.
Borremans Collection / Thierry Borremans P120 T.
CTK Photo / Jiri Krulis P46 B.
Dr Stefan Culer P14 T, P16 B, P21 B.
Daimler AG P314 T, P355 B.
Patrick Dasse P44 T.
Pierre Devillers P52 T.
Ennstal Classic GmbH P348 B, P349 B.
Fastlane.com P259 BL.
Jutta Fausel P64 B, P65, P66 T, P66 B, P67, P73, P78, P83, P86 T, P87, P93, P95, P97 T, P105, P106 T, Back Cover TL.
Raoul Fornezza P197.
Getty Images / Paul-Henri Cahier P185, P186, P287 B, P326.
Getty Images / Gérard Fouet P275 B.
Getty Images / Mark Thompson P354 T.
Getty Images / Stephan Woldron P362.
Getty Images / Hoch Zwei P262.
Giorgio Nada Editore / Franco Villani P241 B.
Grandprixphoto.com / Peter Nygaard P212, P236 B, P283, P332, P359 B.
Luc Ghys Back Cover TR, Back Cover BR.
Historic Motor Prints / Bill Wagenblatt P100, P131, P201 T.
Bengt-Åson Holm P37.

Karl Holzinger P376.
Peter Hoffmann P187 B.
Peter Houston P345 T, P345 B.
Inkart / Fabio van der Sande P350 B.
IPA / Richard Kelley Front Cover.
Ferdi Kräling Motorsport P51, P56, P104, P109 T, P151, P156, P188, P198, P260.
Marchives P110 B.
McKlein Photographic P21 T, P28 T, P36 T, P48 B, P50 B, P64 T, P68 B, P72, P118 B, P125, P174, P249 B, P261, P265 T, P265 B, P266, P267, P268, P269 B, P325, P337, P339 B.
Motoprint.co.za P110 T, P142 B, P307, P343.
Motorsport Images P57 T, P84, P85, P90 B, P103, P107, P115, P118 T, P128, P132, P202 T, P222, P224 T, P230, P254 B, P258, P271, P273, P300 B, P312, P327, P344, P347 B, P352 B.
Motorsport Images / Ercole Colombo P7, P10, P130 B, P163 B, P216, P257, P269 T, P278, P279 B, P310, P317 B.
Motorsport Images / Glenn Dunbar P361 T.
Motorsport Images / Gareth Harford P361 B.
Motorsport Images / LAT P63, P70, P74, P76, P81 T, P82, P92, P94 B, P98 T, P102 B, P106 B, P113 B, P114, P119, P121, P124 T, P124 B, P127 T, P129, P135, P140 B, P141, P142 T, P143, P146, P147 B, P148, P149, P157 T, P158 T, P158 B, P159, P166, P167, P168, P169, P171, P177 B, P179, P181 B, P189 T, P191 B, P192, P193 T, P193 B, P196, P202 B, P203, P205, P206, P207 T, P209 T, P210, P211 T, P215 T, P217 T, P218, P220, P227, P231, P233, P234 B, P237, P238, P243, P244, P251 T, P255, P259 BR, P264 B, P270, P277, P280, P282, P294, P300 T, P303 B, P311, P313, P315 B, P319, P320 T, P322, P324, P339 T, P342, P351 T.
Motorsport Images / Luca Martini P359 T.
Motorsport Images / David Phipps P81 B, P86 B, P108, P109 B, P123, P133 T, P133 B, P140 T, P144, P145 B, P150, P153, P154, P155 B, P161, P162, P163 T, P165, P170, P177 T, P178, P182, P183 T, P184, P191 T, P199, P200, P201 B, P207 B, P219 B, P228 T, P228 B, P229, P235, P236 T, P239, P240 B, P245, P246, P250, P251 B, P252, P256, P289.
Motorsport Images / Rainer W Schlegelmilch P71, P88, P89 B, P96, P98 B, P120 B, P145 T, P147 T, P152, P183 B, P195,

P215 B, P259 T, P281, P285, P301, P303 T, P323.
Motorsport Images / Mirko Stange P358 T.
Motorsport Images / Sutton Images P8, P295, P296 T, P297, P304, P306, P314 B, P316, P320 B, P321, P335 T, P335 B, P336, P351 B.
Motorsportarchiv.at P34 T, P43 T, P46 T, P136 T, P217 B.
Doug Nye P 11.
Oggi / RCS P211 B.
Örebro Stadsarkivs Bildarkiv P53, P54.
Photo-4 s.r.l. P288, P298, P302, P305, P317 T, P331, P333 T, P333 B, P334, P340, P341, P353 B, P356 T, P356 B, P357 B.
Porsche Archive P50 T, P296 B, P299 T, P315 T.
Powerslide / Carl Imber P111.
PressArt / Josef Mayrhofer P59 T, P75 T, P116 T.
ProSports Visuals / Daniele Amaduzzi P173 T, P221, P232, P233 T, P279 T, P284, P286, P290, P291.
Racefoto / Bengt-Åce Gustavsson P101.
Rallye Racing P60, P253 B.
Revs Institute P293, P299 B, P318.
Julian Roberts P263.
Lindsay Ross P328.
Alois Rottensteiner P52 M, P52 B, P57 B.
Sandlerchristian@aon.at / Christian Sandler P14 B, P19 B, P20 T, P20 B, P23 B, P24 B, P59 B, P68 T, P134 T, P134 B, P136 M, P139 T, P139 B, P143 B, P175, P176, P194 T, P194 B.
Scuderia Naftalin / Holger Eklund P47, P48 T.
Shutterstock / ANL / Neville Marriner P11.
Lars-Göran Sjöberg P75 B.
Smugmug P254 T.
Supercharged Collection / Gary Critcher P91.
Technische Museum Wien / Arthur Fenzlau P19 T, P22, P23 T, P27, P32 B, P33 T, P77 T, P97 B, P117.
Technische Museum Wien / Erwin Jellinek P18 T, P38.
Jean-Marc Teissèdre P55 B.
The Grand Prix Library / Geoff Goddard P113 T.
Edwin Van Nes P354 B.
VW Motorsport P35 T.
Peter Windsor P309.

PHOTOGRAPH CREDITS **371**

BIBLIOGRAPHY

PERIODICALS

Australian Motor Racing + GT
Austro Classic
Austro Motor
Autocar
Autodiva
Auto Hebdo
Automobile Historique
Automobil-Revue Zeitungen
Automobilsport
Automundo
Auto Motor und Sport
Autopista
Auto Revue
Autosport
Autosprint
Autoweek
Bilsport
Chequered Flag
Formel V Europa Express
Formel Vau Sport
Grand Prix International
Historic Racing
Illustrerad Motor Sport
Kronen Zeitung
Magyar Hirlip
Motor Sport
Motoring News
Motorsport Aktuell
Oggi
Parabrisas Corsa
Powerslide
Racing Car News
Rallye Racing
Road & Track
Rombo
Speedworld International
Sport Auto (France)
Sport Auto (Germany)
Turbo
Tschechoslowakische Motor-Revue
Vauhdin Maailma
Vee Line
Wheels
Wiener Zeitung

ANNUALS

Autocourse 1971–85
Automobile Year 1971–85
John Player Motorsport Yearbook 1972–76
Marlboro Motorsport Yearbook 1977–78
Motor Racing Year 1971–78
Race Report/Renn Report 1968–70

BOOKS

Peter Biro & George Levy, *F1 Mavericks* (Quarto Publishing, 2019)
Erich Breinsberg, *Der Niki, der Keke und das Genie aus der Vorstadt* (Egoth Sport, 2009)
Tanja Chraust, *Die Internationalen Auto und Motorraden auf dem Innsbrucker Flughafen* (UW Innsbruck, 2007)
Chris Ellard, *The Forgotten Races* (W3 Publications, 2004)
Gerald Donaldson, *The Grand Prix of Canada* (Avon Books, 1984)
Jürg Dubler, *Les Années Fabuleuses de la Formule 3 1964–1970* (Éditions du Palmier, 2014)
Di Athos Evangelisti & Gino Rancati, *Ferrari Mondiale Vincitori* (Fratelli Fabbri Editori, 1975)
Paul Fearnley, *Hunt vs. Lauda* (David Bull, 2013)
Heinz Hemmer & others, *Der Österreichring: Biographie Einer Rennstrecke* (Private, 1989)
Alan Henry, *Brabham: The Grand Prix Cars* (Hazelton, 1985)
Alan Henry, *Ferrari: The Grand Prix Cars* (Hazelton, 1984)
Alan Henry, *Flat-12: The Racing Career of Ferrari's 3-Litre Grand Prix & Sports Cars* (MRP, 1981)
Alan Henry, *March: The Grand Prix & Indy Cars* (Hazelton, 1989)
Alan Henry, *Niki Lauda: Kimberley's Racing Driver Profile* (Lavenham Press, 1986)
Alan Henry, *Niki Lauda: Autocourse Driver Profile* (Hazelton, 1989)
Alan Henry, *Four Seasons at Ferrari* (Breedon Books, 2002)
Peter Higham, *Formula One Car by Car 1980–89* (Evro, 2018)
Graham Howard & Stewart Wilson, *The Official 50-Race History of the Australian Grand Prix* (R&T Publishing, 1986)
Thomas Kessler, Frank Orthey & Lothar Panten, *Formel Vau und Super Vau* (VIEW, 2017)
Mike Lang, *Grand Prix Volumes 2, 3 & 4* (Haynes, 1982–92)
Peter Lanz, *Niki Lauda: Der Weg Zum Triumph* (Ullstein Sachbuch, 1983)
Niki Lauda, *Formula One* (Guild, 1977)
Niki Lauda, *For The Record* (William Kimber, 1978)
Niki Lauda, *Second Time Around* (William Kimber, 1984)
Niki Lauda, *To Hell And Back* (Stanley Paul, 1986)
Hartmut Lehbrink, *Niki Lauda: Von Aussen Nach Innen* (Delius Klassang Verlag, 2014)
Tapani Lehtinen, *Finnish Formula History: From Midgets to Modern Times 1947–1989* (Scuderia Naftalin, 2013)
Mike Lawrence, *March: The Rise & Fall of a Motor Racing Legend* (MRP, 2002)
Pierre Menard & Jacques Vassal, *Niki Lauda: The Rebel* (Chronosports, 2004)
Florian T. Mrazek, *Legende Salzburgring: Im Windschatten der Geschichte* (Verlag Anton Pustet, 2014)
Doug Nye, *The Great Racing Drivers* (Hamlyn, 1977)
Doug Nye, *Autocourse History of the Grand Prix Car 1966–1985* (Hazelton, 1986)
Doug Nye, *McLaren: The Grand Prix, Can-Am & Indy Cars* (Hazelton, 1988)
Ann O'Brien (ed), *The Heavily Censored History of Hesketh Racing* (Great British Media, 1974)
Chas Parker, *Motor Racing at Brands Hatch in the Seventies* (Veloce, 2004)
Martin Pfunder, *Von Semmering Zum Grand Prix – Der Automobilsport in Österreich* (Boehlau Verlag, 2003)
Martin Pfunder, *Die Formel 1 in Österreich* (Boehlau Verlag, 2014)
Alois Rottensteiner & Klaus Neuberger, *Die Niki Lauda Story* (Arlo Verlagsges, 1984)
Peter Schroeder, *McNamara Racing: Der Weg von Lenggries Nach Indianapolis* (VIEW, 2015)
Rob Semmeling, *Rennen! Races! Vitesse!* (OLP, 2014)
Rob Semmeling & Burkhard Kohr, *The Other Green Hell* (Shaker Media, 2010)
Paul Sheldon, *Milestones Behind The Marques* (David & Charles, 1976)
Paul Sheldon & Duncan Rabagliati, *A Record of Grand Prix & Voiturette Racing, Volumes 9, 10, 11 & 12* (St Leonard's Press, 1995)
Hans Tanner with Doug Nye, *Ferrari* (Haynes, 1979)
Jeremy Walton, *Capri: The Development & Competition History of Ford's European GT Car* (Foulis, 1981)
Helmut Zwickl, *Niki Lauda: Reportage Einer Karriere* (Uberreuter, 1975)
Helmut Zwickl & Michael Glöckner, *Ennstal Classic: Autofahren Im Letzten Paradies* (Edition Glöckner & Zwickl, 1996)

INDEX

A1-Ring 350, 355
Abarth 16, 67, 68, 164
Adelaide
　Australian Grand Prix
　　1985 328, 343–345, 346
Agnelli, Gianni 179, 329
Ahrens, Kurt 36
Ahvenisto 47, 363
Air Berlin 11, 360
Akersloot, Han 125, 126
Alesi, Jean 357
Alfa Romeo 24, 51, 58, 59, 60, 86, 103, 117, 136, 234, 241, 247, 265, 271, 278, 281, 283, 286, 288, 289, 291, 292, 293, 295, 307, 325, 333, 334, 336, 337
　GTA 19, 21
　T177 241, 247, 256–257
　T179 271
　183T 295
　184T 313, 320
　184TB 339
　T33/3 36, 49
Alfa Romeo engines 236, 363
　Flat 12 217–218, 225, 234, 237, 244, 245
　V12 247, 248, 249, 250, 255, 257, 262, 265, 266, 267, 270
　Turbo V8 292
Albi 77–78, 363
Alboreto, Michele 277, 280, 290, 291, 295, 296, 298, 303, 310, 313, 316, 320, 321, 323, 324, 325, 326, 327, 331, 335, 336, 339, 341, 368
Alpina 51, 71, 72, 80, 89, 104, 111, 112, 115, 116, 117, 118, 119, 120–121, 122, 125, 126, 128, 129, 359, 363
Alpl (hillclimb) 16–17
Amira Air 11, 360
Amon, Chris 97, 99, 100, 102, 111, 130, 138, 190–191, 193
Andersson, Conny 48
Anderstorp
　Swedish Grand Prix
　　1973 123–124
　　1974 148
　　1975 169–171
　　1976 190–191, 208
　　1977 214, 215
　　1978 234, 235–236
Andretti, Mario 165, 174, 191, 193, 203, 208, 209, 211, 216, 217, 219, 220, 222, 223, 227, 229, 232, 233, 235, 236, 237, 238, 239, 242, 244–245, 247, 252, 255, 256, 264, 271, 313, 346, 366, 368
Argentine Grand Prix
　(Buenos Aires)
　1972 81–82
　1973 113
　1974 139–140
　1975 161
　1977 205
　1978 227
　1979 249–250
Arnoux, René 252, 262, 264, 266, 267, 269, 271, 278, 281, 283, 288, 289, 306, 313, 316, 318, 320, 325, 331, 338
Arundell, Peter 32
Arrows 230, 235, 242, 255, 299, 300, 334, 337, 338, 340
　FA1 234
　A1 257, 259
　A6 296, 305
　A7 323
　A8 335
Ascari, Alberto 9, 187, 218
Ashley, Ian 181
Aspern 22–23, 24, 27–28, 61, 117
ATS (Auto Technisches Spezialzubehör) 215, 230, 234, 257, 262, 282, 284, 287, 292, 301, 306, 313
　HS1 234
　D5 281

Audetto, Daniele 180, 182, 186, 197, 201, 203, 204
Australian Grand Prix (Adelaide) 1985 343–344, 345, 346
Austrian Airlines 8, 11, 360
Austrian Grand Prix (Österreichring)
　1971 66, 73–75
　1972 102–103
　1973 132
　1974 153–154
　1975 175–176
　1976 196–197
　1977 218–219
　1978 240, 242
　1979 267
　1981 274
　1982 288
　1983 302–303, 307
　1984 321–322
　1985 338–340
Austro 21, 22, 24, 27, 28, 29, 30, 31, 33, 34, 39, 40, 41

Bad Mühllacken (hillclimb) 15
Baldi, Mauro 293, 315, 316, 325
Baldwin, Dave 213
Balestre, Jean-Marie 260, 261
Balocco (test track) 225, 234, 241
Barnard, John 7, 10, 274, 285, 290, 299, 300, 319, 330, 338, 360, 366
Basche, Dieter 41
Bathurst — see 'Mount Panorama'
Baumgärtner, Fritz 14, 15, 16, 17, 32
Beatrice Lola — see 'Lola'
Belgian Grand Prix
　1972 (Nivelles) 92
　1973 (Zolder) 10, 121–122, 364
　1974 (Nivelles) 145–146
　1975 (Zolder) 168–169
　1976 (Zolder) 186–188
　1977 (Zolder) 212–213, 214
　1978 (Zolder) 232–233
　1979 (Zolder) 256–257
　1982 (Zolder) 280–281, 290
　1983 (Spa-Francorchamps) 297–298
　1984 (Zolder) 311–312
　1985 (Spa-Francorchamps) 342
Belgrade 28–29
Bell, Derek 66
Bellof, Stefan 316, 332, 337, 338
Belsø, Tom 90
Beltoise, Jean-Pierre 10, 65, 67, 87, 113, 114, 115, 119, 133, 135, 136, 363, 368
Benz 120 HP 346, 355
Berger, Gerhard 335, 338, 357, 359
Bergmann, Kurt 20, 21, 22, 25, 26, 27, 31, 32, 33, 35, 36, 37, 41, 61, 175, 363
Bergner, Paul 51
Bertolini, Enrico 364
Beuttler, Mike 62, 64, 70, 73, 79, 91, 92, 94–95, 98, 99, 103, 109, 363
Birrell, Gerry 54, 64, 76, 79, 85, 87, 88, 90, 91
BMW 16, 24, 28, 29, 32, 60, 80, 89, 115, 136, 137, 156, 256, 261, 263, 346, 347, 356, 363, 365, 366
　1602 51
　2002 23, 40, 89
　Ti 51, 117, 134–135
　2800 CS 71, 72, 89, 103–104
　3.0 CSL 115–117, 118–121, 122, 124–126, 127–128, 129–131, 143–144, 147, 359, 364, 365
　320i Turbo 263
　635 CSi 365
　M1 253, 256, 258, 260, 261, 270, 356, 359, 365, 366
　Procar 7, 253, 256, 257–258, 260–261, 263, 264–265, 266, 268, 269–270, 356, 359, 365
　M3 (E30) 347
　M5 (E28) 347
　Z4 M Coupé GT

BMW (engines) 103, 110
　Four-cylinder turbo 262, 281, 292, 304
Boeing 360
　767 8, 11
Boesel, Raul 278
Böhler, Fritz 41
Bonnier, Joakim 53, 60
Bonnin, Max 52
Bourgoignie, Claude 120
Boutsen, Thierry 300, 305, 323, 334, 335, 337, 340
Bovensiepen, Burkard 80, 89, 125, 126
Brabham 6, 11, 12, 45, 50, 51, 54, 55, 56, 63, 65, 66, 69, 71, 76, 78, 82, 83, 84, 86, 87, 88, 93, 97, 99, 101, 106, 107, 108, 113, 114, 119, 127, 140, 141, 143, 154, 155, 157, 160, 161, 168, 171, 175, 176, 199, 202, 205, 206, 210, 216, 217, 221, 222, 223, 224–225, 226–247, 248–273, 280, 281, 283, 284, 285, 287, 288, 289, 292, 293, 294, 305, 307, 310, 311, 313, 317, 319, 320, 321, 322, 324, 325, 329, 330, 332, 334, 337, 340, 341, 343, 345, 365
　BT18 20
　BT28 46, 48, 52
　BT30 65
　BT36 78, 83
　BT37 121
　BT38 95
　BT44 157, 159
　BT44B 160
　BT45B 217, 219, 224
　BT45C 224, 225, 227–229, 230
　BT46 224, 225, 229–230, 231–240, 242–246, 248, 250
　BT46B (fan car) 234, 235–236, 237, 239, 255
　BT46C 239, 240, 242
　BT48 247, 248–259, 261–266, 267, 268–269, 270–272, 368
　BT49 270, 272–273
　BT50 281
　BT52 282–283, 291
　BT53 313, 323
　BT54 333, 335, 339
　BT55 345
Brambilla, Ernesto 'Tino' 68
Brambilla, Vittorio 63, 65, 165, 168, 169, 174, 176, 188, 199, 200, 201, 206, 211, 216, 217, 236–237, 241, 244
Brands Hatch 51–52, 53, 54, 56–57, 76, 90–91, 98–99, 117, 201, 234, 249, 330, 363, 365
　British Grand Prix
　　1970 51
　　1972 98–99
　　1974 152–153
　　1976 192–194, 208
　　1978 237, 238
　　1982 285–286, 291
　　1984 319–320
　European Grand Prix
　　1983 305–306
　　1985 342
　Race of Champions
　　1973 115
　　1974 141–142, 349
　　1976 182–184
　　1979 254–255
Braun, Rainer 41
Brawn, Ross 8
Brazilian Grand Prix
　1973 (Interlagos) 113–114
　1974 (Interlagos) 140–141
　1975 (Interlagos) 162
　1976 (Interlagos) 181
　1977 (Interlagos) 205–206
　1978 (Jacarepaguá) 227–229
　1979 (Interlagos) 250–251
　1982 (Jacarepaguá) 278, 281
　1983 (Jacarepaguá) 293, 302
　1984 (Jacarepaguá) 308, 309–310
　1985 (Jacarepaguá) 331
Breinsberg, Erich 25, 26, 27, 28, 30, 31, 32, 33, 36, 37, 38, 39
Breyer, Günther 33
Bricarello, Guido 338

British Grand Prix
　1970 (Brands Hatch) 51
　1972 (Brands Hatch) 98–99
　1973 (Silverstone) 10, 128–129, 131
　1974 (Brands Hatch) 152–153
　1975 (Silverstone) 172–174
　1976 (Brands Hatch) 192–194, 208
　1977 (Silverstone) 216
　1978 (Brands Hatch) 237, 238
　1979 (Silverstone) 263–264, 365
　1981 (Silverstone) 274
　1982 (Brands Hatch) 285–286, 291
　1983 (Silverstone) 300–301, 307
　1984 (Brands Hatch) 319–320
　1985 (Silverstone) 336–337
BRM (British Racing Motors) 6, 10, 12, 73, 77, 81, 96, 103, 111, 112, 117, 123, 131, 135, 136, 142, 171, 206, 258, 364, 366
　P160B 111
　P160C 113–114
　P160D 114–115, 117–118
　P160E 117, 119, 121–123, 126–127, 128–129, 130–135
　P180 111, 357
BRM (engines)
　V12 112, 113, 123, 132, 137, 181
Brno 12, 46, 60, 89, 363
Brodner, Berndt 21, 23, 25
Bross, Helmut 29
Broström, Per-Olov 39
Brundle, Martin 309, 334, 335
Budapest 29
Buenos Aires 364
　Argentine Grand Prix
　　1972 81–82
　　1973 113
　　1974 139–140
　　1975 161
　　1977 205
　　1978 227
　　1979 249–250
Bühler, Lazi 36
Bulow, Wolfgang 34
Burton, John 67
Bussek, Walter 21

Caesar's Palace Grand Prix (Las Vegas)
　1981 274
　1982 7, 290–291
Calder Park 327–329
Cambiaghi, Roberto 190
Canadian Grand Prix
　1971 (Mosport) 363
　1972 (Mosport) 108
　1973 (Mosport) 133–134, 137
　1974 (Mosport) 156–157
　1976 (Mosport) 197, 200–201, 202
　1977 (Mosport) 223
　1978 (Montréal) 245–246
　1979 (Montréal) 11, 272
　1982 (Montréal) 283–284
　1983 (Montréal) 300, 307
　1984 (Montréal) 316–317, 329
　1985 (Montréal) 334
Cannon, John 78–79, 95
Catalunya 351
Cecotto, Johnny 365
Cevert, François 85, 91, 103, 122, 124, 134, 135
Chaparral 234
　2K 366
Charlton, Dave 99
Cheever, Eddie 281, 283, 306, 307, 325
Chevrolet Camaro Z28 246–247, 366
Chevron 52, 56, 93, 110, 111
　B15 45, 52
　B17 46
　B19 67, 68
Chiti, Carlo 241
Clark, Jim 9, 350
Clermont-Ferrand
　French Grand Prix
　　1972 96
Colombo, Alberto 234
Coombs, John 62

Cosworth engines 111
　DFV 73, 82, 100, 103, 106, 108, 140, 186, 220, 237, 270, 273, 274, 276, 278, 284, 286, 291, 292, 293, 295, 296, 297, 363
　DFY 295, 300, 301, 302, 303, 307
　FVA 63
Coulon, Jacques 366
Craft, Chris 59, 60, 103, 364
Croker, Terry 59
Croft 51, 363
Crystal Palace 68–69, 91, 92
Culen, Stefan 16
Cuoghi, Ermanno 'Mannu' 11, 145, 223

Dal Bo, Patrick 78
Dallas Grand Prix
　1984 318–319
Daly, Derek 286, 291
Danner, Christian 354, 356
Dayan, Denis 45
de Adamich, Andrea 87, 99, 108, 121–122
de Angelis, Elio 281, 282, 288, 295, 299, 306, 312, 313, 315, 316, 317, 318, 321, 324, 325, 326, 331, 332, 336, 342, 343, 368
de Cadenet, Alain 49, 58
de Cesaris, Andrea 278, 280, 281, 286, 288, 289, 291, 295, 307, 319, 320
della Casa, Ermanno 221
der Clerk, Etienne 29
Dennis, Ron 6, 7, 10, 256, 274, 296, 299, 300, 307, 317, 325, 329, 338, 339, 343, 351, 365
Depailler, Patrick 65, 88, 91, 96, 161, 169, 174, 182, 185, 188, 191, 193, 199, 217, 227, 230, 232, 242, 257, 258, 259
Derflinger, Heinz 136
Detroit Grand Prix
　1982 282–283, 291
　1983 298–299
　1984 317–318
　1985 334–335
Dieden, Gustaf 54
Diepholz 53, 61, 129–131, 363, 364
Dietrich, Christian 31, 37
Dijon-Prenois 148, 260, 263, 264, 265
　French Grand Prix
　　1974 149–150, 365
　　1977 215–216
　　1979 261–263
　　1984 314–315, 329
　Swiss Grand Prix
　　1982 289
Dobratsch (hillclimb) 16
Dolhem, José 149
Donington Park 224, 275, 365
Donington Collection 365
Donohue, Mark 176
Doodson, Mike 309
Dopplerhütte (hillclimb) 25
Draxler, Peter 14
Dubler, Jürg 46, 56, 64
Ducarouge, Gérard 213
Dufferer, Patrick 111
Dungl, Willi 160, 185, 197, 275, 276, 288, 323
Dunlop 37, 71, 202, 328
Dutch Grand Prix (Zandvoort)
　1973 130–131
　1974 148–149
　1975 171–172
　1976 197
　1977 220–221
　1978 242–243
　1978 268–269
　1982 284
　1983 303–304
　1984 322–323
　1985 10, 340–341, 344

Ecclestone, Bernie 6, 10, 11, 12, 202, 223, 236, 259, 261, 268, 270, 272, 318, 345, 366
Edwards, Guy 196

Elford, Vic 50, 67, 68, 366
Engelhartszell (hillclimb) 17
Enna-Pergusa 75, 364
Ennstal Classic
　1995 348–349
　1996 349–350
　2001 353
Ensign 191, 204, 213, 217, 222
　N176 193
　N177 219
Ertl, Harald 39, 47, 196
Estoril
　Portuguese Grand Prix
　　1984 326–327
　　1985 331–332
European Grand Prix
　1983 (Brands Hatch) 305–306
　1984 (Nürburgring) 325–326
　1985 (Brands Hatch) 342, 365
Evans, Bob 171
Eyckmans, Wim 350

Fabi, Teo 288, 310, 323, 324, 337, 340, 343
Fangio, Juan Manuel 9, 183, 313, 324, 356
Ferrari, Enzo 6, 10, 12, 123, 129, 132, 137, 138, 139, 158, 164, 187, 189–190, 199, 203, 204, 208, 214, 272, 350
Ferrari, Piero — see 'Lardi, Piero'
Ferrari 6, 9, 10, 11, 12, 30, 58, 66, 82, 87, 99, 103, 123, 127, 128, 131, 134, 135, 137, 138–159, 160–179, 180–203, 204–223, 224, 225, 226, 227, 228, 229, 231, 232, 234, 238, 244, 245, 247, 250, 255, 256, 258, 262, 264, 266, 267, 271, 272, 277, 279, 283, 284, 285, 286, 288, 292, 293, 304, 306, 307, 310, 311, 313, 316, 318, 319, 321, 324, 325, 327, 329, 331, 335, 336, 338, 341, 349, 353, 360, 361, 365, 366, 368
　126C4 323
　156/85 339
　308 GT4 187
　308 GTB 187, 214
　　308 GTB4 LM 187
　312B3 113
　312B3 123, 137, 138, 139–143, 144–150, 152–159, 161–163, 164, 349–350
　312P 366
　312PB 110, 120, 354
　　312PB-74 137
　312T 158, 160, 162–179, 180, 181, 182, 186, 187, 209, 362
　312T2 11, 12, 179, 180, 181–203, 204–223, 224, 357, 364
　312T3 233, 238, 242, 243, 352
　312T4 259, 271
　'312T6' 208
　365 GTB4 (Daytona) 111
　500 Testa Rossa 348, 349, 350
　512 59;
　　512S 58
　F1 87/88C 357
Ferrari (engines)
　Flat-12 (3-litre) 137, 140, 143, 160, 168, 213, 352
Fiat 137, 139, 179, 187, 208, 329
　127 211
　131 Mirafiori 190
　508 Balilla Coppa d'Oro 214
　Uno Turbo 338
Fillon, Pierre 362
Fiorano (test track) 132, 137, 158, 160, 164, 179, 180, 185, 187, 197, 206, 208, 209, 211, 213, 214, 222, 225
Fittipaldi 194, 206, 246, 248, 281
　F5 213
Fittipaldi, Emerson 76, 78, 90–91, 92, 93, 96, 111, 119, 122, 123, 130, 140, 141, 146, 149, 150, 153, 156, 157, 159, 161, 162, 164, 165, 168, 174, 176, 177, 179, 203, 206, 213, 220, 246, 257, 313
Fittipaldi, Wilson 64, 67, 76, 83, 95, 113, 127, 364

INDEX **373**

Fitzpatrick, John 103
Flammini, Maurizio 185
Flohr, Wolfgang-Peter 347
Florini, Gaetano 187
FlyNiki 11, 360
Follmer, George 130
Ford 11, 80, 103, 136, 137, 160, 247, 360, 366
Capri 103, 115, 117, 119, 125, 126, 128, 366
RS 2600 71, 72, 120, 136
RS 3100 143–144, 146–147, 150–152, 156, 364
3000E 90–91
Escort 33, 164
RS 1600 152
XR3 309
Ford engines 42
BDA 83, 84, 87, 96
BDF 107, 108
Forghieri, Mauro 6, 137, 138, 148, 155, 158, 160, 162, 164, 180, 190, 194, 201, 203, 208, 209, 223
Forster, Martin 17
French Grand Prix
1972 (Clermont-Ferrand) 96
1973 (Paul Ricard) 126–127
1974 (Dijon-Prenois) 149–150, 365
1975 (Paul Ricard) 172
1976 (Paul Ricard) 191–192
1977 (Dijon-Prenois) 215–216
1978 (Paul Ricard) 236–237
1979 (Dijon-Prenois) 261–263
1982 (Paul Ricard) 286–287
1983 (Paul Ricard) 295
1984 (Dijon-Prenois) 314–315, 329
1985 (Paul Ricard) 335–336
Fritzinger, Klaus 126
Fuji 6
Japanese Grand Prix
1976 202–203
1977 223
Furtmayr, Ernst 23, 24, 25

Galli, Nanni 36, 92, 363
Ganley, Howden 70, 124, 130, 131, 134
Gartlan, Malcolm 115, 364
German Grand Prix
1969 (Nürburgring) 34, 41
1972 (Nürburgring) 100
1973 (Nürburgring) 10, 131–132, 364
1974 (Nürburgring) 153, 364
1975 (Nürburgring) 174–175
1976 (Nürburgring) 10, 194, 195–197, 201, 202, 203, 204, 207, 208, 210, 293, 361
1977 (Hockenheim) 217–218
1978 (Hockenheim) 239, 240
1979 (Hockenheim) 265–266
1982 (Hockenheim) 287, 291
1983 (Hockenheim) 301–302, 307
1984 (Hockenheim) 321
1985 (Nürburgring) 337–338
Gethin, Peter 93, 103, 106, 110, 133
Ghedini, Sante 204
Giacomelli, Bruno 222, 238, 247, 256–257, 271, 278, 283, 286, 287, 295, 298, 300, 305
Giunti, Ignazio 36
Glemser, Dieter 143, 147, 150
Glöckner, Michael 348
Goffinet, Bernard 29
Goodwood 92, 103, 106, 237, 352
Goodyear 37, 38, 93, 110, 131, 137, 138, 141, 145, 169, 181, 196, 201, 202, 204, 208, 213, 218, 221, 224, 225, 227, 229, 232, 234, 237, 238, 241, 252, 255, 256, 261, 262, 266, 279, 285, 294, 295, 306, 311, 330, 341, 343
GRAC (Group de Recherches Automobile de Course) 45
Gradassi, Héctor Luis 364
GRD (Group Racing Developments) 88
Greger, Sepp 25
Gregory, Masten 366
Grünsteidl, Herbert 17, 21
Guerrero, Roberto 298, 305
Guglielminetti, Francesco 164
Guiter, François 329
Gunnarson, Sten 54

Haberson, Thomas 36
Haider, Jörg 352
Hailwood, Mike 97, 109, 111
Hämeenlinna — see 'Ahvenisto'
Hamilton, Lewis 11, 360, 362
Hanon, Bernard 329
Hart (engines)
Four-cylinder turbo 292
Hart, Brian 63, 111
Hasemi, Masahiro 203
Haug, Norbert 355
Hawthorne, Bert 85–86
Heidfeld, Nick 351
Hémery, Victor 355
Henry, Alan 11, 322
Henton, Brian 287, 288
Herd, Robin 6, 76, 79, 81, 86
Herzog, René 51
Hesketh 107, 139, 148, 161, 164, 171–172, 175, 176, 196
308 148, 171
Hesnault, François 328
Heyer, Hans 125
Hezemans, Toine 104, 119, 143, 150–152, 156
Hill, Bette 329
Hill, Graham 65, 66, 76, 82, 88, 100, 106, 108, 127, 133, 364
Hill 166, 169
Himmetsburger, Hans 17
Hine, John 67, 68, 111
Hobbs, David 117–118
Hockenheim 6, 27, 30–31, 45, 49–51, 61, 64–65, 85–86, 93, 108–109, 264, 266, 349, 352, 356, 363
German Grand Prix
1977 217–218
1978 239, 240
1979 265–266
1982 287, 291
1983 301–302, 307
1984 321
Hofer, Lambert 16–18, 21, 23, 61
Hogan, John 274
Huber, Günther 21, 71, 72, 369
Hulme, Denny 124, 140
Hunt, James 12, 45, 47, 48, 56, 76, 107, 148, 161, 164, 171–172, 175, 176, 181, 182, 184, 186, 187, 188, 189, 192, 193, 194, 195, 197, 201, 202, 203, 205, 206, 211, 216, 217, 219, 220, 222, 223, 232, 233, 234, 237, 364, 365, 368
Hutchinson, Jeff 309

Ickx, Jacky 82, 87, 103, 113, 119, 123, 131–132, 140, 141–142, 143, 144, 183, 266, 350, 364
Ikuzawa, Tetsu 63
Imola 58, 99–100, 271–272
Italian Grand Prix
1980 271
San Marino Grand Prix
1982 281, 365
1983 295–296
1984 312, 329
1985 332
Indianapolis 313, 366
Indra, Dr Fritz 89, 111
Innsbruck 23–25, 38–39, 117, 134–135
Interlagos 248, 364
Brazilian Grand Prix
1973 113–114
1974 140–141
1975 162
1976 181
1977 205–206
1979 250–251
ISO-Williams 124, 131, 134
IR02 130
Italian Grand Prix
1972 (Monza) 106
1973 (Monza) 132–133
1974 (Monza) 155–156
1975 (Monza) 176–178
1976 (Monza) 10–11, 197–200, 346
1977 (Monza) 221–222
1978 (Monza) 244–245, 247
1979 (Monza) 270–271
1980 (Imola) 271
1982 (Monza) 289–290, 291
1983 (Monza) 7, 304–305
1984 (Monza) 323–324, 329
1985 (Monza) 341–342

Jabouille, Jean-Pierre 244, 252, 256, 262, 271
Jacarepaguá 224
Brazilian Grand Prix
1978 227–229
1982 278, 281
1983 293, 302
1984 308, 309–310
1985 331
Jacobsson, Eddie 52
Jagerhofer, Hannes 352
Jaguar 11, 352, 360
D-type 353
R2C 353
Jane, Bob 328
Japanese Grand Prix
1976 (Fuji) 202–203
1977 (Fuji) 223
Jarama 66–67, 141, 231, 249
Spanish Grand Prix
1972 86–87
1974 144–145
1976 185–186, 188, 192
1977 210
1978 234–235
1979 255
Jarier, Jean-Pierre 70, 110, 157, 161, 164, 166, 169, 171, 181, 182, 215, 230, 252, 257, 259
Järvi, Matti 21
Jaussaud, Jean-Pierre 67, 73, 79, 86, 88, 93, 97, 101
Jenkinson, Denis 187, 351
Joest, Reinhold 60
Johansson, Jean 47, 48
Johansson, Stefan 303, 305, 326, 327
Joisten, Hans-Peter 124–126, 127–128, 364, 369
Jones, Alan 183, 184, 216, 217, 219, 237, 238, 239, 259, 262, 263, 267, 270
Juan Carlos, King of Spain 351

Kaimann 20, 21, 22, 26, 33, 34, 36, 37, 40, 41, 61, 175, 363
Mk3 21, 22, 23–24, 25, 29, 363
Mk4 27–38, 363
Mk5 39, 40–41
Kammerlander, Alfons 16
Karlskoga 53–54
Kasten-Vichtenstein (hillclimb) 17, 18
Kazato, Hiroshi 106
Keegan, Rupert 255, 287
Keele, Roger 56
Keimola 21–22, 47–48, 53, 363
Kelleners, Helmut 55, 60
Kinnekulle-Ring 75
Kinnunen, Leo 55, 59
Klien, Christian 365
Knutsdorp 55
Koinigg, Helmut 17, 136
Kojima 203
Koralpe (hillclimb) 18
Kottingbrünn (test track) 15, 32, 42
Kottulinsky, Freddy 46, 56, 58
Kovalainen, Heiki 355
Kozarowitzky, Mikko 46, 52
Krackowizer, Dr Helmut 275
Krammer, Gerhard 60
Kranefuss, Michael 137, 151
Kussmaul, Roland 296
Kyalami 138, 365
Nine Hours 110–111
South African Grand Prix
1972 82
1973 114
1974 142–143
1975 162–164
1976 182
1977 206–208
1979 251–252
1982 277
1983 306–307
1984 310–311
1985 342–343
Ladoux (test track) 275, 316
Laffite, Jacques 175, 188, 193, 199, 210, 211, 213, 216, 217, 220, 234, 237, 242, 250, 252, 255, 256, 259, 264, 267, 271, 277, 294, 295, 296, 298, 299, 308, 323, 337
Lammers, Jan 252, 253
Lang, Hermann 275
Lardi, Piero 137, 221
Larrousse, Gérard 50, 55, 58, 60, 72, 329
Las Vegas — see 'Caesar's Palace Grand Prix'
Lauda Air 11, 265, 350, 360
LaudaMotion 11, 360
Lauda, Birgit (*née* Wetzinger) (second wife) 361
Lauda, Florian (brother) 361
Lauda, Heinz (uncle) 20
Lauda, Lukas (son) 350, 351, 355
Lauda, Marlene (*née* Knaus) (first wife) 197
Lauda, Matthias (son) 350, 351, 354
Le Mans 187, 292, 366
Learjet 223, 272
Lec 213
Leda 86
Leuze, Helmut 49
Ligier 199, 210, 216, 220, 231, 234, 242, 250, 255, 258, 264, 266, 267, 271, 277, 283, 319, 337
JS5 188, 193
JS7 213, 217
JS7/9 237
JS11 252, 259
JS19 281
Lins, Rudi 58, 59, 60
Liuzzi, Vitantonio 354
Löhner, Horst 22
Lohr, Ellen 349
Lola 59, 67, 117, 118, 345
T70 49, 54, 55, 60
T210 53, 60, 364
Lombardi, Lella 211
Long Beach
United States Grand Prix (West)
1976 183, 184–185, 348, 356, 364
1977 208–210
1978 231
1979 252–253
1982 278–280, 291
1983 294–295, 301
Lotus 9, 46, 56, 65, 67, 76, 78, 79, 92, 93, 96, 99, 111, 115, 119, 131, 134, 139, 140, 144, 146, 147, 149, 152, 159, 164, 168, 176, 184, 190, 191, 203, 208, 216, 219, 220, 221, 222, 223, 227, 230, 232, 234, 235, 237, 238, 242, 244, 245, 247, 248, 255, 264, 271, 272, 282, 288, 292, 295, 299, 312, 315, 316, 317, 318, 321, 325, 326, 327, 331, 332, 336, 337, 340, 342, 343, 345
59 45
69 48, 62, 68
72D 129, 130, 142
77 183, 193
78 204, 209, 211, 212, 213, 216, 217, 219
79 232, 233, 237, 239, 252
91 281
92 296
93T 295
95T 323
Love, John 110
Lowinger, Willy 67, 117, 134
Lunger, Brett 118, 196, 210

Magny-Cours 44–45, 355
Mallory Park 6, 63, 83–84, 93
Mannhalter, Sepp 60
Mansell, Nigel 282, 288, 299, 309, 315, 316, 318, 323, 327, 332, 338, 339, 343
Mantorp Park 36–37, 39, 72–73, 101
March 6, 10, 12, 52, 62, 65, 67, 70, 73, 76, 78, 79, 80, 83, 85, 87, 88, 91, 95, 96, 103, 111, 112, 113, 165, 168, 169, 174, 176, 188, 199, 200, 201, 206, 210, 216, 219, 278, 281, 287
703 47
707 55, 60
711 74–75, 81, 363
712 62
712M 63–71, 72–73, 75–79, 363, 364
721 81–82, 94–95
721G 92, 94–95, 96, 98–99, 100, 102–103, 106, 108–109
721X 86–87, 88–89, 92, 94–95, 96, 98, 158
722 83–85, 87–88, 91, 92, 93, 95–97, 99–100, 101, 104–106, 107, 108–109, 364
72A 95
732 110
73S 103, 110–111, 366
751 169
761 188, 192, 193
Marko, Helmut 17, 20, 21, 22, 24, 25, 31, 34–35, 41, 42, 49, 55, 59, 60, 62, 66, 67, 72, 77, 79, 81, 82, 96, 106, 357, 363, 366
Martini, Giancarlo 190
Martini, Pierluigi 336
Mason, Nick 352
Mass, Jochen 86, 96, 103, 117, 119–120, 128, 143–144, 147, 150–152, 175, 176, 186, 196, 201, 205, 211, 213, 217, 234, 257, 281, 364, 365, 369
Massa, Felipe 354
Matchett, Steve 52
Mateschitz, Dieter 357
Matra 99, 100, 102
MS120C 102
MS120D 102
Matra (engines)
V12 213, 220
Mayer, Teddy 21, 152, 286, 365
McDonnell Douglas DC10 6
McInerney, Brendan 45
McLaren 6, 7, 8, 73, 79, 88, 107, 119, 124, 129, 131, 134, 140, 141, 146, 149, 152, 156, 159, 160, 161, 162, 164, 174, 175, 176, 179, 181, 184, 186, 187, 192, 194, 196, 197, 201, 202, 205, 206, 213, 216, 219, 220, 222, 232, 234, 237, 238, 248, 250, 252, 262, 263, 267, 272, 273, 274, 275, 276–291, 292–307, 308–329, 330–345, 360, 365, 366
M6B 50
M7 55
M8C 60
M12 53, 60
M19A 109
M21 83
M23 133, 146, 157, 160, 165, 181, 188, 192, 193, 207, 211, 217, 365
M26 217, 219, 233, 237
M28 253
MP4 274, 275
MP4/1B 277–291, 299
MP4/1C 292–303, 307
MP4/1D 299, 300, 304
MP4/1E 303–307, 308
MP4/2 290, 299, 308–327, 358
MP4/2B 330–345
MP4/2C 358
MP4/12 351
MP4/98T (two-seater) 351
McNamara 31, 32, 34, 42, 56, 61
Mk3B 32, 43–48, 50, 51–52, 53, 54–55, 56–58, 63, 363
McNamara, Francis 42
McNish, Allan 354
Menzel, Harald 364
Mercedes-Benz 8, 11, 346, 360
190E 2.3-16 314
300SL 9
300SLR 351
450SLC 358
500SL Rallye 358
C-class 349
CLK 355
SLS AMG GT3 346, 357
W154 275
W196 183, 348, 350, 351, 356
Merzario 242
Merzario, Arturo 67, 68, 99, 111, 120, 127, 196, 242
Mezger, Hans 292, 296, 299, 315
Michelin 204, 213, 221, 238, 242, 247, 256, 272, 275, 278, 280, 281, 284, 285, 288, 289, 291, 293, 294, 297, 298, 302, 306, 308, 311, 316, 318, 322, 323, 330
Miedaner, Horst 38
Migault, François 78, 169
Minardi 336
Mini 14, 23
Cooper S 14–17, 18, 21, 25, 32, 33, 363
Misano 138, 338
Mitter, Gerhard 17, 25
Monaco Grand Prix
1972 88–89
1973 6, 122–123, 137
1974 147, 159
1975 166–168, 172
1976 188–189
1977 210–211
1978 231–233, 247
1979 258–259
1982 281–282, 291
1983 297
1984 316, 320, 350
1985 333–334, 344
Montezemolo, Luca di 6, 10, 11, 129, 137, 160, 175, 179, 180, 221, 360
Montjuïc 363
Spanish Grand Prix
1973 119
1975 165–166
Montréal
Canadian Grand Prix
1978 245–246
1979 11, 272
1982 283–284
1983 300, 307
1984 316–317, 329
1985 334
Monza 6, 7, 10–11, 37, 58, 69–70, 115–117, 143, 269, 347, 363, 364
Italian Grand Prix
1972 106
1973 132–133
1974 155–156
1975 176–178
1976 10–11, 197–200, 346
1977 221–222
1978 244–245, 247
1979 270–271
1982 289–290, 291
1983 7, 304–305
1984 323–324, 329
1985 341–342
Moreno, Roberto 328
Moretti, Gianpiero 58
Morgan, Dave 83–84, 93, 99, 107
Moser, Roland 33
Mosley, Max 76, 268
Mosport 364
Canadian Grand Prix
1971 363
1972 108
1973 133–134, 137
1974 156–157
1976 197, 200–201, 202
1977 223
Moss, Stirling 9, 351
Mount Panorama 365
Mugello 180, 190
Muir, Brian 115–117, 118, 122, 126, 364
Müller, Herbert 60
Munich-Neubiberg 40–41
Murray, Gordon 160, 224, 225, 226, 228, 229, 234, 236, 237, 239, 246, 247, 248, 250, 270, 285

Nardò (test track) 208
Neerpasch, Jochen 253, 263, 356
Neuhaus, Jürgen 55, 59
Newman, Paul 366
Nilsson, Gunnar 183, 184, 190, 212, 213, 216, 217, 219, 222, 365
Nissan Pulsar 327–328
Nivelles 95
Belgian Grand Prix
1972 92
1974 145–146
Nogaro 43

Norisring 48–49, 50, 156, 260
Nosetto, Roberto 204
Nürburgring 6, 10, 12, 31, 34–35, 37, 38, 39, 41, 44, 60, 61, 65–66, 73, 189, 313–314, 336, 347, 354, 356, 361, 364, 368, 369
1,000km
1973 122
1974 146–147
European Grand Prix
1984 325–326
German Grand Prix
1969 34, 41
1972 100
1973 131–132, 364
1974 153, 364
1975 174–175
1976 194, 195–197, 201–203, 204, 207, 208, 210, 293
1985 337–338
Nordschleife 12, 18, 34–35, 41, 44, 51, 60, 65, 71, 127, 128, 146, 153, 195, 347, 359, 369
Six Hours
1968 18
1970 51, 363
1971 71
1973 127–128, 359, 364
1974 150–152
24 Hours
1973 124 126
Südschleife 31, 39, 60, 369

Ojjeh, Mansour 290
Oliver, Jackie 73, 124, 129, 215
Olympic 22, 23, 27, 30, 31, 34, 41, 49
Opel
Blitz transporter 21, 363
Rekord ('Black Widow') 32–33, 36, 40
Orthey, Frank 362
Ortner, Hans 16
Osella 283
Österreichring 34, 46, 60, 61, 96–97, 136, 194, 266, 336
1,000km
1969 35–36
1970 59–60
Austrian Grand Prix
1971 73–75
1972 102–103
1973 132
1974 153–154
1975 175–176
1976 196–197
1977 218–219
1978 240, 242
1979 267
1981 274
1982 288
1983 302–303, 307
1984 321–322
1985 338–340
Oulton Park 84, 107

Pace, Carlos 69, 85, 120, 140, 161, 168, 171, 205, 206
Paletti, Riccardo 283
Palliser 56
Palm, Torsten 52, 55
Palmer, Jonathan 319
Pankl, Gerold 24, 26, 27, 28, 29, 38, 39, 42, 43, 44, 45, 51, 53, 56, 60, 89, 103, 104, 117, 134, 363
Parma–Poggio di Berceto (hillclimb) 214
Parnell, R.H.H. 'Tim' 111, 364
Parnelli 165, 174
Parry-Jones, Richard 360
Patrese, Riccardo 230, 234, 235, 238, 242, 280, 281, 283, 285, 288, 289, 294, 295, 307, 325, 333, 334, 336, 337, 339
Pau 65, 363
Paul Ricard 44, 111, 132, 137, 138, 143, 158, 181, 225, 241, 247, 249, 275, 308, 364
French Grand Prix
1973 126–127
1975 172
1976 191–192
1978 236–237
1982 286–287
1983 295

1985 335–336
Pechtl Helmuth 33
Penske 176, 182, 197, 215
PC3 193
Penske, Roger 366
Pescarolo, Henri 66, 86, 87, 108
Peter, Peter 16, 17, 26, 28, 31, 33, 34, 35, 38, 39, 40, 41, 59
Peterson, Ronnie 6, 9, 12, 54, 55, 62, 66, 70, 73, 76, 77–78, 79, 80, 81–82, 83, 85, 86, 87, 92, 95, 99, 100, 103, 104–105, 106, 107, 108, 109, 111, 115, 119, 131, 134, 144, 146, 147, 149, 152, 164, 166–168, 176, 188, 192, 193, 200, 201, 202, 203, 210, 211, 223, 227, 230, 232, 234, 237, 238, 239, 242, 244, 363, 364, 366, 368
Pianta, Giorgio 190
Piccinini, Marco 329
Pilette, Teddy 54, 55
Piper, David 55
Piquet, Nelson 248, 250, 251, 252, 256, 257, 261, 263, 264, 265, 266, 267, 269, 270, 271, 273, 280, 281, 283, 284, 285, 287, 288, 289, 293, 305, 307, 310, 311, 313, 315, 317, 319, 320, 321, 322, 324, 325, 329, 331, 332, 333, 334, 335, 337, 339, 340, 341, 343, 365, 366, 368
Pirelli 241, 345
Pironi, Didier 242, 252, 258, 259, 264, 277, 281, 283, 285, 286, 287
Pirro, Emanuele 347
Porsche 58, 290, 292, 296, 299, 308, 309, 342, 366
907 49
908 54
908/2 48–50, 53–54, 55, 58–60, 61, 363
910 35–36
911 33
911S 6, 17–21, 22–23, 24–25, 363
Carrera RSR 121, 366
917 36, 49
917K 55, 58, 59, 60
917/10 292
917/30 292
935 260
956 296, 299
RSK 19
Porsche, Ferry 299
Portuguese Grand Prix (Estoril)
1984 326–327
1985 331–332
Postlethwaite, Harvey 79, 110, 139
Prinoth, Ernst 37
Procar — see 'BMW M1'
Project Four 7, 256, 260, 261, 263, 264, 266, 268, 270, 273, 274, 365
Prophet, David 53, 60
Prost, Alain 10, 277, 278, 281, 282, 283, 289, 293, 297, 298, 303, 307, 308–327, 329, 330–332, 334, 336–344, 350, 358, 365, 368
Prüller, Heinz 272, 274
Pryce, Tom 166, 175, 176, 206, 207
Pugmeister, Yorn 309
Purley, David 51, 54, 88, 96, 213
Pust, Sigi 19, 20
Pygmée 67, 78, 85

Quester, Dieter 29, 38, 62, 66, 70, 73, 77, 79, 117, 134–135, 136, 357, 365

Ralt RT4 328
Ravaglia, Roberto 365
Red Bull RB3
Red Bull Ring 357, 358, 359, 362
Redman, Brian 58
Rees, Alan 70
Regazzoni, Clay 10, 111, 113, 114, 117, 132, 134, 135, 136, 137, 138, 140, 142, 144, 145, 146, 147, 148–149, 150, 153, 154, 155, 156, 157, 158, 159, 163, 165, 166, 174, 176, 177, 178,

179, 181, 184, 185, 186, 187, 188, 190, 193, 194, 197, 199, 204, 217, 219, 222, 247, 253, 256, 257, 258, 260, 261, 262, 267, 269, 270, 366, 368
Reininghaus, Mariella 145
Reisch, Klaus 19, 21, 23
Reitzle, Wolfgang 360
Renaudo, Fausto 214
Renault 221, 244, 247, 252, 256, 262, 264, 266, 267, 269, 271, 277, 278, 281, 282, 283, 288, 289, 292, 293, 297, 298, 303, 304, 306, 307, 310, 312, 313, 315, 316, 320, 321, 324, 326, 329, 331, 334, 365
RS01 252
RE40 307
RE60 332, 335
RE60B 335, 339
Renault (engines)
V6 turbo 292
Reutemann, Carlos 6, 65, 66, 71, 76, 78, 83–84, 97, 99, 106, 114, 119, 140, 141, 143, 154, 155, 157, 159, 161, 171, 175, 176, 199, 203, 204, 205, 206, 208, 210, 211, 214, 215, 216, 217, 219, 220, 222, 223, 227, 228, 229, 231, 232, 233, 238, 242, 243, 247, 272, 278, 314, 368
Revson, Peter 109, 119, 133
Richards, Jim 328
Rieder, Kurt 136
Riedl, Werner 22, 42, 45, 46, 363
Rindt, Jochen 19, 20, 58, 65, 73, 79, 133, 350
Rindt, Nina 62
Riverside 246–247
Robinson, Peter 342
Rodríguez, Pedro 49, 59
Roebuck, Nigel 362
Roos, Bertil 37
Rosberg, Keke 277, 279, 280, 281, 283, 284, 285, 289, 290–291, 293, 299, 300, 302, 306, 310, 311, 312, 314, 318, 323, 327, 328–329, 331, 332, 336, 338, 339, 340, 343, 366, 376
Rossfeld (hillclimb) 30, 363
Rottensteiner, Alois 52
Rouen-les-Essarts 70–71, 95–96
Royer, Hans 175
RPB (Racing Plast Burträsk) 37, 39
Ruesch, Carlos 97
Rutherford, Johnny 366
Ryan, Terry 329

Sailer, Toni 355
Salazar, Eliseo 284
Salzburgring 38, 67–68, 104–106, 118–119, 143–144, 253, 275, 348, 356, 364, 365
San Marino Grand Prix (Imola)
1982 281, 365
1983 295–296
1984 312, 329
1985 332
Scheckter, Jody 83, 88, 107, 110–111, 117, 129, 134, 146, 153, 156, 157, 159, 169, 172, 175, 183, 184, 188, 191, 193, 194, 199, 200, 201, 207, 208, 209, 210, 216, 217, 218, 219, 220, 222, 223, 230, 232, 233, 234, 237, 238, 250, 255, 258, 267, 268, 271, 272, 366, 369
Schenken, Tim 64, 65, 71, 73, 84, 107
Schmidt, Günther 262
Schneider, Bernd 355
Schnitzer 23, 71, 103, 117, 356
Schörg, Lothar 21, 26, 27, 47, 363
Schreider, Siegfried 45
Schrempp, Jürgen 352
Schumacher, Michael 360
Schuppan, Vern 111, 117
Schurti, Manfred 29, 37
Schuster, Ernst 349, 350
Schütz, Wolfgang 260
Schwab, Alfred 16
Scott, Richard 68, 83, 95
Seitz, Kary 51
Senna, Ayrton 10, 313, 314, 316,

317, 321, 323, 327, 331, 333, 336, 337, 340, 342, 343, 350, 368
Serra, Chico 281
Shadow 124, 127, 129, 161, 164, 166, 171, 175, 176, 181, 182, 207, 215, 216, 217, 219, 229, 238, 246, 252, 366
DN1 130, 133
DN3 157
DN6 366
DN9 253
Siffert, Jo 36
Silingardi, Marino 338
Silverstone 10, 95, 103, 224, 225, 256, 261, 266, 300, 363
British Grand Prix
1973 128–129, 131
1975 172–174
1977 216
1979 263–264, 365
1981 274
1983 300–301, 307
1985 336–337
International Trophy
1973 117–118
1975 164–165
1976 364
1978 230
Sirviö, Lassi 37
Sopron 31–32
South African Grand Prix (Kyalami)
1972 82
1973 114
1974 142–143, 159
1975 162–164
1976 182
1977 206–208
1979 251–252
1982 277
1983 306–307
1984 310–311
1985 342–343
Spa-Francorchamps 12, 92, 119–120
24 Hours
1971 72
1973 128, 364
1,000km
1973 120–121
Belgian Grand Prix
1983 297–298
1985 342
Spanish Grand Prix
1972 (Jarama) 86–87
1973 (Montjuïc) 119
1974 (Jarama) 144–145
1975 (Montjuïc) 165–166
1976 (Jarama) 185–186, 192
1977 (Jarama) 210
1978 (Jarama) 234–235
1979 (Jarama) 255
Spirit 303, 315, 316, 325
201 305
Springer, Alwin 296
Stainz (hillclimb) 20
Stanley, Jean 10
Stanley, Louis 10, 112, 123, 132, 134
Stappert, Dieter 366
Steinemann, Rico 366
Stenzel, Reinhardt 24, 25
Stewart, Jackie 9, 106, 109, 117, 118, 123, 129, 132, 313, 320, 350, 368
Stommelen, Rolf 71, 99, 166, 364
Stone, Bill 91
Stuck, Hans 115, 120–121, 130–131, 143, 144, 147, 156, 200, 210, 216, 219, 229, 238, 246, 257, 260, 261, 262, 264, 268, 269, 270, 366, 369
Stuppacher, Otto 35–36
Sullivan, Danny 305, 366
Surer, Marc 296, 299, 305, 343
Surtees 97, 100, 108, 109, 111, 149, 184, 196, 237
TS10 84, 87, 96, 97
TS16 147, 357
TS19 183, 217
Surtees, John 84, 91, 96, 100, 350
Svensson, Ulf 47, 50–51, 55, 56
Swedish Grand Prix (Anderstorp)
1973 123–124
1974 148
1975 169–171

1976 190–191, 208
1977 214, 215
1978 234, 235–236
Swiss Grand Prix (Dijon-Prenois)
1982 289

TAG (Techniques d'Avant Garde) 290
V6 turbo 7, 292, 296, 299, 302, 303, 304, 305, 306, 307–309, 310, 313, 317, 331, 342, 358
Talbot-Ligier — see 'Ligier'
Tambay, Patrick 219, 237, 252, 253, 284, 286, 288, 293, 306, 307, 315, 321, 324, 325, 331, 332, 335, 339
Tanzi, Calisto 274
Tauplitz (hillclimb) 19
Tecno 45, 65, 92, 138
69 45, 47, 48, 52
PA123 130
Theodore 298
N183 305
Thruxton 58–59, 65, 70, 79, 84–85, 93
Titan 46, 52
Todt, Jean 360
Toleman 285, 288, 292, 293, 295, 300, 316, 321, 326, 327, 340, 343
TG183B 298, 305
TG184 316, 323
Tulln-Langenlebarn 19, 32–33, 60, 77
Tyrrell 103, 106, 109, 118, 122, 124, 129, 132, 134, 146, 148, 153, 156, 161, 169, 172, 175, 182, 184, 185, 191, 194, 199, 201, 210, 217, 223, 227, 230, 232, 242, 252, 258, 277, 280, 287, 288, 290, 291, 298, 303, 332, 337
007 157, 169, 174, 183
009 252, 259
011 296
011B 305
012 334, 335
P34 188, 193, 208, 211

United States Grand Prix (Watkins Glen)
1972 108–109
1973 135
1974 157–159
1975 178–179
United States Grand Prix (East) (Watkins Glen)
1976 201–202
1977 222–223
1978 245, 366
United States Grand Prix (West) (Long Beach)
1976 183, 184–185, 348, 356, 364
1977 208–210
1978 231
1979 252–253
1982 278–280, 291
1983 294–295, 301
Urbanek, Peter 42

Valencia 353
Vallelunga 78–79, 94–95, 138, 142, 158, 180, 181, 224, 225, 363, 364
van Hooydonk, Mike 350
van Lennep, Gijs 55, 121
van Wassenhove, Michael 29
Varano 189–190
Veemax 21
Verdi, Giuseppe 214
Vettel, Sebastian 357, 362
Vigoureux, Etienne 45
Villeneuve, Gilles 217, 223, 231, 232, 233, 244, 245, 247, 255, 256, 258, 259, 262, 264, 266, 267, 271, 272, 279, 281, 352
Vogelberger, Alfred 22, 23, 27, 29, 34, 37, 41
Völker, Herbert 274
von Wendt, Karl 48, 49
VW Beetle 30

Walding (hillclimb) 20
Walker, Alistair 65

Walkinshaw, Tom 52
Warr, Peter 159
Warren, Martin 52
Warwick, Derek 285, 288, 293, 310, 312, 313, 315, 316, 318, 320, 321, 325, 326, 331, 332, 334, 335, 365
Watkins Glen
United States Grand Prix
1972 108–109
1973 135
1974 157–159
1975 178–179
United States Grand Prix (East)
1976 201–202
1977 222–223
1978 245, 366
Watson, John 6–8, 69, 73, 75, 76, 97, 157, 182, 193, 197, 205, 206, 210, 216, 217, 224, 225, 227, 228, 229, 231, 232, 234, 236, 237, 240, 245, 247, 250, 274, 275, 277, 278, 280, 281, 282, 283, 290–291, 293, 294–295, 297, 299, 302, 305, 306, 307, 313, 314, 365, 368
Wauters, Koen 350
Webber, Mark 357
Weber, Michel 59
Weissach 292, 296, 299, 314, 342
Werner, Hannelore 57
Westbury, Peter 65, 66, 76, 78, 99
Wheatcroft, Tom 111, 365
Williams 175, 238, 239, 262, 267, 269, 274, 277, 278, 279, 281, 283, 284, 285, 286, 289, 290, 291, 293, 294, 296, 298, 299, 302, 306, 310, 312, 318, 323, 327, 331, 332, 336, 338, 340, 343
FW05 183
FW06 237, 253
FW07 259
FW08C 296
FW09B 323
FW10 339
Williams, Frank 69
Williamson, Roger 111, 171
Wimille, Jean-Pierre 9
Windsor, Peter 309
Winkelhock, Manfred 268, 281, 282, 287, 301, 306, 309, 313
Wisell, Reine 76, 88
Wolf 207, 208, 210, 216, 218, 219, 221, 222, 230, 232, 234, 238, 262
WR1 207, 209, 217
WR3 219
WR5 233, 237, 238
Wolf Williams 196
Wolf, Walter 221
Wolff, Toto 8, 358
Wollek, Bob 95, 99, 106
Woodman, Vince 91

Zandvoort 56, 60, 103–104, 169, 213, 268, 364
Dutch Grand Prix
1973 130–131, 137
1974 148–149
1975 171–172
1976 197, 202
1977 220–221
1978 242–243
1979 268–269
1982 284
1983 303–304
1984 322–323
1985 10, 340–341, 344
Zarges, Holger 25
Zasada, Sobieslaw 358
Zeltweg 35
Zolder 29, 57–58, 189, 261, 265
Belgian Grand Prix
1973 121–122, 364
1975 168–169
1976 186–188
1977 212–213, 214
1978 232–233
1979 256–257
1982 280–281, 290
1984 311–312
Zorzi, Renzo 207, 211
Zunino, Ricardo 272
Zwickl, Helmut 272, 273, 348, 349

INDEX **375**

AFTERWORD
KURT BERGMANN

Niki was one of eight of my drivers who made it to Formula 1. They were all quick, but Niki was also diligent and very ambitious. He pushed himself, worked with the mechanics to make his car faster, with the sponsors to have enough money at his disposal, with me as a team owner and designer so that he could always maximise his advantage — and he was never satisfied. There was something special going on; we all felt the energy that flowed from him.

This was the case in 1969 when the young star drove straight to second place behind our veteran Erich Breinsberg and even won two races. During a race at the Aspern airfield, he overturned his car and when we got there, he called out from underneath it, 'I can drive in the afternoon.' We quickly repaired it and he was soon behind the wheel again.

Fifty years later, we were still friends and he visited regularly when the Formula 1 teams came to Austria. He never changed; he was always at full throttle. With his driven personality, he kept his environment in motion and always continued to push his team forward. The five world titles with Mercedes-Benz were no coincidence.

I am pleased that this book features not only his achievements in Formula 1 but also shows that he competed widely as a racing driver and that he often drove many things in parallel. On some race weekends, the name Lauda appeared in several classes in the programme.

Niki did not win his last race and sadly left us too early; for me he remains the greatest motor sportsman our country has produced.

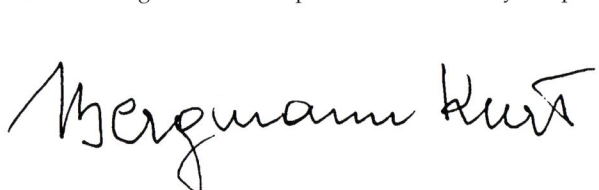

Bergmann Kurt

ABOVE Kurt Bergmann and Niki Lauda pictured together at the Kaimann boss's 80th birthday celebrations in Vienna. Both giants of Austrian motor sport, they remained friends for over 50 years.

AUTHOR'S NOTE

Kurt Bergmann is a modest but charismatic former motor mechanic and motorcycle racer who was known by friends and admirers only as 'Master' in the local Viennese jargon. In the 1960s he was the founder, designer and driving force behind the Kaimann Racing Team, whose cars became the benchmark in European Formula Vee and Super Vee racing throughout the 1970s.

He was the first professional works team owner to recognise the young Niki Lauda's latent talent and gave him his break in single-seater competition. He also nurtured the early careers of Formula 1 drivers Dieter Quester, Helmut Marko, Harald Ertl, Helmut Koinigg, Jochen Mass, Jo Gartner and Keke Rosberg. Bergmann was prepared to take risks with young talent, albeit on a highly selective basis; he was later to comment that all his junior drivers would deliver scrap metal back to him at some point, with the average being two write-offs each. The young Lauda certainly contributed to that statistic, but the shrewd Bergmann also quickly spotted his commitment and extraordinary technical understanding; even in the earliest days Lauda would spend hours in discussion with the mechanics.

Erich Breinsberg's book *Der Niki, der Keke und das Genie aus der Vorhaus* opens with Bergmann's comment to Lauda at Hockenheim in 1969: 'You can become something.' In his own Foreword to the same book, Lauda wrote of Bergmann: 'He was the most important man for me. He was the stirrup in the great race for all of us; without him, I would not have got any further.'

376 NIKI LAUDA